Cultures of Fear

Anthropology, Culture and Society

Series Editors:
Professor Vered Amit, Concordia University
and
Dr Jon P. Mitchell, University of Sussex

Published titles include:

Home Spaces, Street Styles:
Contesting Power and Identity
in a South African City
LESLIE J. BANK

On the Game:
Women and Sex Work
SOPHIE DAY

Slave of Allah:
Zacarias Moussaoui vs the USA
KATHERINE C. DONAHUE

A History of Anthropology
THOMAS HYLLAND ERIKSEN
AND FINN SIVERT NIELSEN

Ethnicity and Nationalism:
Anthropological Perspectives
Second Edition
THOMAS HYLLAND ERIKSEN

Globalisation:
Studies in Anthropology
Edited by THOMAS HYLLAND ERIKSEN

Small Places, Large Issues:
An Introduction to Social
and Cultural Anthropology
Second Edition
THOMAS HYLLAND ERIKSEN

What is Anthropology?
THOMAS HYLLAND ERIKSEN

Anthropology, Development and
the Post-Modern Challenge
KATY GARDNER AND DAVID LEWIS

Corruption:
Anthropological Perspectives
Edited by DIETER HALLER
AND CRIS SHORE

Culture and Well-Being:
Anthropological Approaches to
Freedom and Political Ethics
Edited by ALBERTO CORSIN JIMENEZ

Fair Trade and a Global Commodity:
Coffee in Costa Rica
PETER LUETCHFORD

The Will of the Many:
How the Alterglobalisation Movement
is Changing the Face of Democracy
MARIANNE MAECKELBERGH

The Aid Effect:
Giving and Governing in
International Development
Edited by DAVID MOSSE
AND DAVID LEWIS

Cultivating Development:
An Ethnography of Aid Policy
and Practice
DAVID MOSSE

Anthropology, Art and
Cultural Production
MARUŠKA SVAŠEK

Race and Sex in Latin America
PETER WADE

Anthropology at the Dawn
of the Cold War:
The Influence of Foundations,
McCarthyism and the CIA
Edited by DUSTIN M. WAX

Learning Politics from Sivaram:
The Life and Death of a Revolutionary
Tamil Journalist in Sri Lanka
MARK P. WHITAKER

CULTURES OF FEAR

A Critical Reader

Edited by
Uli Linke and Danielle Taana Smith

PlutoPress
www.plutobooks.com

First published 2009 by Pluto Press
345 Archway Road, London N6 5AA and
175 Fifth Avenue, New York, NY 10010

www.plutobooks.com

Distributed in the United States of America exclusively by
Palgrave Macmillan, a division of St. Martin's Press LLC,
175 Fifth Avenue, New York, NY 10010

British Library Cataloguing in Publication Data
A catalogue record for this book is available from the British Library

ISBN   978 0 7453 2966 6   Hardback
ISBN   978 0 7453 2965 9   Paperback

Library of Congress Cataloging in Publication Data applied for

This book is printed on paper suitable for recycling and made from fully managed
and sustained forest sources. Logging, pulping and manufacturing processes are
expected to conform to the environmental standards of the country of origin.
The paper may contain up to 70 percent post-consumer waste.

10   9   8   7   6   5   4   3   2   1

Designed and produced for Pluto Press by
Chase Publishing Services Ltd, 33 Livonia Road, Sidmouth, EX10 9JB, England
Typeset from disk by Stanford DTP Services, Northampton, England
Printed and bound in the European Union by
CPI Antony Rowe, Chippenham and Eastbourne

Contents

Acknowledgments

Uli Linke, and Danielle Taana Smith, "Fear: a Conceptual Framework." Copyright © Pluto Press, 2009.

Noam Chomsky's "The New War against Terror" is an abridged version of the transcript of a lecture given at the Massachusetts Institute of Technology (MIT) Technology and Culture forum, October 18, 2001. It is available online at: <http://www.chomsky.info/talks/20011018.htm.> Reproduced by permission of the author. Copyright © 2001 and 2009 by Noam Chomsky.

Joseph Masco's "Engineering Ruins and Affect" is an excerpted version of "'Survival is Your Business': Engineering Ruins and Affect in Nuclear America," *Cultural Anthropology*, 23(2), 2008: 361–398. Reproduced by permission of the American Anthropological Association. DOI: 10.1111/j.1548-1360.2008.00012.x. Not for sale or further reproduction.

David L. Altheide's chapter is an abridged version of "Terrorism and the Politics of Fear," *Cultural Studies–Critical Methodologies*, 6(4): 415–439. Copyright © 2006 by SAGE Publications. Reprinted by permission of SAGE Publications.

Slavoj Žižek's "Welcome to the Desert of the Real!" is taken from an essay posted on *The Global Site* (University of Sussex), September 15, 2001. Copyright © 2001 and 2009 by Slavoj Žižek. Reproduced by permission of the author.

Lucia Ann McSpadden and John R. MacArthur's "Human Rights and Complex Emergencies" is excerpted from the *Bulletin of the National Association for the Practice of Anthropology*, 21: 36–55. DOI:10.1525/napa.2001.21.1.36. Reproduced by permission of the American Anthropological Association. Not for sale or further reproduction.

Liisa H. Malkki's "Speechless Emissaries: Refugees, Humanitarianism, and Dehistoricization" is an excerpted version of her article in *Cultural Anthropology* 11(3), 1996: 377–404. Reproduced by permission of the American Anthropological Association. Not for sale or further reproduction.

Doug Henry's "Trauma and Vulnerability During War" is excerpted from "Violence and the Body: Somatic Expressions of Trauma and Vulnerability During War," *Medical Anthropology*

University Press 2008: 321–351. Copyright © Cambridge University Press, reproduced with permission. The author thanks Regina Muehlhaeuser for her skillful abridgement.

Cynthia Enloe's "Militarizing Women's Lives" is an excerpt from "When Soldiers Rape," in *Maneuvers: The International Politics of Militarizing Women's Lives*, Berkeley: The University of California Press, 2000: 108–152. Copyright © 2000 The Regents of the University of California. Reproduced by permission of the University of California Press.

Meredeth Turshen's chapter is based on "The Political Economy of Violence against Women during Armed Conflict in Uganda," *Social Research: An International Quarterly of the Social Sciences* 67(3): 805–824. Copyright © 2000 The New School For Social Research. Reproduced by permission of The New School for Social Research; <www.socres.org>.

Susan Sontag's "Regarding the Torture of Others" was first published in *The New York Times Magazine*, May 23, 2004. Copyright © 2004 by Susan Sontag, reprinted with permission of The Wiley Agency LLC.

Arthur Kleinman and Joan Kleinman's chapter, "Cultural Appropriations of Suffering," is an abridgement of "The Appeal of Experience, the Dismay of Images: Cultural Appropriations of Suffering in Our Times," *Daedalus: Journal of the American Academy of Arts and Sciences* 125(1), 1996: 1–23. Copyright © 1996 and 2009 by Arthur Kleinman and Joan Kleinman. Reproduced by permission of the authors.

Henry A. Giroux's chapter, "The Biopolitics of Disposability," is from "Violence, Katrina, and the Biopolitics of Disposability," *Theory, Culture & Society* 24(7–8), 2007: 305–309. Copyright © 2007 Theory, Culture & Society Ltd. Reprinted by permission of SAGE Publications.

Nicholas Mirzoeff's "Empire of Camps" is reprinted with permission from *Watching Babylon: The War in Iraq and Global Visual Culture* by Nicholas Mirzoeff, New York: Routledge, 2005: 143–157. Copyright © 2005 and 2009 by Nicholas Mirzoeff.

Series Preface

Anthropology is a discipline based upon in-depth ethnographic works that deal with wider theoretical issues in the context of particular, local conditions—to paraphrase an important volume from the series: *large issues* explored in *small places*. The series has a particular mission: to publish work that moves away from old-style descriptive ethnography—that is strongly area-studies oriented—and offer genuine theoretical arguments that are of interest to a much wider readership but which are nevertheless located and grounded in solid ethnographic research. If anthropology is to argue itself a place in the contemporary intellectual world then it must surely be through such research.

We start from the question: "What can this ethnographic material tell us about the bigger theoretical issues that concern the social sciences"; rather than "What can these theoretical ideas tell us about the ethnographic context." Put this way round, such work becomes *about* large issues, *set in* a (relatively) small place, rather than detailed description of a small place for its own sake. As Clifford Geertz once said: "anthropologists don't study villages; they study *in* villages."

By place we mean not only geographical locale, but also other types of "place"—within political, economic, religious or other social systems. We therefore publish work based on ethnography within political and religious movements, occupational or class groups, youth, development agencies, nationalists; but also work that is more thematically based—on kinship, landscape, the state, violence, corruption, the self. The series publishes four kinds of volume—ethnographic monographs; comparative texts; edited collections; and shorter, polemic essays.

We publish work from all traditions of anthropology, and all parts of the world, which combines theoretical debate with empirical evidence to demonstrate anthropology's unique position in contemporary scholarship and the contemporary world.

Professor Vered Amit
Dr Jon P. Mitchell

1

Fear: A Conceptual Framework

Uli Linke and Danielle Taana Smith

Washington (CNN) – A Muslim family was removed from an airliner after passengers became concerned about a conversation they thought they overheard "of the safest place to sit." AirTran officials refused to rebook them, even after FBI investigators cleared them of wrongdoing.

> 1pm Thursday [January 1, 2009]: AirTran flight 175 was preparing for takeoff from Reagan National Airport outside of Washington DC, a flight destined for Orlando, Florida. Among the passengers were Atif Irfan, his brother Kashif Irfan, their wives, a sister and three children, ages 7, 4, and 2; they were headed to Orlando to meet with family and attend a religious retreat. "The conversation, as we were walking through the plane trying to find our seats, was just about where the safest place in an airplane is," Sahin said.
>
> While the plane was still at the gate, an F.B.I. agent boarded the plane and asked Irfan and his wife to leave the plane. Passengers were informed that there was a "security situation"—a "breach of security"—on the plane. The rest of the family was removed 15 or 20 minutes later, along with a family friend, Abdul Aziz, a Library of Congress attorney, who was coincidentally taking the same flight and had been seen talking to the family. "I guess it's just a situation of guilt by association," Aziz said. "They see one Muslim talking to another Muslim and they automatically assume something wrong is going on."
>
> The conversation did not contain the words "bomb," "explosion," "terror" or other words that might have aroused suspicion, Irfan said. (Ahlers 2009)

*   *   *

Washington DC (*The New York Times*) ... But passengers sitting behind them evidently overheard the ["safest" seat] remark, saw

1

Mr. Irfan's beard and his wife's head scarf, and grew concerned. ... The worried passengers contacted flight attendants, who contacted Transportation Security Administration officials and soon Mr. Irfan and his wife were off the plane and being questioned in the jet way. Next, the nine Muslim passengers—all but one are United States-born American citizens—were taken to a quarantine area in the passenger lounge where they were questioned by FBI agents. Mr. Irfan's three small nephews were denied access to food in the family's carry-on luggage. ...

"To be honest, as Muslims, we do understand how to deal with this, we realize this is an unfortunate aspect in our lives," Mr. Irfan said. "Whenever we get on a plane, because of the color of our skin, people tend to look at us with a wary eye anyway." (Robbins 2009)

* * *

Irfan said he and the others think they were profiled because of their appearance. He said five of the six adults in the party are of South Asian descent, and all six are traditionally Muslim in appearance. (Garder 2009)

* * *

According to Inayet Sahin: "There is a climate of fear that is present. When you are on the [Washington] beltway it says, 'Report any suspicious activity.' When you come into the airport, it says, 'Report any suspicious activity.' So people, you know, are just afraid, looking for suspicious activity." (Ahlers 2009)

* * *

AirTran defended its handling of the situation. In a statement issued, the company said:

At departure time, the Captain of flight 175 informed the airline that there were two federal air marshals onboard who contacted local and federal Washington law enforcement officials for a security related issue onboard the aircraft involving verbal comments made by a passenger and overheard by other passengers. The airline then advised the Transport Security Administration (T.S.A.). It was determined that all 104 passengers onboard must deplane and passengers, crew, baggage and the aircraft should be re-screened. After the re-screening of the passengers, crew, bags and the aircraft, 95 passengers were allowed to reboard the aircraft and nine were detained for interrogation by the local law enforcement officials, the F.B.I. and the Transport Security Administration. ... AirTran Airways complied with all Transport Security Administration, law enforcement and Homeland Security directives and had no discretion in the matter. (Robbins 2009)

"Security," "safety," "protection," and "defense." These are among the terms circulated as part of a global public discourse of fear which encourages proactive military action, legitimates war as a surgical intervention, and authorizes faraway acts of violence as a means of national border fortification. The securocratic language of the contemporary western state is war talk: it not only empowers a state's military reach across national borders, but diminishes civil society, abandons human rights, diplomacy, and visions of peace. In US-American militarized media productions, the figure of the enemy outsider is conflated with the terrorist, who is imagined as a syncretic figure, as Muslim-Arab-Black. In this terrain of propaganda, mediatized militarism invigorates a montage of fear and race, recuperating an Africanist Orientalism that resonates across the Atlantic divide, into Europe, and worldwide.

The attacks on New York and Washington in 2001 and the ensuing declaration of the "war on terror" by the United States have had significant consequences for global social life. Anti-terrorist policies designed in the interest of national security and border protection forged a climate of unprecedented state-legitimated terror against phantasmatic others: US visions of the "axis of evil" or the figure of "the terrorist" are as illusive as reactive—fueling a popular desire for fortified borders. But these ideological fantasies about fortification and border protection are not merely discursive machinations. They are grounded in the operational logic of an expansive capitalist empire that seeks to disguise inherent instabilities and contradictions by a turn to war on terror. In the United States, the shifting configurations between politics, power, and capital have encouraged a rigid nationalism and vigilant patriotism.

But in the neoliberal global order, the economic requirements of mobility, flexibility, and deterritorialization collide with the state's political commitment to securitize space. In this context, the imperatives of national security not only restructure the terrain of the biosocial (Giroux, Chapter 20 this volume) by an appeal to racial hierarchies but alter the essence of the border regime. As Miriam Ticktin observes, "the struggle to define citizenship and the borders of the nation-state is now also a struggle to define the threshold of humanity and of life itself" (Chapter 9 this volume). The ubiquity of borders and the liquidity of empire are symptomatic of this current reality of the capitalist security state: a nation form, founded on fear, in which policing, surveillance, and militarism have become companions to normal life.

In such a context of heightened security measures and scenarios of threat, this book explores how fear has become a central feature of global social life: it shapes those societies at the very core of the "war on terror" (the United States, the European Union, Australia) as well as those national communities pushed to the margins by globalization, violence, and armed conflict (El Salvador, Mozambique, Uganda). In this chapter, we present a conceptual framework for the intercultural study of fear. Our discussion takes the following format. First, we map out the scope of this volume by a focus on a global logic of fear. Second, we explore the possibilities for a cultural analytics of fear by a heuristic focus on European border regimes. Third, we elaborate how a culture of fear is normalized in everyday social life to emerge as an ontological praxis. Fourth, we outline the organization of the book's contents, giving particular attention to the thematic grouping of essays. Since each of the volume's thematic sections begins with a separate introduction to explain our choice of focus and texts, this chapter provides an account of the book's overarching conceptual frame.

A GLOBAL LOGIC OF FEAR

In this book, we expand contemporary discussions about the entanglements of political terror, national security, and human life not only by a comparative, transnational, and global perspective but also by moving beyond more narrowly focused terrorism-security debates. Our collection of essays provides a critical exploration of the formation and normalization of fear in global contexts of war and armed conflict. Our aim is to enable readers to engage the political, social, and cultural dimensions of fear with a humanistic and judicious approach.

This undertaking requires a particular conception of fear. We conceive of "cultures of fear" in terms of the regimes of terror that are discursively, strategically, and experientially imposed on human beings entrapped in the increasingly volatile contact zones between political systems, militarized communities, and administrative apparatuses. Cultures of fear have a political grounding: negative emotions like fear or terror are produced and sustained to govern populations within the carceral spaces of militarized societies. In this sense, an emergent cultural system of fear cannot be understood solely as a byproduct of violence or as an inevitable symptom of war. Forms of terror are artifacts of history, society, and global politics. Cultures of fear and states of terror are affective tools of government that come into being as a modus of population management deployed by military, political, and administrative actors (Masco, Chapter 3 this volume). With our selection of chapters, we reveal the similar logics of fear that governments, humanitarian agencies, and extremist organizations use to monitor, control, and contain human beings in various zones of violence.

This book offers a comprehensive examination of the cultural manifestations of fear across the globe: the studies range from North America and Europe to Latin America, Africa, Asia, and Australia. Our goal is to provide readers with a deeper understanding of the cultural modus of fear: what forms it takes, how it is perpetrated, in what contexts it occurs, and what marks and traces it leaves on the bodies and minds of ordinary people. Our investigation is thus less concerned with specific acts of violence perpetrated in different parts of the world. Rather, we explore the formation of a global logic of fear under conditions of war and in the aftermath of political violence. We seek to illuminate the parameters, practices, and discourses that support the contemporary complex of terror-fear in societies worldwide. Our collection of essays shows that reification, normalization, and sublimation are among the procedures variously deployed by securocratic, bureaucratic, technocratic, militaristic, and mediatized forms of social governance in different parts of the globe. In exploring the deeper, often hidden, impact of cultures of fear, we reveal the common linkages between seemingly dissimilar conditions of violence that structure the lives of human beings—as citizens, immigrants, and refugees—in the contemporary world.

FEAR AS A BORDER REGIME

How does a global logic of fear take local form? How is the relationship between the security state and the biopolitics of privilege, race, and fear made evident in militarized societies? How do neoliberal security states sustain the fortification of borders in different parts of the world? These are among the central questions addressed by our collection of essays. The perpetual formation of militarized violence, racist terror, and destructive dehumanization across the globe makes it imperative, as Simon Gikandi proposed, to confront the imperial machination "on its home ground" (1996: 27). Accordingly, we are persuaded to take the pertinent task of critical analysis back to the centers of global power, beginning with Europe and the United States. But while committed to this endeavor, we further argue that there is an urgency to widen the scope of such an analysis. There is a need to incorporate a transnational perspective to uncover the global hegemony of terror that structures the relations between subjects, communities, and nations. Following Noam Chomsky (Chapter 2 in this volume), the political history of globalization, including the violent reach of Western imperialism, requires us to rethink existing notions about the geographies of security and threat. In the contemporary world order, as Chomsky points out, the spaces and places where terror is enacted and where cultures of fear take form are not disparate, self-contained political geographies. Transnational flows of capital, media, migration, soldiers, sex, and weapons connect local situations to global networks and global centers of power. This analytic position is shared by other contributors to this volume. For example, by a focus on the global proliferation of US military bases, Cynthia Enloe (Chapter 16) documents how the traffic in sex and gendered violence impacts emergent cultures of fear in local communities across the world, from Okinawa in Japan to South Korea and Chile. By investigating the underground abuse of children by UN peacekeeping forces in Mozambique, Carolyn Nordstrom (Chapter 13) likewise uncovers how the local sex trade is driven by multinational industries with global connections. Although locally situated, cultures of fear are shaped by the dynamics of global power relations.

The essays in this volume approach the subject of fear from different angles, along various analytic trajectories. Positional perspectives illuminate the workings of fear in disparate societal frames and ethnographic contexts: military violence and armed conflict, the aftermath of war, the impact of international intervention, refugee camps, the quest for asylum, and the border protection by security states. What do these distinct settings have in common? How do we connect or assemble anthropological insights from separate places, situations, and events toward an integrated understanding of a global culture of fear? Based on a cohesive analysis of an exemplary case, we can identify those prevailing parameters that organize the ways in which cultures of fear are formed, sustained, and normalized. In the following, we examine the violent procedures of empire through the specters of a culture of fear that govern the borders of Europe. Our discussion is guided by the following questions: What spaces, borders, and enemies are imagined or manufactured to serve as catalysts for protective militarism? How are populations governed, monitored, and disciplined in the realm of global security? And how is an emergent culture of fear linked to the proliferation of border regimes?

Cultures of Fear: Borders and Others

In studying cultures of fear and regimes of terror as situated "imaginative geographies," Stephen Graham describes "the ways in which imperialist societies tend to be constructed through normalizing, binary judgments about both 'foreign' territories and the 'home' spaces which sit at the 'heart of empire'" (2006: 255). The "binaries of place attachment" serve to demarcate a putative "us" in opposition to "the other", "who become the legitimate target for military power. ...Very often, such polarizations are manufactured and recycled discursively through racist and imperial state and military discourses and propaganda, backed up by popular cultural representations" (256). Such mutually exclusive imaginings of a securitized 'inside' and a threatening 'outside' are enforced by border regimes that monitor, protect, and sustain cultural notions of relative human worth. As we suggest in this book, cultures of fear rely on this performative capacity of borders.

We therefore begin with an inquiry into the meaning of political borders. How do borders perform their designated task of inclusion and exclusion? Do we envision borders as geophysical entities or as legal, political, symbolic and social forms? In what societal spaces can we locate borders? Following Etienne Balibar, we need to speak of a "regime of borders," "both in the middle of the European space and at its extremities" (2004: 13). Indeed, any modern state recognizes or creates "borderlines," as Balibar asserts, "which allow it to clearly distinguish between the national (domestic) and the foreigner" (4). The outer borders of Europe, as mapped out by single states, incontestably have a geospatial dimension, a territorial reference or landmark, a footprint just beyond no-man's land, where "the entrance of asylum seekers and migrants into the European 'common space'" can be regulated and controlled (14). But on the ground, where matters of belonging and exclusion are decided, borderlines also acquire tangible form as legal, political, and social contact zones (Ticktin, Chapter 9 in this volume). European Union territories, like other federated entities (the United States), are defined by "open" borders in the interior—the so-called Schengen space—where European citizens can traverse national borders without passport or identity checks. This inner "open" space, which guarantees the freedom of mobility for nationals, is protected by the simultaneous fortification of exterior borders. This is one snapshot of fortress Europe: an imagined political community with an interior borderland that is envisioned as open, liberal, democratic, and an exterior security border that is monitored, policed, and protected against refugees, immigrants, non-Europeans, and political enemies.

But such a binary juxtaposition of internal openness (no policing) and exterior closure (border militarism) is misleading (Williksen, Chapter 14 in this volume). For in the process of monitoring, capturing, and detaining unwanted populations—the dark-skinned migrants from the global south—external border guarding has become a militarized regime that extends into the very center of Europe: into European "securocratic public space" (Feldman 2004). As in the United States, the regime of borders in Europe is not confined to a fixed periphery, but comes into evidence as a decentered, dislocated, and ubiquitous process of exclusion. Let us elaborate by a look at detention centers. In September 2008, the European Parliament approved a new set of common rules for expelling undocumented migrants from European Union space. Under the new guidelines, these "illegals" can be held in specialized detention camps for up to 18 months before being deported.

The regime of borders, which includes the camps, is expansive, amorphous: it reaches into all contact zones between state officials and non-citizen subjects, both outside and inside of European space. A cartographic view of the location of the camps is revealing: the "empire of camps," as termed by Nicholas Mirzoeff (Chapter 21 in this volume), extends throughout North Africa, southwest Asia, the eastern parts of Eastern Europe and western Asia; it demarcates Europe's southern and eastern security borders and extends into all interior borderlands, with notable concentrations in Poland, Germany, Switzerland, the Netherlands, and Great Britain (Migreurop 2009). An analysis of Europe's border regimes therefore requires a focus on "the contradictory effects of the violent security policies waged" *by Europe* within its interior borderlands and "'*in the name of Europe*' by the bordering countries, now aggravated by the conjuncture of the 'global war on terror'" (Balibar 2004: 15).

Europe's political borders may be conceived as a militarized machinery, a violent procedure for tracking and containment that is subject to the operations of a state apparatus: migrants can be envisioned either as a valued labor force or as a potential threat to life and safety. As such, border regimes have a dual disposition:

> [O]n the one hand, a *violent process of exclusion* whose main instrument (not the only one) is the quasi-military enforcement of "security borders", which recreates the figure of the *stranger as political enemy*, ... which is potentially exterministic; on the other hand, a *"civil" process of elaboration of differences*, which clearly involves ... a basic aporia concerning the self-understanding of Europe's "identity" and "community". (Balibar 2004: 14)

Producing Cultures of Fear: Exclusion as a Form of Terror

Cultures of fear are founded on border regimes, processes of exclusion that can be enforced by political and military means. In what ways does the performative violence of border guarding in Europe come into evidence? According to documentation provided by various humanitarian organizations, border militarism in Europe has resulted in close to 9,000 deaths of undesirable border crossers between 1993 to 2007 (United for Intercultural Action 2007). This figure includes "statistics of the permanent increase of death cases in some sensitive areas of the 'periphery' (such as the Gibraltar strait, the sea shores of Sicily and the Adriatic, some passages of the Alps and the Carpaths, the English Channel and Tunnel, and so on), which are recorded officially as casualties or tragic accidents" (Balibar 2004: 15). In addition to recording the fatalities of border militarism in Europe's periphery, these statistics also include the deaths of migrants in Europe's interior. Refugees, migrants, and asylum seekers are imprisoned, tortured, and killed, even after they enter the presumed zones of safety in Europe, in detention camps and police custody:

> In January 2005, while detained in a police station in Dessau, Germany, Oury Jalloh (from Sierra Leone) was burned alive in a holding cell, found with his hands and feet chained to a bed, his nose broken, and his pants pulled down to his ankles. A month later, his death was declared an accidental suicide, with a notation by the chief of police: "Blacks just happen to burn longer". (Jansen 2008)

This murder is not an isolated case. In Europe's interior, the border regime is violent and often deadly. Detainees (primarily young black men) are murdered in state custody: in the camp, the holding cell, the police station. The most often used methods of killing (based on a review of hundreds of cases) include the following: asphyxiation (hanging, suffocation with an object, strangulation, manual choking), the use of sedatives, waterboarding, drowning in police custody (by pushing a water hose down the victim's throat), forcible drug-induced vomiting (as practiced in Germany), being set on fire or dying in a fire (at airport detention centers or in police custody), and the denial of medical treatment. These murders by European state officials are pronounced and recorded as accidents or suicides. We suggest that we must rethink such practices, following Noam Chomsky (Chapter 2 in this volume), in terms of a "silent genocide."

In analyzing the tactics of border militarism in Europe, some scholars proposed that there is a need "to expand the model of 'war' to the study of the violent processes of control and suppression which target 'illegal migrations' and also affect asylum seekers at the 'outer borders'" (Balibar 2004: 15). But this border war, as we have suggested, is not confined to the periphery. It extends its reach into the very center of Europe, where predatory state terror unfolds in the detention camp and the police station, in holding cells, in police custody, in airplanes, airports, and in prisons. In addition, we argue that Europe's border regime, and the concomitant border war, is not limited to the carceral spaces of state detention. It takes effect in all those public places where migrants are policed, monitored, and violated by ordinary European citizens: the street, the park, the subway, and so on. But this biopolitical extension of the border regime, the border war's penetration into the vernacular spaces of everyday life, remains largely unrecorded. Such observations are supported by many contributors to this volume, such as Cynthia Cockburn (Chapter 11), who speaks of an unacknowledged "continuum" of violence and fear.

Implementing a Culture of Fear: Rendering Others Visible

Cultures of fear are founded on a politics of borders that enables the systematic inclusion and exclusion of specific population groups. But the everyday work of terror requires visible signifiers: abject difference comes to be visually marked. In the public realm, a binary code of race, sex, and space (ghetto, slum, camp) is implanted into vernacular looking-relations, used to identify the Other on sight (Giroux (Chapter 20), Kleinman and Kleinman (Chapter 19), Malkki (Chapter 7) and Sontag (Chapter 18) in this volume).

Similarly, European border regimes are encoded by a cultural logic of othering that sustains the fortification of Europe as a hegemonic white space. The regime of borders, as a violent process of exclusion, as Paul Gilroy observed, implicates the European Union in the explicit construction of a "white fortress" (2000: 247), a "bleached, politically fortified space" (2004: xii). Border militarism, as a way of guarding whiteness, has extended its reach into the political and social interior of Europe, into the everyday zones of national life. In Europe, violent exclusion proceeds by what Jonathan Inda (with view to the US-Mexican border) termed "border prophylaxis": by spatial enclosures (camps), surveillance, and by "governing through crime" (2006: 116) and race. This conflation of blackness and criminality has several important consequences. African immigrants (by extension Black Europeans) are forced to inhabit the figure of the "illegal alien," the enemy "outsider," the "welfare sponger," "pimp," "drug dealer," and the "diseased body"; they are treated accordingly. Random passport and identity checks, arbitrary arrests, body searches, physical abuse, torture, and sexual humiliation are perpetrated by state officials and police with increasing frequency since September 11, 2001. In Europe's white public space, the black and dark-skinned signifier is continuously monitored. In this panoptic theater of race, the figure of the black-terrorist-criminal is conjured on sight.

In Europe's interior "borderlands," in those everyday zones of contact that Gloria Anzaldúa envisioned as "open wound[s]," "where the Third World grates against the first and bleeds" (in Fine et al. 2007: 76; see Anzaldúa 1987: 25), we see an intensi-fication of racial violence and street terror against those whose physical appearance is rejected as non-European. Perceived "as a threat to the [white] body politic" (Campt 2005: 83), black and brown people are brutalized and killed by ordinary Europeans. The attacks appear to be opportunistic encounter-killings (on a train, in front of a pub, on a street, in a park, on a streetcar or subway), perpetrated by close-contact violence: the victim is kicked or beaten to death, stabbed, dowsed with alcohol and burned, bashed with a rock, pushed through a glass door or thrown out of a window. Europe's border war has transfigured the space of the street into a zone of terror.

In this carceral terrain of white-on-black violence, fear becomes a central experience. In the words of one young African man: "I cannot move freely and avoid certain places; I am always afraid" (Men-schenrechtsverein 2002). Europe's "violent security policies ... [want to] install migrants in a condition of permanent insecurity" (Balibar 2004: 15). In Europe's border war, the securocratic apparatus not only includes peripheral borderlines, camps, prisons, and holding cells, but all public places. By policing the perceptual anti-citizen across European Union territory—from the outer perimeter to the camp to the street—border militarism has become commonplace: it has been implanted into the security habitus of the mundane.

Border regimes fabricate cultures of fear through panoptic markers of difference. This observation is attested by the various studies in this volume: the creation of "diseased" and "disabled" African bodies in France (Ticktin, Chapter 9); the vision of "proper" refugees imposed by international aid workers in Tanzania (Malkki, Chapter 7); the sexual targeting of "Asian girls" in Okinawa by US soldiers (Enloe, Chapter 16); the denial of humanity to grieving survivors of war in Sierra Leone (Henry, Chapter 8); the 'disposability' of black bodies in the United States (Giroux, Chapter 20); or the terror focused on "boys in rural areas" of El Salvador who come under suspicion of being soldiers (Dickson-Gómez, Chapter 12). The exclusionary capacity of border regimes is evident beyond fixed geographies.

Normalizing Fear: Monitoring and Surveillance

Analytic insights about Europe's securocratic terror can be transported to other political terrains, whether Japan, Tanzania, Australia, or the United States (see Enloe (Chapter 16), Malkki (Chapter 7), Giroux (Chapter 20), Sontag (Chapter 18), and Mirzoeff (Chapter 21), this volume). As we have seen, the border regime's focus on postulated biopolitical threats is effective in mobilizing public support for and participation in the everyday regimes of terror. In some cases, such a penetration of the security state into the everyday, vernacular spaces of social life is accelerated by enhanced technologies of surveillance and the panoptic regimes erected in militarized space (Masco, Chapter 3 this volume).

The fusion of national security and border protection has taken an electronic turn in some nations, as for instance, in the United States. Camera surveillance of the US-Mexican border has gone online: ordinary citizens can now participate in the policing of national space by accessing the World Wide Web (Rotstein 2008). Computerized, privatized, and global, the US border war is fought by techno-prosthetic means:

In a controversial program aimed at enhancing border security, Texas sheriffs have erected a series of surveillance cameras along the Rio Grande and connected them to the Internet. Thousands of people are now virtual Border Patrol agents—and they're on the lookout for drug smugglers and illegal immigrants. ...

Online border patrolling is about as sexy as real-life police work—hours of tedium punctuated by minutes of high excitement. On Blueservo's Web site, each camera focuses on an area that's known for illegal crossing. Next to a real-time view of a grassy meadow is the message: "Look for individuals on foot carrying backpacks." A shot of a border highway says, "If you see movement from the right to the left, please report this activity." When a citizen spots suspicious activity, they click a button on the Web site and write a report. That message goes to the corresponding sheriff's office. The sheriff may handle the problem or call the U.S. Border Patrol.

To date, more than 43,000 people have logged on and become, as the Web site calls them, "virtual Texas deputies." ... But effective or not, more than 43,000 pairs of eyes are watching the Texas-Mexico border through blueservo.net. (Burnett 2009)

The violence of the US border regime has been turned into an ontological practice by a new political technology of the senses. Anyone, anywhere across the globe, can participate in the surveillance-terror of the US border regime: as "TechnoPatriots," as "virtual Texas deputies" or as "Armchair Warriors." Virtual eyes watching, 24/7, with a militarized gaze that is trained on the nation's southern periphery to monitor the borderland for signs of black or brown bodies, whose movements are criminalized and treated as a national security threat. These moving targets, who appear as blips on someone's computer screen, are effectively dehumanized.

The surveillance and capture of disenfranchised human subjects has become a national pastime in centers of global power. Security patriotism and fear of the phantasmatic terrorist are deeply embedded in Western popular culture and the global public sphere. Similar principles of othering and dehumanization are uncovered by the contributors to this book (Wood (Chapter 15), Turshen (Chapter 17), Dickson-Gómez (Chapter 12), Sontag (Chapter 18), Giroux (Chapter 20), Ticktin (Chapter 9), Mirzoeff (Chapter 21), and Kleinman and Kleinman (Chapter 19) in this volume). Race, sex, and space are conjured as elemental signs of difference, turning marked subjects into targets of political violence and everyday terror.

FEAR AS AN ONTOLOGICAL PRAXIS

The contents of our book are not confined to the study of terrorism or political violence in a conventional sense. We seek to provide a novel approach to the formation and normalization of cultures of fear under conditions of political violence, including war and armed conflict. Our emphasis is on the multiple ways in which regimes of terror and fear are manufactured and performed in the daily lives of ordinary people. We uncover how the production of fear is normalized and essentialized through the reification of the threat of violence, including the theater of terrorism (see Chomsky (Chapter 2), Altheide (Chapter 4), Brison (Chapter 10), Cockburn (Chapter 11), and Žižek (Chapter 5) in this volume). In turn, we examine the manner in which the use of terror is legitimated by states, institutions, and military actors. Throughout this volume we ask how the tactics of fear come into evidence as an ontological praxis—on the ground, at borders, transit hubs, and within a nation's interior, in the everyday performances of social life.

Our book explores the various mechanisms whereby cultures of fear are anchored to the border regimes of a given political system. We show how globalization practices, partnered with the militarization of society, have serious repercussions for the government of social life in local settings. This is especially evident in post-conflict situations, in the aftermath of violence, when human beings, traumatized by bodily injury and by the loss of their families and homes, need to maneuver through purported zones of safety. But these zones of safety, as suggested by the contributors to this volume, are often unsafe, governed by fear (see McSpadden and MacArthur (Chapter 6), Malkki (Chapter 7), Henry (Chapter 8), and Nordstrom (Chapter 13) in this volume). The logic of fear may be imposed on local situations by several factors: these range from the perpetual threat of 'raw' violence inflicted by presumed enemies to the conditions of crisis and uncertainty imposed by state officials, whose assessments regarding a refugee's identity, trauma condition, health, poverty status, eligibility for resource allocation, and asylum or extradition "dictate who may live and who must die" (Mbembe 2003: 11). Minimally, such interventions inhibit subjects' durable ability to shape a life or to imagine a future (Dickson-Gómez (Chapter 12), Ticktin (Chapter 9), and Williksen (Chapter 14) in this volume). New border security measures, biometric technologies, and the surveillance of public space as well as the criminalization of designated populations in emergent border regimes continue to challenge the possibilities for building a global democratic future.

CULTURES OF FEAR: ORGANIZATION OF CONTENTS

Our volume is divided into five thematic sections, thereby illuminating significant analytic connections between distinct essays. The integrating themes are cultures of fear, states of terror, zones of violence, intimacies of suffering, and normalizing terror. Each section begins with a focused introduction that explicates the respective issues and essays. Based on this organizing framework, we have assembled essays by leading scholars and thinkers that investigate the everyday regimes of fear in a global context.

- In Part I, we emphasize the formative dimensions of cultures of fear. The essays by Noam Chomsky, Joseph Masco, David Altheide, and Slavoj Žižek highlight the ways in which the US security state operates in a global theater, securing national support for violence by a culture of fear embedded in scenarios of threat and terror, national media discourse, and popular culture.
- In Part II, we broaden our focus by analyzing emergent states of terror in different countries. Studies by Lucia Ann McSpadden and John MacArthur, Liisa Malkki, Doug Henry, and Miriam Ticktin show how the administration of western aid to refugees in the aftermath of terror-warfare pushes the boundaries of fear into the zones of safety in both Africa and Europe.
- Part III further explores the shifting boundaries of fear within flexible zones of violence. The essays by Susan Brison, Cynthia Cockburn, Julia Dickson-Gómez, Carolyn Nordstrom, and Solrun Williksen document the international syndication of fear that haunts Latin America, Africa, Europe, and the United States, where terror runs through national communities with devastating effects on families and children.
- Part IV reveals how sexual suffering and fear are consequences of the synchronized organization of militarized masculinities and the tactical deployment of soldiers' bodies as weapons. The essays by Elisabeth Wood, Cynthia Enloe, Meredeth Turshen, and Susan Sontag integrate documented cases of military sexual terror into a global analysis.

- In Part V, we conclude with an examination of the ways in which cultures of fear are normalized. The essays by Arthur Kleinman and Joan Kleinman, Henry Giroux, and Nicholas Mirzoeff explore the linkages between the commoditization of fear in a global media market and the political disempowerment of populations worldwide. Panoptic regimes, militarized societies, and security states collude to negate a sense of shared humanity between privileged and disenfranchised populations.

Focused on the formation and normalization of cultures of fear, our collection of essays enables readers to think through the various dimensions of war and terror and to acquire an enhanced understanding of the impact of fear on the lives of men, women, and children in different parts of the world. Our book is designed for a broad interdisciplinary readership concerned with the humanitarian consequences of war, armed conflict, and terror.

REFERENCES

Ahlers, Mike M. (2009) "'Safest' Seat Remarks Get Muslim Family Kicked off Plane." CNN, January 2. Online at: <http://www.cnn.com/2009/US/01/01/family.grounded/index.html>. Accessed January 15, 2009.

Anzaldúa, Gloria (1987) *Borderlands/La Frontera*. 2nd ed, San Francisco: Aunt Lute.

Balibar, Etienne (2004) "Europe as Borderland." The Alexander von Humboldt Lecture in Human Geography, University of Nijmegen, November 10, 2004. Online at: <http://www.ru.nl/socgeo/colloquium/Europe%20as%20Borderland.pdf>. Accessed June 2008.

Burnett, John (2009) "A New Way to Patrol the Texas Border: Virtually." National Public Radio, February 29. Online at: <http://www.npr.org/templates/story/story.php?storyId=101050132&sc=emaf>. Accessed March 3, 2009.

Campt, Tina M. (2005) "Converging Specters of an Other Within." In Patricia Mazón and Reinhild Steingröver (eds.), *Not so Plain as Black and White*. Rochester: Rochester University Press: 82–106.

Feldman, Allen (2004) "Securocratic Wars of Public Safety." *Interventions* 6(3): 330–350.

Fine, Michael, Jaffe-Walter, Reva, Pedraza, Pedro, Futch, Valerie and Stoudt, Brett (2007) "Swimming: On Oxygen, Resistance, and Possibility for Immigrant Youth under Siege." *Anthropology & Education Quarterly* 38(1): 76–96.

Gardner, Amy (2009) "9 Muslim Passengers Removed from Plane." *Washington Post*, January 2: B1. Online at: <http://www.washingtonpost.com/wp-dyn/content/article/2009/01/01/AR2009010101932.html?hpid=topnews>. Accessed January 15, 2009.

Gikandi, Simon (1996) *Maps of Englishness*. New York: Columbia University Press.

Gilroy, Paul (2000) *Between Camps*. London: Penguin.

Gilroy, Paul (2004) "Migrancy, Culture, and a New Map of Europe." In Heike Raphael-Hernandez (ed.), *Blackening Europe*. New York: Routledge: xi–xxii.

Graham, Stephen (2006) "Cities and the 'War on Terror'." *International Journal of Urban and Regional Research* 30(2): 255–276.

Inda, Jonathan Xavier (2006) "Border Prophylaxis." *Cultural Dynamics* 18(2): 115–132.

Jansen, Frank (2008) "Rassistische Polizei–Landtag prüft Vorwürfe." *tagespiegel.de*, February 14. Online at: <http://www.tagesspiegel.de/politik/deutschland/rechtsextremismus/Sachsen-Anhalt;art2647,2476264>. Accessed June 2008.

Mbembe, A. (2003) "Necropolitics." *Public Culture* 15(1): 11–40.

Menschenrechtsverein (2002) "Wenn die Polizei Schwarz sieht ...Der ganz normale Alltag." *Augenauf* (November). Online at <http://www.augenauf.ch/bs/archiv/poldiv/021100.htm>. Accessed July 2, 2008.

Migreurop (2009) "Carte des Camps 2007." Online at: <http://www.migreurop.org>. Accessed March 4, 2009.

Robbins, Liz (2009) "Muslim Family Excluded From AirTran Flight." *New York Times*, January 2. Online at: <http://thelede.blogs.nytimes.com/2009/01/02/muslim-family-excluded-from-airtran-flight>. Accessed January 15, 2009.

Rotstein, Arthur H. (2008) "'TechnoPatriots' use Internet to Watch Border for Migrants." *Tuscon Citizen*, April 19.

United for Intercultural Action (2007) "List of 8855 Documented Refugee Deaths through Fortress Europe: 1993–2007." *United for Intercultural Action*, March 14. Online at: <http://www.unitedagainstracism.org>. Accessed August 2008.

Part I

Cultures of Fear

Cultures of Fear: Introduction

Uli Linke and Danielle Taana Smith

The coercive reach of American imperialism, with its capture of markets, anti-democratic practices, and war-centered economies, has produced far-reaching consequences for global social life. Burned landscapes, wounded bodies, and devastated lives are symptomatic of the predatory forays of empire in the twenty-first century. In the contemporary world order, as in the past, political power is birthed by violence: civil wars, proxy wars, paramilitary wars, wars between states, guerilla wars, revolutionary wars, counterinsurgency wars, and 'humanitarian' border wars. But in this era of globalization, terror warfare and civilian suffering cannot be regarded as random events: terror is intimately linked to the logic of a capitalist world system that is commandeered by the conglomerate interests of US global patronage and policing. Acts of resistance have fueled a climate of unprecedented state-legitimated violence, such as the war on terror, which not only produces new social conditions for militancy but also gives rise to new terrains of security and defense that have influenced the domestic political process of every nation. In Part I, we examine the effects of militarized violence through the specters of a culture of fear that impacts communities across the globe. The essays in this section explore the formation of fear as an emergent social reality or sociological fact that is simultaneously deployed as a powerful discourse to govern populations on a global, national, and local level.

The opening essay by Noam Chomsky (Massachusetts Institute of Technology) offers a critical assessment of the global entanglements of terror, nationalism, and empire-building with a sobering look at the implications of western state violence past and present. Contemporary world events have historical precedents and contexts, and so do acts of terror. Following a case-by-case account of European policies and US-American campaigns of mass devastation in much of Asia, Africa, and the Americas, Chomsky sketches the long-term consequences of western militarism and possible future outcomes. Chomsky's global summation brings to light the traces of a succinct political grammar: terrorism, as defined by the world community, has historically been practiced by western governments, including the United States. Western military interventions, covert operations, participation in proxy wars, and allegiances forged with repressive regimes have caused death and destruction across the world. Resistance movements are obliterated as the United States responds with its "new war on terrorism." According to Chomsky, the contemporary terror-state is enabled by manufacturing national warrior-heroes *and* indifference to global human suffering, much of it among the world's poorest people whose histories are never known or soon forgotten. Terrorism ends, Chomsky concludes, by not participating in state terror.

The subsequent essay by Joseph Masco (University of Chicago) shifts our attention to the interior machinations of empire. With a focus on the United States, Masco shows how an entire nation can be emotionally mobilized to support and execute the programmatic agenda of a militaristic "security state." Looking into the past, Masco argues that a regime of emotions was strategically orchestrated during the Cold War, a time when a visual culture of ruination and nuclear annihilation was deployed by the security state in an attempt to govern the US-American public through the production of fear. What was the national cultural work performed by the mass circulation of images of a nuclear-bombed United States since 1945? The political discourse of fear was to create a docile population that could be seduced into obedience by the state's illusory promise of protection, food, and collective survival after a catastrophic war. Although the machination of *negative* affect initially emerged as a central arena of nation-building in the nuclear age, Masco follows the visual deployment of nuclear fear on film from the early Cold War project of civil defense through the "war on terror." Masco shows that the management of fear remains a central tool of the contemporary national security state. His research demonstrates that the atomic bomb, as a weapon of mass destruction, plays a primary role in the United States as a means of militarizing everyday life and, ultimately, justifying an agenda of war.

Our insights on the politics of fear as an ingredient of state power are further enhanced by David L. Altheide (Arizona State University), whose essay illuminates the formation of insecurity in the twenty-first century. Altheide inquires how public sentiments about terrorism, crime, and victimization are influenced by mass media, especially during the aftermath of the terrorist attacks on 9/11. From a comparative study of news reports about terrorism in five prominent US-American newspapers, Altheide concludes that a fearful awareness of danger and an unsettling sense of the failure of national security have become central features of everyday life. By tracking changes in the prevalent usage of concepts such as fear, victim, terror, and crime before and after September 11, Altheide's research reveals the techniques whereby the media has amplified, even brought about, a national discourse of fear. When such a discourse of fear, which distorts language and experience, inhabits the national imagination and is staged in a global theater, the implications for social control become apparent.

The concluding essay by Slavoj Žižek (University of Ljubljana) complicates the cultural analysis of fear by shifting our attention to the political theater of capitalist fantasy. With a focus on US-America, Žižek depicts a consumption-driven society which sees and experiences the real world through a fantasmatic screen. He contends that "in late capitalist consumerist society," as in the United States, "'real social life' *itself somehow acquires the features of a staged fake*" (see p.70), a disneyfied habitat that nourishes an illusory sense of security and self-contentment. By drawing on popular cultural references, Žižek points to the synchrony between real-world politics, national imagination, and the dream world of media. Behind the obvious expressions of political liberalism and consumer capitalism lie deeper, hidden forms of systemic violence with which supposedly peace-loving western democracies are irrevocably complicit—a system that secretly feeds on violence. The dreamworld enterprise of capitalism thus is inherently unstable. Its perpetuation depends on containing or subverting the "American paranoiac fantasy" of sudden disillusionment. What happens, asks Žižek, when this chimera is partially, though perhaps only momentarily shattered? In reaction to the violence of 9/11, the United States responded with a global war on terror. The eventual public disclosure of the secret "empire of camps," the use of torture and sexual abuse, the disposability of racialized citizen-subjects, and the state's abandonment of civil-human rights have further destabilized the fantasmatic cocoon. But how will it end? What possible futures can be envisioned? Should we anticipate a retreat into a fortified fantasmatic dreamworld-sanctuary that is oblivious to the suffering of others or a realist acceptance of the necessity for global responsibility?

2
The New War Against Terror

Noam Chomsky

During these [past] 200 years, we, the United States expelled or mostly exterminated the indigenous population, that's many millions of people, conquered half of Mexico, carried out depredations all over the region, Caribbean and Central America, sometimes beyond, conquered Hawaii and the Philippines, killing several 100,000 Filipinos in the process. Since World War II, it has extended its reach around the world in ways I don't have to describe. But it was always killing someone else, the fighting was somewhere else, it was others who were getting slaughtered. Not here. Not the national territory.

EUROPE

In the case of Europe, the change is even more dramatic because its history is even more horrendous than ours. We are an offshoot of Europe, basically. For hundreds of years, Europe has been casually slaughtering people all over the world. That's how they conquered the world, not by handing out candy to babies. During this period, Europe did suffer murderous wars, but that was European killers murdering one another. The main sport of Europe for hundreds of years was slaughtering one another. The only reason that it came to an end in 1945, was ... it had nothing to do with Democracy or not making war with each other and other fashionable notions. It had to do with the fact that everyone understood that the next time they played the game it was going to be the end for the world. Because the Europeans, including us, had developed such massive weapons of destruction that that game just had to be over. And it goes back hundreds of years. In the seventeenth century, about probably 40 percent of the entire population of Germany was wiped out in one war.

But during this whole bloody murderous period, it was Europeans slaughtering each other, and Europeans slaughtering people elsewhere. The Congo didn't attack Belgium, India didn't attack England, Algeria didn't attack France. It's uniform. There are again small exceptions, but pretty small in scale, certainly invisible in the scale of what Europe and we were doing to the rest of the world. This is the first change. The first time that the guns have been pointed the other way. And in my opinion that's probably why you see such different reactions on the two sides of the Irish Sea which I have noticed, incidentally, in many interviews on both sides, national radio on both sides. The world looks very different depending on whether you are holding the lash or whether you are being whipped by it for hundreds of years, very different. So I think the shock and surprise in Europe and its offshoots, like here [regarding the September 11 attacks], is very understandable. It is a historic event but regrettably not in scale, in something else and a reason why the rest of the world ... most of the rest of the world looks at it quite differently. Not lacking sympathy for the victims of the atrocity or being horrified by them, that's almost uniform, but viewing it from a different perspective. Something we might want to understand.

WHAT IS THE WAR AGAINST TERRORISM?

[...] The war against terrorism has been described in high places as a struggle against a plague, a cancer which is spread by barbarians, by "depraved opponents of civilization itself." That's a feeling that I share. The words I'm quoting, however, happen to be from 20 years ago. Those are ... that's President Reagan and his Secretary of State. The Reagan administration came into office 20 years ago declaring that the war against international terrorism would be the core of our foreign policy ... describing it in terms of the kind I just mentioned and others. And it was the core of our foreign policy. The Reagan administration responded to this plague spread by depraved opponents of civilization itself by creating an extraordinary international terrorist network, totally unprecedented in scale, which carried out massive atrocities all over the world.

THE REAGAN-US WAR AGAINST NICARAGUA

But I'll just mention one case which is totally uncontroversial, so we might as well not argue about it, by no means the most extreme but uncontroversial. It's uncontroversial because of the judgments of the highest international authorities: the International Court of

Justice, the World Court, and the UN Security Council. So this one is uncontroversial, at least among people who have some minimal concern for international law, human rights, justice and other things like that. And now I'll leave you an exercise. You can estimate the size of that category by simply asking how often this uncontroversial case has been mentioned in the commentary of the last month. And it's a particularly relevant one, not only because it is uncontroversial, but because it does offer a precedent as to how a law-abiding state would respond to ... did respond in fact to international terrorism, which is uncontroversial. And was even more extreme than the events of September 11. I'm talking about the Reagan-US war against Nicaragua which left tens of thousands of people dead, the country ruined, perhaps beyond recovery.

NICARAGUA'S RESPONSE

Nicaragua did respond. They didn't respond by setting off bombs in Washington. They responded by taking it to the World Court, presenting a case, they had no problem putting together evidence. The World Court accepted their case, ruled in their favor, ... condemned what they called the "unlawful use of force," which is another word for international terrorism, by the United States, ordered the United States to terminate the crime and to pay massive reparations. The United States, of course, dismissed the court judgment with total contempt and announced that it would not accept the jurisdiction of the court henceforth. Nicaragua then went to the UN Security Council which considered a resolution calling on all states to observe international law. No one was mentioned but everyone understood. The United States vetoed the resolution. It now stands as the only state on record which has both been condemned by the World Court for international terrorism and has vetoed a Security Council resolution calling on states to observe international law. Nicaragua then went to the General Assembly where there is technically no veto but a negative US vote amounts to a veto. It passed a similar resolution with only the United States, Israel, and El Salvador opposed. The following year, this time the United States could only rally Israel to the cause, so two votes were cast opposed to observing international law. At that point, Nicaragua couldn't do anything lawful. It tried all the measures. They don't work in a world that is ruled by force.

This case is uncontroversial but it's by no means the most extreme. We gain a lot of insight into our own culture and society and what's happening now by asking "how much we know about all this? How much we talk about it? How much you learn about it in school? How much is it all over the front pages?" And this is only the beginning. The United States responded to the World Court and the Security Council by immediately escalating the war very quickly, that was a bipartisan decision, incidentally. The terms of the war were also changed. For the first time there were official orders given ... official orders to the terrorist army to attack what are called "soft targets," meaning undefended civilian targets, and to keep away from the Nicaraguan army. They were able to do that because the United States had total control of the air over Nicaragua and the mercenary army was supplied with advanced communication equipment, it wasn't a guerilla army in the normal sense and could get instructions about the disposition of the Nicaraguan army forces so they could attack agricultural collectives, health clinics, and so on ... soft targets with impunity. Those were the official orders.

WHAT WAS THE REACTION HERE?

What was the reaction? It was known. There was a reaction to it. The policy was regarded as sensible by left-liberal opinion. So Michael Kinsley, who represents the left in mainstream discussion, wrote an article in which he said that we shouldn't be too quick to criticize this policy as Human Rights Watch had just done. He said a "sensible policy" must "meet the test of cost benefit analysis"—that is, I'm quoting now, that is the analysis of "the amount of blood and misery that will be poured in, and the likelihood that democracy will emerge at the other end." Democracy as the US understands the term, which is graphically illustrated in the surrounding countries. Notice that it is axiomatic that the United States, US elites, have the right to conduct the analysis and to pursue the project if it passes their tests. And it did pass their tests. It worked. When Nicaragua finally succumbed to superpower assault, commentators openly and cheerfully lauded the success of the methods that were adopted and described them accurately. So I'll quote *Time* magazine just to pick one. They lauded the success of the methods adopted: "to wreck the economy and prosecute a long and deadly proxy war until the exhausted natives overthrow the unwanted government themselves," with a cost to us that is "minimal," and leaving the victims "with wrecked bridges, sabotaged power stations, and ruined farms," and thus providing the US candidate with a "winning issue": "ending the impoverishment of the people of Nicaragua."

The *New York Times* had a headline saying "Americans United in Joy" at this outcome.

TERRORISM WORKS—TERRORISM IS NOT THE WEAPON OF THE WEAK

That is the culture in which we live and it reveals several facts. One is the fact that terrorism works. It doesn't fail. It works. Violence usually works. That's world history. Secondly, it's a very serious analytic error to say, as is commonly done, that terrorism is the weapon of the weak. Like other means of violence, it's primarily a weapon of the strong, overwhelmingly, in fact. It is held to be a weapon of the weak because the strong also control the doctrinal systems and their terror doesn't count as terror. Now that's close to universal. I can't think of a historical exception, even the worst mass murderers view the world that way. So pick the Nazis. They weren't carrying out terror in occupied Europe. They were protecting the local population from the terrorisms of the partisans. And like other resistance movements, there was terrorism. The Nazis were carrying out counter terror. Furthermore, the United States essentially agreed with that. After the war, the US army did extensive studies of Nazi counter-terror operations in Europe. First I should say that the US picked them up and began carrying them out itself, often against the same targets, the former resistance. But the military also studied the Nazi methods, published interesting studies, sometimes critical of them because they were inefficiently carried out, so a critical analysis, you didn't do this right, you did that right, but those methods, with the advice of Wehrmacht officers who were brought over here, became the manuals of counterinsurgency, of counter-terror, of low-intensity conflict, as it is called, and are the manuals, and are the procedures that are being used. So it's not just that the Nazis did it. It's that it was regarded as the right thing to do by the leaders of western civilization, that is, us, who then proceeded to do it themselves. Terrorism is not the weapon of the weak. It is the weapon of those who are against "us" whoever "us" happens to be. *And if you can find a historical exception to that, I'd be interested in seeing it.*

NATURE OF OUR CULTURE—HOW WE REGARD TERRORISM

Well, an interesting indication of the nature of our culture, our high culture, is the way in which all of this is regarded. One way it's regarded is just suppressing it. So almost nobody has ever heard of it. And the power of American propaganda and doctrine is so strong that even among the victims it's barely known. I mean, when you talk about this to people in Argentina, you have to remind them. Oh, yeah, that happened, we forgot about it. It's deeply suppressed. The sheer consequences of the monopoly of violence can be very powerful in ideological and other terms. [...]

COLOMBIA AND TURKEY

The worst human rights violator in the 1990s is Colombia, by a long shot. It's also, by far, the leading recipient of US military aid in the 1990s, maintaining the terror and human rights violations. In 1999, Colombia replaced Turkey as the leading recipient of US arms worldwide, that is excluding Israel and Egypt which are a separate category. And that tells us a lot more about the war on terror right now, in fact.

Why was Turkey getting such a huge flow of US arms? Well if you take a look at the flow of US arms to Turkey, Turkey always got a lot of US arms. It's strategically placed, a member of NATO, and so on. But the arms flow to Turkey went up very sharply in 1984. It didn't have anything to do with the Cold War. I mean Russia was collapsing. And it stayed high from 1984 to 1999 when it reduced and it was replaced in the lead by Colombia. What happened from 1984 to 1999? Well, in 1984, [Turkey] launched a major terrorist war against Kurds in southeastern Turkey. And that's when US aid went up, military aid. And this was not pistols. This was jet planes, tanks, military training, and so on. And it stayed high as the atrocities escalated through the 1990s. Aid followed it. The peak year was 1997. In 1997, US military aid to Turkey was more than that in the entire period 1950 to 1983, that is the Cold War period, which is an indication of how much the Cold War has affected policy. And the results were awesome. This led to two to three million refugees. Some of the worst ethnic cleansing of the late 1990s. Tens of thousands of people killed, 3,500 towns and villages destroyed, way more than Kosovo, even under NATO bombs. And the United States was providing 80 percent of the arms, increasing as the atrocities increased, peaking in 1997. It declined in 1999 because, once again, terror worked as it usually does when carried out by its major agents, mainly the powerful. So by 1999, Turkish terror, called of course counter-terror, but as I said, that's universal, had worked. Therefore Turkey was replaced by Colombia which had not yet succeeded in its terrorist war. And therefore had to move into first place as a recipient of US arms.

SELF-CONGRATULATION ON THE PART OF WESTERN INTELLECTUALS

Well, what makes this all particularly striking is that all of this was taking place right in the midst of a huge flood of self-congratulation on the part of Western intellectuals which probably has no counterpart in history. I mean you all remember it. It was just a couple [of] years ago. Massive self-adulation about how for the first time in history we are so magnificent; that we are standing up for principles and values; dedicated to ending inhumanity everywhere in the new era of this-and-that, and so-on-and-so-forth. And we certainly can't tolerate atrocities right near the borders of NATO. That was repeated over and over. [It is] only within the borders of NATO where we can not only tolerate much worse atrocities but contribute to them. Another insight into Western civilization and our own is how often was this brought up? Try to look. I won't repeat it. But it's instructive. It's a pretty impressive feat for a propaganda system to carry this off in a free society. It's pretty amazing. I don't think you could do this in a totalitarian state.

TURKEY IS VERY GRATEFUL

Prime Minister Ecevit announced that Turkey would join the coalition against terror, very enthusiastically, even more so than others. In fact, he said they would contribute troops which others have not [been] willing to do. And he explained why. He said, We owe a debt of gratitude to the United States because the United States was the only country that was willing to contribute so massively to our own, in his words, "counter-terrorist" war, that is, to our own massive ethnic cleansing and atrocities and terror. Other countries helped a little, but they stayed back. The United States, on the other hand, contributed enthusiastically and decisively and was able to do so because of the silence, servility might be the right word, of the educated classes who could easily find out about it. It's a free country after all. You can read human rights reports. You can read all sorts of stuff. But we chose to contribute to the atrocities and Turkey is very happy, they owe us a debt of gratitude for that and therefore will contribute troops just as they did during the war in Serbia. Turkey was very much praised for using its F-16s, which we supplied, to bomb Serbia exactly as it had been doing with the same planes against its own population up until the time when it finally succeeded in crushing internal terror, as they called it. And as usual, as always, resistance does include terror. It's true of the American Revolution. That's true of every case I know. Just as it's true that those who have a monopoly of violence talk about themselves as carrying out counter-terror.

THE COALITION—INCLUDING ALGERIA, RUSSIA, CHINA, INDONESIA

Now that's pretty impressive and that has to do with the coalition that is now being organized to fight the war against terror. And it's very interesting to see how that coalition is being described. So have a look at this morning's *Christian Science Monitor* [a month after September 11, 2001]. That's a good newspaper. One of the best international newspapers, with real coverage of the world. The lead story, the front-page story, is about how the United States, you know people used to dislike the United States but now they are beginning to respect it, and they are very happy about the way that the US is leading the war against terror. And the prime example, well in fact the only serious example, the others are a joke, is Algeria. Turns out that Algeria is very enthusiastic about the US war against terror. The person who wrote the article is an expert on Africa. He must know that Algeria is one of the most vicious terrorist states in the world and has been carrying out horrendous terror against its own population in the past couple of years, in fact. For a while, this was under wraps. But it was finally exposed in France by defectors from the Algerian army. It's all over the place there and in England and so on. But here, we're very proud because one of the worst terrorist states in the world is now enthusiastically welcoming the US war on terror and in fact is cheering on the United States to lead the war. That shows how popular we are getting.

And if you look at the coalition that is being formed against terror it tells you a lot more. A leading member of the coalition is Russia which is delighted to have the United States support its murderous terrorist war in Chechnya instead of occasionally criticizing it in the background. China is joining enthusiastically. It's delighted to have support for the atrocities it's carrying out in western China against what it calls Muslim secessionists. Turkey, as I mentioned, is very happy with the war against terror. They are experts. [Like] Algeria, Indonesia is delighted to have even more US support for atrocities it is carrying out in Aceh and elsewhere. Now we can run through the list, the list of the states that have joined the coalition against terror is quite impressive. They have a characteristic in common. They are certainly among the leading terrorist states in the world. And they happen to be led by the world champion.

WHAT IS TERRORISM?

[...] A brief statement of it taken from a US army manual, is fair enough, is that terror is the calculated use of violence or the threat of violence to attain political or religious ideological goals through intimidation, coercion, or instilling fear. That's terrorism. That's a fair enough definition. [...]

But there's a problem. If you use the official definition of terrorism in the comprehensive treaty you are going to get completely the wrong results. So that can't be done. In fact, it is even worse than that. If you take a look at the definition of low-intensity warfare which is official US policy you find that it is a very close paraphrase of what I just read. In fact, low-intensity conflict is just another name for terrorism. That's why all countries, as far as I know, call whatever horrendous acts they are carrying out, counter terrorism. We happen to call it counterinsurgency or low-intensity conflict. [...]

WHY DID THE UNITED STATES AND ISRAEL VOTE AGAINST A MAJOR RESOLUTION CONDEMNING TERRORISM?

There are some other problems. Some of them came up in December 1987, at the peak of the first war on terrorism, that's when the furor over the plague was peaking. The United Nations General Assembly passed a very strong resolution against terrorism, condemning the plague in the strongest terms, calling on every state to fight against it in every possible way. It passed unanimously. One country, Honduras, abstained. Two votes against; the usual two, United States and Israel. Why should the United States and Israel vote against a major resolution condemning terrorism in the strongest terms, in fact pretty much the terms that the Reagan administration was using? Well, there is a reason. There is one paragraph in that long resolution which says that nothing in this resolution infringes on the rights of people, struggling against racist and colonialist regimes or foreign military occupation, to continue with their resistance with the assistance of others, other states, states outside in their just cause. Well, the United States and Israel can't accept that. The main reason that they couldn't at the time was because of South Africa. South Africa was an ally, officially called an ally.

There was a terrorist force in South Africa. It was called the African National Congress. They were a terrorist force officially. South Africa, in contrast, was an ally and we certainly couldn't support actions by a terrorist group struggling against a racist regime. That would be impossible.

And of course there is another one. Namely the Israeli occupied territories, now going into their 35th year. Supported primarily by the United States in blocking a diplomatic settlement for 30 years now, and it still is. And you can't have that. There was another one at the time. Israel was occupying southern Lebanon and was being combated by what the US calls a terrorist force, Hizbullah, which in fact succeeded in driving Israel out of Lebanon. And we can't allow anyone to struggle against a military occupation when it is one that we support, so therefore the US and Israel had to vote against the major UN resolution on terrorism. And I mentioned before that a US vote against ... is essentially a veto. Which is only half the story. It also vetoes it from history. So none of this was ever reported and none of it appeared in the annals of terrorism. If you look at the scholarly work on terrorism and so on, nothing that I just mentioned appears. The reason is that it has got the wrong people holding the guns. You have to carefully hone the definitions and the scholarship and so on so that you come out with the right conclusions; otherwise it is not respectable scholarship and honorable journalism. Well, these are some of problems that are hampering the effort to develop a comprehensive treaty against terrorism. [...]

THE LIKELY PERPETRATORS

Well, with regard to the perpetrators, in a certain sense we are not really clear. [...]

Where do they come from? We know all about that. Nobody knows about that better than the CIA because it helped organize them and it nurtured them for a long time. They were brought together in the 1980s, actually by the CIA and its associates elsewhere: Pakistan, Britain, France, Saudi Arabia, Egypt, China were involved, they may have been involved a little bit earlier, maybe by 1978. The idea was to try to harass the Russians, the common enemy. According to President Carter's National Security Advisor, Zbigniew Brzezinski, the US got involved in mid-1979. Do you remember, just to put the dates right, that Russia invaded Afghanistan in December 1979? OK. According to Brzezinski, the US support for the mojahedin fighting against the government began six months earlier. He is very proud of that. He says we drew the Russians into, in his words, an Afghan trap, by supporting the mojahedin, getting them to invade, getting them into the trap. Now then we could develop this terrific mercenary army. Not a small one, maybe 100,000 men or so bringing together the best killers they could find, who were radical Islamist fanatics from around North Africa, Saudi Arabia ... anywhere they could find them. They were often called the Afghanis but many of them, like bin Laden, were not Afghans. They were brought by the CIA and its friends from elsewhere. Whether Brzezinski is telling the truth or not, I don't know. He may have been bragging, he is apparently very proud of it, knowing the consequences incidentally. But maybe it's true. We'll know someday, if the documents are ever released. Anyway, that's his perception. By January 1980 it is not even in doubt that the US was organizing the Afghanis and this massive military force to try to cause the Russians maximal trouble. It was a legitimate thing for the Afghanis to fight the Russian invasion. But the US intervention was not helping the Afghanis. In fact, it helped destroy the country and much more. The Afghanis, so called, had their own ... and did force the Russians to withdraw, finally. Although many analysts believe that it probably delayed their withdrawal because they were trying to get out of it. Anyway, whatever, they did withdraw.

Meanwhile, the terrorist forces that the CIA was organizing, arming, and training were pursuing their own agenda, right away. It was no secret. One of the first acts was in 1981 when they assassinated the President of Egypt, who was one of the most enthusiastic of their creators. In 1983, one suicide bomber, who may or may not have been connected, it's pretty shadowy, nobody knows. But one suicide bomber drove the US army-military out of Lebanon. And it continued. They have their own agenda. The US was happy to mobilize them to fight its cause but meanwhile they were doing their own thing. They were very clear about it. After 1989, when the Russians had withdrawn, they simply turned elsewhere. Since then they have been fighting in Chechnya, Western China, Bosnia, Kashmir, South East Asia, North Africa, all over the place.

THEY ARE TELLING US WHAT THEY THINK

The United States wants to silence the one free television channel in the Arab world because it's broadcasting a whole range of things, from [Colin] Powell over to Osama bin Laden. So the US is now joining the repressive regimes of the Arab world that try to shut it up. But if you listen to it, if you listen to what bin Laden says, it's worth it. [...] Their prime enemy is what they call the corrupt and oppressive authoritarian brutal regimes of the Arab world and when they say that they get quite a resonance in the region. They also want to defend and they want to replace them by properly Islamist governments. That's where they lose the people of the region. But up till then, they are with them. From their point of view, even Saudi Arabia, the most extreme fundamentalist state in the world, I suppose, short of the Taliban, which is an offshoot, even that's not Islamist enough for them. OK, at that point, they get very little support, but up until that point they get plenty of support. Also they want to defend Muslims elsewhere. They hate the Russians like poison, but as soon as the Russians pulled out of Afghanistan, they stopped carrying out terrorist acts in Russia as they had been doing with CIA backing before that within Russia, not just in Afghanistan. They did move over to Chechnya. But there they are defending Muslims against a Russian invasion. Same with all the other places I mentioned. From their point of view, they are defending the Muslims against the infidels. [...]

WHAT ARE THE POLICY OPTIONS?

Well, there are a number. A narrow policy option from the beginning was to follow the advice of really far-out radicals like the Pope. The Vatican immediately said, look it's a horrible terrorist crime. In the case of crime, you try to find the perpetrators, you bring them to justice, you try them. You don't kill innocent civilians. Like if somebody robs my house and I think the guy who did it is probably in the neighborhood across the street, I don't go out with an assault rifle and kill everyone in that neighborhood. That's not the way you deal with crime, whether it's a small crime like this one or really massive one like the US terrorist war against Nicaragua. [...] And there are plenty of other precedents.

IRA BOMBS IN LONDON

When the IRA set off bombs in London, which is pretty serious business, Britain could have, apart from the fact that it was unfeasible, let's put that aside, one possible response would have been to destroy Boston, which is the source of most of the financing. And of course to wipe out West Belfast. Well, you know, quite apart from the feasibility, it would have been criminal idiocy. The way to deal with it was pretty much what they did. You know, find the perpetrators; bring them to trial; and look for the reasons. Because these things don't come out of nowhere. They come from something. Whether it is a crime in the streets or a monstrous terrorist crime or anything else. There's reasons. And usually if you look at the reasons, some of them are legitimate and ought to be addressed, independently of the crime, they ought to be addressed because they are legitimate. And that's the way to deal with it. There are many such examples. [...]

LEADERLESS RESISTANCE

You know, it could be that the people who did it, killed themselves. Nobody knows this better than the CIA. These are decentralized, nonhierarchic networks. They follow a principle that is called "leaderless resistance." That's the principle that has been developed by the Christian Right terrorists in the United States. It's called leaderless resistance. You have small groups that do things. They don't talk to anybody else. There is a kind of general background of assumptions and then you do it. Actually, people in the antiwar movement are very familiar with it. We used to call them affinity groups. If you assume correctly that whatever group you are in is being penetrated by the FBI, when something serious is happening, you don't do it in a meeting. You do it with some people you know and trust, an affinity group, and then it doesn't get penetrated. That's one of the reasons why the FBI has never been able to figure out what's going on in any of the popular movements. And other intelligence agencies are the same. They can't. That's leaderless resistance or affinity groups, and decentralized networks are extremely hard to penetrate. And it's quite possible that they just don't know. When Osama bin Laden claims he wasn't involved, that's entirely possible. In fact, it's pretty hard to imagine how a guy in a cave in Afghanistan, who doesn't even have a radio or a telephone, could have planned a highly sophisticated operation like that. Chances are it's part of the background. You know, like other leaderless resistance terrorist groups. Which means it's going to be extremely difficult to find evidence. [...]

AN EASY WAY TO REDUCE THE LEVEL OF TERROR

We certainly want to reduce the level of terror, certainly not escalate it. There is one easy way to do that and therefore it is never discussed.

Namely stop participating in it. That would automatically reduce the level of terror enormously. But that you can't discuss. Well we ought to make it possible to discuss it. So that's one easy way to reduce the level of terror.

Beyond that, we should rethink the kinds of policies, and Afghanistan is not the only one, in which we organize and train terrorist armies. That has effects. We're seeing some of these effects now. September 11 is one. Rethink it.

Rethink the policies that are creating a reservoir of support. Exactly what the bankers, lawyers and so on are saying in places like Saudi Arabia. On the streets it's much more bitter, as you can imagine. That's possible. You know, those policies aren't graven in stone.

It's hard to find many rays of light in the last couple of weeks but one of them is that there is an increased openness. Lots of issues are open for discussion, even in elite circles, certainly among the general public. [...] I think there is much more openness and willingness to think about things that were under the rug and so on. These are opportunities and they should be used, at least by people who accept the goal of trying to reduce the level of violence and terror, including potential threats that are extremely severe and could make even September 11 pale into insignificance.

3
Engineering Ruins and Affect

Joseph Masco

Has any nation-state invested as profoundly in ruins as Cold War America? Although many societies have experienced moments of self-doubt about the future, perhaps even contemplating the ruins that might be left behind as testament to their existence, it took American ingenuity to transform ruination into a form of nation-building. In this regard, the invention of the atomic bomb proved to be utterly transformative for the United States: it not only provided the inspiration for a new US geopolitical strategy—one that quickly enveloped the earth in advanced military technology and colonized everyday life with the minute-to-minute possibility of nuclear war. The bomb also provided officials with a new means of engaging and disciplining citizens in everyday life. For US policymakers, the Cold War arms race transformed the apocalypse into a technoscientific project and a geopolitical paradigm, but also a powerful new domestic political resource.

Put differently, a new kind of social contract was formed in the first decade of the nuclear age in the United States, one based not on the protection and improvement of everyday life but, rather, on the national contemplation of ruins. Known initially as "civil defense," the project of building the bomb and communicating its power to the world turned engineering ruins into a form of (inter)national theater. Nuclear explosions matched with large-scale emergency response exercises became a means of developing the bomb as well as imagining nuclear warfare (see Glasstone and Dolan 1977; Kahn 1960; Vanderbilt 2002). This "test program" would ultimately transform the United States into the most nuclear-bombed country on earth, distributing its environmental, economic, and health effects to each and every US citizen (Masco 2006). By the mid-1950s it was no longer a perverse exercise to imagine one's own home and city devastated, on fire, and in ruins; it was a formidable public ritual—a core act of governance, technoscientific practice, and democratic participation. Indeed, in the early Cold War United

States, it became a civic obligation to collectively imagine, and at times theatrically enact through "civil defense," the physical destruction of the nation-state.

It is this specific nationalization of death that I wish to explore in this article, assessing not only the first collective formulations of nuclear fear in the United States but also the residues and legacies of that project for contemporary American society. For today, we live in a world populated with newly charred landscapes and a production of ruins that speaks directly to this foundational moment in US national culture (see Stoler with Bond 2006). The notions of preemption and emergency response that inform the George W. Bush administration's "war on terror" derive meaning from the promises and institutions built by the Cold War security state. Indeed, the logics of nuclear fear informing that multigenerational state and nation-building enterprise exist now as a largely inchoate, but deeply embedded, set of assumptions about power and threat. How Americans have come to understand mass death at home and abroad, I argue, has much to do with the legacies of the Cold War nuclear project, and the peculiar psychosocial consequences of attempting to build the nation through the contemplation of nuclear ruins. [...]

In the aftermath of the terrorist attacks on New York and Washington DC on September 11, 2001, the affective coordinates of the Cold War arms race provided specific ideological resources to the state, which once again mobilized the image of a United States in nuclear ruins to enable war. Ultimately, this article follows Walter Benjamin's (1969: 242) call to interrogate the aestheticized politics that enable increasing militarization and that allow citizens to experience their own destruction as an "aesthetic pleasure of the first order."

BE AFRAID BUT DON'T PANIC!

Nuclear ruins are never the end of the story in the United States but, rather, always offer a new beginning. In the early Cold War period, ruins become the markers of a new kind of social intimacy grounded in highly detailed renderings of theatrically rehearsed mass violence. The intent of these public spectacles—nuclear detonations, city evacuations, and duck-and-cover drills—was not defense in the classic sense of avoiding violence or destruction but rather a psychological reprogramming of the US public for life in a nuclear age. The central project of the early nuclear state was to link US institutions—military, industrial, legislative, and academic—for the production of the bomb, while calibrating public perceptions of the nuclear danger to enable that project. This effort to think through the disaster colonized everyday life as well as the future, while fundamentally missing the actual disaster (see Blanchot 1995). The scripting of disaster in the imagination has profound social effects: it defines the conditions of insecurity, renders other threats invisible, and articulates the terms of both value and loss. In the United States, civil defense was always a willful act of fabulation, an official fantasy designed to promote an image of nuclear war that would be, above all things, politically useful. It also installed an idea of an American community under total and unending threat, creating the terms for a new kind of nation-building that demanded an unprecedented level of militarism in everyday life as the minimum basis for "security."

After the Soviets' first nuclear detonation in 1949, US policymakers committed to a new geopolitical strategy that would ultimately dominate US foreign policy for the remainder of the twentieth century. The policy of "containment," as formalized in National Security Council 68 (known as NSC 68), proposed, in response to the Soviet bomb, a total mobilization of American society based on the experience of World War II. National Security Council 68 articulates the terms of a permanent wartime posture funded by an ever-expanding domestic economy, transforming consumerism into the engine of a new kind of militarized geopolitics. National Security Council 68 identifies internal dissent as perhaps the greatest threat to the project of "Cold War" and calls for a new campaign to discipline citizens for life under the constant shadow of nuclear war. Thus, in Washington, DC, nuclear fear was immediately understood not only to be the basis of US military power, but also a means of installing a new normative reality within the United States, one that could consolidate political power at the federal level. The nuclear danger became a complex new political ideology, both mobilizing the global project of Cold War (fought increasingly on covert terms) and installing a powerful means of controlling domestic political debates over the terms of security. By focusing Americans on an imminent end of the nation-state, federal authorities mobilized the bomb to create the "Cold War consensus" of anticommunism, capitalism, and military expansion. [...]

A long "Cold War" consequently required not only a new geopolitics powered by nuclear weapons but also new forms of psychological discipline at home. Indeed, one of the earliest and most profound projects of the Cold War state was thus to deploy the bomb as a mechanism for accessing and controlling the emotions of citizens (see Orr 2006).

As Guy Oakes has documented (1994: 47), the civil defense programs of the early Cold War were designed to "emotionally manage" US citizens through nuclear fear. The formal goal of this state program was to transform "nuclear terror," which was interpreted by US officials as a paralyzing emotion, into "nuclear fear," an affective state that would allow citizens to function in a time of crisis (see Associated Universities 1952, as well as Oakes 1994: 62–63). By militarizing everyday life through nuclear fear, the Cold War state sought to both normalize and politically deploy an image of catastrophic risk. Rather than offering citizens an image of safety or of a war that could end in victory, the early Cold War state sought instead to calibrate everyday American life to the minute-to-minute possibility of nuclear warfare. In addition to turning the domestic space of the home into the front line of the Cold War, civil defense argued that citizens should be prepared every second of the day to deal with a potential nuclear attack. In doing so, the Civil Defense Program shifted responsibility for nuclear war from the state to its citizens by making public panic the enemy, not nuclear war itself. It was, in other words, up to citizens to take responsibility for their own survival in the nuclear age. As Val Peterson, the first head of the US Civil Defense Administration, argued in 1953:

> Ninety per cent of all emergency measures after an atomic blast will depend on the prevention of panic among the survivors in the first 90 seconds. Like the A-bomb, panic is fissionable. It can produce a chain reaction more deeply destructive than any explosive known. If there is an ultimate weapon, it may well be mass panic—not the A-bomb. (Peterson 1953)

Panic is fissionable. This idea that emotional self-regulation was the single most important issue during a nuclear attack (not to mention the 90-second window on success or failure), sought quite formally to turn all Americans into docile bodies that would automatically support the goals of the security state. Civil defense planners sought ultimately to saturate the public space with a specific idea about nuclear war, one that would nationalize mass death and transform postnuclear ruins into a new American frontier, simply another arena for citizens to assert their civic spirit and ingenuity. At the heart of the project was an effort to install psychological defenses against the exploding bomb, as well as a belief in the possibility of national unity in a postnuclear environment—all via the contemplation of nuclear ruins.

Indeed, as the Eisenhower administration promoted an idea of "Atoms for Peace" around the world to emphasize the benefits of nuclear energy and provide a positive face to atomic science, it pursued an opposite emotional management strategy within the United States (Craig 1998; Hewlett and Holl 1989; Osgood 2006). The domestic solution to the Soviet nuclear arsenal was a new kind of social-engineering project, pursued with help from the advertising industry, to teach citizens a specific kind of nuclear fear while normalizing the nuclear crisis. The goal, as a top-secret study on the "human effects of nuclear weapons development" put it in 1956, was an "emotional adaptation" of the citizenry to nuclear crisis, a program of "psychological defense" aimed at "feelings" that would unify the nation in the face of apocalyptic everyday threat (Panel on The Human Effects of Nuclear Weapons Development 1956). This took the form of the largest domestic propaganda campaign to date in US history (Garrison 2006: 36). Designed to mobilize all Americans for a long Cold War, the civil defense effort involved town meetings and education programs in every public school; it also sought to take full advantage of mass media—television, radio, and, particularly, film. By the mid-1950s, the Federal Civil Defense Agency (FCDA) saturated newspapers and magazines with nuclear war planning advertisements and could claim that its radio broadcasts reached an estimated audience of 175 million Americans per year.

As the campaign evolved, the Federal Civil Defense Agency turned increasingly to film, creating a library of short subjects on nuclear destruction and civil defense that was shown across the country in schools, churches, community halls, and movie theaters. The Federal Civil Defense Agency concluded in 1955 that "each picture will be seen by a minimum of 20,000,000 persons, giving an anticipated aggregate audience of more than half a billion for the civil defense film program of 1955" (1956: 78). A key to winning the Cold War was producing the bomb not only for military use but also in cinematic form for the American public. It is important to recognize that the circulation of these images relied on a simultaneous censorship of images from the atomic bombings of Hiroshima and Nagasaki in 1945. US authorities made available images of destroyed buildings from Japan but withheld the detailed effects of the atomic bomb on the human body, as well as some firsthand accounts of the aftermath. An immediate project of the nuclear state was thus to calibrate the image of atomic warfare for the American public through the mass circulation of certain images of the bomb and the censorship of all others. In this way, officials sought to mobilize the power of mass media to transform nuclear attack from an unthinkable apocalypse into an opportunity for psychological self-management, civic responsibility, and ultimately, governance. Civil defense ultimately sought to produce an "atomic bomb-proof" society in which nuclear conflict was normalized along side all other threats, making public support for the Cold War sustainable.

Civil defense theorists argued that citizens could only achieve this contradictory state of productive fear (simultaneously mobilized and normalized) by gaining intimacy with nuclear warfare itself, by becoming familiar with language of nuclear effects from blast, heat, and fire to radioactive fallout. As the RAND analyst I. I. Janis put it, the goal of civil defense was ultimately an "emotional inoculation" of the US public (1951: 220). This inoculation, he cautioned, needed to be finely calibrated: the simulated nuclear destruction in civil defense exercises, as well as the atomic test film footage released to the public, had to be formidable enough to mobilize citizens but not so terrifying as to invalidate the concept of defense altogether (a distinct challenge in an age of increasingly powerful thermonuclear weapons which offered no hope of survival to most urban residents). A central project of civil defense was thus to produce fear but not terror, anxiety but not panic, to inform about nuclear science but not fully educate about nuclear war. The microregulation of a national community at the emotional level was the goal. Put differently, alongside the invention of a new security state grounded in nuclear weapons came a new public culture of insecurity in the United States: figuring the United States as global nuclear superpower was coterminous with a domestic campaign to reveal the United States as completely vulnerable, creating a citizen–state relationship increasingly mediated by forms of inchoate but everpresent nuclear fear.

Indeed, one of the first US civil defense projects of the Cold War was to make every US city a target, and every US citizen a potential victim of nuclear attack. The Federal Civil Defense Agency circulated increasingly detailed maps of the likely targets of a Soviet nuclear attack through the 1950s, listing the cities in order of population and ranking them as potential targets. In one 1955 map, the top 70 Soviet targets include major population centers as well as military bases in the United States—revealing not only the vulnerability of large cities to the bomb but also the increasingly wide distribution of military industrial sites across the continental United States. As the size of US and Soviet bombs, and the means of delivery, grew (from bombers to intercontinental ballistic missiles [ICBMs]), so too did the highly publicized target lists. Thomas J. Martin and Donald C. Latham's 1963 civil defense textbook, *Strategy for Survival*, for example, presented a case for 303 ground zeros in the United States in case of nuclear war. Designating 303 US cities and towns that would be likely targets of nuclear attack, they concluded that:

> No one can predict that any one or combination of these cities would be attacked in any future war. Thus, it might appear that we are trying to know the unknowable, to predict the unpredictable, to impose a logical rationale upon war which is, itself, illogical and irrational. But such an inference is incorrect. It was shown in Chapter 5 that there are good reasons to believe that a large fraction of these cities would be attacked in a future war—but what specific cities would be included in this fraction? Because there is no precise answer to this question, civil defense planning must assume that all could be potential targets. Any other approach is thermonuclear Russian Roulette played with 100 million American lives. (Martin and Latham 1963: 182)

Thermonuclear Russian roulette. Marking every population center with over 50,000 people a likely target, Martin and Latham saw no "safe" area in the United States. From New York to Topeka, from Los Angeles to Waco, from Albuquerque to Anchorage—each community could increasingly argue that it was a "first strike" target of Soviet attack. Indeed, citizens were informed from multiple media sources that their community—indeed, their very living room—was the literal front line of the Cold War, with Soviet thermonuclear warheads poised to attack.

From 1953 to 1961, the yearly centerpiece of the civil defense program was a simulated nuclear attack on the United States directed by federal authorities. Cities were designated as victims of nuclear warfare, allowing civic leaders and politicians to lead theatrical evacuations of the city for television cameras, followed by media discussions of blast damage versus fire damage versus fallout, and the expected casualty rates if the attack had been "real." In 1955, for example, the "Operation Alert" scenario involved 60 cities hit by a variety of atomic and hydrogen bombs, producing over eight million instant deaths and another eight million radiation victims over the coming weeks. It imagined 25 million homeless and fallout covering some 63,000 square miles of the United States (FCDA 1956; see also Krugler 2006: 126). Each year Americans acted out their own incineration in this manner, with public officials cheerfully evacuating cities and evaluating emergency planning, while nuclear detonations in Nevada and the South Pacific provided new images of fireballs and mushroom clouds to reinforce the concept of imminent nuclear threat. The early Cold War state sought to install a specific idea of the bomb in the American imagination through these public spectacles, creating a new psychosocial space caught between the utopian promise of US technoscience and the minute-to-minute threat of thermonuclear incineration. It sought to make mass death an intimate psychological experience while simultaneously claiming that thermonuclear war could be planned for alongside tornados, floods, and traffic accidents. Civil defense ultimately sought to make nuclear war a space of nation-building, and thereby bring this new form of death under the control of the state.

Here is how one of the most widely circulated US Civil Defense films of the
1950s, *Let's Face It*, described the problem posed by nuclear warfare:

> The tremendous effects of heat and blast on modern structures raise important questions concerning their durability and safety. Likewise, the amount of damage done to our industrial potential will have a serious effect upon our ability to recover from an atomic attack. Transportation facilities are vital to a modern city. The nation's lifeblood could be cut if its traffic arteries were severed. These questions are of great interest not only to citizens in metropolitan centers but also to those in rural areas who may be in a danger zone because of radioactive fallout from today's larger weapons. We could get many of the answers to these questions by constructing a complete city at our Nevada Proving Ground and then exploding a nuclear bomb over it. We could study the effects of damage over a wide area, under all conditions, and plan civil defense activities accordingly. But such a gigantic undertaking is not feasible.

The problem voiced here is ultimately one of scientific detail: how can the security state prepare to survive a nuclear attack if it does not know precisely how every aspect of American life would respond to both the effects of the bomb and the resulting social confusion?

But after denying the possibility of building an entire city in Nevada simply to destroy it, the narrator of *Let's Face It* reveals that the nuclear state has, in fact, done just that:

> Instead we build representative units of a test city. With steel and stone and brick and mortar, with precision and skill—as though it were to last a thousand years. But it is a weird, fantastic city. A creation right out of science fiction. A city like no other on the face of the earth. Homes, neat and clean and completely furnished, that will never be occupied. Bridges, massive girders of steel spanning the empty desert. Railway tracks that lead to nowhere, for this is the end of the line. But every element of these tests is carefully planned in these tests as to its design and location in the area. A variety of materials and building techniques are often represented in a single structure. Every brick, beam, and board will have its story to tell. When pieced together these will give some of the answers, and some of the information we need to survive in the nuclear age.

A *weird, fantastic city*. This test city was also an idealized model of the contemporary American suburb, and by publicizing its atomic destruction the state was involved in an explicit act of psychological manipulation. As we shall see, the Nevada Test Site was the location of nuclear war "simulations" involving real nuclear explosions, and model American cities destroyed in real time for a national audience. Each ruin in these national melodramas—each element of bombed US material culture—was presented as a key to solving the "problem" of nuclear warfare, a means of cracking the code for survival in nuclear conflict. But in this effort to control a specific idea of death, the civil defense strategy also forced citizens to confront the logics of the nuclear state, allowing many to reclaim and reinvest these same ruins with a counternarrative and critique. Thus, real and imagined nuclear ruins became the foundation for competing ideas of national community, producing resistance to, as well as normalization of, a militarized society. But, although the early Cold War effort to produce an "atomic bomb-proof" society may have failed, as we shall see, the psychosocial legacies of this moment continue to haunt and inform US national culture. In the remainder of this article, I offer a history of nuclear ruins in the United States as a means both of recovering the affective coordinates of the nuclear security state, and exploring the lasting impacts of the Cold War "emotional management" strategy on American society.

"CUE FOR SURVIVAL"

On May 5, 1955, 100 million Americans watched live on television a "typical" suburban community blown to bits by an atomic bomb (see FCDA 1955, 1956). Many watched from homes and apartments that were the explicit models for the test city, and saw mannequin families posed in casual everyday moments (at the kitchen table, on the couch, in bed—or watching TV) experience the atomic blast. "Operation Cue" was the largest of the civil defense spectacles staged at the Nevada Test Site: it promised not only to demonstrate the power of the exploding bomb but also to show citizens exactly what a postnuclear American city would look like. In addition to the live television coverage, film footage was widely distributed in the years after the test, with versions shown in movie theaters and replayed on television. Some of the most powerful and enduring US images of atomic destruction were crafted during Operation Cue and remain in circulation to this day. Thus, in important ways, the broken buildings and charred rubble produced in Operation Cue continue to structure contemporary US perceptions of postnuclear ruins, constituting a kind of *ur*-text for the nuclear age.

As an experiment, Operation Cue was designed to test residences, shelter designs, utilities, mobile housing, vehicles, warning systems, as well as a variety of domestic items, under atomic blast. Linked to each of these objects was a specific test program and research team drawn from Los Alamos Scientific Laboratory, the Atomic Energy Commission and the Federal Civil Defense Agency. A variety of Federal Civil Defense Agency exercises were conducted in the aftermath of the explosion as well, including rescue operations, fire control, aircraft evacuations, communication and sanitation efforts, and mass feeding. The test city was designed as a "representative" American community, and was made up of a variety of current building styles (ramblers, two-story brick houses, as well as trailers and mobile homes), a variety of utilities (from electronic towers to propane systems), numerous bomb shelter designs, as well as efforts to protect records (such as a variety of office safes). Over 150 industrial associations participated in the test, insuring that the very latest consumer items from cars to furniture, clothing to dishware, televisions to radio, were installed in the brand-new houses. Hundreds of civilian participants were invited to inhabit not the pristine pre-test city but the post-test atomic ruins: civilians were simultaneously witnesses and test subjects, serving as representative "Americans" and individuals to be tested by viewing the blast and participating in mass feeding and emergency operations. The formal inhabitants of Operation Cue were the mannequin families, dressed and theatrically posed to suggest everyday life activities, communicating through their posture and dress that the bombing was an unexpected intrusion into an intimate home space.

Operation Cue was designed to appeal to a domestic audience, and particularly to women. Unlike previous civil defense films, *Operation Cue* (FCDA 1955, 15 minutes) has a female narrator—Joan Collins—who promises to see the test "through my own eyes and the eye of the average citizen." In its effort to produce a "bomb-proof" society, the Federal Civil Defense Agency was concerned with documenting the effects of the bomb against every detail of middle-class, white, suburban life. The media strategy involved recalibrating domestic life by turning the nuclear family into a nuclearized family, preprogrammed for life before, during, and after a nuclear war. Gender roles were reinforced by dividing up responsibility for food and security in a time of nuclear crisis between women and men. Similarly, the civil defense campaigns in public schools were designed to deploy children to educate their parents about civil defense. Normative gender roles were used to reinforce the idea that nuclear crisis was not an exceptional condition but one that could be incorporated into everyday life with minor changes in household technique and a "can do" American spirit.

Of particular concern in Operation Cue, for example, were food tests and mass feeding programs. In each of the model homes, the pantries and refrigerators were stocked with food. In her film voiceover, Collins underscores Operation Cue's address to women, announcing: "As a mother and housewife, I was particularly interested in the food test program, a test that included canned and packaged food." Additionally, food in various forms of packaging was buried along the desert test site, to expose it to radiation, and some of the mannequin families were posed to be involved in food preparation at the time of the detonation. Conceptually, the argument was that at any moment of the day—while enjoying one's breakfast for example—the bomb could drop. The Federal Civil Defense Agency sought, as McEnaney argues (2000: 109), to create a "paramilitary housewife," emotionally and materially in control of her home and thinking about postnuclear social life. Formally, the Federal Civil Defense Agency was interested in whether or not food would be too contaminated in the immediate aftermath of a blast to eat, and also what kinds of techniques would be needed to feed large groups of homeless, injured, and traumatized people.

Within this scheme of crisis management, food was positioned as a primary means of calming individual anxieties and establishing social authority (McEnaney 2000: 111). Informally, the goal was to saturate the domestic space of the home with nuclear logics and civic obligations, to militarize men, women, and children to withstand either a very long nuclear confrontation or a very short nuclear war. [...]

Indeed, documenting evidence of material survival after the atomic blast was ultimately the point of Operation Cue. The mass feeding project, for example, pulled equipment from the wreckage after the test, as well as the food from refrigerators and buried canned goods, and served them to assembled participants: this emergency meal consisted of roast beef, tomato juice, baked beans, and coffee (FDCA 1955: 67). The destruction of a model American community thus became the occasion of a giant picnic, with each item of food marked as having survived the atomic bomb, and each witness positioned as a postnuclear survivor. Additionally, the emergency rescue group pulled damaged mannequins from out of the rubble and practiced medical and evacuation techniques on them, eventually flying several charred and broken dummies to offsite hospitals by charter plane. The formal message of Operation Cue was that the postnuclear environment would be only as chaotic as citizens allowed, that resources (food, shelter, and medical) would still be present, and that society—if not the nation-state—would continue. Nuclear war was ultimately presented as a state of mind that could be incorporated into one's normative reality—it was simply a matter of emotional preparation and mental discipline.

The mannequin families that were intact after the explosion were soon on a national tour, complete with tattered and scorched clothing. J. C. Penney's department stores, which provided the garments, displayed these postnuclear families in its stores around the country with a sign declaring "this could be you!" Inverting a standard advertising appeal, it was not the blue suit or polkadot dress that was to be the focal point of viewers' identification. Rather, it was the mannequin as survivor, whose very existence seemed to illustrate that you could indeed "beat the a-bomb", as one civil defense film of the era promised. Invited to contemplate life within a postnuclear ruin as the docile mannequins of civil defense, the national audience for Operation Cue was caught in a sea of mixed messages about the power of the state to control the bomb. This kind of ritual enactment did not resolve the problem of the bomb but, rather, focused citizens on emotional self-discipline through nuclear fear. It asked them to live on the knife's edge of a psychotic contradiction—an everyday life founded simultaneously in total threat and absolute normality—with the stakes being nothing less than survival itself.

Indeed, although Operation Cue was billed as a test of "the things we use in everyday life," the full intent of the test was to nationalize nuclear fear and install a new civic understanding via the contemplation of mass destruction and death. Consider the narrative of Mr Arthur F. Landstreet (the general manager of the Hotel King Cotton in Memphis, Tennessee) who volunteered to crouch down in a trench at the Nevada Test Site about 10,000 feet from ground zero and experience the nuclear detonation in Operation Cue. After the explosion, he explained why it was important for ordinary citizens to be tested on the front line of a nuclear detonation:

> Apparently the reason for stationing civilians at Position Baker was to find out what the actual reaction from citizens who were not schooled in the atomic field would be, and to get some idea of what the ordinary citizen might be able to endure under similar conditions. This idea was part of the total pattern to condition civilians for what they might be expected to experience in case of atomic attack. ... Every step of the bomb burst was explained over and over from the moment of the first flash of light until the devastating blast. We were asked to make time tests from the trench to our jeeps. We did this time after time, endeavoring to create more speed and less loss of motion. We were told that this was necessary because, if the bomb exploded directly over us with practically no wind, the fallout would drop immediately downward, and we would be alerted to get out of the territory. We would have about 5 minutes to get at least 2.5 to 3 miles distant, so it was necessary that we learn every move perfectly. (FCDA 1955: 75)

The total pattern to condition civilians. Physical reactions to the nuclear explosion are privileged in Mr Landstreet's account, but a corollary project is also revealed, that of training the participants not to think in a case of emergency but simply to act. If the first project was an emotional management effort to familiarize citizens with the exploding bomb—to psychologically inoculate them against their own apocalyptic imagination—the later effort sought simply to control those same bodies, to train and time their response to official commands. The atomic bomb extended the docility of the citizen-subject to new levels, as civil defense sought to absorb the everyday within a new normative reality imbued with the potential for an imminent and total destruction.

This short-circuiting of the brain, and willingness to take orders under the sign of nuclear emergency, reveals the broader scope of the civil defense project: anesthetizing as well as protecting, producing docility as well as agency. This effort to document the potentialities of life in a postnuclear environment met with almost immediate resistance. In addition to the mounting scientific challenges to the claims of civil defense, a "mothers against the bomb" movement started in 1959 when two young mothers in New York refused to participate in Operation Alert by simply taking their children to Central Park rather than the fallout shelter (Garrison 2006: 93–95). The widely publicized effects of radioactive fallout in the 1950s as well as the move from atomic to thermonuclear weapons provided ample evidence that Operation Cue was not, in the end, a "realistic" portrait of nuclear warfare. [...]

Thus, as a scientific test of "everyday objects," Operation Cue had less value over time, as the effects of blast and radiation in increasingly powerful weapons rendered civil defense almost immediately obsolete as a security concept. In Cold War ideology, however, the promise of nuclear ruins was deployed by the state to secure the possibility of a postnuclear remainder, and with it, the inevitable reconstitution of social order. The discourse of "obliteration" here, however, reveals the technoscientific limitations of that ideological project, as the destructive reality of thermonuclear warfare radically limits the possibility of a postnuclear United States.

After the 1963 Partial Test Ban Treaty, the visual effects of the bomb were eliminated as atomic testing went underground. The elimination of aboveground tests had two immediate effects: (1) it changed the terms of the public discourse about the bomb, as the state no longer had to rationalize the constant production of mushroom clouds and the related health concerns over radioactive fallout to US citizens, and (2) it locked in place the visual record of the bomb. Thus, the visual record of the 1945–63 aboveground test program, with its deep implication in manipulating public opinions and emotions, remains the visual record of the bomb to this day. As science, Operation Cue was always questionable, but as national theater it remains a much more productive enterprise: it created an idealized consumer dream space and fused it with the bomb, creating the very vocabulary for thinking about the nuclear emergency that continues to inform US politics. Thus, the motto of

Operation Cue "Survival Is Your Business" is not an ironic moment of atomic kitsch, but rather reveals the formal project of the nuclear state, underscoring the link between the production of threat, its militarized response, and the Cold War economic program. As an emotional management campaign, civil defense proved extraordinarily influential, installing within American national culture a set of ideas, images, and assumptions about nuclear weapons that continued to inform Cold War politics, and that remain powerful to this day. [...]

EPILOGUE

Reclaiming the emotional history of the atomic bomb is crucial today, as nuclear fear has been amplified to enable a variety of political projects at precisely the moment American memory of the bomb has become impossibly blurred. In the United States, nuclear fear has recently been used to justify preemptive war and unlimited domestic surveillance, a worldwide system of secret prisons, and the practices of rendition, torture, and assassination. But what today do Americans actually know or remember about the bomb? We live not in the ruins produced by Soviet ICBMs but, rather, in the emotional ruins of the Cold War as an intellectual and social project. The half-century-long project to install and articulate the nation through contemplating its violent end has colonized the present. The terrorist attacks on New York and Washington, DC in 2001 may have produced a political consensus that "the Cold War is over" and a formal declaration of a counterterrorism project. But American reactions to those attacks were structured by a multigenerational state project to harness the fear of mass death to divergent political and military industrial agendas. [...]

US citizens live today in the emotional residues of the Cold War nuclear arms race, which can only address them as fearful docile bodies. Thus, even in the twenty-first century, Americans remain caught between terror and fear, trapped in the psychosocial space defined by the once and future promise of nuclear ruins.

REFERENCES

Associated Universities (1952) *Report of the Project East River*. New York: Associated Universities.

Benjamin, Walter (1969) "The Work of Art in the Age of Mechanical Reproduction." In *Illuminations*, New York: Schocken Books: 217–251.

Blanchot, Maurice (1995) *The Writing of Disaster*. Lincoln: University of Nebraska Press.

Craig, Campbell (1998) *Destroying the Village*. New York: Columbia University Press.

Federal Civil Defense Administration (FCDA) (1955) *Operation Cue: The Atomic Test Program*. Washington DC: Government Printing Office.

FCDA (1956) *Annual Report for 1955*. Washington DC: Government Printing Office.

Garrison, Dee (2006) *Bracing for Armageddon*. Oxford: Oxford University Press.

Glasstone, Samuel and Philip J. Dolan (eds.) (1977) *The Effects of Nuclear Weapons*. 3rd edition. Washington DC: US Department of Defense and US Department of Energy.

Hewlett, Richard G., and Jack M. Holl (1989) *Atoms for Peace and War 1953–1961*. Berkeley: University of California Press.

Janis, Irving L. (1951) *Air War and Emotional Stress*. New York: McGraw-Hill.

Kahn, Herman (1960) *On Thermonuclear War*. Princeton: Princeton University Press.

Krugler, David F. (2006) *This Is Only a Test*. New York: Palgrave Books.

Martin, Thomas J. and Donald C. Latham (1963) *Strategy for Survival*. Tucson: University of Arizona Press.

Masco, Joseph (2006) *The Nuclear Borderlands*. Princeton: Princeton University Press.

McEnaney, Laura (2000) *Civil Defense Begins at Home*. Princeton: Princeton University Press.

Oakes, Guy (1994) *The Imaginary War*. New York: Oxford University Press.

Orr, Jackie (2006) *The Panic Diaries*. Durham: Duke University Press.

Osgood, Kenneth (2006) *Total Cold War*. Lawrence: University Press of Kansas.

Panel on the Human Effects of Nuclear Weapons Development (1956) *The Human Effects of Nuclear Weapons Development*. Washington DC: A Report to the President and the National Security Council.

Peterson, Val (1953) "Panic: The Ultimate Weapon?" *Collier's*, August 21: 99–107.

Stoler, Ann Laura, with David Bond (2006) "Refractions off Empire." *Radical History Review* 95(Spring): 93–107.

Vanderbilt, Tom (2002) *Survival City*. New York: Princeton Architectural Press.

4
Terrorism and the Politics of Fear

David L. Altheide

> Al Qaeda is to terror what the Mafia is to crime.
> > *George W. Bush*

> If we make the wrong choice, the danger is that we will get hit again, that we'll be hit in a way that is devastating.
> > *Dick Cheney*

> He has conviction. ... He's taking the fight to the terrorists. ... I love my kids. I want my kids to be safe.
> > *Undecided voter 'leaning' toward Bush*

George W. Bush's reelection in 2004 was preordained when his handlers were able to convince true believers that citizens killed in the 9/11 attacks were victims of al-Qaeda-aided-by-Iraq-that-had-weapons-of-mass-destruction. Many Americans, and the majority of Bush supporters, continued to believe that Iraq was involved in the 9/11 hijackings and was prepared to use stockpiles of weapons of mass destruction against the United States despite incontrovertible evidence to the contrary (Kull 2004; Kull, Ramsay, and Lewis 2002). It was not evidence that drove Bush supporters; it was emotions consonant with the mass mediated politics of fear nurtured by decades of crime control efforts. The architect of the 9/11 attacks, Osama bin Laden, remains free (at this writing), whereas an estimated 15,000 to 100,000 Iraqis, mostly women and children, have been killed (BBC 2004). As Vice President Cheney's comment (above) indicates, the Bush campaign celebrated the victims of 9/11 and warned that more US citizens would die if the Iraq War did not continue. Fear has great political utility in joining terrorism with nonconformity, deviance, and crime as a threat (Hornqvist 2004). The politics of fear have transformed terrorism as a tactic to terrorism as a world condition, and now, as Giroux suggests, "the rhetoric of terrorism is important because it operates on many registers to both address and inflict human misery" (2003: 5).

This article examines these events as products of the politics of fear, or decision-makers' promotion and use of audience beliefs and assumptions about danger, risk, and fear, to achieve certain goals. The particular focus is on how fear as a topic was presented in news reports about terrorism and victimization and, more generally, how news reports about terrorism in five nationally prominent newspapers reflect the terms and discourse associated with the politics of fear. I wish to examine the conceptual and empirical support for the politics of fear thesis, which may be stated as follows: The terms *crime*, *victim*, and *fear* are joined with news reports about terrorism to construct a public discourse that reflects symbolic relationships about order, danger, and threat which may be exploited by political decision makers. [...]

NEWS AND THE DISCOURSE OF FEAR

The discourse of fear has been constructed through news and popular culture accounts. The main focus of the discourse of fear in the United States for the past 30 years or so has been crime. News reports about crime and fear have contributed to the approach taken by many social scientists in studying how crime is linked with fear. [...]

Criminal victimization, including numerous crime myths (predators, stranger danger, random violence; Best 1999) contributed to the cultural foundation of the politics of fear, particularly the belief that we were all actual or potential victims and needed to be protected from the source of fear—criminals or terrorists (Garland 2001). Politicians and state control agencies, working with news media as "news sources," have done much to capitalize on this concern and to promote a sense of insecurity and reliance on formal agents of social control—and related businesses—to provide surveillance, protection, revenge, and punishment to protect us, to save us (Chiricos et al. 1997; Ericson et al. 1991; Surette 1992). Hornqvist suggests that a security perspective overrules mere law, especially as numerous instances of deviance and violations are perceived to be threatening social order:

> First, the central factor is not what acts an individual may have committed, but rather which group an individual may belong to. Is he a drug addict? Is she an activist? Refugee? Muslim? Arab? ... Second, according to security logic, it is not the behaviour itself that is of interest, but rather what this might be perceived as

indicating: does it mean that the individual constitutes a risk? ...
(2004: 39)

The mass media and popular culture are best conceived of as key
elements of our symbolic environment rather than independent
causes and effects. News does not merely set agendas; rather,
consistent with symbolic interaction theory, news that relies on
certain symbols and promotes particular relationships between
words, deeds, and issues also guides the perspectives, frameworks,
language, and discourse that we use in relating to certain problems
as well as related issues. My focus in this article is on news that
guides discourse. [...]

Tracking the emergence of new "connections" during a period
of time is one way to assess the process of the social construction
of reality. Research documents how fear and crime have been
joined. Crime and threats to the public order—and therefore, all
good citizens—are part of the focus of fear, but the topics change
throughout time. What they all have in common is pointing to
the "Other," the outsider, the nonmember, the alien. However,
Schwalbe et al. (2000) have shown that "othering" is part of a
social process whereby a dominant group defines into existence an
inferior group. This requires the establishment and "group sense"
of symbolic boundaries of membership. These boundaries occur
through institutional processes that are grounded in everyday
situations and encounters, including language, discourse, accounts,
and conversation. Knowledge and skill at using "what everyone
like us knows" involves formal and informal socialization so that
members acquire the coinage of cultural capital with which they
can purchase acceptance, allegiance, and belonging. Part of this
language involves the discourse of fear:

> Discourse is more than talk and writing; it is a way of talking
> and writing. To regulate discourse is to impose a set of formal or
> informal rules about what can be said, how it can be said, and
> who can say what to whom. ... The ultimate consequence is a
> regulation of action. ... When a form of discourse is established
> as standard practice, it becomes a tool for reproducing inequality,
> because it can serve not only to regulate thought and emotion,
> but also to identify Others and thus to maintain boundaries as
> well. (Schwalbe et al. 2000: 433–434)

Fear, crime, terrorism, and victimization are experienced and known vicariously through the mass media by audience members. Information technology, entertainment programming, and perspectives are incorporated into a media logic that is part of the everyday life of audience members. Media logic is defined as a form of communication and the process through which media transmit and communicate information. Elements of this form include the distinctive features of each medium and the formats used by these media for the organization, the style in which it is presented, the focus or emphasis on particular characteristics of behavior, and the grammar of media communication. [...]

News formats, or the way of selecting, organizing, and presenting information, shape audience assumptions and preferences for certain kinds of information. The mass media are important in shaping public agendas by influencing what people think about and how events and issues are packaged and presented. Certain news forms have been developed as packages or "frames" for transforming some experience into reports that will be recognized and accepted by the audience as "news." Previous research has shown how the "problem frame" was encouraged by communication formats and in turn has promoted the use of "fear" throughout American society (Altheide 1997). Other work has demonstrated that the linkage of crime with fear has promoted a discourse of fear, or the pervasive communication, symbolic awareness, and expectation that danger and risk are a central feature of everyday life (Altheide 1997, 2002a; Altheide and Michalowski 1999; Ericson and Haggerty 1997).

It is not fear of crime, then, that is most critical. It is what this fear can expand to, what it can become. Sociologists have observed that we are becoming "armored." Social life changes when more people live behind walls, hire guards, drive armored vehicles (sport utility vehicles), wear "armored" clothing—No Fear!—("big soled shoes"), carry mace, handguns, and take martial arts classes. Indeed, many symbolic interactionists would assert that acting in certain ways provides the meaning or interpretation of fear. The problem is that these activities reaffirm and help produce a sense of disorder that our actions perpetuate. We then rely more on formal agents of social control to "save us" by "policing them", the "Others", who have challenged our faith.

The major impact of the discourse of fear is to promote a sense of disorder and a belief that "things are out of control". Ferraro (1995) suggests that fear reproduces itself or becomes a self-fulfilling prophecy. Social life can become more hostile when social actors define their situations as "fearful" and engage in speech communities through the discourse of fear. And people come to share an identity as competent "fear realists" as family members, friends, neighbors, and colleagues socially construct their effective environments with fear. Behavior becomes constrained, community activism may focus more on "block watch" programs and quasi-vigilantism, and we continue to avoid "downtowns" and many parts of our social world because of "what everyone knows." In short, the discourse of fear incorporates crime reflexively; the agents, targets, and character of fear are constituted through the processes that communicate fear.

Fear is part of our everyday discourse, even though we enjoy unprecedented levels of health, safety, and life expectancy. And now we "play with it." More of our "play worlds" come from the mass media. News reports are merging with TV reality programs and crime dramas ripped from the front pages that in turn provide templates for looking at everyday life. [...]

Stories of assaults and kidnappings blasted across headlines—even when false or greatly distorted—make it difficult for frightened citizens to believe that schools are one of the safest places in American society. It is becoming more common to "play out" scenarios of danger and fear that audiences assume to be quite commonplace. Researchers find that many of these hoaxes rely on stereotypes of marginalized groups (poor people and racial minorities). The oppositions that become part of the discourse of fear can be illustrated in another way as well. Repetitious news reports that make connections between fear, children, schools, and suspected assailants who fit stereotypes are easy to accept even when they are false. Katheryn Russell's (1998) study of 67 publicized racially tinged hoaxes between 1987 and 1996 illustrates how storytellers frame their accounts in social identities that are legitimated by numerous reports and stereotypes of marginalized groups (racial minorities). For example, in 1990 a George Washington University student reported that another student had been raped by two Black men with "particularly bad body odor" to "highlight the problems of safety for women."

Examples of crime hoaxes abound, but so do false terrorism reports. I have more in mind than the hundreds of "false reports" of anthrax that followed 9/11 attacks on the United States in 2001. When people "pretend" that they have been assaulted, abducted, or in some way harmed by strangers, they are acting out a morality play that has become part of a discourse of fear or the notion that fear and danger are pervasive. Indeed, a student's project in New

York City involved placing black boxes in the subway to elicit citizens' concerns:

> At the same time it turned out that those 37 black boxes with the word "Fear" on them, which mysteriously turned up attached to girders and walls in the Union Square subway station last Wednesday, were, as you may have guessed from the start, an art project. The boxes, which spread panic and caused the police to shut the station for hours and call in the bomb squad, turn out to be the work of Clinton Boisvert, a 25-year-old freshman at the School of Visual Arts in Manhattan, who surrendered Monday to the Manhattan district attorney's office, which intends to prosecute him on charges of reckless endangerment. (Kimmelman 2002: 1)

METHODS AND MATERIALS

This article draws from several research projects that used qualitative content analysis to track the discourse of fear over time and across different topics (crime, drugs, children, immigrants) presented in various newspapers (Altheide 1996, 1997; Altheide and Michalowski 1999). One way to approach these questions is by "tracking discourse," a qualitative document analysis technique that tracks words, themes, and frames during a period of time, across different issues, and across different news media.

The aim in this study was to compare coverage of terrorism with crime and victim and note how these may be related to use of the word *fear*. [...] The research design called for comparing several newspapers' coverage of fear, crime, terrorism, and victim (in headlines and reports) at two 18-month time periods before and after September 11, 2001. The research design also called for including several major newspapers. The first newspaper examined was the *Los Angeles Times*. Subsequently, students in a seminar project obtained data from the *New York Times, Washington Post, San Francisco Chronicle*, and *USA Today*. News reports were selected using Lexis/Nexis materials. News reports were selected according to search criteria that would identify articles with the words *fear, victim, crime,* and *terrorism* in various relationships or within several words of one another. For example, we examined reports with *fear* in headlines and *victim* in the body of the article. [...]

NEWS SOURCES AND THE POLITICS OF FEAR

A politics of fear rests on the discourse of fear. The politics of fear serves as a conceptual linkage for power, propaganda, news and popular culture, and an array of intimidating symbols and experiences, such as crime and terrorism. [...]

Numerous public opinion polls indicated that audiences were influenced by news media reports about the attacks as well as the interpretations of the causes, the culprits, and ultimately the support for various US military actions. For example, one study of the perceptions and knowledge of audiences and their primary source of news found that gross misperceptions of key facts were related to support of the war with Iraq. Misperceptions were operationalized as stating that clear evidence was found linking Iraq to al-Qaeda, that weapons of mass destruction had been found, and that world opinion favored the Iraq war. Many of these misperceptions were consistent with news reports, particularly with those on Fox News. The authors conclude the following:

> From the perspective of democratic process, the findings of this study are cause for concern. ... What is worrisome is that it appears that the President has the capacity to lead members of the public to assume false beliefs in support of his position. ... In the case of the Iraq War, among those who did not hold false beliefs, only a small minority supported the decision to go to war. ... It also appears that the media cannot necessarily be counted on to play the critical role of doggedly challenging the administration. (Kull et al. 2002: 596–597)

The White House influence on news content was aided by other government and military officials who also dominated news reports about terrorism and fear.

> But how men and women interpret and respond to their fear—these are more than unconscious, personal reactions to imagined or even real dangers. They are also choices made under the influence of belief and ideology, in the shadow of elites and powerful institutions. There is, then, a politics of fear. Since September 11, that politics has followed two distinct tracks: First, state officials and media pundits have defined and interpreted the objects of Americans' fears—Islamic fundamentalism and terrorism—in anti-political or non-political terms, which has

raised the level of popular nervousness; and, second, these same elites have generated a fear of speaking out not only against the war and US foreign policy but also against a whole range of established institutions. (Robin 2002: 5)

Newspapers as well as TV network news relied heavily on administration sources that directed the focus and language of news coverage. This was particularly apparent with those persons interviewed. A study by the *Columbia Journalism Review* documented this trend: "According to numbers from the media analyst Andrew Tyndall, of the 414 stories on Iraq broadcast on NBC, ABC, and CBS from last September to February, all but thirty-four originated at the White House, Pentagon, and State Department. So we end up with too much of the 'official' truth" (Cunningham 2003: 24). An analysis by *Fairness and Accuracy in Reporting* (2003) of network news interviewees one week before and one week after Secretary of State Colin Powell addressed the United Nations about Iraq's alleged possession of weapons of mass destruction found that two thirds of the guests were from the United States, with 75 percent of these being current or former government or military officials, and only one—Senator Kennedy—expressed skepticism or opposition to the impending war with Iraq.

The news media played a major role in promoting the politics of fear following the September 11 attacks. Dan Rather, CBS anchorman, acknowledged the pressure to comply with propaganda and that many of the tough questions were not being asked. Rather told a British journalist the following:

It is an obscene comparison ... but you know there was a time in South Africa that people would put flaming tires around people's necks if they dissented. And in some ways the fear is that you will be necklaced here, you will have a flaming tire of lack of patriotism put around your neck. ... Now it is that fear that keeps journalists from asking the toughest of the tough questions. ...

It starts with a feeling of patriotism within oneself. It carries through with a certain knowledge that the country as a whole—and for all the right reasons—felt and continues to feel this surge of patriotism. ...

Limiting access, limiting information to cover the backsides of those who are in charge of the war, is extremely dangerous and cannot and should not be accepted. And I am sorry to say that, up to and including the moment of this interview, that overwhelmingly it has been accepted by the American people. And the current administration revels in that, they relish that and they take refuge in that. (Engel 2002: 4)

Even news magazines like *Newsweek* concurred that the news was being managed: "News management is at the heart of the administration's shake-up of Iraq policy. The National Security Council recently created four new committees to handle the situation in Iraq. One is devoted entirely to media coordination—stopping the bad news from overwhelming the good" (Wolfe and Norland 2003: 32).

Very dramatically, journalists cried on camera, wore flag lapels, and often referred to those involved in planning and fighting the Afghanistan and Iraq wars as "we." Moreover, they invoked routinely the claim that the "world is different," security and safety can no longer be taken for granted, and many sacrifices would have to be made (Altheide 2004). Numerous observers raised serious questions about the role that journalism played in covering the attacks, the wars with Afghanistan and Iraq that followed, and the increased surveillance and control of United States citizens. [...]

The news reports that were published by a compliant press stressed fear of terrorism. The collective identity of victims of terrorist attacks was promoted by news reports stressing communal suffering as well as opportunities to participate in helping survivors and in defeating terrorism (Altheide 2004). More traditional and culturally resonant narratives about crime, drugs, and evil were transformed into the "terror story." Sorrow, suffering, empathy, and pain were merged with fear and vengeance. National character was played out in scenarios of heroics, sacrifice, suffering, marketing, and spending (Denzin and Lincoln 2003). Patriotic responses to the attacks were joined with commercialism and pleas for donations as well as support for an ill-defined and nebulous "war on terrorism" that referred to an idea as well as a tactic or method. Building on a foundation of fear, citizens who saw the repetitive visuals of the World Trade Center attacks generously followed governmental directives to donate blood, supplies, and money to the immediate victims of the attacks. They were also urged to travel, purchase items, and engage in numerous patriotic rituals, while civil liberties were compromised and critics were warned by the Attorney General to not "give ammunition to America's enemies." This was the context for constructing the politics of fear.

NEWS AND THE POLITICS OF FEAR

The politics of fear did not begin with September 11 in 2001; the politics of fear was extended from a long history associating fear with crime. A central argument of previous research (Altheide 2002b) was that fear is cumulatively integrated into topics throughout time and indeed becomes so strongly associated with certain topics that, on repetition, is joined with that term—as with an invisible hyphen—and eventually the term *fear* is no longer stated but is simply implied. Examples from previous work include gangs, drugs, and in some cases even crime, although crime continues to be heavily associated with fear (Altheide 2002b). Of course, fear is also connected to many other issues in social life, but the close connection with crime led to increased use and familiarity of fear in public discourse (Altheide 2002b; Furedi 1997). My aim here is to show the continuity between major events—the attacks of September 11—and a history of crime reporting emphasizing fear and social control. [...] Building on previous work, I was interested in whether fear and terrorism were strongly associated with articles featuring fear in headlines. Of course, they were, but to varying degrees. Tracking changes in the use of *fear, crime, terrorism,* and *victim* in several newspapers 18 months before and after September 11 reveals the following changes:

> There was a dramatic increase in linking terrorism to fear.
> Coverage of crime and fear persisted but at a very low rate.
> There was a large increase in linking terrorism to victim.

First, the five newspapers that provided data for this project varied considerably in the increases of *fear* in headlines and *crime* in report. The *Los Angeles Times*, which already had a strong "base" in crime reporting, showed the least increase (32 percent), whereas *USA Today* (73 percent), *New York Times* (85 percent), and *Washington Post* (116 percent) all trailed the most massive increase in crime reporting by the *San Francisco Chronicle* (181 percent). [...] The relevance of terrorism and sensitivity to crime can be illustrated by an editorial on October 15, 2002, "Media Feeding the Fear," which was about the "Tarot Card" serial killer who was shooting people seemingly at random. In this and subsequent reports by other news media, shooting people is linked to terrorism, and the shooters are labeled as terrorists.

This inexplicable string of murders has triggered yet another disappointing overreaction from the media. But this is different from the Chandra Levy or O. J. Simpson overreactions. We are a different country from the one that weathered those stories. We feel more vulnerable to terrorism, and no matter how you cut it, this killer is a terrorist. His purpose, or at least one of them, is to spread terror. And the media playing right into his hands, as if September 11 never happened.

> "We may be entering a time when what has been ghettoized in Israel and the Middle East breaks its boundaries," says UC Berkeley dean of journalism Orville Schell, referring to suicide bombers and other acts of terrorism. "The unspoken thought is, 'What if this guy is a Muslim?' The media is feeding this most paranoid fear of all but without acknowledging it." ...
>
> The national climate of fear, energized by this psycho sniper, demands that the media examine its decisions more critically than ever. What kind of coverage serves the public interest? What information helps, and more important what harms? (Ryan 2002: A23)

Next, [my research] shows the massive increase in reports that associated fear with terrorism. Fear in headlines and terrorism in news reports greatly exceeded the increases in fear and crime. Four of the five newspapers (the exception was the *Washington Post*) increased the linkage of fear with terrorism by more than 1,000 percent. [...] The resulting measures reflected a foundational politics of fear that promoted a new public discourse and justification for altering everyday life and social interaction. [...]

Similar to propaganda, messages about fear are repetitious, stereotypical of outside "threats" and especially suspect and "evil Others." These messages also have a resonance of moral panic, with the implication that action must be taken to not only defeat a specific enemy but to also save civilization (Hunt 1997). Because so much is at stake, it follows that drastic measures must be taken, that compromises with individual liberty and even perspectives about "rights," the limits of law, and ethics must be "qualified" and held in abeyance in view of the threat. In addition to propaganda effects, the constant use of fear pervades crises and normal times; it becomes part of the taken-for-granted world of "how things are," and one consequence is that it begins to influence how we perceive and talk about everyday life, including mundane as well as significant events.

Tracking this discourse shows that fear pervades our popular culture and is influencing how we view events and experience. [...]

DISCUSSION

The discourse of fear now includes terrorism as well as victimization and crime. Terrorism and fear have been joined through victimization. Crime established a solid baseline in its association with fear, and it continues to grow, but it is terrorism that now occupies the most news space. The primary reason for this, as noted above in the discussion of news sources, is that government officials dominate the sources relied on by journalists. When journalists rely heavily on government and military officials to not only discuss an immediate war or military campaign but also for information about the security of the country, rationale for more surveillance of citizens, and comments about related domestic and international issues, then the body politic is symbolically cultivated to plant more reports and symbols about the politics of fear. This is particularly true during periods of war, such as the ongoing war with Iraq. Messages that the war on terrorism and the importance of homeland security, including periodic elevated "terror alerts," will not end soon lead journalists to turn to administration news sources for information about the most recent casualties, operations, reactions to counterattacks, and the omnipresent reports about soldiers who have perished and those who are still in peril. In this sense, news updates from authoritative sources quickly merge with orchestrated propaganda efforts.

Terrorism plays well with audiences accustomed to the discourse of fear as well as political leadership oriented to social policy geared to protecting those audiences from crime. I am proposing, then, that the discourse of fear is a key element of social fears involving crime and other dreaded outcomes in the postmodern world. As rhetoricians have noted, terrorism is easily included within this perspective: "Terrorism, then, is first and foremost discourse. There is a sense in which the terrorist event must be reported by the media in order for it to have transpired at all" (Zulaika and Douglass 1996: 14). Terrorism is more than a narrative, but its essence is the definition of the situation, one that extends beyond the present into a distal future, gray but known. The forebodingness of events (September 11 attacks) is cast as a terrible trend, as an inevitability, but the power comes from the uncertainty of "when" and "where."

Like the prospective victims of crime in the future, citizens will be made terrorist victims in the future.

Terrorism—and especially the attacks of September 11—enabled political actors to expand the definition of the situation to all Americans as victims. Moreover, all those fighting to protect actual and potential victims should be permitted to do their work, unimpeded by any concerns about civil liberties or adding context and complexity to the simple analysis that was offered: Evil people were attacking good people, and evil had to be destroyed. [...]

Victims are a byproduct of fear and the discourse of fear. I contend that fear and victim are linked through social power, responsibility, and identity. The linkage involves concerns about safety and perceptions of risk. Thus, President Bush was relying on more than skilled speechwriters in connecting the mafia and terrorism; he was also relying on the audience's acceptance of mythical mafia dons and godfathers depicted in entertainment to grease the conceptual slide of terrorism as a similar threat. What audiences were presumed to share, then, was the sense that terrorism, like crime—especially mafia crime—was a monstrous black hand that was invisible, omnipresent, all-powerful and could only be stopped by a stronger force if ordinary Americans were to survive. I refer specifically to the role and identity of victim, as held by numerous audiences, who expect victims to perform certain activities, speak a certain language, and in general follow a cultural script of "dependence," "lacking," and "powerlessness" while relying on state-sponsored social institutions to save and support them (Garland 2001). [...]

As noted above, the politics of fear refer to decision-makers' promotion and use of audience beliefs and assumptions about danger, risk, and fear to achieve certain goals. The politics of fear promotes attacking a target (crime, terrorism), anticipates further victimization, curtails civil liberties, and stifles dissent as being unresponsive to citizen needs or even "unpatriotic." The Homeland Security Office advised the American people to buy duct tape and plastic sheeting as a barrier to terrorism. This advisory had little to do with chemical protection and much to do with the politics of fear. [...]

Symbolic links are made between an event, a threat, the avowed character, and purpose of the terrorists, who, like criminals, are constructed as lacking any reason, moral foundation, and purpose except to kill and terrify. Not likely to be ravaged by childhood diseases or workplace injuries, postindustrial citizens are prime potential victims; viewing mass-mediated scenarios of crime, mayhem, and destruction, they have no option but to believe and wait and wait:

> The most typical mode of terrorism discourse in the United States has been, indeed, one of Waiting for Terror. ... That which captivates every mind is something so meaningless that it may never happen, yet we are forced to compulsively talk about it while awaiting its arrival. In the theater of the absurd, "no significance" becomes the only significance. ... When something does happen, after decades during which the absent horror has been omnipresent through the theater of waiting, the vent becomes anecdotal evidence to corroborate what has been intuited all along—the by-now permanent catastrophe of autonomous Terror consisting of the waiting for terror. (Zulaika and Douglass 1996: 26)

There can be no fear without actual victims or potential victims. In the postmodern age, victim is a status and representation and not merely a person or someone who has suffered as a result of some personal, social, or physical calamity. Massive and concerted efforts by moral entrepreneurs to have their causes adopted and legitimated as "core social issues" worthy of attention have led to the wholesale adaptation and refinement of the use of the problem frame to promote victimization (Best 1995). Often couching their causes as battles for justice, moral entrepreneurs seek to promote new social definitions of right and wrong (Johnson 1995). As suggested above with the examples of hoaxes, victims are entertaining, and that is why they abound. They are evocative, bringing forth tears, joy, and vicarious emotional experience. But victim is more. Victim is now a status, a position that opens to all people who live in a symbolic environment marked by the discourse of fear (Chermak 1995). We are all potential victims, often vying for official recognition and legitimacy.

CONCLUSION

This study documents how fear and terrorism have been joined with victimization since the September 11 attacks. I argue that expanding the discourse of fear to include terrorism is consistent with an emergent politics of fear. I suggest that the politics of fear is a dominant motif for news and popular culture. Moreover, within this framework, news reporting about crime and terrorism are linked with victimization narratives that make crime, danger, and fear very relevant to everyday life experiences. [...]

The politics of fear as public discourse represents an emergent feature of the symbolic environment: Moral entrepreneurs' claims-making is easier to market to audiences anchored in fear and victimization as features of crime and terrorism. The politics of fear can be theoretically useful in understanding the relevance of mass mediated fear in contemporary popular culture and political life. This concept is useful for clarifying the closer ties between entertainment-oriented news and popular culture, on one hand, and media-savvy state officials. The politics of fear joined crime with victimization through the "drug war," interdiction and surveillance policies, and grand narratives that reflected numerous cultural myths about moral and social "disorder." We are in the midst of an emerging politics of fear that discourages criticism, promotes caution, and reliance on careful procedures. [...]

Skillful propaganda and the cooperation of the most powerful news media enabled simple lies to explain complex events. Like entertaining crime reporting, anticipation of wars, attacks, and the constant vigilance to be on guard is gratifying for most citizens who are seeking protection within the symbolic order of the politics of fear. The skillful use of heightened "terrorist alerts" to demand attention to the task at hand is critical in avoiding any detractor. And that is the key point: An otherwise sensible or cautionary remark that signals one is aware, rational, and weighing alternatives marks one as a detractor, someone who is "against the United States."

REFERENCES

Altheide, D. L. (1996) *Qualitative Media Analysis*. Thousand Oaks: Sage.

Altheide, D. L. (1997) "The News Media, the Problem Frame, and the Production of Fear." *Sociological Quarterly* 38(4): 646–668.

Altheide, D. L. (2002a) "Children and the Discourse of Fear." *Symbolic Interaction* 25(2): 229–250.

Altheide, D. L. (2002b) *Creating Fear*. Hawthorne: Aldine de Gruyter.

Altheide, D. L. (2004) "Consuming Terrorism." *Symbolic Interaction* 27(3): 289–308.

Altheide, D. L., and R. S. Michalowski (1999) "Fear in the News." *Sociological Quarterly* 40(3): 475–503.

Altheide, D. L., and R. P. Snow (1979) *Media Logic*. Beverly Hills: Sage.

BBC (2004) "Iraq Death Toll 'Soared Post-War'." BBC Newscast, October 29. Online at: <http://news.bbc.co.uk/2/hi/middle_east/3962969.stm>. Accessed January 5, 2006.

Best, J. (ed.) (1995) *Images of Issues*. Hawthorne: Aldine de Gruyter.

Best, J. (1999) *Random Violence*. Berkeley: University of California Press.

Chermak, S. (1995) *Victims in the News*. Boulder: Westview.

Chiricos, T., S. Eschholz and M. Gertz (1997) "Crime, News, and Fear of Crime." *Social Problems* 44(3): 342–357.

Cunningham, B. (2003) "Re-Thinking Objectivity." *Columbia Journalism Review* (July/August): 24–32.

Denzin, N. K., and Y. S. Lincoln (eds.) (2003) *9/11 in American Culture*. Lanham: Rowman and Littlefield.

Engel, M. (2002) "War on Afghanistan." *Guardian*, May 17: 4.

Ericson, R. V., P. M. Baranek, and J. B. L. Chan (1991) *Representing Order*. Toronto: University of Toronto Press.

Ericson, R. V., and K. D. Haggerty (1997) *Policing the Risk Society*. Toronto: University of Toronto Press.

Fairness and Accuracy in Reporting (2003) "Iraq Crisis." Online at: <http://www.fair.org/reports/iraq-sources.html>.

Ferraro, K. F. (1995) *Fear of Crime*. Albany: State University of New York Press.

Furedi, F. (1997) *Culture of Fear*. London: Cassell.

Garland, D. (2001) *The Culture of Control*. Chicago: University of Chicago Press.

Giroux, H. A. (2003) *The Abandoned Generation*. New York: Palgrave Macmillan.

Hornqvist, M. (2004) "The Birth of Public Order Policy." *Race and Class* 46(1): 30–52.

Hunt, A. 1997 "'Moral Panic' and Moral Language in the Media." *British Journal of Sociology* 48(4): 629–648.

Johnson, J. M. (1995) "Horror Stories and the Construction of Child Abuse." In J. Best (ed.), *Images of Issues*. Hawthorne: Aldine de Gruyter: 17–31.

Kimmelman, M. (2002) "In New York, Art is Crime, and Crime becomes Art." *The New York Times*, December 18. Online at: <http://www.nytimes.com/2002/12/18/arts/design/18FEAR.html?ex=1041231425&ei=1&en=14502da3abfe7b7f>. Accessed January 6, 2006.

Kull, S. (2004) "U.S. Public Beliefs and Attitudes about Iraq." Online Reports, August 20 Online at: <http://www.pipa.org/OnlineReports/Iraq/Report08_20_04.pdf>. Accessed January 6, 2006.

Kull, S., C. Ramsay, and E. Lewis (2002) "Misperceptions, the Media, and the Iraq War." *Political Science Quarterly* 118(4): 569–598.

Robin, C. (2001) "Primal Fear." *Theory and Event* 5(4).

Russell, K. K. (1998) *The Color of Crime*. New York: New York University Press.

Ryan, J. (2002) "Media Feeding the Fear." *San Francisco Chronicle*, October 15: A23.

Schwalbe, M., S. Godwin, D. Holden, D. Schrock, S. Thompson, and M. Wolkomir (2000) "Generic Processes in the Reproduction of Inequality." *Social Forces* 79(2): 419–452.

Snow, R. P. (1983) *Creating Media Culture*. Beverly Hills: Sage.

Surette, R. (1992) *Media, Crime, and Criminal Justice*. Pacific Grove: Brooks/Cole.

Wolfe, R. and R. Norland (2003) "Bush's News War." *Newsweek*, October 27: 32.

Zulaika, J. and W. A. Douglass (1996) *Terror and Taboo*. New York: Routledge.

5
Welcome to the Desert of the Real!

Slavoj Žižek

The ultimate American paranoiac fantasy is that of an individual living in a small idyllic Californian city, a consumerist paradise, who suddenly starts to suspect that the world he lives in is a fake, a spectacle staged to convince him that he lives in a real world, while all people around him are effectively actors and extras in a gigantic show. The most recent example of this is Peter Weir's *The Truman Show* (1998), with Jim Carrey playing the small town clerk who gradually discovers the truth that he is the hero of a 24-hour permanent TV show: his hometown is constructed on a gigantic studio set, with cameras following him permanently. Among its predecessors, it is worth mentioning Philip Dick's *Time Out of Joint* (1959), in which a hero living a modest daily life in a small idyllic Californian city of the late 1950s, gradually discovers that the whole town is a fake staged to keep him satisfied. ... The underlying experience of *Time Out of Joint* and of *The Truman Show* is that the late capitalist consumerist Californian paradise is, in its very hyper-reality, in a way IRREAL, substanceless, deprived of the material inertia.

So it is not only that Hollywood stages a semblance of real life deprived of the weight and inertia of materiality—in the late capitalist consumerist society, "real social life" *itself somehow acquires the features of a staged fake*, with our neighbors behaving in "real" life as stage actors and extras. ... Again, the ultimate truth of the capitalist utilitarian de-spiritualized universe is the de-materialization of the "real life" itself, its reversal into a spectral show. Among others, Christopher Isherwood gave expression to this unreality of American daily life, exemplified by the motel room: "American motels are unreal! /... / they are deliberately designed to be unreal. /... / The Europeans hate us because we've retired to live inside our advertisements, like hermits going into caves to contemplate." Peter Sloterdijk's notion of the "sphere" is here literally realized, as the gigantic metal sphere that envelopes and isolates the entire city.

Years ago, a series of science fiction films like *Zardoz* or *Logan's Run* forecasted today's postmodern predicament by extending this fantasy to the community itself: the isolated group living an aseptic life in a secluded area longs for the experience of the real world of material decay.

The Wachowski brothers' hit *The Matrix* (1999) brought this logic to its climax: the material reality we all experience and see around us is a virtual one, generated and coordinated by a gigantic mega-computer to which we are all attached; when the hero (played by Keanu Reeves) awakens into the "real reality," he sees a desolate landscape littered with burned ruins—what remained of Chicago after a global war. The resistance leader Morpheus utters the ironic greeting: "Welcome to the desert of the real."

Was it not something of a similar order that took place in New York on September 11? Its citizens were introduced to the "desert of the real"—to us, corrupted by Hollywood, the landscape and the shots we saw of the collapsing towers could not but remind us of the most breathtaking scenes in the catastrophe's big productions. When we hear how the bombings were a totally unexpected shock, how the unimaginable Impossible happened, one should recall the other defining catastrophe from the beginning of the twentieth century, that of the *Titanic*: it was also a shock, but the space for it was already prepared in ideological fantasizing, since the *Titanic* was the symbol of the might of nineteenth-century industrial civilization. Does the same not hold also for these bombings? Not only were the media bombarding us all the time with the talk about the terrorist threat; this threat was also obviously libidinally invested—just recall the series of movies from *Escape From New York* to *Independence Day*. Therein resides the rationale of the often-mentioned association of the attacks with Hollywood disaster movies: the unthinkable that happened was the object of fantasy, so that, in a way, *America got what it fantasized about*, and this was the greatest surprise.

It is precisely now, when we are dealing with the raw Real of a catastrophe, that we should bear in mind the ideological and fantasmatic coordinates which determine its perception. If there is any symbolism in the collapse of the WTC towers, it is not so much the old-fashioned notion of the "center of financial capitalism," but, rather, the notion that the two WTC towers stood for the center of VIRTUAL capitalism, of financial speculations disconnected from the sphere of material production. The shattering impact of the bombings can only be accounted for against the background of the borderline which today separates the digitalized First World from the Third World "desert of the real." It is the awareness that we live in an insulated artificial universe which generates the notion that some ominous agent is threatening us all the time with total destruction.

Is, consequently, Osama bin Laden, the suspected mastermind behind the bombings, not the real-life counterpart of Ernst Stavro Blofeld, the master-criminal in many of the James Bond films, involved in the acts of global destruction? What one should recall here is that the only place in Hollywood films where we see the production process in all its intensity is when James Bond penetrates the master-criminal's secret domain and locates there the site of intense labor (distilling and packaging drugs, constructing a rocket that will destroy New York ...). When the master-criminal, after capturing Bond, usually takes him on a tour of his illegal factory, is this not the closest Hollywood comes to the socialist-realist proud presentation of the production in a factory? And the function of Bond's intervention, of course, is to explode in fireballs this site of production, allowing us to return to the daily semblance of our existence in a world with the "disappearing working class." Is it not that, in the exploding WTC towers, that this violence directed at the threatening Outside turned back at us?

The safe Sphere in which Americans live is experienced as under threat from the Outside of terrorist attackers who are ruthlessly self-sacrificing AND cowards, cunningly intelligent AND primitive barbarians. Whenever we encounter such a purely evil Outside, we should gather the courage to endorse the Hegelian lesson: in this pure Outside, we should recognize the distilled version of our own essence. For the last five centuries, the (relative) prosperity and peace of the "civilized" West was bought by the export of ruthless violence and destruction into the "barbarian" Outside: the long story from the conquest of America to the slaughter in Congo. Cruel and indifferent as it may sound, we should also, now more than ever, bear in mind that the actual effect of these bombings is much more symbolic than real: in Africa, EVERY SINGLE DAY more people die of AIDS than all the victims of the WTC collapse, and their death could have been easily cut back with relatively small financial means. The US just got the taste of what goes on around the world on a daily basis, from Sarajevo to Grozny, from Rwanda and Congo to Sierra Leone. If one adds to the situation in New York rapist gangs and a dozen or so snipers blindly targeting people who walk along the streets, one gets an idea about what Sarajevo was a decade ago.

It is when we watched on a TV screen the two WTC towers collapsing that it became possible to experience the falsity of "reality TV shows": even if these shows are "for real," people still act in them—they simply *play themselves*. The standard disclaimer in a novel ("characters in this text are a fiction, every resemblance with real life characters is purely contingent") holds also for the participants in the reality soaps: what we see there are fictional characters, even if they play themselves for real. Of course, the "return to the Real" can be given different twists: one already hears some conservatives claim that what made us so vulnerable is our very openness—with the inevitable conclusion lurking in the background that, if we are to protect our "way of life," we will have to sacrifice some of our freedoms which were "misused" by the enemies of freedom. This logic should be rejected *tout court*: is it not a fact that our First World "open" countries are the most controlled countries in the entire history of humanity? In the United Kingdom, all public spaces, from buses to shopping malls, are constantly videotaped, not to mention the almost total control of all forms of digital communication.

Along the same lines, rightist commentators like George Will also immediately proclaimed the end of the American "holiday from history"—the impact of reality shattering the isolated tower of the liberal tolerant attitude and the cultural studies focus on textuality. Now we are forced to strike back, to deal with real enemies in the real world. ... However, WHOM to strike? Whatever the response, it will never hit the RIGHT target, bringing us full satisfaction. The ridiculousness of America attacking Afghanistan cannot but strike the eye: if the greatest power in the world will destroy one of the poorest countries in which peasants barely survive on barren hills, will this not be the ultimate case of the impotent acting out? Afghanistan is otherwise an ideal target: a country ALREADY reduced to rubble, with no infrastructure, repeatedly destroyed by war for the last two decades. ... One cannot avoid the surmise that the choice of Afghanistan will be also determined by economic considerations: is it not the best procedure to act out one's anger at a country for which no one cares and where there is nothing to destroy? Unfortunately, the possible choice of Afghanistan recalls the anecdote about the madman who searches for the lost key beneath a street light; when asked why he was there when he lost the key in a dark corner behind him, he answers: "But it is easier to search under strong light!"

To succumb to the urge to act now and retaliate means precisely to avoid confronting the true dimensions of what occurred on September 11—it means an act whose true aim is to lull us into the secure conviction that nothing has REALLY changed. The true long-term threat are further acts of mass terror in comparison to which the memory of the WTC collapse will pale—acts less spectacular, but much more horrifying. What about bacteriological warfare, what about the use of lethal gas, what about the prospect of DNA terrorism (developing poisons which will affect only people who share a determinate genome)? Instead of a quick acting out, one should confront these difficult questions: What will "war" mean in the twenty-first century? Who will be "them", if they are, clearly, neither states nor criminal gangs?

There is a partial truth in the notion of the "clash of civilizations" attested here—witness the surprise of the average American: "How is it possible that these people display and practice such a disregard for their own lives?" Is the obverse of this surprise not the rather sad fact that we, in the First World countries, find it more and more difficult even to imagine a public or universal Cause for which one would be ready to sacrifice one's life? When, after the bombings, even the Taliban foreign minister said that he can "feel the pain" of the American children, did he not thereby confirm the hegemonic ideological role of Bill Clinton's trademark phrase? It effectively appears as if the split between First World and Third World runs more and more along the lines of the opposition between leading a long satisfying life full of material and cultural wealth, and dedicating one's life to some transcendent Cause. However, this notion of the "clash of civilizations" has to be thoroughly rejected: what we are witnessing today are rather clashes WITHIN each civilization. Furthermore, a brief look at the comparative history of Islam and Christianity tells us that the "human rights record" of Islam (to use this anachronistic term) is much better than that of Christianity: in the past centuries, Islam was significantly more tolerant towards other religions than Christianity. NOW it is also the time to remember that it was through the Arabs that, in the Middle Ages, we in Western Europe regained access to our Ancient Greek legacy. While in no way excusing today's acts of horror, these facts nonetheless clearly demonstrate that we are not dealing with a feature inscribed into Islam "as such," but with the outcome of modern socio-political conditions.

Every feature attributed to the Other is already present at the very heart of the US: murderous fanaticism? There are today in the US itself more than two million Rightist populist "funda-mentalists" who also practice terror of their own, legitimized by (their understanding of) Christianity. Since America is in a way "harboring" them, should the US Army have punished the US themselves after the Oklahoma bombing? And what about the way Jerry Falwell and Pat Robertson reacted to the bombings, perceiving them as a sign that God suspended protection of the US because of the sinful lives of Americans, putting the blame on hedonist materialism, liberalism, and rampant sexuality, and claiming that America got what it deserved? America as a safe haven? When a New Yorker commented on how, after the bombings, one could no longer walk safely on the city's streets, the irony of it was that, well before the bombings, the streets of New York were well-known for the dangers of being attacked or, at least, mugged—if anything, the bombings gave rise to a new sense of solidarity, with scenes of young African-Americans helping an old Jewish gentleman to cross the street, scenes unimaginable a couple of days previously.

Now, in the days immediately following the bombings, it is as if we dwell in the unique time between a traumatic event and its symbolic impact, like in those brief moments after we are deeply cut, and before the full extent of the pain strikes us—it is open how the events will be symbolized, what their symbolic efficiency will be, what acts they will be evoked to justify. Even here, in these moments of utmost tension, this link is not automatic but contingent. There are already the first bad omens, like the sudden resurrection, in public discourse, of the old Cold War term "free world": the struggle is now the one between the "free world" and the forces of darkness and terror. The question to be asked here is, of course: Who then belongs to the UNFREE world? Are, say, China or Egypt part of this free world? The actual message is, of course, that the old division between the Western liberal-democratic countries and all the others has again been enforced.

The day after the bombing, I got a message from a journal which was just about to publish a longer text of mine on Lenin, telling me that they had decided to postpone its publication—they considered it inopportune to publish a text on Lenin immediately after the bombing. Does this not point towards the ominous ideological reart-iculations which will follow, with a new *Berufsverbot* (prohibition to employ radicals) much stronger and more widespread than the one in the Germany of the 1970s? These days, one often hears the phrase that the struggle is now the one for democracy—true, but not quite in the way this phrase is usually meant. Already, some leftist friends of mine have written to me that, in these difficult moments, it is better to keep one's head down and not push forward with our agenda. Against this temptation to duck out the crisis, one should insist that NOW the Left should provide a better analysis—otherwise, it will concede in advance its political AND ethical defeat in the face of the acts of quite genuine ordinary popular heroism (like the passengers who, in a model of a rational ethical act, overtook the kidnappers and provoked the early crash of the plane [United Airlines Flight 93]: if one is condemned to die soon, one should gather the strength and die in such a way as to prevent other people dying ...).

So what about the phrase that reverberates everywhere, "Nothing will be the same after September 11"? Significantly, this phrase is never further elaborated—it is just an empty gesture of saying something "deep" without really knowing what we want to say. So our first reaction to it should be: Really? Is it, rather, not that the only thing that effectively changed was that America was forced to realize the kind of world it was part of? On the other hand, such changes in perception are never without consequences, since the way we perceive our situation determines the way we act in it. Recall the processes of collapse of a political regime, say, the collapse of the Communist regimes in Eastern Europe in 1990: at a certain moment, people all of a sudden became aware that the game was over, that the Communists were lost. The break was purely symbolic, nothing changed "in reality"—and, nonetheless, from this moment on, the final collapse of the regime was just a question of days. ... What if something of the same order DID occur on September 11?

We don't yet know what consequences in economy, ideology, politics, and war this event will have, but one thing is certain: the US, which till now perceived itself as an island exempted from this kind of violence, witnessing this kind of thing only from the safe distance of the TV screen, is now directly involved. So the alternative is: will Americans decide to fortify further their "sphere," or to risk stepping out of it? Either America will persist in, strengthen even, the deeply *immoral* attitude of "Why should this happen to us? Things like this don't happen HERE!" leading to more aggression towards the threatening Outside, in short, to a paranoiac acting out. Or US-America will finally risk stepping through the fantasmatic screen separating it from the Outside World, accepting its arrival into the Real World, making the long-overdue move from "A thing like this should not happen HERE!" to "A thing like this should not happen ANYWHERE!" Therein resides the true lesson of the bombings: the only way to ensure that it will not happen HERE again is to prevent it going on ANYWHERE ELSE.

America's "holiday from history" was a fake: America's peace was bought by the catastrophes going on elsewhere. These days, the predominant point of view is that of an innocent gaze confronting unspeakable Evil which struck from the Outside—and, again, apropos this gaze, one should gather strength and apply to it also Hegel's well-known dictum that the Evil resides (also) in the innocent gaze itself which perceives Evil all around itself.

In the electoral campaign, President Bush named Jesus Christ as the most important person in his life. Now he has a unique chance to prove that he meant it seriously: for him, as for all Americans today, "Love thy neighbor!" means "Love the Muslims!" OR IT MEANS NOTHING AT ALL.

Part II

States of Terror

States of Terror: Introduction

Uli Linke and Danielle Taana Smith

There is a disturbing side to contemporary global politics: while enhancing peace and solidarity within and between some societies, worldwide governance has also promoted war, militarism, and armed conflict. Transnational alliances among some nations amplify the exclusion, marginalization, and destruction of others. The legacy of racial, national, and ethnic violence continues to devastate communities throughout the world. In Part II, we examine how situations of terror are managed by western intervention. The readings included in this section reveal that states of terror tend to reverberate beyond the immediate devastation of catastrophic events into the fabricated zones of safety. Humanitarian organizations, administrative bodies, and government bureaucracies acting in the perceived best interests of victimized groups perpetuate or prolong the experience of terror by imposing conditions of dependency, surveillance, containment, detention, and the annihilation of personhood. The formation of terror operates on multiple levels of dehumanization of the victim-survivors of armed conflict, who are seeking refuge abroad and at home.

The opening essay by Lucia Ann McSpadden (Pacific School of Religion) and John R. MacArthur (Centers for Disease Control) invites us to rethink global futures with an uncompromising commitment to human rights. War, genocide, acts of violence, economic collapse, poverty, and ecological disasters are catastrophic events with devastating consequences for communities and individuals. Forms of torture and terror often result in mass population displacement as people abandon their homes in search of protection. Such events rise to the level of *complex emergencies*, as McSpadden and MacArthur assert, when they are enmeshed with ongoing and systemic human rights abuses. Humanitarian emergencies are likewise considered *complex* because intervention or assistance entails much more than meeting the basic survival needs of single individuals. The enduring effects of trauma are magnified by societal power imbalances and status differentials with regard to gender, age, disability, social dependency, and access to resources, and become "especially problematic when the entire group of refugees is experiencing limited resources, fear and anxiety, concern for survival, depression, and sorrow because of severe loss" (see p.87). With careful attention to the complex requirements of safety, dignity, and health, McSpadden and MacArthur propose that international relief organizations safeguard critical human rights concerns throughout all phases of contact with disenfranchised populations.

Effective strategies for securing sustainable futures must take into account that displaced populations are never an undifferentiated mass, but human beings who are culturally and historically situated, as members of social communities, with distinct trauma experiences and coping strategies. Based on fieldwork in refugee camps in Tanzania, Liisa Malkki (Stanford University) demonstrates how the administrative management of traumatized communities has disempowering effects. Western humanitarian intervention has increasingly focused on refugees as "passive objects" of assistance and management (see p.114). Malkki describes what happens when international aid workers embrace a liberal approach that portrays refugees through images of an undifferentiated "raw" or "bare" humanity: human beings are stripped of their memories, histories, and identities, and as such are rendered voiceless. Their testimonies are appropriated by relief organizations to be rewritten, reimagined, and retold to the rest of the world in order to solicit funding. "Proper refugees," refugees of concern to relief organizations and the "compassionate" public, as Malkki points out, are those who conform to the figure of an "exemplary victim." In this signifying process, refugees are stripped of their personhood. As a generic category, they are viewed as "universal man, universal woman, universal child, and, taken together, universal family" (see p.101). Such a "dehistoricizing universalism" tends to envision traumatized people in terms of units, categories, rubrics, negating individual subjects' lives and identities. When human beings do not conform to the preconceived notion of the refugee or victim and do not behave in accordance with corresponding expectations, the allocation of resources by humanitarian organizations dwindles. Malkki shows how the portrayal of refugees effectively serves to entrench their helplessness.

The subsequent essay by Doug Henry (University of North Texas) shows how experiences of anxiety, fear, and loss are magnified when a peoples' remembrance of violence is contested. Drawing on ethnographic research among war survivors along the Sierra Leone–Guinea border, Henry reveals how the suffering body assumes political, social, and emotional meanings in the aftermath of trauma. As a mimetic battleground, the body in pain provides survivors with the ability to express their experience of terror. In turn, work performed on the body, for example remedies used to soothe an aching heart, also effects emotional healing. But in refugee camps, the survivor's body becomes a site of intervention by international relief workers. Local understandings of pain are rejected by western-trained medical practitioners, whose biomedical models of illness trivialize and negate culture-specific articulations of embodied terror as "erroneous" or "irrational." In this context, as Henry suggests, humanitarian medical assistance tends to impede rather than promote the alleviation of suffering among traumatized communities.

In a critical ethnography about immigration practices in France, Miriam Ticktin (New School of Social Research) examines the role of humanitarianism and compassion in a country that makes illness a primary means by which undocumented persons can obtain temporary legal status. Ticktin shows how humanitarianism has been appropriated by the French state to govern non-citizen subjects. France grants residency permits to foreign nationals with life-threatening pathologies, who cannot receive treatment in their home countries. While taking temporary custody of those in medical need, France has restricted other possibilities of immigration that permit work, education, and life. In a final act of desperation, those seeking a right to life resort to endangering their health to remain in France. Undocumented immigrants, as Ticktin observes, are forced "to trade in biological integrity for political recognition" (2006: 33). Based on her work in hospitals, state medical offices, and clinics in Paris, Ticktin uncovers the devastating consequences of a political system that produces diseased and disabled citizens and enacts a limited version of what it means to be human. Reduced to mere physical bodies, undocumented migrants are subjected to extreme vulnerabilities and indignities as they are forced to endure acts of political violence and human rights abuses within yet another state of terror in Europe.

REFERENCE

Ticktin, Miriam (2006) "Where Ethics and Politics Meet: The Violence of Humanitarianism in France." *American Ethnologist* 33(1): 33–49.

6
Human Rights and Complex Emergencies

Lucia Ann McSpadden and John R. MacArthur

> Within a system which denies the existence of basic human rights, fear tends to be the order of the day. Fear of imprisonment, fear of torture, fear of death, fear of losing friends, family, property or means of livelihood, fear of poverty, fear of isolation, fear of failure.
>
> *Aung San Suu Kyi, Nobel Peace Prize Winner,*
> *Freedom from Fear (1991: 184)*

Human rights abuses are embedded within complex humanitarian emergencies. The terse term *complex emergencies* describes local, regional, national, and international systems overwhelmed by the rapid, large-scale movement of people fleeing actual or anticipated human rights abuses.

Recent figures from the US Committee on Refugees state that there are more than 35 million persons uprooted worldwide—an increase of five million over 1998 (US Committee for Refugees 2000). As the United Nations High Commissioner for Refugees stresses, "violations of human rights are a major—indeed, the major—cause of mass population displacement" in spite of politicians', media's, governments', and even nongovernmental organizations' assertions to the contrary (UNHCR 1995b: 58).

The origins of population displacement have changed since the fall of the former Soviet Union. In the past, persons fled because of political ideological differences, individual acts of persecution, and/or to escape proxy wars being fought by global superpowers in developing countries. During the past decade, we have seen flight stem from a different set of circumstances: intrastate conflicts, often fueled by ethnic or religious antagonisms, weakened states because of poverty and economic collapse, and ecological disasters.

Torture and other abuses have a direct (and indirect) link to mass population displacement. People leave their homes in an attempt to seek protection from widespread violence originating from either intentional targeting or getting caught between warring groups. Yet, in spite of international agreements, over 93 countries still practice torture (Basoglu 1993). Human rights, within complex emergencies during the initial phases of humanitarian relief, are the focus of our discussion. Our concern is with the planning and implementation of the response system, especially as it affects health and wellbeing. Our intent is to provide anthropologists and other social scientists, especially those with medical expertise engaged in these efforts, with brief descriptions and analyses of selected human rights concerns within complex emergencies. We offer some suggestions for protecting the human rights of the persons we intend to help.

BACKGROUND

The protection of human rights has been prominent on the international agenda since World War II, and was a founding principle in the establishment of the United Nations (UN) in 1945. The standards for human rights were codified in the Universal Declaration of Human Rights, the International Covenant of Civil and Political Rights, and the International Covenant on Economic, Social and Cultural Rights (Mann et al. 1994). A number of other UN conventions have built upon this foundation in the ensuing years, covering such areas as discrimination, child rights and torture. With the establishment of the office of the UN High Commissioner for Human Rights in December 1993, global attention towards human rights has been intensified.

According to the United Nations' Universal Declaration of Human Rights, "all human beings ... without distinction of any kind" (1948: 6–9) have a right to life, liberty, and security of person. They have the right not to be subjected to torture, slavery, or arbitrary detention or exile. They have the right to own property, to move freely within the borders of their country, and to be protected against arbitrary interference in their personal and family life. One's honor and reputation are not to be attacked. The family is recognized as the fundamental social group and thus entitled to protection as a human right (United Nations 1948).

Although the protection of human rights was the foundation of the 1951 UN Convention and the 1967 Protocol Relating to the Status of Refugees, as well as the primary responsibility of the Office of the UN High Commissioner for Refugees (McSpadden and Choi 1998), few relief workers understand the international laws enacted to protect refugees. Furthermore, even with an understanding of the laws, aid organizations have not developed clear policies for their personnel when they become aware of human rights violations (Waldman and Martone 1999). With violence impelling people to flee, humanitarian relief organizations have a growing awareness of the need to be more sensitive to human rights violations within the populations being served. As civilians are increasingly the targets of such abuses, the health consequences—both physical and psychological—are a growing concern for public health workers (Waldman and Martone 1999). These consequences are obvious; for example, people who survive torture have health problems (Mann et al. 1994). What are less evident or given less attention are possible human rights abuses within international and local responses to these complex emergencies.

Complex humanitarian emergencies require the rapid response of the local and international communities. Since the morbidity and mortality rates within the displaced population are very high during the acute phase of the emergency, emphasis is placed on public health interventions. The three central functions of public health include: assessing needs and problems; developing strategies to address areas of priority; and implementing public health programs aimed at combating these problems (Institute of Medicine 1988). When a relief team conducts public health programs comprising each of these areas, there may be possible infringements if a human rights perspective is not used (Mann et al. 1994). For example, programs in mental health and reproductive health are among the most neglected (Dick and Simmonds 1983; Waldman and Martone 1999), thus restricting the displaced population's right to health. Other rights are just not recognized in spite of rhetoric about the right to live in safety and dignity.

Our discussion is organized around the following topics, chosen because they are factors of dominance, inequity and/or marginalization affecting health, wellbeing, and treatment of diseases: power imbalances; protection; access to resources; rights of the host communities; gender; and the roles of the anthropologist. In addition, as torture may be a prominent feature of the complex emergency, and because of the need for certain skills to address displaced populations, we also discuss the issue of interviewing torture survivors. There is overlap in these topics; it is for convenience and focus that we separate them. These are also factors that anthropologists may well have the expertise to investigate and analyze.

POWER IMBALANCES

Human rights abuses typically originate from pervasive and systemic power imbalances within the socioeconomic/political/cultural system. These power imbalances most often are embedded within the social structures of the society. When we speak of vulnerable groups such as young children, the elderly, women, the physically disabled, people with chronic or acute illnesses, or mentally disabled or unaccompanied minors, we are speaking of power imbalances. These persons are vulnerable because they cannot exert the same level of authority, influence, or access as other groups within their social system. They are dependent socially and economically, and this dependency is only enhanced by the effects of displacement in a complex emergency.

At first glance, speaking of such vulnerable groups in medical or health terms is obvious; there are specific needs that need attention and response. Adequate food for malnourished children is essential. People with malaria should be treated and, where possible, the spread of malarial transmission halted or diminished. Pregnant women need specialized care. Infant diarrhea must be prevented or treated rapidly. However, these medical needs also place persons in a less powerful position within their own society; others must look out for and care for them. This social dependency is especially problematic when the entire group of refugees is experiencing limited resources, fear and anxiety, concern for survival, depression, and sorrow because of severe loss. [...]

A common power imbalance experience is to have men in higher status social positions become the spokespersons for men and women of lesser status. These "patrons" become the resource brokers, interpreting to health and aid workers the social and health situation, needs of people and suggested ways of responding. Most often the responses suggested and the role of the spokesperson itself enhance the power differentials of that spokesperson within his community. If the spokesperson represents a particular segment of the community, it is not surprising that his interventions will, in some fashion, enhance the wellbeing of his own group, even if such consequences are not intentional or devious. He knows his own people best and can express their situation and needs. Status differentials, by definition, indicate to those within the social system that some people are more important than others, and likely to be more valuable if resources are limited.

Of course the power imbalances present in the delivery of humanitarian assistance and immediate relief within complex emergencies are, in stark reality, simply there. People are basically powerless to provide for their own, possibly life-threatening, needs; the humanitarian relief system has the resources—material and human—for immediate response to the most pressing of these needs. Given the very real situation of a complex emergency, there is no way around that. It is how basic life services and ongoing medical, educational and economic aid are provided. Given the power differentials embedded in the humanitarian relief system, the typical approach is to maintain control over the refugees rather than consulting them as responsible equals (Harrell-Bond 1999). It is here—in sharing responsibility in identifying issues, in decision making and in planning responses that allow the refugees as much control over their lives as possible—that addresses some of the power imbalance. Emphasizing community participation—for example, in accessing health status, linking to community healers, involving community leaders and developing refugee health teams—is an approach that turns as much control as possible over to the refugees (MacArthur et al. 2000). The implication is that humanitarian aid workers should use human rights as a measure of their work. [...]

PROTECTION

Protection is basic to human rights: It is the first priority (Toole and Waldman 1997). The various humanitarian responses in a complex emergency are protection from the terror and threats causing the flight.

People are often threatened, intimidated, and hurt, yet many times the displaced find it difficult to express these fears or talk with strangers: "Who are you?" and "Why do you want to talk with me?" Such fear was pervasive in Goma camp with Rwandan refugees and in the Cambodian border camps in Thailand controlled by the Khmer Rouge.

Unfortunately, protection concerns follow people into areas of refuge. Problems can come in the form of infiltrators from the country of origin or refuge. The fear of such persons is pervasive in mass displacement and settlement. Lack of trust is rampant, and for good reason. As the Burmese military launched an offensive against the Karenni, mortar shells fell close to one of the refugee camps located in Thailand. Since the camp was situated very close to the border, the refugees fled deeper into Thai territory for safety. The local Thai officials, reluctant to have the camp relocate further inland, dispersed a militia group to relocate the camp to an area 5 kilometers from the border and close to a Burmese army encampment. When the Karenni refused to move to an area they felt to be unsafe, the militia threatened to kill the refugees. They emphasized these threats by beating on the walls of the houses with their rifles. (MacArthur 1995)

The political nature of mass displacement often means that there are opposing factions within a refugee camp. UNHCR attempts to keep arms and armed groups out of camps, often by setting up locked camps and monitoring who comes in and out. However, in a rapid mass displacement such as the arrival of 10,000 Rwandan refugees daily into the camp at Goma in 1994, the systems were overwhelmed. In Goma, the very persons who had participated in the slaughter of Tutsis and moderate Hutus were in the camp with arms. When there are threats to protection at this level, the situation is beyond the scope of humanitarian relief agencies and must be dealt with at the state and multinational levels.

Sometimes protection problems arise from hostility between different ethnic or religious groups:

Somalis were pouring into Kenya, over land and by sea. Those coming in small boats landed near Mombasa on the Indian Ocean. There were two camps, one in a rural area and one housed at an abandoned school right in the heart of Mombasa. The school-based camp, with space for only a few hundred persons, had people coming in steadily over a period of several days. UNHCR had not even had time to register them, to know much about them. As we walked through the camp a woman ran up to us, a mixture of anger and fear on her face, almost screaming in her attempt to communicate with us. She was a member of one clan; all the other people in the school were from another, rival clan. They were threatening her, preventing her from getting food and water, pushing and shoving her. She was hysterical with fear. (McSpadden 1992)

In camps housing Kosovar refugees, Roma refugees were threatened and assaulted. Although oppressed minorities themselves, they were accused by the Kosovo Albanians of joining with the Serbs in the destruction of homes, killing, and threats.

Sometimes camp authorities, wielding significant power, can use that power for their own benefit or for political ends. Physical threats are not uncommon. If there is hostility or suspicion on the part of the host country towards the refugees, the camp authorities become representatives of possible threat.

Sitting in a small hut that had been turned into a little cafe, we drank warm cokes and talked with Ethiopian refugees who were planning to start a school for young children. The conversation was animated. Suddenly people fell silent; my colleague leaned over and said "Don't say anything more; just talk about nothing." I looked up and saw that a Kenyan, a camp staff, had entered the cafe. Apparently, he had been following us around the camp noting with whom we talked. We began to talk among ourselves, ignoring the refugees so as not to cause them problems. (McSpadden 1992)

ACCESS TO RESOURCES

Necessities basic for life are essential resources: water, food, shelter, and medicine. Organizing access is a major task of the camp administration and humanitarian relief agencies, requiring intricate planning and well-coordinated efforts among UN agencies, NGOs, and state authorities. Public health and relief agencies' policies can directly affect the human rights of the population. Not only can establishing security measures assure protection, but also developing public health interventions with a human rights perspective can further protect the population from abuse. For example, ensuring the quantity and quality of food and water is necessary; however, making them available to everyone is another matter (Prothero 1994). Incorporating this perspective into the planning heightens awareness of vulnerable populations and thus strategies aimed at overcoming barriers may be developed.

In spite of the desire to give refugees an active role in the planning and implementation of relief programs, caution is essential. Camp staff from the host country or refugee leaders may control food distribution and other resources and benefits. They may demand payment of money, sexual favors, or support for particular political activities (UNHCR 1999).

The refugee camp was located far enough away from a trading center that supplies—food, medicine, clothing, basic living needs—had to be trucked in daily. Driving to the camp one day we happened to follow directly behind a supply truck as it pulled up to the gate of the locked camp. The camp guard held out his hand to the driver, obviously expecting a "financial donation" in order to open the gate. Seeing us watching him, he suddenly pulled his hand back and waved the truck through. (McSpadden 1992)

The physical realities of getting resources, especially food and water, can threaten the health, psychological and physical wellbeing of vulnerable persons. In households with only one healthy or strong adult, the rest of the household—elderly, children, incapacitated—must depend on that one person. If this person weakens or is denied access to food, medicine or other necessities through intimidation, discriminatory practices, or ineffective organization of service delivery, the basic wellbeing of all members is threatened. A subtle and deleterious factor in delivering health care is the frequent demeaning behavior of well-educated medical personnel towards persons who are illiterate and/or rural people.

The internal power relations within households themselves affect access to resources. These power relations are typically structured according to cultural mores and vary from group to group. Who is expected to gather the food? Who is entitled to eat first and most? Who shares with whom and why? If there is not enough food, what happens? Analyzing such dynamics in order to ameliorate the inequities is a major contribution of the anthropologist.

One of the most effective ways to identify problems regarding access to resources is to encourage the refugees to organize themselves, and have meetings to address the problems (UNHCR 1999). However, in so doing, some marginalized groups will continue to be ignored by those in power. [...]

THE RIGHTS OF THE HOST COMMUNITY

The Right to Food, Shelter, and Health Care

Complex humanitarian emergencies often occur quickly with large numbers of persons becoming displaced from the security of their homes. These people are not able to carry many personal items and often travel long distances with little food and water. Hunger, thirst, exposure, abuse, and disease all contribute to poor health upon arrival in the host country.

When tens of thousands of fleeing persons cross an international border and settle in an encampment, the degree of disruption on the local community can be devastating. The sociopolitical and economic relationships in frontier regions are not capable of withstanding such an influx of human beings. Because the host country is often poor, there are few local resources to provide assistance to the population of concern. Thus, in order to ensure that the basic needs of the displaced persons are met, an outpouring of international relief efforts follows. When international aid arrives, the need for vehicles, office space, food, and building supplies increases tremendously. With the increase in demand, there follows the inevitable increase in prices. This can have a devastating affect on the local population.

With the outpouring of large funds for assistance programs, the basic needs of the refugees are met and mortality falls. When death rates drop, the humanitarian emergency progresses into a maintenance phase that relief agencies describe as the "relief to development continuum" (Demusz 1998). Other projects develop during this phase, such as capacity building by training of essential personnel (for example, medics, nurses, health educators, teachers), elaborate water and sanitation projects and microenterprises. Each of these is aimed at producing a "self-sustainable" refugee. In certain situations, the relief efforts go far beyond what is available in the country of origin and/or refuge, and exceeds what will be available if/when repatriation occurs.

Article 25 of the Universal Declaration of Human Rights states that "everyone has the right to a standard of living adequate for the health and well-being of himself and of his family, including food, clothing, housing, and medical care" (UN 1948: 8). The response of the international community to aid refugees and internally displaced persons addresses this right. Although these efforts are substantial and often done with the best of intentions, one must question the ethics of establishing programs that will create aid dependency.

Aid brings another problem as well. If the local community is poor, as is often the case, they lack many of the very basic needs that the refugee community lacks: food, water, security, and shelter. Unfortunately, it is not always easy to include the local community into the budget submitted to the donor nations. Thus, either the local villagers are completely left out of the aid process or merely given token gestures of support. This creates an imbalance in the distribution of resources and may build feelings of tremendous resentment on the part of the host community, leading to subsequent political problems and even hostilities.

When addressing the relief needs of the displaced community, it is imperative to be aware of the socioeconomic situation of the refugee's country of origin and the host villagers. A human rights perspective to relief ensures that both the refugees and the host villages have access to adequate health care, food, clothing, and shelter. All efforts should be made to not only focus efforts on the displaced population, but also on the often-neglected villagers surrounding the refugee camps.

GENDER

Although taking gender into consideration when planning for the delivery of humanitarian aid has been accepted as necessary, it would seem that operationalizing a gender perspective is typically problematical, since it requires "transforming the protection agenda itself" (Minear 1999). Some of this difficulty is because of a lack of understanding of what one means when talking about gender as a significant factor in the provision of humanitarian aid.

Women and Men: Social Relationships and Power

A gender perspective requires an analysis of how social power and responsibility are differentially constructed for men and women within a given society or cultural group. A gender focus necessitates that the different needs, vulnerabilities and capacities of women and men be recognized and responded to specifically or program-matically (Indra 1999). At its best, this approach helps us to put into focus inequalities involving both women and men. When gender inequities are faced, humanitarian aid workers are often challenged by the socially powerful to overlook the consequences of such inequities. Those who benefit frequently insist that "our cultural values must be honored; you have no right as an outsider to question our values." However, a commitment to protect human rights requires that the safety and dignity of the person be protected, even if this means challenging accepted cultural norms. [...]

Gender Inequities and Humanitarian Aid

Typically, a society is structured so that women have less access to resources and social power. Within the domain of humanitarian aid "most assistance is camp administered and most administrators are men" (Harrell-Bond 1999: 40–62). When a gender focus was introduced into humanitarian aid delivery, women in greatest need were the targets; for example, food was now distributed to the poorest of women. This was an "add women and stir" approach; there were no questions about power relations (Indra 1999).

With a power relationship focus, there is now more attention to social justice and the improvement of the quality of life for women and men. For example, an approach to household analysis would not assume that all persons benefit equally when food aid, medicine or tools are distributed to families. One would look at internal power relations in the family and ask how needs are met, keeping in mind that most of the "vulnerable groups" of concern—young children, elderly, the severely ill—are in the care of women. Harrell-Bond (1999) reports situations in which, when women in camps were given control over ration distribution, the system worked out more fairly.

Women sometimes have wider social networks than men; the consequence can be that in a complex emergency with limited resources, male-headed households could be worse off than female-headed households:

> The camp system was being overwhelmed by the daily, almost hourly arrival of hundreds of Somalis. There was not enough staff; the sanitary facilities were inadequate; shelter had not yet been constructed. In the corner of a crowded room a man sat with a three month old baby in his arms and a four year old daughter by his side. His wife had died two hours before; he was sitting and staring into space. Some women in the room were preparing food; children were running around. He seemed to be unnoticed. The baby will die, it is clear. (McSpadden 1992)

Women and Girls Have Special Health and Protection Needs

Without question, refugee women and girls have special health and protection needs. Surprisingly, however, "in most emergency situations, gender-specific mortality data has not been collected ... [although] a number of authors have described increased risk of both morbidity and mortality among women in refugee and displaced populations" (Toole and Waldman 1997: 292). Women, particularly those of childbearing age, will likely need preferential access to medical services in order to provide an "integrated package of growth monitoring, immunization, antenatal and postnatal care, treatment of common ailments, and health promotion" (307). For example, Gilles et al. (1969) describe malaria as a major cause of maternal mortality, abortion, stillbirths, premature birth, and low birth weight babies, thus special programs aimed at reducing malaria in pregnancy should be developed.

Consistent sexual vulnerability is the reality for women and girls in complex emergencies. Women and girls may experience physical and sexual attacks and abuse even after arriving at the camp. UNHCR, for example, reported 192 cases of rape of Somali refugee women in Kenyan camps over a seven-month period in 1993, and estimated that several thousand more rape cases went unreported (Toole and Waldman 1997). The basic layout of the camp again and again is a health-related factor that affects the safety of women: distance to latrines, lighting, and clearing of shrubs that obscure visibility and encourage rape (UNHCR 1995a).

Refugee women who are unable to feed, clothe, and shelter themselves and their children are more vulnerable to manipulation and to physical and sexual abuse. If monetary bribes are necessary in order to get water or food, as was reported by Ethiopian refugees in camps in Djibouti, women will predictably experience sexual harassment. Reports consistently indicate that women are forced into prostitution to get life necessities for themselves and for their children (Moussa 1993). Domestic violence often increases in camps as men, having lost status and control over their lives, take out their anger on their wives and children.

As we walked into Utunge camp near Mombasa, we saw persons huddled under trees. The UNHCR staff said the refugees were arriving in such large numbers that there were not enough blue tents to shelter them. In the distance were huts that the earlier arrivals had built. As we walked on, a Somali woman rushed up to the UNHCR staff woman and began to complain loudly. The UNHCR staff, a Pakistani woman, turned to the men gathered around watching and asked them to translate for the woman. No one responded; the woman continued to press her dilemma. Again the staff asked the men to translate. Finally one did. It seemed that the woman had been given a tent for herself and her children, but the tent had been taken away by some of the men. She was without shelter. No wonder the men did not want to translate! (McSpadden 1992)

All of these are issues of wellbeing, health, safety, and life resources. Sexual assault and endangerment, in addition, are issues of respect and dignity. Given the sensitivity of sexual issues and the continued threat when rape or other sexual harassment is revealed while the perpetrators are still present, it is essential that women staff or women social scientists be used when discussing this with the refugee women.

In addition, consulting with women regarding the realities of camp life, such as the type and location of water points, the location and means of collecting fuel for cooking and heating, the distribution of food, and the location of basic services such as latrines or medical facilities, is needed for protection. Men cannot speak for women. Participation of the women, especially in groups, is a process that promotes dignity and protection (UNHCR 1999).

In summary, a gender perspective involves social relationships and responsibilities of both men and women. Often one is more powerful or more "valued" in the culture; frequently, but not always, this is the man. Consistently, the less powerful are at risk. [...]

SURVIVORS OF HUMAN RIGHTS ABUSE

Refugees can be traumatized by both abuse suffered in their home country and/or the effects of forced migration (Basoglu et al. 1994; Holtz 1998). Those conducting interviews in this population should be aware of how the population became displaced, the psychological sequelae survivors may have, interviewing techniques, possible interventions, as well as recognizing interviewer countertransference.

Process of Torture/Human Rights Abuses

Many displaced people have suffered extreme human rights abuses, including torture. The twentieth century has seen torture reemerge as a tool of authoritarian states. Up to 35 percent of the world's refugees have experienced torture. It is one of the most severe forms of human rights abuse that can lead to profound psychological sequelae (Baker 1992). Torture is a sociopolitical phenomenon. It is often, but not always, aimed at the destruction of enemies of the state. Through the detention and abuse of the prisoner, the state acts to inflict societal trauma. Often the person abducted and tortured holds a position of respect in the community. The aim of the torturer is not to kill the victims, but rather to subject them to dehumanizing experiences. [...]

The Nature of Flight

The decision to leave one's home does not come easily and is often influenced by a complex set of circumstances. Prior to fleeing, torture survivors live in a state of unrest and insecurity. They experience upheaval of their families, homes and communities and the loss of previous societal roles and status. The survivor often arrives at an international border with very few personal belongings; upon crossing the border they "officially" become refugees. Loss of material items compounds their feelings of despair. The nature of the journey may include fear of discovery, hunger, further torture, rape, robbery, disease, and other difficulties adding to their overall psychological stress. Often on arrival, the new site for a refuge camp is still not secure, there may be resentment on behalf of the host country and the refugee must confront linguistic, financial, and cultural obstacles (Cunningham et al. 1990).

Psychological Effects

It is important for social scientists not only to recognize the reasons for flight but also to acquaint themselves with some of the potential psychological manifestations of either surviving torture or other human rights abuses. Psychological sequelae can manifest themselves in a variety of ways. Cultural differences may lead to variability in how these symptoms present. [...]

Interviewing Survivors

The interview process in a complex humanitarian emergency can vary depending on the objective of the project. The relief agency might ask a social scientist to assist in further understanding the nature of the refugees' belief system. This information will allow the agency to adopt culturally specific and appropriate interventions in such areas as public health, education, capacity building, or job skills training. The interviewing used to gather this information must be done with utmost sensitivity. [...] It is imperative that the interview is always constructed in such a manner as to allow the survivor to set acceptable parameters, rules, and expectations of the process.

Interventions to Regain Control

The role of the social scientist in complex emergencies is multifaceted. Relief workers with a human rights perspective can be advocates for the displaced population. Awareness of and sensitivity to both the culture of relief agencies and displaced populations allow the urging of the inclusion of human rights into all aspects of programmatic planning and implementation. Although mental health disorders are among the leading medical problems in refugee situations, it is rare to find mental health professionals as a part of the initial relief team.

While social scientists are not trained in psychological assessment and intervention, there are techniques that can be employed to assist a survivor of torture. A safe, predictable environment with available, culturally appropriate social support will enhance the recovery process. [...]

Interviewer's Personal Feelings/Countertransference

When involved in a large assessment of a displaced population where the population has been exposed to a tremendous level of human rights abuse, the interviewer may find the experience emotionally overwhelming. Not only is the work exhausting, often lasting twelve or more hours a day for multiple days, but the interviewing process often exposes the interviewer to stories that go beyond the realm of what society would classify as normal human experiences. This can lead to secondary trauma in the persons taking the abuse histories. [...]

ROLES FOR THE ANTHROPOLOGIST

Protection is the fundamental human rights issue. For protection to be effective, information is necessary. Gathering such information requires sensitivity to the life-threatening and respect-demeaning conditions faced by the refugees. Awareness of the possibilities of human rights abuses is necessary. These abuses may be embedded within the system, because of the system being overwhelmed or a lack of understanding of the issues on the part of those controlling the system. In bringing such abuses to light and analyzing their causes, anthropologists can be effective advocates for protecting human rights. [...]

It is equally important to become well informed about the demands upon humanitarian aid staff: their responsibilities, authority, and limits. The ability to carry out human rights-focused research can make an enormous contribution to overextended staff operating under intense time frames. The literature is replete with assertions that data necessary for planning appropriate public health interventions are often lacking; for example, morbidity and mortality data for displaced women (Waldman and Martone 1999). There are numerous calls for the well-planned pursuit of answers to many important questions, as well as for the sharing of such information with key organizations, in order to enhance cooperation and delivery of services. Social scientists, especially medical anthropologists, are trained, and as members of a team, well positioned, to contribute to these needs. Even within a complex emergency there are ways of protecting the lives of vulnerable people. Social scientists can contribute significantly to identifying points of threat to human rights; these must not be ignored any more than one would consider ignoring the absence of water, food, and shelter. Social scientists should take a major role in ensuring effective protection.

REFERENCES

Baker, Ron (1992) "Psychosocial Consequences for Tortured Refugees Seeking Asylum and Refugee Status in Europe." In Metin Basoglu (ed.), *Torture and Its Consequences.* New York: Cambridge University Press: 83–106.

Basoglu, Metin (1993) "Prevention of Torture and Care of Survivors." *Journal of the American Medical Association* 270(5): 606–611.

Basoglu, Metin, M. Parker, O. Parker, E. Ozmen, I. Marks, C. Incesu, D. Sahin, and N. Sarimurat (1994) "Psychological Effects of Torture." *American Journal of Psychiatry* 151(1): 76–81.

Cunningham, Margaret, Derrick Silove, and Victor Storm (1990) "Counseling Survivors of Torture and Refugee Trauma." *Australian Family Physician* 19(4): 501–504, 506, 509–510.

Demusz, Kerry (1998) "From Relief to Development." *Journal of Refugee Studies* 11(3): 231–244.

Dick, Bruce, and Stephanie Simmonds (1983) "Refugee Health Care?" *Disasters* 7(4): 291–303.

Gilles, H. M., J. B. Lawson, M. Sibelas, A. Voller, and N. Allan (1969) "Malaria, Anaemia and Pregnancy." *Annals of Tropical Medicine and Parasitology* 63(2): 245–63.

Harrell-Bond, Barbara E. (1999) "Interview with Barbara Harrell-Bond." In Doreen Indra (ed.), *Engendering Forced Migration.* New York: Berghahn Books: 40–62.

Holtz, Timothy H. (1998) "Refugee Trauma Versus Torture Trauma." *Journal of Nervous and Mental Disease* 186(1): 24–34.

Indra, Doreen (1999) "Not a 'Room of One's Own'." In Doreen Indra (ed.), *Engendering Forced Migration.* New York: Berghahn Books: 1–22.

Institute of Medicine (1988) *Future of Public Health.* Washington DC: National Academy Press.

Kyi, Aung San Suu (1991) *Freedom from Fear.* London: Penguin Books.

MacArthur, John R. (1995) "Field Notes." Unpublished MS, International Rescue Committee, Thailand.

MacArthur, John R., Holly A. Williams, and Peter B. Bloland (2000) "Malaria Control in Complex Humanitarian Emergencies." *Refuge* 18(5): 4–10.

Mann, Jonathan M., Lawrence Gostin, Sofia Gruskin, Troyen Brennan, Zita Lazzarini, and Harvey V. Fineberg (1994) "Health and Human Rights." *Health and Human Rights* 1(1): 6–23.

McSpadden, Lucia Ann (1992) *Refugee Camps in Kenya.* New York: Church World Service.

McSpadden, Lucia Ann, and Ayok A. Choi (1998) "Generating the Political Will for Protecting the Rights of Refugees." In C. F. Alger (ed.), *The Future of the United Nations System.* Tokyo: United Nations University Press: 282–314.

Minear, Larry (1999) "Partnerships in the Protection of Refugees and Other People at Risk." In *New Issues in Refugee Research*. Working Paper No. 13. Geneva: UNHCR Centre for Documentation and Research.

Moussa, Helene (1993) *Storm and Sanctuary*. Dundas: Artemis Enterprises.

Prothero, R. Mansell (1994) "Forced Movements of Population and Health Hazards in Tropical Africa." *International Journal of Epidemiology* 23(4): 657–664.

Toole, Michael J., and Ronald J. Waldman (1997) "The Public Health Aspects of Complex Emergencies and Refugee Situations." *Annual Review of Public Health* 18: 283–312.

United Nations (1948) "Universal Declaration of Human Rights." In Center for the Study of Human Rights (ed.), *Twenty-Five Human Rights Documents*. New York: Columbia University Press: 6–9.

UNHCR (United Nations High Commissioner for Refugees) (1995a) *Sexual Violence against Refugees*. Geneva: UNHCR.

UNHCR (1995b) *The State of the World's Refugees*. London: Oxford University Press.

UNHCR (1999) *Protecting Refugees*. Geneva: UNHCR.

US Committee for Refugees (2000) *World Refugee Survey 2000*. Washington DC: USCR.

Waldman, Ronald, and Gerald Martone (1999) "Public Health and Complex Emergencies." *American Journal of Public Health* 89(10): 1483–1485.

7
Speechless Emissaries

Liisa H. Malkki

Massive displacements of people due to political violence and the sight—on television and in newspapers—of refugees as a miserable "sea of humanity" have come to seem more and more common. If these displacements, and media representations of them, appear familiar, so too does the range of humanitarian interventions routinely activated by the movement of people. The purpose of this essay is to explore the forms typically taken by humanitarian interventions that focus on refugees as their object of knowledge, assistance, and management, and to trace the effects of these forms of intervention at several different levels. [...]

The central purpose here is to examine some of the specific effects of the contemporary dehistoricizing constitution of the refugee as a singular category of humanity within the international order of things. Much as in the case of the local refugee administrators in Dar es Salaam, one important effect of the bureaucratized humanitarian interventions that are set in motion by large population displacements is to leach out the histories and the politics of specific refugees' circumstances. Refugees stop being specific persons and become pure victims in general: universal man, universal woman, universal child, and, taken together, universal family (Barthes 1980). Of course, refugee populations usually consist of people in urgent need who have been victimized in numerous ways. The problem is that the necessary delivery of relief and also long-term assistance is accompanied by a host of other, unannounced social processes and practices that are dehistoricizing. This dehistoricizing universalism creates a context in which it is difficult for people in the refugee category to be approached as historical actors rather than simply as mute victims. It can strip from them the authority to give credible narrative evidence or testimony about their own condition in politically and institutionally consequential forums. [...]

The intent here is not to dismiss humanitarian interventions as useless. The alternatives to humanitarianism that come most easily to mind—utter, uninformed indifference or repressive, undemocratic, mercenary logics—are clearly terrible. But precisely because international interventions (humanitarian and otherwise) are increasingly important, we should have better ways of conceptualizing, designing, and challenging them. This is why it is useful to examine the idea of a universal, ahistorical humanity that forms the basis of much of contemporary progressive politics. [...]

REFUGEE STATUS AS LIVED BY HUTU REFUGEES IN MISHAMO, TANZANIA

The tens of thousands of Hutu refugees who fled the mass killings by the Tutsi-dominated army in Burundi in 1972 have, for the most part, been living in refugee camps ever since. A much smaller group of these 1972 refugees (some 20,000–30,000) settled spontaneously in and around Kigoma township, and have thus had no experience of prolonged residence inside a refugee camp. [...] The social status of being a refugee had a very pronounced salience in the camp refugees' life-worlds, while in town it generally did not. In Mishamo it was indispensable to understanding something of the social and political meaning given collectively to refugeeness and to exile by the camp inhabitants. In contrast, for the people I have called the town refugees, refugee status was generally not a collectively heroized or positively valued aspect of one's social person. Insofar as it was considered relevant at all, it was more often a liability than a protective or positive status.

I have examined this contrast at length elsewhere (Malkki 1995a). But even in its simplest outlines, the case suggests that the elaboration of legal refugee status into a social condition or a moral identity does not occur in an automatic or predictable way, and that even people who fled originally from the "same place" can, and often do, come to define the meaning of refugee status differently, depending on the specific lived circumstances of their exile. In what follows I will focus only on the camp refugees' social imagination of refugeeness because it was their definitions that most directly challenged the refugee administrators' visions of the same.

The most unusual and prominent social fact about the camp of Mishamo was that the refugees who had lived within its confines for so many years were still in 1985–86 continually engaged in an urgent, collective process of constructing and reconstructing a true history of their trajectory as "a people." This was an oppositional process, setting itself against state-approved versions of the history of Burundi. The narrative production of this history in exile was sweeping. [...]

The Hutu refugees' narratives outlined the lost features of the "autochthonous," "original" Burundi nation and the primordial social harmony that was believed to have prevailed among the original [Hutu] inhabitants. The narratives of the past then located the coming of the Tutsi in time and space: they were remembered as the pastoral "foreigners from the North" who came in search of new pastures for their cattle "only 400 years ago." There followed the progressive theft of power from the [Hutu] "natives" by Tutsi ruse and trickery, and the emergence of an extractive, oppressive social hierarchy. The refugees' historical narratives moved on to the colonial era, concentrating mainly on the period of Belgian administration, and defined the end of formal colonial rule as the defeat of the departing Belgians by Tutsi trickery. The culminating chapter in the refugees' historical narratives of the Burundian past amounted to a vast and painful documentation of the mass killings of people belonging to the Hutu category by Burundi's (mainly Tutsi) army—and, eventually, by Tutsi civilians—in 1972. So many years later, the historical and personal memory of the apocalyptic violence and terror of that era still had a sharp and shocking salience in people's everyday lives. [...]

The camp refugees saw themselves as a nation in exile. And they thought of exile as an era of moral trials and hardships that would enable them to reclaim the "homeland" in Burundi at some moment in the future. [...]

Conversations about refugeeness and exile with people in Mishamo began to suggest over time that refugeeness was seen as a matter of becoming. They often explained that in the initial stages of exile, the Hutu were not yet true refugees, refugees properly speaking. What they had to say strongly suggested that, socially, there was such a thing as a novice refugee. True or mature refugeeness, then, entailed a cumulative process embedded in history and experience. It had to do, if I have understood correctly, with a certain level of self-knowledge, and the camp was a privileged site for the elaboration of such a knowledge.

Another indication that refugeeness had come to be interiorized as an aspect of people's identities in Mishamo was that it was considered to be inherited from one generation to another as long as the Hutu lived in exile. To quote one person, "If I am a refugee here, of course my child is a refugee also—and so is his child, and his child, until we go back to our native country." This vision, of course, fit well into the narratives of history and exile that were so central in the everyday life of the refugee camp, but it was quite different from the legal definition, and also from the ideal trajectory of refugeeness usually constructed by the staffs of the international aid organizations.

Being a refugee also naturally suggested, even demanded, certain kinds of social conduct and moral stances, while precluding others. Thus, for example, many refugees in Mishamo, in the camp, were continually angered by the conduct of those among them who engaged in commerce—those who had become "merchant refugees." (And, in fact, the most prominent Hutu merchant refugees mostly lived outside the camps, among the so-called spontaneously settling refugees in Kigoma and Ujiji, and in other towns). As one person exclaimed: "We have not come here to make commerce. We are refugees." This sense of outrage was echoed by another man: "[The merchant refugees,] they became rich. They have cabarets, hotels, restaurants ... *being refugees*." As we will see momentarily, the camp refugees and their administrators agreed on the point that a rich refugee was a contradiction in terms; but they came to this conclusion from different premises. The camp refugees recognized that wealth would likely root people in the here and now, making them forget that they were in exile, and thus properly rooted elsewhere. In a curious way, wealth and commerce made people "this-worldly"—while the "other world," of course, was the homeland. And refugeeness, ideally, was an integral part of the process of a future return just as it was inevitably linked to the past. It should be noted, too, that commerce put Hutu in the position of exploiting other Hutu, thus challenging their corporate solidarity.

This brief account of the social construction and moral imagination of refugeeness in Mishamo has, perhaps, been sufficient to show in what sense refugee identity can be shaped by historical and political context. Why the Hutu had to flee, what the history of political struggle had been in Burundi, how the refugees expected to help bring about a new political order in Burundi: all these were issues inextricably tied to the social meaning of exile. It would therefore have been impossible for them to concentrate only on life within the confines of their camp, as if the camp were not itself deeply within history.

THE SOCIAL IMAGINATION OF REFUGEE STATUS AMONG REFUGEE ADMINISTRATORS IN TANZANIA

Throughout my field research in Tanzania I was offered crucially important assistance by the United Nations High Commissioner for

Refugees (UNHCR) and the Tanganyika Christian Refugee Service, that is, by the people who—along with officials of the Tanzanian Ministry of Home Affairs—were charged with administering and assisting the Hutu refugees. The United Nations' office funded the greatest part of the refugee projects, while the Tanganyika Christian Refugee Service was the principal implementing agency. [...]

When I had completed one year of field research in rural western Tanzania in late 1986 and returned to Dar es Salaam in preparation for my departure from Tanzania, the director of the Tanganyika Christian Refugee Service invited me to his home to speak to staff about my research. [...] At the evening gathering on the terrace of the director's home, I gave an account of what I had heard and thought in the course of the short year in western Tanzania, knowing that numerous people in my audience had much longer experience of living in Tanzania. I spoke about the fact that the Hutu refugees in Mishamo saw exile in Tanzania first and foremost not as a tragedy, but as a useful, productive period of hardships that would teach and purify them, and thereby help them to grow powerful enough to return to their homeland on their own terms. That the refugees considered they had undergone hardship in Tanzania was evident, and I tried to give an account of this also. I spoke about the antagonisms that had developed in Mishamo Refugee Settlement as a result of the highly hierarchical social organization within it, about resentment over practices that were considered extractive of the refugees' agricultural labor power, about the control of movement through Leave Passes, about the scarcity of secondary and higher education for refugee children, and so on. The most important point I was trying to convey was that the experiential reality of the refugee camp was powerfully shaped by the narrative memory of relationships and antagonisms located in the past in Burundi, antagonisms between the Hutu peasant majority there and the minority Tutsi category that at the time predominated in the military and government. That is, the camp was a site of intense historicity, and to be a refugee was a historicizing and politicizing condition. To study this historicity, I said, had become one of my main activities during the fieldwork.

I knew as I spoke that my findings were in some measure incommensurable with the language of project evaluations and "development" discourse in which refugee issues were so often framed (Ferguson 1994). The results of my research were listened to politely but were clearly not received as particularly useful information by the Tanganyika Christian Refugee Service staff, who were my audience that evening. What I reported was not completely novel to them. Several among them—especially the Tanzanian staff—had previously heard aspects of the grand historical narrative of the Hutu as a people in exile. [...] But this historical knowledge, this narrative evidence, was, to all intents and purposes, irrelevant and unusable by the organization. Moreover, when it did become relevant to daily operations, it was as a potential trouble factor threatening to complicate the administering of the projects.

My presentation in the director's garden provoked a spirited discussion of what a real refugee was, or ought to be—and whether the Hutu who had come to Tanzania in 1972 still fit the picture. One of the guests heard in my presentation evidence that the Hutu refugees were ungrateful recipients of international assistance, and was moved to challenge the refugee status of the Hutu on grounds of material, economic wellbeing:

> Nowhere else in Africa do these people [refugees] receive their own land to cultivate. Not in Sudan, not in Somalia. They say that these people are refugees; they should not have all the same rights as citizens.

Another employee added, "In fact, their standard of living is higher than in the Tanzanian villages!" While both clearly were referring to complex questions regarding the distribution of poverty, there was also an evident moral intent to say that a real or proper refugee should not be well off. Later in the same discussion the director himself commented:

> I should show you a film the Norwegians made of the Burundi refugees when they first came. One was showing a bullet wound, someone else a cut, torn clothes, dirty. ... They had nothing. ... These people don't look like refugees anymore. If you go to Mishamo [refugee camp] as a visitor, you will think these are just ordinary villagers.

It was not uncommon to hear similar comments from other refugee administrators, whether of the Tanganyika Christian Refugee Service or the United Nations. There was a pronounced tendency to try to identify and fix the "real" refugee on extralegal grounds. And one key terrain where this took place was that of the *visual image* of the refugee, making it possible to claim that given people were not real refugees because they did not look (or conduct themselves) like real refugees. This suggests that refugee status was implicitly understood to involve a performative dimension. The symbolic, social significance of the Hutu refugees' early wounds and physical problems for their administrators emerged only gradually, in the course of numerous exchanges with the Tanganyika Christian Refugee Service and United Nations staff. It appeared that the staff—in an effort to do their jobs properly and to direct assistance where it might be needed most—were in some manner trying to identify *exemplary victims*.

Frantz Fanon has observed that for "the native," "objectivity is always against him" (in McClintock 1992: 97). For the refugee, much the same might be said. In his or her case, wounds speak louder than words. Wounds are accepted as objective evidence, as more reliable sources of knowledge than the words of the people on whose bodies those wounds are found. So the ideal construct, the "real refugee," was imagined as a particular kind of person: a victim whose judgment and reason had been compromised by his or her experiences. This was a tragic, and sometimes repulsive, figure who could be deciphered and healed only by professionals, and who was opaque even (or perhaps especially) to himself or herself.

This set of expectations about the communicative efficacy (Tambiah 1985: 123–166) of corporeal wounds—and of the presumed unreliability of the refugees' own narrative firsthand accounts of political violence—should be seen in relation to more general social expectations and interventions directed at refugees in Tanzania. What was conspicuously absent from all the documentary accumulation generated in the refugee camps was an official record of what the refugees themselves said about their own histories and their present predicament.

They were frequently regarded as simply unreliable informants. There was also a more general tendency among some (though by no means all) administrators to characterize the refugees as dishonest, prone to exaggeration, even crafty and untrustworthy. So, in a sense, they had to be cared for and understood obliquely, *despite themselves*. Their bodies were made to speak to doctors and other professionals, for the bodies could give a more reliable and relevant accounting than the refugees' "stories." I often heard the Hutu refugees characterized as persons who were always "telling stories."

Writing in the 1930s, Ernst Bloch defined "realism" as "the cult of the immediately ascertainable fact" (in Feldman 1994: 406). This useful phrase accurately describes how the figure of the refugee comes to be knowable: it is necessary to cut through "the stories" to get to "the bare facts." It is here that physical, non-narrative evidence assumes such astonishing power. It has all the authority of an "immediately ascertainable fact." In contrast, the political and moral history of displacement that most Hutu in Mishamo themselves insisted on constructing was generally rejected by their administrators as too messy, subjective, unmanageable, hysterical— as just "stories." Set against an ostensibly knowable, visible medical history of injuries or illness, a political history snaking its way from Burundi to Tanzania, from the past to the here and now, weaving people into complex loyalties and unseen relations, presented itself as unstable and unknowable—and as ultimately, or, properly, irrelevant to the practical efforts to administer and care for large refugee populations.

In this manner history tended to get leached out of the figure of the refugee, as imagined by their administrators. This active process of dehistoricization was inevitably also a project of depoliticization. For to speak about the past, about the historical trajectory that had led the Hutu as refugees into the western Tanzanian countryside, was to speak about politics. This could not be encouraged by the camp administrators (whether the Ministry of Home Affairs, the Tanganyika Christian Refugee Service, or the United Nations); political activism and refugee status were mutually exclusive here, as they are in international refugee law more generally.

The conversation at the Tanganyika Christian Refugee Service director's home illustrates how the everyday language and practices of those very people who worked with the Hutu because of their refugee status continually acted to destabilize the solidity of the legal category, as documented in the refugees' identity papers. This desta- bilization occurred along several different axes. On the one hand, there was a continual, informal monitoring of signs of decreasing refugeeness. As the visible signs of one's social refugeeness faded, one's worthiness as a recipient of material assistance was likely to decrease. But there was more to it than that. What emerges from this and other accounts is that the refugees were thought to be at their purest when they first arrived, and when their condition was visibly at its worst. So, instead of refugee status imagined as a state of being attained gradually (as the Hutu camp refugees themselves saw it) or as a legal status that one has or has not, the administrators tended to imagine refugee status as a processual condition that was at its purest and most recognizable early in exile, and was thereafter subject to gradual adulteration over time. All this added up, in a subtle way, to the barely noticeable but nevertheless powerful constitution of the real or true refugee—an ideal figure of which any actual refugees were always imperfect instantiations.

REFUGEES AS OBJECTS OF HUMANITARIAN INTERVENTION

The case of Tanzania in the mid-1980s facilitates the effort of identifying (even if tentatively) certain key features in the constitution of the archetypal refugee at the more general level of humanitarian policy discourse. I take as a starting point the observation that there has emerged, in the post-World War II era, a substantially standardized way of talking about and handling "refugee problems" among national governments, relief and refugee agencies, and other non-governmental organizations (Malkki 1995b). I would also suggest that these standardizing discursive and representational forms (or, perhaps more precisely, tendencies) have made their way into journalism and all of the media that report on refugees. As a result, it is possible to discern transnational commonalities in both the textual and the visual representation of refugees. Such trans-nationally mobile representations are often very easily translated and shared across nation-state borders. And because they are shared among the institutions that locate, fund, and administer refugee projects, these representations can reasonably be expected to carry significant consequences. One of the most far-reaching, important consequences of these established representational practices is the systematic, even if unintended, silencing of persons who find themselves in the classificatory space of "refugee." That is, refugees suffer from a peculiar kind of speechlessness in the face of the national and international organizations whose object of care and control they are. Their accounts are disqualified almost a priori, while the languages of refugee relief, policy science, and "development" claim the production of authoritative narratives about the refugees. In what follows I attempt to look a little more closely at the systemic underpinnings of this form of silencing and speechlessness. I approach this phenomenon from several different directions, starting with a brief look at the complex effects of the visual representation of refugees, especially in the media of photography and documentary film.

The visual representation of refugees appears to have become a singularly translatable and mobile mode of knowledge about them. Indeed, it is not farfetched to say that a vigorous, transnational, largely philanthropic traffic in images and visual signs of refugeeness has gradually emerged in the last half-century. Pictures of refugees are now a key vehicle in the elaboration of a transnational social imagination of refugeeness. The visual representation of displacement occurs in many arenas: among refugee administrators (as we have seen); in applied and other academic scholarship; among journalists; in the publications of humanitarian and international organizations (United Nations *Refugees Magazine*); in television fund-raising drives; and even in fashion advertising (I once saw a fashion spread in a Finnish women's weekly magazine, *Anna*, entitled "The Refugee Look"). This global visual field of often quite standardized representational practices is surprisingly important in its effects, for it is connected at many points to the de facto inability of particular refugees to represent themselves authoritatively in the inter- and transnational institutional domains where funds and resources circulate.

The first thing to be noted about the mutual relationship between image and narrative, spectacle and self-representation, is that photographs and other visual representations of refugees are far more common than is the reproduction in print of what particular refugees have said. There are more established institutional contexts, uses, and conventions for pictures of refugees than for displaced persons' own narrative accounts of exile. Indeed, some of these visual conventions seem to speed up the evaporation of history and narrativity.

Mass displacements are often captured as a "sea" or "blur of humanity" (Lamb 1994: H5) or as a "vast and throbbing mass" (Warrick 1994: E1), especially in Africa. Black bodies are pressed together impossibly close in a confusing, frantic mass. An utter human uniformity is hammered into the viewer's retina. This is a spectacle of "raw," "bare" humanity. It in no way helps one to realize that each of the persons in the photograph has a name, opinions, relatives, and histories, or that each has reasons for being where he is now: inside the frame of [a] photograph.

Feldman's essay on "cultural anesthesia" explores these kinds of mass images:

> Generalities of bodies—dead, wounded, starving, diseased, and homeless—are pressed against the television screen as mass articles. In their pervasive depersonalization, this *anonymous corporeality* functions as an allegory of the elephantine, "archaic," and violent histories of external and internal subalterns. (1994: 407; emphasis added)

This "anonymous corporeality" is a precise characterization of what happens to refugees in the regimes of representation under discussion here. No names, no funny faces, no distinguishing marks, no esoteric details of personal style enter, as a rule, into the frame of pictures of refugees when they are being imagined as a sea of humanity.

Of course, this anonymous corporeality is not necessarily just a feature of mass scenes; it is equally visible in another conventionalized image of refugees: women and children. This sentimentalized, composite figure—at once feminine and maternal, childlike and innocent—is an image that we use to cut across cultural and political difference, when our intent is to address the very heart of our humanity.

Elsewhere I have also suggested that the visual prominence of women and children as embodiments of refugeeness has to do not just with the fact that most refugees are women and children, but with the institutional, international expectation of a certain kind of *helplessness* as a refugee characteristic (Malkki 1995a: 11). In an article entitled "The Refugee Experience: Defining the Parameters of a Field of Study," Barry Stein notes that "refugees are helped because they are helpless; they must display their need and helplessness" (1981: 327). This vision of helplessness is vitally linked to the constitution of speechlessness among refugees: helpless victims need protection, need someone to speak for them. In a sense, the imagined sea of humanity assumes a similar helplessness and speechlessness.

The bodies and faces of refugees that flicker onto our television screens and the glossy refugee portraiture in news magazines and wall calendars constitute spectacles that preclude the "involved" narratives and historical or political details that originate among refugees. It becomes difficult to trace a connection between me/us—the consumers of images—and them—the sea of humanity (Calhoun 1995: xiii). Or, more precisely, it becomes difficult to trace a connection, a relationship, other than that of a bare, "mere," common underlying humanity: "We are all human, after all." [...] One cannot help but feel horror and profound sadness, I think, in the face of such images or in the knowledge that such social circumstances do exist. But it is also possible and, indeed, useful to notice that in their overpowering philanthropic universalism, in their insistence on the secondariness and unknowability of *details* of specific histories and specific cultural or political contexts, such forms of representation deny the very particulars that make of people something other than anonymous bodies, mere human beings.

At first it is difficult to see what might be so problematic in seeing the suffering of people with the eyes of "humanitarian concern" and "human compassion." It is surely better than having no compassion or simply looking the other way. But this is not the issue. The issue is that the established practices of humanitarian representation and intervention are not timeless, unchangeable, or in any way absolute. On the contrary, these practices are embedded in long and complicated histories of their own—histories of charity and philanthropy, histories of international law, peacekeeping, and diplomacy, histories of banishment and legal protection, histories of empires and colonial rule, histories of civilizational and emancipatory discourses and missionary work, histories of World Bank and other development initiatives in Africa, and much more. These humanitarian representational practices and the standardized interventions that go with them have the effect, as they currently stand, of producing anonymous corporeality and speechlessness. That is, these practices tend actively to displace, muffle, and pulverize history, in the sense that the Hutu refugees in Mishamo understood history. And they tend to hide the political, or political-economic, connections that link television viewers' own history with that of "those poor people over there" (see Calhoun 1995; Ferguson 1995).

These processes were in grotesque evidence when the most recent large refugee movements from Burundi began to be photographed in the world's newspapers. In the October 25, 1993, issue of the *Los Angeles Times*, on what the paper calls its "Second Front Page," there was a large photograph of women and children laden with bundles. Underneath was a slim caption:

> Hutu tribe refugees cross the border near Rwanda after walking more than 37 miles from Burundi. Tribal violence is believed to have flared up between the Tutsi and Hutu after a Burundi military coup overthrew and killed President Melchior Ndadaye on Thursday. On Sunday, 4,000 people marched through the streets of Bujumbura, the capital, calling for the release of the bodies of the president and of others killed in the coup. (*Los Angeles Times* 1993: A3)

The photo was a very large one, but there was no story to go with it. It was as if this grouping of people—women clothed in colorful cotton wraps, children in ragged T-shirts and shorts, walking barefoot out of Burundi—had just become generic refugees and generic Africans in whose societies tribal violence periodically flares up. It was as if this was all the context that might be required. Whoever got close enough to this cluster of people to take that photograph could have asked them to explain (if not in Kirundi, perhaps in French, or certainly through an interpreter) what had happened to them and what they had witnessed. Instead, there was almost no news from Burundi at all—only this large Associated Press photograph. And this small group of speechless emissaries was allowed to go on its way.

This newspaper photograph helps us to see how "the refugee" is commonly constituted as a figure who is thought to "speak" to us in a particular way: wordlessly. Just the refugee's physical presence is "telling" of his or her immediate history of violence. So we tend to assume, at any rate.

But it is not just that photographs displace narrative testimony. When there is testimony about refugees, it mostly does what the photographs do: it silences the refugees. For it tends to be testimony by "refugee experts" and "relief officials" (or even by those ever ready "well-placed western diplomatic sources"), not by refugees themselves. How often have we seen the media image of a (usually white) UN official standing in a dusty landscape, perhaps in Africa, surrounded by milling crowds of black people peering into the camera, and benevolently, efficiently, giving a rundown on their numbers, their diseases, their nutritional needs, their crops, and their birth and mortality rates? This mode of what may be called a "clinical humanitarianism" looks for all the world like an exhaustive report on the displaced masses; and the official is surely trying to be informative, as well as to balance honesty and diplomacy. And yet the scene and the expert voice operate precisely to erase knowledge. In constructing a raw humanity and a pure helplessness, this spectacle all but blocks the possibility of persons stepping forward from the milling crowds, asking for the microphone, and addressing the glassy eye of the camera: "Now, if I may, Sir/ Madam, there are numerous things that you have not considered, many details about our history and political circumstances that might assist you in helping us." Such details easily appear as mere quibbles, fine points, and posturing in the face of the other, very powerful narrative of emergency relief, humanitarian intervention, and "raw" human needs.

The visual conventions for representing refugees and the language of raw human needs both have the effect of constructing refugees as a bare humanity even as a merely biological or demographic presence. This mode of humanitarianism acts to trivialize and silence history and politics—a silencing that can legitimately be described as dehumanizing in most contexts. And yet the mechanisms involved here are more complex than that. For one might argue that what these representational practices do is not strictly to dehumanize, but to humanize in a particular mode. A mere, bare, naked, or minimal humanity is set up. This is a vision of humanity that repels elements that fail to fit into the logic of its framework.

THE STAKES IN THE HUMANITARIAN INTERVENTIONS IN RWANDA, BURUNDI, AND BEYOND

The vast displacements of people that occurred in the wake of the fighting and the genocide of 1994 in Rwanda are a good example of what is at stake in the constitution of refugees as such passive objects of humanitarian intervention. [...]

The genocide in Rwanda has already happened; it is not possible to go back and change interventions or omissions of the past. But the dangerous effects of silencing are still all too salient in currently unfolding events in the region. The Hutu refugees from Rwanda are still in Zaire, Tanzania, and elsewhere, and, as of this writing (February 1996), refusing repatriation, still the objects of concerted efforts from the Zairean government, the United Nations, and various other agencies to push them back where they "belong." The effects of such silencing are detectable in neighboring Burundi, also. By ignoring the continual political persecution, intimidation, and killings occurring in that country, the "international community" risks coming face to face with another Rwanda-like period of terror there and finding that nothing that could have been done has been done (Balzar 1994).

But preventive measures do not come easily in the conventional logic of the "humanitarian operation." For humanitarian help to be mobilized, the disaster usually must have happened already. When refugees and orphans have been produced, then the site for intervention is visible. Otherwise, the matter is "political" (or a "domestic" issue in a sovereign state) and thus beyond the realm of humanitarian intervention (Waal 1994: 10).

CONCLUSION

[...] These forms and practices of humanitarianism do not represent the best of all possible worlds, and it is politically and intellectually possible to try to come up with something better. Especially in the face of the political crisis in Rwanda, and the very real possibility that the political situation in Burundi will soon become much worse than it already is, it is necessary to do better. Perhaps a part (a crucial part) of the improvement is to be found in a radically "historicizing humanism" that insists on acknowledging not only human suffering but also narrative authority, historical agency, and political memory. Barthes's call for a progressive humanism (1980: 101) addressed this very issue, as do Foucault's later writings; he suggested why it is more useful to seek to connect people through history and historicity than through a human essence (or "human nature"). This is not to make a simple, romantic argument about "giving the people a voice"; for one would find underneath the silence not a voice waiting to be liberated but ever deeper historical layers of silencing and bitter, complicated regional struggles over history and truth.

It is a historicizing (and politicizing) humanism that would require us, politically and analytically, to examine our cherished notions of mankind and the human community, humanitarianism and humanitarian "crises," human rights and international justice. For if humanism can only constitute itself on the bodies of dehistoricized, archetypal refugees and other similarly styled victims—if clinical and philanthropic modes of humanitarianism are the only options— then citizenship in this human community itself remains curiously, indecently, outside of history.

REFERENCES

Balzar, John (1994) "Burundi Battles Its Demons in Fight to Survive." *Los Angeles Times*, August 15: A3, A10.

Barthes, Roland (1980) *Mythologies*. New York: Hill and Wang.

Calhoun, Craig (1995) "Foreword." In Micheline R. Ishay, *Internationalism and Its Betrayal*. Minneapolis: University of Minnesota Press: ix–xiv.

Feldman, Allen (1994) "On Cultural Anesthesia." *American Ethnologist* 21: 404–418.

Ferguson, James (1994) *The Anti-Politics Machine*. Minneapolis: University of Minnesota Press.

Ferguson, James (1995) "From African Socialism to Scientific Capitalism." In D. B. Moore and G. J. Schmitz (eds.), *Debating Development Discourse*. New York: St Martin's Press: 129–148.

Ferguson, James (1997) "Paradoxes of Sovereignty and Independence." In Karen Fog Olwig and Kirsten Hastrup (eds.), *Siting Culture*. New York: Routledge: 123–141.

Lamb, David (1994) "Threading through a Surreal World on the Way to Tragedy in Rwanda." *Los Angeles Times*, June 14: H1, H5.

Los Angeles Times (1993) "Burundi Refugees Enter Rwanda." October 25: A3.

Malkki, Liisa (1995a) *Purity and Exile*. Chicago: University of Chicago Press.

Malkki, Liisa (1995b) "Refugees and Exile." *Annual Review of Anthropology* 24: 495–523.

McClintock, Anne (1992) "The Angel of Progress." *Social Text* 10(2–3): 84–98.

Stein, Barry (1981) "The Refugee Experience." *International Migration Review* 15(1): 320–330.

Tambiah, Stanley (1985) *Culture, Thought, and Social Action*. Cambridge MA: Harvard University Press.

de Waal, Alex (1994) "A Lesson to Learn from Rwanda." Helsinki: United Nations University/World Institute for Development Economics Research 2194 (December 28): 9–10.

Warrick, Pamela (1994) "Tipper Gore's Mission of Mercy." *Los Angeles Times*, August 15: El, E2.

8
Trauma and Vulnerability during War

Doug Henry

In March 1991, an attack on a small southern village by a group of armed Sierra Leoneans, Liberians, and Burkinabés calling themselves the Revolutionary United Front began an 11-year conflict in Sierra Leone. Although initially supported by the National Patriotic Front of Liberia, apparently as retribution for Sierra Leone's support of the Economic Community of West African States' multilateral military wing's activities in Liberia, the Revolutionary United Front quickly claimed its own populist agenda for political reform. However, their tactic of targeting civilians, and the failure of genuine political reforms to produce a lasting ceasefire, fueled popular skepticism about the legitimacy of claims by the Revolutionary United Front. Numerous attempts were made at ceasefires, brokered amnesties, negotiated settlements, boycotts, and political power sharing (Henry 2005), yet there were still hit-and-run guerilla attacks, highway ambushes, burned and looted houses, destroyed or confiscated crops, rapes, maiming, and mass human rights violations. Infrastructural damage to the country has been enormous (Hoffman 2004); people everywhere witnessed their homes, schools, clinics, bridges, mosques, churches, and social institutions being damaged or destroyed. [...]

This article explores the contested nature of the body and bodily illness during the social and political violence in Sierra Leone from 1991 through 2002. I conducted ethnographic research among mostly Mende speakers along the Sierra Leone–Guinea border during the conflict. The Mende are one of the two largest ethnic groups in Sierra Leone, occupying the largest part of the south and southeast of the country. Because the original combatants entered from Liberia to the south and east, Mende people in these areas have been somewhat disproportionately affected by the conflict (Henry 2000). Drawing on this research, I document how spectacular acts of violence represented attempts to wrest control of self and identity away from those displaced by the war. As Carolyn Nordstrom writes: "Identity, self, and personhood, as well as physical bodies, are strategic targets of war" (1998: 105). War attempts to take from people ways in which they recognize themselves as human. When separated from its previous context of place and history, the body, as the "existential ground" of culture, becomes the referent on which new classifications are created and contested (Coker 2004).

The article also considers emic interpretations and contested meanings of the illness hypertension, or *haypatɛnsi*, among the displaced. I document how discussions of *haypatɛnsi* allowed horrific subjective experiences to become mediated, enabling survivors to understand and express the pain of their situation and begin reestablishing order and control. As Gay Becker, Yewoubdar Beyene, and Pauline Ken (2000) note, illness narratives can represent "cultural documents" that allow difficult subjective experiences to become apprehended and mediated. Even these discussions of illness, however, involved competition over control of meanings and prescriptive models with medical practitioners. [...]

Anthropological literature has often been critical of medicalizing terms and labels because this does little to advance understanding of the meaning of suffering for victims and survivors; instead, experience and personal expression of conflict are privileged as authentic forms of knowledge. Such criticisms encourage anthropological examination into the "reality" of war, the profound personal perceptions and shared experiences of war's survivors. This is challenging, because violence is, of course, experienced differently by different people (Nordstrom 1998). In Sierra Leone, the girl who was gang raped by soldiers experienced the war differently from the boy who was kidnapped by rebels and forced to carry ammunition by foot 60 miles to a battle zone. There have been, however, collective experiences, shared sufferings, and social struggles.

Illness narratives about trauma and war can be useful in approaching how embodied distress or suffering become manifest and how people begin to come to terms with violence done to their lives. Both terror and healing are acts of embodied narration; they address how the self "speaks" during times of violent unrest (Young 1997). Janis Jenkins (1996), for example, uses narrative to demonstrate how violence can become part of the bodily experience of refugees, women in particular. She discusses how Salvadoran women often represent trauma narratives in ways that are either very extreme or very mundane, but finds that these are simply different ways of expressing the same profound emotional response. She quotes one woman: "Then I would feel my heart, *pum*, *pum*,

pum. If you are fearful it can make you sick. ... I feel that my body isn't me. It can cause a person to go crazy" (Jenkins 1991: 148).

My choice of narrative as a method to convey traumatic experiences was made less by personal choice but by how people around me related their experiences. People rarely shied away from telling me about their encounters with violence. [Rather, they proceeded] tracing a rent fabric back to the crucial moment where some "tear" occurred, realizing a history that, although not necessarily explaining an event, mapped it in time and space as if to say: "*This* is where things began to go wrong." Carina Perelli (1992) calls these "blood memories," when life becomes broken into a before and after of discontinuities and disruptions. Consciousness is suddenly robbed of the social rationality and normality that previously structured its existence. For Feldman (1995), this break is the moment of "existential vertigo," where one's previously held referents are abruptly and violently dissociated, and social conventions and identities unexpectedly flounder. [...]

THE WAR AND ITS REALITY IN SIERRA LEONE—VIOLENCE EMBODIED

Everyone I met remembered acutely where they were and what they were doing at the moment they came face to face with violence, even if it had first occurred years before. Amara, who I met in a refugee camp in Guinea, narrated his experiences from seven years before as though it had just happened to him a day ago:

> I was in Sembehun, sponsoring some boys to mine diamonds, and doing just well enough to take care of my family. One morning as I was coming back from clearing my farm, I saw that rebels had entered the town. I turned and started to go back, but it was too late—they saw me, and put a knife at my chest. "Where's your gun?" they asked. But I didn't have a gun. ... Then they made us all stare at the sky, and started taking my children away. I begged them, telling them I had a farm and needed my children to help me. ... Then the commander came. He was a Liberian; he slapped me hard, and then they carried away my kids. (Amara, Kolomba Camp)

Amara, like others, remembered the "immediacy" of the moments, the unexpected and sudden disruption in the routine fabric of everyday life—the sudden dissolution and disappearance of families after a normal day of farming, and of limited, mortal abilities to protect and provide for them.

Over half of Sierra Leone's population became displaced at least once during the conflict, some many more times, scattered either internally within the country or across the border in Guinea or Liberia. Estimates of those killed usually range between 50,000 and 75,000; thousands more lost limbs in violent amputations, as rebels hacked off body parts of thousands of innocent civilians in a campaign of terror. Thousands more children and youths were forcibly conscripted at the warfront and trained to be guides, carriers, bodyguards, or fighters; some were forced to commit horrible atrocities against family or village, thus severing their ties to home. Abduction and sexual violence against girls became common. Civilians were often targets of the violence, as combatants sought to use bodily violence to destroy self-constructions of identity and personhood. David, a displaced husband I met, with three wives and eight children, talked about the harsh corporal beatings that became normal during the war, perpetrated as much by soldiers sworn to protect people as they were by rebels:

> I returned to Buedu in November 1992, the same month the Sierra Leonean military recaptured Buedu from the rebels. (Shaking his head.) We thought our ordeals were over when the soldiers got there; unfortunately, we were very wrong. Things really intensified. Our own soldiers said we were collaborators, arrested us, beat us. ... They were afraid of us who could read and write; we became very serious suspects ... they said we were up to nothing better, and that we shouldn't have stayed there (under rebel occupation). ... They would really tie me tight; sometimes they would beat you and knock you over, and the knots were so tight that it would take some time before you could move your hands again—sometimes it would take a whole month. (Chuckling.) Once my wives had to hand feed me, because I couldn't move my fingers!
>
> [So] later on, whatever little that remained that the rebels hadn't taken away, they took—our beds, chairs—they carted every single thing away. They even started removing the zinc roofs from houses, which they took over to Daru, and started selling it on the market ... sometimes they even went to the same spots rebels had to sell things. (David, Kenema town)

One strategy of combatants in Sierra Leone was to control people, terrorizing them through dramatic and symbolic violence of the body—limb amputations, severed heads paraded on sticks, rape, body mutilation, stories of cannibalistic acts, and violations of cultural taboo. [...]

Idioms of power and terror attempted to transform individual bodies into political ones, using individuals in symbolic ways to express structural domination through torture, interrogation, dismemberment, rape, or scarification (Turshen and Twagiramariya 1998). During part of the Sierra Leone conflict, for instance, the state (at that time a military–rebel alliance that had gained power by coup d'état) maintained control for a time by expressing in Sierra Leone's Krio *sivilyan noh gǎt blohd* (civilians don't have blood), meaning, in context, that civilians are less than human, without rights, as compared to the junta soldiers. Jenkins (1991), Linda Green (1995), and Glen Perice (1997) all discuss how fear and terror may be instruments used by the state for defining and structuring a social milieu, accomplished through rumor-mongering, deaths, or disappearances.

Combatants also attacked traditional symbols of the social and political body. For instance, rebels would enter indiscriminately into sacred men's and women's society bushes to scatter sacred items, dress in society-devil costumes, and mock their dances. Inasmuch as these institutions normally provide established structure, rules, and mechanisms for settling disputes and keeping peace during ordinary times, attacks on them were direct challenges to their social and political authority and attempts to destroy collective methods for coping with stress. The attacks thus undermined the security and sense of order with which these societies are typically associated.

> Even our sacred areas, they burned sacred houses, destroyed sacred things, and mocked our devils. They upset the whole thing. What women weren't supposed to see, they saw. Sacred places, where women weren't supposed to go—EH! When a war comes behind you, who wouldn't show you a hiding place?! But the rebels exposed most of these things. (Brima, Kolomba Camp, Guinea)

Part of what was so worrisome about events like these was that they dramatized the fact that rebels possessed knowledge of the same societies that people associated with hidden order, yet they seemed unconcerned by the proper control of that knowledge (Ferme 2001). As mentioned above, some of the younger rebels had been captured and conscripted as children, before the time of their own managed induction into the Poro [a secret society in Sierra Leone and Liberia]. The thought that these youths might possess important secrets, but not the discipline to respect them, was frightening (see Ellis 2001).

One of the traditional functions of the Poro has been to train its initiates in the arts and diplomacy of war (Little 1949). In colonial times, it effectively mobilized armed resistance to disrupt the unpopular "hut tax." In some places early in the war, local communities did attempt to respond to local rebel incursions through the Poro, yet this almost invariably backfired; this was thought to be because some of the Poro's own members were among the invading rebels. Instead, local society heads became frequent targets of rebels, as were other community authorities such as chiefs, family heads, policemen, and school principals; sometimes they would be forcibly sodomized, branded with Revolutionary United Front slogans, or executed. All these were deliberate attempts to attack or overturn shared values, ideological norms, and traditional institutions. (These tactics have not been unique to Sierra Leone but are similar to those used by Renamo in Mozambique, the Contras in Nicaragua, and British-trained military forces in colonial Rhodesia.)

Although civilians and social institutions were targeted, the immediate point of contact was always the body. Bodies became loci of contested control between rebels, soldiers, and civilians, as each attempted to replace personal selfhood and humanity with inscribed social, political, and gender ideology (Green 1998). Severed hands, ears, and limbs became testaments to attempts to remove the self from self-conceptions, separating people from their previous experiences of living in their bodies. The boy who had the rebel acronym RUF (Revolutionary United Front) seared into a permanent scar across his chest, the girl who became pregnant from a soldier rape, and others, became walking examples of deliberate attempts to violate the body's personal intimacy, challenging the personal control of the self with a narration by the body politic (Feldman 1991).

The following story came from Foday, a man in his early twenties, who had been kidnapped by rebels and forced to spy, fight, and carry heavy loads. I met him in the Kamboi Hotel in Kenema, a shell of a building with no walls that was serving as a temporary rehabilitation camp for former rebel combatants who had left or escaped the cause. Foday's story reminds one of a cult, where loyalty was created during trials born of fear, bodily injury, hard training, and initiation:

Sometimes they'd make us walk with loads, sometimes over 30 miles a day ... if we complained, they made us dig a hole, and then stay in it all day and night. They said if we came out they'd shoot us. ... The killing was awful. Lots of recruits were killed. Sometimes they would just pile about 20 bodies in a hole. And if you tried to run into the bush to escape, they'd take a machete and cut you all over your body, sometimes scarring "RUF" [Revolutionary United Front] across your forehead. That way they could say, "This one, he won't run again." Because any man you came across would know that you were a rebel!

The control exerted by combatants on individuals or groups was carefully managed by cultivating fear, through the threat of further violence, or through the horror of the threat suggested. Those threats that could violate norms of personhood and identity were particularly horrifying. This included the fear of seeing cannibalism or being coerced to take part in it, as a victim or participant. This was very real for those under rebel control, paralyzing them with fear, and making escape seem a dicey, if not ludicrous, proposition. I talked to Foday about this:

(Me) Did you ever see *bohni hinda* (cannibalism)?

(Foday) Bohni hinda? Yes! When they'd eat people! Yes, they'd kill them and eat them. ... They were the "outside" people (the Liberians)! If they'd want people's power for themselves, they'd ... pull their skin off, and carry it away! Really I never saw it; we just heard about it. The common rebels would just kill you and leave you in the road.

Significantly, Foday associates this activity with the Liberians among the rebel leadership, hardly surprising given the growing international realization of Liberian political profiteering from illegally smuggled Sierra Leonean diamonds (Campbell 2002; Smillie et al. 2000). Cannibalism has been a trope referenced throughout Sierra Leonean political history (MacCormack 1983). In Mende, this is called *bohni hinda*, literally "cannibalism business," and is commonly believed to be a method by which those in power traffic in body parts to maintain personal authority, power, and charisma. Anthony Gittins (1987) notes that eating human flesh is an accusation that can fall on powerful people if their dependents are excessively exploited or if they demonstrate excessive individualism. Collective accusations of *bohni hinda* can function as "weapons of the weak" in rallying support to counterbalance this power. Yet, although the optimistic may note that stories or rumors of cannibalism could be a "weapon" controlled by captives to express disfavor with the rebels, it is also true that the stories played into rebel plans by spreading terror.

HYPERTENSION

For several months in 1997, Kenema, the town near the internally displaced persons' (IDP) camp in which I lived, became the site of near-daily street battles between a coalition of soldiers and rebels that had taken over the government by military coup and the civilian militia Kamajohs, who remained loyal to the previous government and fought for its reinstallation. The atmosphere was agonizingly tense; automatic gunfire nearby and the boom of rocket-propelled grenades kept us all near our houses for security for days on end, although at night drunk or stoned soldiers would routinely break into homes. Dead bodies would appear on the streets in the morning.

When I first began fieldwork in this setting, I was amazed at how many people seemed to be suffering from "heart problems." Young people, but especially the old, seemed to suffer from what had become locally understood as an epidemic, and the pharmacy in town could not keep Inderal (a western-manufactured beta-blocker-class drug, pilfered from World Health Organization relief supplies and sold to local pharmacies) in stock, before it would sell out again. Various heart complaints had come to be associated with the war, or with the violence and fear that people experienced; conditions or sicknesses previously known in Mende as "spoiled heart," "heart cramps," or "heart pain" had come to be grouped together under the more general Mendecized syndrome *haypatɛnsi*.

Specifically, a spoiled heart is considered spoiled in the sense that it has been torn apart by a tremendous amount of worry, suffering, or sadness. One local healer named Moriba described it, "You can't sleep; you remember too much. Because you know it's the heart that distributes blood ... so the spoiled heart spreads through your whole body." Similarly, heart pain and heart cramps are seen as being emotional in nature, from sadness, uneasiness, or "too much feeling." Put together, *haypatɛnsi* results from too much anxiety and dwelling on losses suffered during the war. [...]

Although the word *haypatɛnsi* originated from the western clinical category, it has taken on local Mende meanings since the beginning of the Sierra Leone war. It has very different meanings than the western biomedical notion of hypertension, which insists that the disease is a "silent killer," one largely genetic, with no manifesting symptoms. Western clinicians insist that no one who has hypertension can tell so unless diagnosed by a medical practitioner with a blood pressure cuff. Local claims of hypertensive knowledge become attributed to "a lack of awareness" by medical practitioners (Sharlin et al. 1993). The Mende understanding, in contrast, is one in which people could more actively participate in their diagnosis and treatment; people very much recognized and associated environmental cues and symptoms with the disease. How people interpreted those cues and symptoms became crucial in understanding how they came to terms with the illness and what they could do about it.

Especially during an outbreak of dramatic violence, *haypatɛnsi* could "attack" the body much as a rebel force could attack a village; the heart could begin to beat heavily or quickly, to burn and cramp, or simply to hurt. Collectively, these symptoms would represent *haypatɛnsi*, expressed in Mende as *haypatɛnsi lo nya ma* or "hypertension is on me." An older man, Mohammed, described its onset in the same kind of language people used to describe war:

> It attacks you like asthma; you can really hear it in your chest—
> "*fwoh, fwoh, fwoh*"... especially when you hear those guns
> and RPGs explode ... like these past few days of fighting here
> in town, when they shoot their guns—that *KPOW! KPOW!*
> *KPOW!* sound, and then you begin to feel it. At times you can
> experience a blackout; it's like it covers your face and you can't
> see anything.

The symptoms described are an almost audible noise in your chest, a churning kind of sound, "fwoh, fwoh, fwoh." Mohammed mirrors this with the repetitive sound of automatic gunfire heard in a village attack. There is one churn of the heart for every bullet fired; one is presented as an echo of the other, as what is heard and seen outside becomes internally manifest.

Outside of Kenema, I met Fatmata, a former rebel captive then living in a temporary reintegration center. At least two of Fatmata's children were dead when I met her, and two more were missing. She was the official "chairlady" of the center and the recent girlfriend of a relief worker assigned to the camp. This allowed her to live somewhat better than most inside—she had some cash and slept in a lockable room with a foam pad instead of on a straw mat in the open on a hard concrete floor. At our time of meeting, Fatmata did not know where her husband was, having not seen him for two years after he had been taken by rebels and forced to fight with them. She gave testimony of days of hard labor and terror among women, and illnesses she associated with it:

> The way they (the Revolutionary United Front) traveled with us, over hills, along roads, we really felt it; it was too far ... they wouldn't just send us out alone; there was always a man there with a gun watching over us, to make sure we wouldn't escape. And sometimes they would mark you, so that you wouldn't try to escape. They would just mark you "RUF" [Revolutionary United Front], sometimes carving it with a razor across your arm or head. ... And the sicknesses we had there, that really wasn't easy. Lots of people died from dysentery. And "heart problems," too, there were lots of heart problems from worrying so much. When you worry so much, your heart doesn't sleep, it doesn't rest. And every now and then you'd hear that gun sound, and not know what you should do. You're always afraid. All that time we were in the bush, I always had fear in my heart. Even at night, when we'd lay down, I could never seem to sleep more than one hour. Always my heart was worried, always afraid of attack. *Because inside your heart, that's where everything is* (emphasis added).

Aside from fear, hypertension was often expressed in association with symptoms like an excess of "heat" in the heart. A different woman, Sia, described it: "Your blood is hot, and it rises. The blood begins to flow very fast ... and it's too warm, much warmer than normal. ... All here (pointing to her chest) burns. And your belly gets hot, too, like if you mixed pepper with water and then drank it."

The symptom of heat is a common image in Mende, much like it is here, invoked to describe anger. Whereas an American might describe an angry person as "hot tempered," a Mende person would say "Their heart is warm." However, to talk of peace or reconciliation in Mende is to have a "cool heart." That hypertension is framed in these very meaningful, socially evocative terms indicates its position at the center of both personal and social bodies. The illness comes to represent the war and the compromised situations that people find themselves in because of their tremendous losses.

Not everyone was equally vulnerable; hypertension was considered mainly a risk for the middle-and older-aged population, who had lost not only loved ones during the fighting but also much of their previous capabilities to support self and family. It affected men and women equally. It was said to have existed before the conflict, but not nearly so much as now, when worries about food, shelter, and security are paramount:

> You can't catch it from another person—you get it from worrying, when you have too many worries. All that fright, and the worry about the problems that keep coming up—everyday you have problems, problems everywhere, everyday, and you worry and think, think, think, think, and your mind doesn't rest (Sia).
>
> When you think a lot, over-thinking, your blood pressure seems to rise. Thinking about your past. Thinking about the way you were. Especially if you were somebody that was relatively affluent before, thinking about the things you had, and then now you find yourself in the condition where you have nobody to come to your aid. (David)

Local understandings did, however, compete and interact with a similar sounding but very different biomedical categorization—the hypertension of the pharmacists and the Western clinical category. Local pharmacists and medical practitioners in the town outside the refugee camp were quite happy to offer their own diagnoses and opinions on the medical and epidemiological aspects of hypertension. The medical interpretation is that *haypatɛnsi* and hypertension are the same thing, that the former word is simply indicative of a rural Mende person's inability to pronounce the "truer" Western clinical word.

The medical conception did not comment on the war directly, but more often faulted people's diet, where practitioners fostered the popular belief that foreign relief supply items ("strange" food items provided by the World Food Program, like bulgur wheat or cornmeal) were, in fact, unhealthy for refugees to be eating, causing bodily stress simply because people were not adapted to them. By diagnosing hypertension, often without a blood pressure cuff, pharmacists, nurse practitioners, and dispensers alike asserted their authority over "bodily facts" (in this case, nutrition), in effect mystifying the social components of war, loss, and displacement, and placing the sickness entirely inside the individual (see Kleinman 1980). By prescribing Inderal, they fostered a local demand for a medicine that supported their own profits and interests.

The situation I encountered contrasts with what Barbara Harrell-Bond (1986) found in her work in the 1980s in Sudanese displacement camps. For Harrell-Bond, it was traditional medical practitioners who were eager to assert false claims. She likens them to "back-street abortionists," calling them "quacks" and "opportunists" eager to exploit a hole left by limited humanitarian emergency health services (Harrell-Bond and Van Damme 1997). She argues for more research into what healers are actually doing and cautions that some in the relief community might romanticize traditional health care.

My research more often found the exact opposite in Sierra Leone and Guinea. The camps where I worked had all been around for several years, and the healers in them were so well integrated into the camp community fabric that quacks and charlatans had been easily discovered and dealt with through fines, ostracism, or simply loss of clients. In my situation, it was rather pharmacists in the nearby town asserting biomedical authority who were less well-regulated and more able to profit from the illnesses of displaced refugees, by diagnosing *haypatɛnsi* as hypertension again, most often without a blood pressure cuff. Inderal was locally desirable because it took effect so quickly, but it was problematic in that its effects also wore off very quickly and required money for a further dose.

Not everyone was easily taken in by the pharmaceutical prescription. The local construction of *haypatɛnsi* very much recognized the congruence of both personal and social components; this allowed people to assert more agency, in effect resisting the dominance and blame of the pharmaceutical or biomedical models. The differences were significant, not just in the etiologies I have mentioned but in the treatments that each prescribed. Only *haypatɛnsi* recognized a social component to its symptoms, and only *haypatɛnsi* recognized a cure spanning both personal and political realms. In response to my often-asked question, "If you don't have Inderal, how do you treat your hypertension?" people would invariably say things like:

You relax, take your time, and settle down.

You have to keep a "cool" heart, and not let things upset you ...

You can't worry too much, and you need a lot of rest.

One young woman in particular made all this fit together in my mind when she said, "Only peace can cure *haypatɛnsi*, there's no medicine for that." All of these self-prescriptions suggest that long-term treatment of *haypatɛnsi* lies at exactly the same location where people learn to cope with the long-term effects of violence— learning to treat one's hypertension is coming to terms with one's grief and losses suffered from the war. Most importantly, these treatments address symptoms that Inderal does not—violence and the tremendous suffering and loss that it entails is not a short-term phenomenon; its effects are chronic and last for years after any single physical event (Nordstrom 1997). People living in violence live with chronic warfare, chronic economic insecurity, and prolonged states of terror. That an illness like *haypatɛnsi* comes to represent and express this is not at all surprising; symptoms that may be labeled "erroneous" or "irrational" by a medical model are, in fact, adaptive responses to terrible circumstances.

CONCLUSION

War brings tremendous suffering and illness, revealed both in very direct ways like visible wounds, severed limbs, or dead bodies, but also in innumerable indirect ways: somatic expressions of fear, exposure, and vulnerability. Because war and political conflict are often directed toward a group, the violence is collectively experienced yet also uniquely and individually manifest. Individual bodies can become idioms through which expressions of deeply personal and social trauma become manifest. In these formulations, the individual body is not something that is merely subject to violence; rather it articulates with violence, as a site of transformative action. Bodies do not simply express trauma; they are a place where identity and meaning can be actively reconfigured into socially and personally acceptable ways for understanding, coping, and creatively managing trauma (Ranger 1992; Reynolds 1990). Thus, illness beliefs, healing systems, indigenous medicines, and healing rituals can provide important coping resources, allowing for the re-creation of a healthy body in a stable universe. [...]

Allen Feldman suggests that, ultimately, anthropology's greatest contribution to studies of violence may lie not in the construction of grand and conclusive metatheories, but in the illumination of alternatives to violence, what he calls "counter-labyrinths" of coping, and "counter-memories" against fear (1995). I propose that the local understanding and treatment of hypertension has become one such alternative for war survivors in Sierra Leone. [...] That some healers from the clinical sector attempted to pull the understanding of *haypatɛnsi* more within their own nutritional or medical domain is really another kind of violence, a hijacking-for-profit of local people's own attempts to deal with the chronic instability around them and to reorder their own worlds. These wartime events are located at the intersection of mind, body, and a social state in turmoil, where personal and social referents have been turned upside down. Yet all offer avenues of recourse, ways to publicly express pain and to begin the road toward long-term peace.

REFERENCES

Becker, Gay, Yewoubdar Beyene, and Pauline Ken (2000) "Memory, Trauma, and Embodied Distress." *Ethos* 28(3): 320–345.

Campbell, Greg (2002) *Blood Diamonds*. Boulder: Westview Press.

Coker, Elizabeth (2004) "Traveling Pains." *Culture, Medicine, and Psychiatry* 28(1): 15–39.

Feldman, Allen (1991) *Formations of Violence*. Chicago: University of Chicago Press.

Feldman, Allen (1995) "Ethnographic States of Emergency." In A. Robben and C. Nordstrom (eds.), *Fieldwork under Fire*. Berkeley: University of California Press: 224–253.

Ferme, Mariane C. (2001) *The Underneath of Things*. Berkeley: University of California Press.

Gittins, Anthony (1987) *Mende Religion*. Nettetal: Steyler Verlag.

Green, Linda (1995) *The Routinization of Fear in Rural Guatemala*. Saskatoon: University of Saskatchewan Press.

Green, Linda (1998) "Lived Lives and Social Suffering." *Medical Anthropology Quarterly* 12(1): 3–7.

Harrell-Bond, Barbara (1986) *Imposing Aid*. Oxford: Oxford University Press.

Harrell-Bond, Barbara and Wim Van Damme (1997) "The Health of Refugees: Are Traditional Medicines an Answer?" *Curare, Special Issue: Women and Health* 11(97): 385–392.

Henry, Doug (2000) *Embodied Violence*. Unpublished PhD dissertation, Department of Anthropology, Southern Methodist University, Dallas.

Henry, Doug (2005) "The Legacy of the Tank, the Violence of Peace." *Anthropological Quarterly* 78(2): 443–456.

Hoffman, Danny (2004) "The Civilian Target in Sierra Leone and Liberia." *African Affairs* 103(411): 211–227.

Jenkins, Janis (1991) "The State Construction of Affect." *Culture, Medicine, and Psychiatry* 15(2): 139–165.

Jenkins, Janis (1996) "The Impress of Extremity." In Caroline Brettell and Caroline Sargent (eds.), *Gender and Health*. New York: Prentice Hall: 278–291.

Kleinman, Arthur (1980) *Patients and Healers in the Context of Culture*. Berkeley: University of California Press.

Little, Kenneth (1949) "The Role of the Secret Society in Cultural Specialization." *American Anthropologist* 51(2): 199–212.

MacCormack, Carol (1983) "Human Leopards and Crocodiles." In P. Brown and D. Tuzin (eds.), *The Ethnography of Cannibalism*. Washington DC: Society for Psychological Anthropology: 51–60.

Nordstrom, Carolyn (1997) *A Different Kind of War Story*. Philadelphia: University of Pennsylvania Press.

Nordstrom, Carolyn (1998) "Terror Warfare and the Medicine of Peace." *Medical Anthropology Quarterly* 12(1): 103–121.

Perelli, Carina (1992) "Settling Accounts with Blood Memory: The Case of Argentina." *Social Research* 59(2): 414–451.

Perice, Glen (1997) "Rumors and Politics in Haiti." *Anthropological Quarterly* 70(1): 1–10.

Ranger, Terrence (1992) "War, Violence, and Healing in Zimbabwe." *Journal of Southern African Studies* 18(3): 698–707.

Reynolds, Pamela (1990) "Children of Tribulation." *Africa* 60(1): 1–38.

Sharlin, Kenneth, G. Health, E. Ford, and T. Welty (1993) "Hypertension and Blood Pressure Awareness among the American Indians of the Northern Plains." *Ethnicity and Disease* 3(3): 337–343.

Smillie, Ian, Lansana Gberie, and Ralph Hazleton (2000) *The Heart of the Matter*. Ottawa: Partnership Africa–Canada.

Turshen, Meredith, and C. Twagiramariya (eds.) (1998) *What Women Do in Wartime*. London: Zed Books.

Young, Alan (1997) "Suffering and the Origins of Traumatic Memory." In Arthur Kleinman, V. Das, and Margaret Lock (eds.), *Social Suffering*. Berkeley: University of California Press: 245–260.

9
The Violence of Humanitarianism

Miriam Ticktin

While I was conducting fieldwork in Paris, the former president of the gay-rights activist group Act-Up Paris told me that he had received phone calls from undocumented immigrants inquiring how they could infect themselves with HIV and thereby obtain legal status in France. Although this particular account of self-infection is anecdotal, the rhetoric of willed self-infection can be located in the larger reality I observed during the course of my research between 1999 and 2001: I increasingly saw undocumented immigrants, or *les sans papiers* (those without papers), turn to physical injury or infection to claim the basic rights supposedly granted to all "human beings." This tendency to turn to illness for papers occurred in the wake of the limited success of the social movement by and for undocumented immigrants in France to secure basic human rights. It also coincided with the introduction of a humanitarian clause in French law—what I call the "illness clause"—that gives people with serious illnesses the right to stay in France and receive treatment.

In this article, I examine the role of humanitarianism and compassion in the development of an ethical configuration that has made illness a primary means by which to obtain papers in France. I open with the HIV anecdote to introduce the notion of the often unintended consequences of ethical discourses such as humanitarianism or practices that claim to further social justice. More broadly, I use this example as an entryway into what I see as an incipient or emergent ethical configuration in which people end up trading in biological integrity for political recognition. [...]

THE SHIFT FROM HUMAN RIGHTS TO HUMANITARIANISM

The issue of illegal immigration erupted into the French public imagination in 1996, when a powerful social movement calling for basic human rights for illegal immigrants gained world media attention through the occupation by 300 African immigrants of the Saint Bernard church in Paris. The ensuing violent eviction by French police of the immigrants, many of whom were women and children, caused an uproar. The movement organized by and for these immigrants changed their labeling from illegal immigrants to *les sans papiers*—those undocumented, "without papers." This was a self-conscious move away from the image of criminality and suspicion associated with clandestinity to one of people deprived of basic human rights, and the movement played on the idea of this happening in what the French themselves like to think of as the "home of human rights." [...]

The French, therefore, have much invested in their identity as global moral leaders, especially in today's climate in which geopolitics and moral codes are intimately intertwined. Perhaps even more important for my purposes is the distinction between human rights and humanitarianism—a distinction that is not always evident in the US context but is more clear in the French one. My goal here in laying out the somewhat analytical distinction between humanitarianism and human rights is to examine what happens when humanitarianism is forced to take on a primary role in government, largely subsuming a system based on rights. Without advocating a regime of human rights at the expense of humanitarianism, I am interested in the consequences of a humanitarian logic filling in for the failure of rights discourses and practices.

Although both human rights and humanitarianism are complexly constituted transnational institutions, practices, and discursive regimes, in a broad sense, human rights institutions are largely grounded in law, constructed to further legal claims, responsibility, and accountability, whereas humanitarianism is more about the ethical and moral imperative to bring relief to those suffering and to save lives; here, the appeal to law remains opportunistic. Although both are clearly universalist discourses, they are based on different forms of action and, hence, often institute and protect different ideas of humanity. The political discourse of human rights has its origins in the French Revolution and the Enlightenment movement away from religion and toward a secular vision of humanity, whereas humanitarianism was initially a form of religiously inflected charity. [...]

The French situation reveals such a shift in emphasis from rights to the practices of humanitarianism in regulating immigration. The issue of *les sans papiers* was one of the major platforms on which the Socialists entered into power in 1997; Prime Minister Lionel Jospin's government promised to deal with *les sans papiers* more generously, respecting their basic human rights. Despite this rhetoric, the promised reexamination of cases of undocumented immigrants in 1997 and the new law in 1998 on the entry and residence of foreigners were both much less generous than promised. The reexamination of cases on the basis of more-favorable criteria—an "amnesty" of sorts—gave only 80,000 people papers, fewer than half of those who had applied, and many still found themselves without papers, despite fulfilling the required criteria. Struggles are ongoing for the basic right to freedom of movement in the new borderless Europe, the right to housing and autonomy, and the right to be free from violence and exploitation. [...]

The larger context is one in which refugees have been increasingly viewed with suspicion by both the French state and the French public and conflated with economic migrants. This conflation has been made explicit in recent policies of restricting asylum to control migration flows, joining two processes that should be entirely independent. As Hubert Védrine, the minister of foreign affairs, stated, "The practice [of asylum] followed must maintain a just balance with our desire to control migration flows" (1997; cf. Delouvin 2000: 70). More broadly, asylum policies must be seen as part of prohibitionist, restrictive immigration policies, in which the state seeks to close all doors. In this climate of closure, many examples can be cited of human rights violations by the state itself, not to mention by nonstate actors; for instance, immigrants are imprisoned in detention centers without trial, despite condemnations of the inhumane and insalubrious conditions in the centers. Similarly, immigration officials are known to be utterly arbitrary in their dealings. [...]

Paradoxically, this arbitrariness was exaggerated by the new law that went into effect in 1998, which added the right to "private and family life" (Article 12bis) to the two previously existing conditions for legal immigration—family reunification and asylum. Drissia, a 50-year-old woman of Moroccan origin I met through an activist group for undocumented women, revealed to me the extent of this paradoxical situation. In the absence of a spouse or children in France that would allow one to enter under the family reunification clause, the new law (Article 12bis.3) gives those who have lived in France for ten consecutive years the right to papers. Residency, however, must be proven, not simply declared. Drissia had been in France for over ten years, which qualified her for papers; yet, despite what immigrants-rights' lawyers believed was proof of her uninterrupted presence on French soil, her request had been turned down multiple times. I saw her alternate between tears and deep anger, often in one sentence, at the sheer frustration of being treated as though she did not exist. As Drissia's case illustrates, what counts as proof of uninterrupted presence is unclear—it depends on the interpretation of each immigration official. For people who have been trying to erase any trace of their presence so as not to be deported, providing official proof of each month of residence for over ten years is a nearly impossible task—practically a contradiction in terms.

The inscription of this article in the law, thus, in many ways simply legitimized the arbitrariness practiced by the *préfectures* (local governments), working along the lines of what immigrant-rights lawyer Danielle Lochak (2001) calls a "humanitarian" logic rather than a juridical one. Law always involves interpretation, and it is always enacted in specific contexts that help determine its meaning; the difference here is that, because the law is so open-ended, those asking for the protection it affords are entirely dependent on eliciting the compassion or pity of those enacting it. [...]

As increasingly restrictive legislation has forced borders closed, transforming the so-called open European space into Fortress Europe, the black market and informal economies have grown, and labor conditions are otherwise changing to favor temporary, insecure forms of labor with no legal protection. In this sense, the increased demand for workers in the agricultural, garment, and construction industries in France is met by closed juridical doors: Undocumented immigrants are desired precisely because they can be denied all rights. [It is a] tension between industry wanting and needing labor and the nation-state refusing to let people legally onto its territory. The French state is complicit in this process, having passed laws that produce a category of persons who are neither legalizable nor deportable. [...]

How does this political economy relate to the shift to humanitarianism? Both the discourse and practice of medical humanitarianism have followed this flow of exploitable labor from the South into the urban centers of the industrialized North; just as Médecins Sans Frontières (Doctors without Borders) started by intervening in crises of governance and economy in the South, so, too, it now intervenes in industrialized centers like Paris—cities in which it has established offices for local concerns. Just as it protects a particular vision of life in war-torn zones, working to ease the immediacy of suffering, so, too, it now intervenes to ease suffering when the larger societal and political structures of the North fail to do their job—when they let increasingly large portions of their population fall through the cracks. Here, medical humanitarianism governs the less desirable portions of the population when the state abandons them. In this sense, ethical systems in the form of medical humanitarianism are part of the transnational circulation of capital and labor, linking the political economy of immigration to the political economy of health and illness.

THE ILLNESS CLAUSE

The illness clause emerged as an alternative to human rights discourse and discourses of social injury for those whose appeals to rights did not easily coincide with state interests or whose positioning has not allowed their claims to be heard. To reiterate, the 1998 amendment grants legal residency permits to those already living in France who have pathologies that entail life-threatening consequences if they are declared unable to receive proper treatment in their home countries; the goal is to permit them to receive treatment in France. Indeed, it was the lobbying of medical humanitarian groups (such as Médecins sans Frontières and Médecins du Monde—Doctors of the World) that helped turn the illness clause into law in France. [...] Only in 1998 did the Ministry of Health officially become involved in the immigration process. [...]

I followed undocumented immigrants through the different steps of the trajectory to papers: To access the illness clause, the persons "without papers" are referred by their own doctors to immigration authorities and then by the immigration officers at the *préfectures* (local governments) to state health officials. It is ultimately the job of these officials to ascertain if people's conditions are of sufficient gravity to merit granting papers for treatment in France, although the permits are actually issued by the *préfectures*, with the understanding that they rely on the state health officials' opinions. The state office in which I did a large part of my research is one of the few in which nurses receive *les sans papiers* in person. Other offices receive undocumented immigrants' files by mail; the files are initially sorted through either by nurses or administrators and then passed to doctors. The state medical doctor can recommend that a medical certificate be granted for varying lengths of time, from a period of three months to an indeterminate (long-term) period, depending on the illness and the doctor's interpretation of the length of treatment needed. People can claim citizenship after a period of five years on the basis of their residency on French soil; thus, continual renewal of illness permits may eventually lead undocumented immigrants to citizenship.

The process is multilayered, taking different shapes and forms in different locations—very little about it is systematic. As noted, the law states that people should receive papers if they suffer from a pathology that has life-threatening consequences and they do not have access to treatment in their own country. Yet there are no lists of life-threatening pathologies and no easily accessible information on whether people can receive treatment in their home countries. The doctors are urged to contact the *Direction de la Population et des Migrations* (Office of Population and Migration) for information. But no source takes into account people's substantive ability to access medical treatment:

Do they live far away from city centers?
Do they have the means of transport to hospitals or doctors?
Do they have the money to get treatment or to continue treatment if it involves subsequent trips to medical facilities?

These questions are not addressed in the guidelines. They are asked at the discretion of the medical officials receiving the case or at the local government office beforehand. Already, one sees the discretionary power of the nurses, doctors, and immigration officials and the advantages and disadvantages that persons "without papers" derive from being able to interact face to face with state officials. Ultimately, the immigration officers at the local government level make the decision about who will receive an illness permit and for what duration, and although, in theory, they should follow the advice of state doctors, they do not necessarily do so. Thus, although legalizing the process was an attempt to systematize the arbitrary treatment of *les sans papiers*, in practice, the illness clause has made little difference to the nature of the process. Instead, a different logic has been instituted, one based on benevolence and compassion.

With the possibility of obtaining papers effectively shut off to new immigrants and refugees—who, as I have mentioned, are seen as either criminal or economically burdensome—those already in France without papers have turned to the illness clause as a means to ease the exploitation that is a regular part of being undocumented, believing—rightly or wrongly—that papers will solve all their problems. [...]

How does the French state reconcile the denial of papers to immigrants who are perceived to be economically burdensome with the decision to give papers and social services to immigrants who are sick? Stated otherwise, why is it that illness is allowed to travel across borders, whereas poverty cannot? [...]

State officials and doctors confirmed to me that the space of pure life honored in the illness clause is conceived of in opposition to political community. [...] As proof that this clause is humanitarian and apolitical in nature and that it remains in the realm of the private, the French state does not automatically include a work permit with the illness visa—initial attempts to do so rendered the clause too politically contentious. [...] The visa given for illness is thereby isolated from all other aspects of life—it is narrowly focused on the healing of suffering, injured, or disabled bodies, disqualifying its recipients from taking any economic, social, or political role in French society.

Consequently, those who gain entry on the basis of chronic illness, such as those who are HIV-positive and who are fully capable of sustaining a full-time job, are for the most part not given the right to work. Although their papers formally allow them to rent apartments, open bank accounts, and travel on the metro without the risk of being arrested and deported, they do not have the substantive means to rent apartments, and they have nothing to put in bank accounts and no money to buy metro tickets. Ironically, in the name of human dignity, the French state indirectly sanctions work on the black market. In this sense, a doctor named Isabelle, who worked at one of the clinics for undocumented immigrants where I observed, suggested that, in her experience, the illness clause was "a curse." It was worse than nothing because it gave people hope, and yet, because work permits were not granted with the papers, it paved the way for greater exploitation of their misery, making them work in situations of virtual slavery and prostitution. She suggested that politicians got rich on the backs of those working on the black market: "Why else are they not deported?" she asked. "It must mean that it is profitable for the state to keep them." [...]

With humanitarianism as the driving logic, only the suffering or sick body is seen as a legitimate manifestation of a common humanity, worthy of recognition in the form of rights; this view is based on a belief in the legitimacy, fixity, and universality of biology. [...]

DISEASED AND DISABLED SUBJECTS

This shift to seeing the suffering body as more legitimate than the threatened or deprived person reveals the desire to recognize the universality of biological life above all else; that is, to find common humanity in apolitical suffering, a universal humanity that exists beyond the specificities of political and social life. Indeed, according to Giorgio Agamben (1998), humanitarianism as a practice cannot help but grasp human life in the figure of "bare life," thereby reproducing the very idea of a form of life distinct from political life. Liisa Malkki has ethnographically confirmed this tendency, demonstrating how humanitarian practices make refugees into "universal man"—how they set up a "bare, naked or minimal humanity" (1996: 390). Of course, humanitarianism does work to reduce people to "pure victims" (Malkki 1996), making it easier for them to be configured as objects of charity rather than of law. Yet, when one looks closely at this process, one sees that bare life and political life actually combine in new ways as a result of humanitarian practices, particularly when humanitarianism takes over the space of political action and responsibility. In other words, people elide victimhood and reduction to bare life in interesting, albeit troublesome, ways; political action is constituted as a series of biological compromises. More to the point, however, is whether this type of political action can be considered desirable or acceptable. [...]

Contradictory subject positions emerge from a politics based on this belief in the universality of life, but only as biological life. At one end of the spectrum are the persons who infect themselves with HIV in an effort to be treated like human beings, to be granted legal recognition and, hence, acknowledged as part of humanity, willfully disabling themselves to live more fully. If willed infection is at one end of the spectrum, at the other end is the person who refuses the possibility of treatment. [...]

For instance, one day as I sat with the state nurses while they attended to undocumented patients requesting papers to stay and receive treatment in France, I watched as a woman named Amina refused to even speak the name of her illness. The nurses questioned her many times: "What do you have?" they asked. "What are your symptoms?" She shook her head and said nothing. Originally from Mali, Amina had come with her baby strapped onto her back in a colorful wrap, and she spent her time unraveling herself and the baby to change his diapers, responding distractedly to the nurses' questions. She handed over a slew of documents, both medical and legal—the telltale pile of papers that all those who are "paperless" must carry wherever they go—a cruel irony, indeed; after the nurses had thumbed through the majority of her documents, their attitude suddenly changed from mild annoyance to care and concern. And one nurse asked her again, "Do you really not know what you have?" This time, Amina responded that, yes, yes, of course, she did. She left it at that—the illness remained unnamed. The nurses promised her papers and told her to take care of herself and the baby. When she left, I was told that both Amina and her baby were HIV-positive.

This phenomenon was explained to the nurses and me by another woman named Fatoumata, who also opened up exceedingly hesitantly when questioned. Fatoumata had recently been released from prison. She had been arrested on drug-related charges and had been infected with HIV through needle use. She told us about the many infected African women in Paris who simply reject the opportunity to obtain a visa that would not only grant them basic rights, such as the right to housing, but would also permit and pay for their regimen of triple therapy—a visa that would literally provide them with both the right to live and life itself. The stigma of HIV/AIDS is so great in their communities that they would rather compromise their bodily integrity and pay with their lives than live ostracized and without dignity. Fatoumata had a tough exterior, but when she mentioned her inability to trust her closest family or friends with the news that she was HIV-positive, she began to cry softly.

In talking to Fatoumata, I became aware of the gendered nature of the stigma of HIV/AIDS among African communities in France. All pregnant women in France must, by law, be tested for HIV, whereas men are never forced to get tested. Thus, more women find out about their illness than do men, leading to an unequal gender dynamic and a particularly gendered stigma in African communities. Indeed, this dynamic has the consequence of increasing the numbers of women granted papers through the illness clause; it also results in more women than men having to lead double lives, hiding their diagnosis from their loved ones, or leading lives that define them solely in terms of their illness, existing outside all community affiliation except for the patient groups they may belong to. In other words, this stigma creates a subject position for women, in particular, in which their reason for living becomes their illness—it becomes their only source of social recognition—yet it is also their death sentence.

Further illuminating the various subject positions created by the structural situation that favors suffering and sick bodies, the nurses told me about cases of people purposely not treating their illnesses, prolonging them to keep their legal status. As mentioned, legal papers are initially granted as temporary permits that can be renewed. Even something as simple as a cataract can serve the purpose of prolonging one's stay. Of course, it means that the advantages of legality are exchanged for the difficulties of living one's life partially blind. I say this with an added caveat, in that those who do not treat themselves often have good structural reasons for not doing so, such as not having sufficient money to cover the costs, or the time, or the means to get to and from the hospital. The nurses themselves agreed that a patient's reasons for not pursuing treatment were not always clear. The point here is still valid, however; one must remain diseased to remain in France and to eventually claim citizenship. Both the medical officials and undocumented immigrants realize this.

Each of the cases mentioned plays on different configurations of bodily integrity and human dignity. Along this spectrum are other unanticipated subject positions. For instance, one of the doctors I worked with treated a patient who took on the identity of a person who had AIDS, including taking the person's medication—in fact, he literally stole the identity of a friend of his who died of AIDS. He did this to get French papers—to obtain legal recognition that enabled both a life free from daily violence and a modicum of human dignity. Paradoxically, his dignity was not recognized, in the sense of his unique, individual self; he preferred to give up that identity to get legal recognition as someone else, again complicating theories of the liberal individual that ground notions of French citizenship.

Finally, the case of a Senegalese woman named Aicha illustrates the results of a politics of humanitarianism that creates political subjects, albeit with limited political choices. Aicha had a thyroid tumor and a serious skin condition aggravated by heat. She left her family in Senegal, including her five children, to live in France and treat her condition. Aicha had lived in France during her first marriage and, thus, had some knowledge of the medical system. Her illnesses were chronic, however; she needed both the thyroid medication and the skin creams on a constant basis, and neither medication was readily available in Senegal. She left her life and family, ironically, to protect what the French law calls her right to "private and family life"; not only was she not legally permitted to bring her children to France, but she was also not given papers to work, transforming her life into a monotony of shelters in which she slept at night—shelters force people out at 8am—and cafés and parks in which she sat during the day to pass the time.

The nurses and doctors at the hospital clinic for the disenfranchised where Aicha received treatment were her main source of community—and even their friendship and support were contingent. As she stood outside, they complained to me that they did not need to see her anymore and wished she would leave space for other patients. In their understandable desire to give others a chance at health and bodily integrity, the larger structural reality of which they are a part dictates that they deprive Aicha of her only source of humanity that goes beyond biological life. Occasionally, she wondered aloud to me whether her life was worth living—what kind of life was it, she asked, with no family, no work, no money, no fulfillment, and nothing to wake up to each morning except one's illnesses, the simultaneously driving and disabling force of her life? She cannot escape her state of injury, which is not only named as such but also embodied. She is just one of the new subjects produced by the French nation-state—given life by the consequences of ethical regimes such as humanitarianism that are both created and circumscribed by global capitalism. [...]

In this emergent ethics, those with cancer, HIV, polio, or tuberculosis—and even occasionally those with more explicitly socially and politically grounded injuries such as rape or disfigurement—become the most mobile, the most able to travel without hiding themselves in the cold-storage containers of trucks or making mad dashes through the English Channel tunnel or across the straits of Gibraltar. Such notions of the mobility of the disabled or injured—indeed, the emergence of the disabled as the modal subject of political economy—force reexamination of ideas of who is "able bodied" and what able-bodiedness actually signifies, and, even more broadly, what good health or wellbeing signifies. The standard of able-bodiedness as the norm and the ideal is herein exposed as fictional, constructed and normativized for a certain type of economic and civic functionality. Indeed, the assumption that the normative human is able-bodied begs redefinition of who is included in the category of "human." [...]

Although the ill and disabled are not entirely stripped of their political or social qualities, they exemplify the dangers of humanitarian government insofar as it limits one's political and social choices and capacities—it forces one to conceal one's political self, all the while drawing on that self. In fact, the paradox of willed infection or disability suggests that undocumented immigrants can act in one of two ways: They can choose to suffer from exploitation, exclusion, and poverty, or they can suffer from illness. But what kind of choice is this, and what kind of humanity does it sustain? [...]

THE NEW POLITICS OF COMPASSION: A LIMITED HUMANITY

Dr Amara, who worked at the clinic for undocumented immigrants that I had been observing, suggested to me that I might be interested in a paradox he had witnessed. He explained to me that several of his HIV-positive patients had stopped taking their medication once they had received their papers, despite having received papers to gain access to the medication. This seemingly incomprehensible act reveals the violence at the heart of this story: Without political recognition, undocumented immigrants exist as a form of "living dead" (Mbembe 2003; Petryna 2002: 3), in a state that, in the immediacy and intensity of their struggle for survival, is indistinguishable from the threat of physical death. The difference between the type of future each remedy guarantees—papers or medication— is elided. In this sense, it is unclear to both doctors and patients which is the more virulent form of suffering—no papers or no medication. The conflation of the two reveals a new territory in which the politics of immigration and citizenship is at once a politics of life and death. In this scene, biological life and political life have taken on equal significance—life as someone sick is interchangeable with life as a politically recognized subject. Indeed, being sick is what is required to be a political subject. [...]

In shifting the politics of immigration to a politics of humanitarianism, those who enact the humanitarian clauses suddenly wield great power—they become the gatekeepers. In this case, they include the state nurses and doctors as well as the medical establishment more broadly. In the state office where I observed, the medical officials went beyond seeing if a person had a disease; they explicitly joined social and medical, knowing that in the cases they treated, to cure the medical, one must inevitably deal with the social—they are inextricably intertwined. Yet the medical officials also admitted to being constrained by their relationship with the *préfecture*; despite acting out of a desire to further a notion of social justice, they could not simply let everyone in, because they were being monitored. [...] The nurses and doctors realized that, to be kept in the decision-making circles, they had to maintain legitimacy—and their legitimacy depended on only letting in people who suffer from pathologies that have life-threatening consequences.

Yet what qualifies as "life-threatening" when life itself remains undefined? As I have already demonstrated, biological life is more malleable in its abstractness than those who insist on its universality may realize. There is room for play. Life is ultimately defined quite pragmatically, by the particular context in which requests for papers are received and by those applying the clause. As noted, this is a relatively arbitrary process, one that changes case by case, location by location, and this is precisely because of the nature of the task: How does one protect "life"—the broadest of concepts? [...]

The face-to-face interaction between the nurses and *les sans papiers* largely determined how "life-threatening" was interpreted in the particular state office where I observed and, thus, who was granted permits for illness. The personal interaction allowed for compassion to be evoked—it allowed the undocumented persons to appear as people, not simply as files or pathologies. It allowed for their social realities to be included in the judgment. Yet a face-to-face encounter allows for performances on both sides, and if one does not perform in the desired manner, one may be penalized and excluded.

The dilemmas and the evocation of compassion arose for nurses and doctors with the more complicated cases—often chronic or psychiatric. The following story, described to me by the nurses, illustrates the way that humanitarianism often depends on compassion to ground a larger politics. Although I was not present in this instance, I witnessed many similar cases, and I use the story here to reveal as much about the nurses as about *les sans papiers* they describe. In the late 1990s, a young Algerian woman named Fatima came to Paris after having been raped and disfigured by her uncle. The background to this violence was the death of her primary caretaker, her grandmother, which forced her into the care of her uncle and aunt. Both her uncle and aunt blamed her for the rape. Fatima was therefore sent to France, where her mother was living. The nurses said that she looked horrible. They decided to give her temporary papers to receive medical care. When the treatment was finished and her permit about to expire, Fatima returned to the state medical office to ask for a renewal of her papers. As they later explained to me, the nurses understood that she would return to a "pitiful" life in Algeria; she would be forever shamed because of her rape and, hence, unmarriageable. According to them, her life would be one of ostracization and loneliness. They decided that, in the face of this reality, they would rather grant her authorization to stay in France for treatment for an indeterminate period—which meant, effectively, forever, if she so chose, renewing her illness permit until she could apply for citizenship. The treatment they prescribed was psychological—she was considered to be suffering from trauma. They were very clear when talking to me that this decision crossed over into the realm of social justice; but they saw themselves inevitably implicated in moral decision-making, which they believe is required at a fundamental level in caring for people's health and wellbeing.

I deeply respect the medical officials for allowing their view of health to include the social and for allowing the disenfranchised to remain when all other doors were and are increasingly closed. Clearly, however, the health officials' decisions are not based on laws, or rules, or rights. Ultimately, they are within the discretion of the person who receives the case. The state medical officials' decisions are, thus, based at least in part on a notion of humanitarianism and compassion or, as may happen, the lack thereof. I found that the result depended on the way the *sans papiers*' story was told and on the emotions evoked. Indeed—perhaps unsurprisingly—I found that compassion is elicited differently according to race and gender. Some people's stories of suffering do not strike a chord with the nurses or doctors.

Thus, for instance, I sat with the nurses as a 25-year-old Algerian man came in one day. Not long after he entered the office, he started crying. He claimed that he had had a heart attack a few days earlier, which the nurse, Felicia, pointed out was not true. He had a heart murmur, she said, looking down at his file. He said that he could not go on. If he was sent to Algeria, who would take care of his wife and his mother? "Last week I was going to commit suicide," he said. "I've never done anything to anyone, I haven't committed a crime and still they do this to us, they break up couples!" I could tell Felicia was getting impatient. Her tone of voice changed. The man told a long story about his mother, who was a healer, and his wife, who was sick, and he kept saying how unfair it was to have a heart attack at his age! He was worked up and kept repeating himself. When he left, Felicia said "*son nez est grand comme un bec*" (his nose is as large as a beak), gesturing toward her own nose, pretending it was growing, insinuating that the man was lying. She claimed his marriage was one of convenience because the wife was 39 and he was only 25. Why Felicia was immediately so suspicious is hard to say. The man certainly exaggerated, and his story did not make complete sense. But, then, he was distraught and crying.

At the time, I was surprised by Felicia's reaction because she rarely lost patience, and I concluded that the man must have elicited a negative feeling in her—nothing concrete, because to me, the message he conveyed largely rang true. As Arendt (1990) notes, compassion is most effective in face-to-face interactions, when those who do not suffer come face to face with those who do. In the state medical offices, however, the suffering is not always immediately apparent—the immigrant has to make a case for it, either in person or in his or her file, as the emotional commitment involved in compassion is dependent on the ability of the nurses to imagine the suffering. [...] In Fatima's case, compassion was clearly based on a familiar Orientalist narrative about pitiful Muslim women. In other words, compassion depends on circulating narratives, images, and histories and often on maintaining an unequal power relation between nurse and patient and citizen and foreigner—distinctions that are already heavily gendered and racialized. To be accepted as a French subject on the basis of compassion, one must be accepted as plausible; and images of the Other inform the legitimacy of one's performance. Algerian men are depicted in the French public imaginary as violent and deceitful and as oppressive to women. These images are the colonial legacy and in some ways have become all the more intense since the bitter war of Algerian independence from French colonial rule. [...]

CONCLUSION: AN ANTI-ENLIGHTENMENT UNIVERSALITY?

My ethnographic research demonstrates the difference between bare life as conceived and practiced: Although, in theory, bare life may be the grounding of humanitarian action and the sovereign exception, the concept is enacted differently in differing places, both creating and requiring new realms of biosociality. The politics of humanitarianism, thus, show how conceptions of bare life blend with politics and the near impossibility of getting beyond socially embedded and mediated interpretations of life. In this particular instance, humanitarianism leads to a politics of life and death, quite literally, in which one's death warrant in the form of AIDS can secure life in France, and citizenship is only given to those who remain diseased. In this sense, one must see the medical realm as an important new site of sovereign power, in which doctors, nurses, and state officials become gatekeepers not only to the nation-state but also, more importantly, to the very concept of "humanity," in the sense that humanitarianism protects individuals by virtue of their membership of humanity. [...]

The citizens produced by the joining of humanitarian ethics and politics have inequality literally inscribed on their bodies. They are forever marked and interpellated as sick, as already handicapped— they can never realize equality. This politics of humanitarianism shows itself to be a politics of universality, but an anti-Enlightenment universality—one that sets biological life against explicitly rational, political beings. Immigrants are stripped of their legal personas when identified solely as suffering bodies, and, as such, they cannot be protected by law; they are rendered politically irrelevant. And although they may be liberated from suffering, they are not liberated into full citizenship. [...]

One can be either a citizen or human but not both—once one is affirmed as part of humanity and protected by humanitarian clauses, one loses one's political and social rights. Here, for instance, the people entering France through the humanitarian clause come from already marginalized backgrounds, primarily from former colonies; this process thus reinforces racial hierarchies while casting France as benevolent. Indeed, the postcolonial space created through this politics of humanitarianism continues in the manner of its colonial predecessors, reconfigured for ever-greater forms of exclusion. [...]

Rights entail a concept of justice, which includes standards of obligation and implies equality between individuals. Humanitarianism is about the exception rather than the rule, about generosity rather than entitlement. The regime of humanitarianism is based on engaging other people in relationships of empathy and in this way demonstrating one's common humanity; this is an ethics that, when taken to the extreme, entails selling one's suffering, bartering for membership with one's life and body. As the political body loses legitimacy in an increasingly globalized world in which national sovereignty is at stake and borders of all kinds are zealously guarded, the supposedly apolitical suffering body is becoming the most legitimate political vehicle in the fight for a broader concept of social justice; our task is not only to understand the consequences of this shift but also to form a response to it.

REFERENCES

Agamben, Giorgio (1998) *Homo Sacer*. Trans. Daniel Heller-Roazen. Stanford: Stanford University Press.

Arendt, Hannah (1990) *On Revolution*. Harmondsworth: Penguin Books.

Delouvin, Patrick (2000) "The Evolution of Asylum in France." *Journal of Refugee Studies* 13(1): 61–73.

Lochak, Danielle (2001) "L'humanitaire perversion de l'etat de droit." *Sciences Sociales et Santé* 19(4): 35–42.

Malkki, Liisa (1996) "Speechless Emissaries." *Cultural Anthropology* 11(3): 377–404.

Mbembe, Achille (2003) "Necropolitics." *Public Culture* 15(1): 11–40.

Petryna, Adriana (2002) *Life Exposed*. Princeton: Princeton University Press.

Ticktin, Miriam (2005) "Policing and Humanitarianism in France." *Interventions: International Journal of Postcolonial Studies* 7(3): 347–368.

Védrine, Hubert (1997) Address to the Law Commission. Paris, November 6.

Part III
Zones of Violence

Zones of Violence: Introduction

Uli Linke and Danielle Taana Smith

Although practices of violence are historically situated, regimes of terror cannot be understood exclusively as products of local traditions or religious fanaticism. War and terror are contemporary manifestations of the collusion of political interests, cultural values, and economic and social inequalities. In Part III, by rethinking violence in these terms, we examine the connections between different regimes of terror both at home and internationally. What is the relation between global military and domestic violence? How is gender implicated in practices of war and terror transnationally? How is terror against women and ethnic or religious minorities deployed by different states as a strategy of war and as a politics of fear? How do human rights norms and paradigms intervene in situations of war and terror within and across nations? The collection of essays in this section not only imparts a global understanding of what seem to be local situations, but also reveals that in this era of postmodernist governance, there exists an uncanny continuum of violence within nations and between nations. Conventional distinctions between "victims" and "perpetrators" no longer apply. The boundaries separating peacekeepers from war-makers and soldiers from torturers have become unsettled and diffuse, erasing the traditional taxonomies with their concomitant indexical markers of gender, space, and state. In these ubiquitous zones of violence, where national welfare is secured by warfare, where security means war on terror, and where every person may be both a potential target and a terrorist, emergent states of paranoia have pushed realistic visions of peace to the margins of awareness.

In the opening essay, Susan J. Brison (Dartmouth College) demonstrates the importance of a feminist approach for a critical analysis of terror. Taking the terrorist attacks of 9/11 as her point of departure, Brison offers a glimpse into the gendered dimensions of military culture. Although some men may be terrorists, others in their roles as police officers, firefighters, and soldiers are celebrated as heroic protectors. While culture-specific notions of masculinity may encourage the brutalization of target (enemy) populations, they also furnish justifications for these acts to enhance national glory. But according to Brison, these simplifications require a critical reassessment. Political discourse propagates gender ideologies: men, not women, are given the power to determine which bodies are valued and protected and which bodies are attacked and destroyed. Although couched in appeals to nationalist, racist, and religious affections, militarist masculinity operates with oppressive gender norms. The privileges of masculinity, whether protective, murderous, or heroic, are contingent on misogynist values that permeate the entire social system.

Gender blindness tends to obscure awareness of the fact that the perpetration of male terror is significant or analytically relevant. In her essay, Cynthia Cockburn (City University, London) discusses these issues from a critical feminist perspective. When seen through the lens of gender, practices of violence can be traced along a continuum, from instances of domestic abuse to the possibilities of global conflict. Drawing on comparative research, Cockburn shows how cultures of masculinity produce similar patterns of powerlessness and terror across disparate domains: "gender links violence at different points on a scale reaching from the personal to the international, from the home and the back street to the maneuvers of the tank column and the sortie of the stealth bomber: battering and marital rape, confinement, 'dowry' burnings, honor killings, and genital mutilation in peacetime; military rape, sequestration, prostitution, and sexualized torture in war" (see p.170). Cultures of masculinity not only sustain power imbalances between men and women but infuse institutions like the family, the military, the state, and multinational corporations with forms of violence that extend from peacetime to wartime. Cockburn maintains that long-term peace-building is possible only by attention being given to the multiple ways that constitute relations of power and gender along the trajectories of terror.

Following this line of enquiry, Julia Dickson-Gómez (Medical College of Wisconsin) examines the impact of modern guerilla warfare on ordinary people. With a focus on El Salvador's civil war, Dickson-Gómez shows that the devastating effects of war reach far beyond the wounds sustained by bodies and buildings. Extreme forms of violence and terror have long-term effects on children, families, and communities. Warfare, in this case guerilla war, is not confined to the limits of a designated front zone. Military, political, and ideological battles are waged in and through communities, often with the assistance of children, who are recruited as soldiers. In El Salvador, as in other armed conflicts around the world, children are traumatized on multiple levels; as witnesses, victims, perpetrators, and soldiers. Used as military targets to enhance communal terror, children are brutalized, tortured, and maimed, forced to witness the execution of family members, their bodies left for public display as a reminder of the penalty for allegedly conspiring with the enemy. With promises of protection, revenge, and food for themselves and others, children are inducted into combat and forced to fight. As Dickson-Gómez documents, child soldiers suffer additional traumatization by having to take part in acts of violence judged morally wrong. In the aftermath of civil war, forced displacement, continued poverty, revenge killings, normalized male aggression, and the effects of unresolved trauma contribute to difficulties of community rebuilding.

The essay by Carolyn Nordstrom (Notre Dame) similarly examines the effects of war on children but with a focus on girls. Based on long-term research in Mozambique, Nordstrom uncovers the predicament of girls and young women, who endure frequent, prolonged, and extreme forms of abuse, yet these experiences are discounted, hidden from public view. The suffering of girls in war zones, Nordstrom observes, remains largely invisible. This erasure of female trauma from public memory has political implications: public secrecy obscures the existence of child trafficking and sexual abuse, and serves to protect those that benefit from the exploitation of children. In this manner, sexual servitude remains widespread even in the aftermath of war, as Nordstrom documents with examples of the sexual abuse of children, primarily girls, by United Nations' peacekeeping forces. Meaningful prosecution and punishment of the perpetrators remains unlikely since such practices are often sanctioned by those in positions of power and authority. Nordstrom reveals that the conscription of girls into forced labor and sex is driven by multinational industries with global connections. The local exploitation of children is linked to networks of violence that penetrate through boundaries of war and peace. In consequence, Nordstrom works to dismantle our preconceived notions of disparate arenas of security and threat. She contends that: "Any hard and fast divisions between 'war (zones)' and 'peace (zones)' are not only misleading but also dangerously wrong. Such divisions obscure the processes by which abuses of power and privilege—and by extension the solutions to these abuses—can be carried out" (see p.197). In conclusion, Nordstrom unravels a global system within which the local abuse of girls in war and the international procurement of child prostitutes are intimately enmeshed along a trajectory of profiteering and human suffering.

The concluding essay by Solrun Williksen (Norwegian University of Science and Technology) recounts the experiences of an adolescent girl in flight, who escapes emotional and physical abuse on one continent only to endure a different form of terror on another. In a daunting journey through Europe, she encounters a world where terror is administered by state representatives: border patrols, the police, immigration officials, prison guards. After a year of traveling in hiding, living in the shadows, always fearing discovery and deportation, Ada is finally detained in Norway, where her petition for asylum is contingent on her ability to provide a believable biographical account. But historical truth-telling, as a narrative genre, is inherently problematic for trauma survivors, whose memories are both painful and incomplete. For immigration officials, however, a compelling testimonial must be coherent, mapped in time and space, and verifiable by a physical record, including fingerprints, ID cards, scars on the body. Fearing uncertainty, terrified by the possibility of extradition, the girl's efforts are focused on her narrative performance, struggling for words to give shape and meaning to what has happened. How to make a life?

10
Gender, Terrorism, and War

Susan J. Brison

"We are all New Yorkers," *Le Monde* (2001) proclaimed. "We are all Yankees," said a baseball fan in Chicago (Coffey 2001). After September 11, there seemed to be a sudden, if short-lived, consensus about who "we" were: we saw the same things at the time of the attacks, and we remembered the same images. And when an airliner crashed in Queens on November 12, 2001 we thought it, too, was a terrorist attack. As a commentator on Cable News Network pointed out that afternoon: "We can't help but see it that way."

The appearance of a unified group identity forged by the memory of September 11 quickly dissipated with the resurgence of *other* cultural memories—particularly those inflected by nationality, race, and religion. But gender was not mentioned much, at least in public responses to the attacks. Amid all the attention to the apparent religious and political motivations for the attacks, the media didn't find it particularly significant that the perpetrators were all men. I suppose I shouldn't have been surprised; since wars and terrorist attacks are virtually always initiated and carried out by men, this was not exactly news. But wasn't it noteworthy that young male Muslim suicide bombers "are usually ... told that they will be greeted by 70 dark-eyed virgins in heaven" (Sacks 2001: 1)? That the three hijackers who were at a Daytona Beach strip club and sports bar on Monday night and who had attracted FBI attention by allegedly saying "'Wait until tomorrow, America is going to see bloodshed'" had just "spent a few hundred dollars on lap dances and drinks" (Wilgoren 2001: 1)? *USA Today* commented on the apparent hypocrisy of Islamic fundamentalists engaging in such decadent western behavior but not on what such behavior means when routinely engaged in by "our" men. Why, I wondered, was so much attention being paid to the influence of Islam on the suicide hijackers and virtually none paid to the influence of gender norms? The perpetrators were Muslim men. Why did women of color in the United States have to fear being victims of hate crimes if they

155

identified themselves as Muslim by wearing scarves in public, while white men here felt free, as always, to go wherever they wanted?

Of course, I am not suggesting that all men are somehow more culpable than women in this attack, any more than I would suggest that all Muslims are more culpable than non-Muslims. Although only men were apparently implicated in this attack, to hold all men responsible would be just as misguided as the view of those who considered the attack to justify perpetrating hate crimes at home—and waging war abroad—against Muslims.

This is not to say that we should ignore the gendered aspects of the attack and our responses to it: *The Times* of London reported, on October 9, in an article titled "Elated Airmen Feel like Football Heroes," that "for one US airman, dropping some of the first bombs on Afghanistan from a B1 bomber was 'like being a football player on Super Bowl day'," and that "an aircraft commander described the start of the war as 'pretty dog-gone exciting'" (Whitworth 2001: 9). In a November 23 article in *USA Today*, we learned that "the Miami Dolphins cheerleaders arrived Wednesday to sign autographs, pose for pictures and dance on the ship's hangar deck" (Stone 2001: 4A). When I was in high school, during the final years of the Vietnam War, football was talked about as if it were war ("Kill Rahway!" "Kill Rahway!" shouted the cheerleaders at the pep rallies). Now war is talked about as if it were football.

Afghan fighters' ideals of masculinity were also in evidence: when Kabul fell, the *New York Times* (2001) ran a series of photos of a captured Taliban fighter who had been tortured, beaten, shot, and beaten some more: although it was not mentioned, one photo showed him naked and bloody from the waist down—clearly the victim of sexual violence, most likely castration. The accompanying article said there was some concern on the part of US officials that the Northern Alliance *might* be getting a little out of hand (*New York Times* 2001: B1). And on December 11, *USA Today* reported that the battered al-Qaeda soldiers remained "cocky and belligerent"—"My dear brothers, your sisters could fight better than you!" blared a voice over a walkie-talkie, an insult conveyed to the anti-Taliban forces (Keley 2001: 1).

That "boys will be boys" in a time of war was taken for granted, although journalists did seem to see the misogyny in Mohammed Atta's suicide note, and Robert McElvaine, a history professor, wrote in the *Washington Post* that "a kind of religion motivates the Taliban, but the religion in question, I'd say, is not Islam [but] insecure masculinity. These men are terrified of women" (Dowd 2001: 13).

But if the enemy's masculinity was "insecure," back home in the United States, masculinity, having been sorely tested, emerged newly secure and celebrated. What women *really* want, we were told, is brawny firefighters and police officers—strong men to protect them (against whom? other strong men?). Michael Kimmel, in a piece in the *Chronicle of Higher Education*, observed that these masculine men, who were so recently maligned by feminists for excluding women from their ranks, turned out to be heroes, saving lives, risking and losing their own (Kimmel 2001). Yes, *and* they also fought long and hard to keep women out of their ranks. Why can't we keep these two thoughts in our heads at once?

I don't really think we're all New Yorkers, and I'm not a fan of the Yankees or any other sports team for that matter. But I do think that all of us—including the women who were kept out of the firehouses and the 343 firefighters who were killed by the suicide hijackers, the Taliban, and the Northern Alliance, and the lap dancers and the fighter pilots—are victims of oppressive gender norms. Some of us are murdered because of them. I can't help but see it that way.

REFERENCES

Coffey, Wayne (2001) "Sports Salutes." *Daily News* (New York), September 23: 110.
Dowd, Maureen (2001) "Liberties: Cleopatra and Osama." *New York Times*, November 18 (section 4): 13.
Keley, Jack (2001) "'Chaos' in War's Final Push." *USA Today*, December 11: 1.
Kimmel, Michael (2001) "Declarations of War." *Chronicle of Higher Education*, October 26: B18–B19.
Le Monde (2001) "We Are All New Yorkers." September 13: 1.
New York Times (2001) "A Nation Challenged: Witness to Execution." November 13: B1.
Sacks, Kevin, with Jim Yardley (2001) "After the Attacks: The Suspects; US Says Hijackers Lived in the Open with Deadly Secret." *New York Times*, September 14: 1.
Stone, Andrea (2001) "No Turkey on Carrier until Bombing Day Is Through." *USA Today*, November 23: 4A.
Whitworth, Damien (2001) "Elated Airmen Feel like Football Heroes." *The Times* (London), October 9: 9.
Wilgoren, Jodi (2001) "After the Attacks: The Hijackers; A Terrorist Profile Emerges That Confounds the Experts." *New York Times*, September 15: 1.

11
The Continuum of Violence

Cynthia Cockburn

"War is imminent," "the war is over." We are used to speaking of "war" as if peace and war simply replace each other at given moments in time. The reality, however, is different. Preparation for war and dealing with the after-effects of war contaminate so-called peacetime, while efforts towards peace often coexist with war-fighting. This became particularly clear to me as I read deeply into the feminist literature on militarization and war, which by now draws examples from many different forms of armed conflict. A feminist analysis suggests that gender is a relation of power underpinned by violence. Since gender relations shape the dynamics of every site of human interaction, from the household to the international arena, a gender lens tends to reveal a connectedness between the many kinds and occasions of violence. One seems to flow into the next, as if they were a continuum.

UNEASY PEACE: BEFORE THE ONSET OF VIOLENCE

For example, if we look with hindsight at societies that have exploded into political violence or armed conflict, it is possible to see warning signs. Three such phenomena are economic distress; militarization; and divisive shifts in ideology in the way identities are represented.

Economic Distress

It was Johan Galtung who first introduced the concept of "structural violence." He maintained that "conflict is much more than what meets the naked eye as 'trouble', direct violence. There is also the violence frozen into structures, and the culture that legitimizes violence" (1996: viii). Violence exists whenever the potential development of an individual or group is held back by the conditions of a relationship, and in particular by the uneven distribution of power and resources (80). "Structural violence" usefully alerts us to look at the ways that strong states and economic actors can achieve their will over weaker countries, classes, groups, and individuals without recourse to weapons. Although this was not Galtung's main point, the notion prompts us to look again at male-dominant gender relations. Long before a man uses physical violence against a woman, she may experience "structural violence" in a marriage in which her husband or a constraining patriarchal community holds power over her. Structural violence may refer to an oppression so life-threatening that outbreaks of physical resistance seem justified. It explains the persistence of struggles against very high odds, as in anticolonial insurgencies.

In many societies that experienced political violence or armed conflict in the 1990s, it was possible to see in the 1980s an intensification of structural violence, of inequality between nations and within them. There were adverse changes in the world economy. The abrupt rise in oil prices of the 1970s was followed in the 1980s by recession, falling commodity prices, higher interest rates, and increased protectionism in developed countries. Poorer countries were hardest hit. Their indebtedness grew (Ahooja-Patel 1991). We saw the stress induced by forced economic liberalization and structural adjustment priming violence in societies continents apart; murderous communalism in India (Chenoy 1998), and imploding power vacuums in Africa (Turshen and Twagiramariya 1998). Economic distress does not necessarily lead to violence, but combined with other factors, such as the rise of nationalist movements in the former Yugoslavia in the 1980s, it may precipitate it (Woodward 1995).

Feminist analysis of these and similar situations has pointed out many gendered phenomena. Depressed wages and high unemployment among male breadwinners destabilizes relations in the family. Young men are at risk of being attracted or forced toward crime and militarism. Reductions in welfare spending and loss of subsistence farming hit women especially hard. Female-headed families make up about one-third of rural households, and these rarely have access either to credit or to the labor inputs required to increase production (Vickers 1991: 61).

Militarization and Arming

In societies that will later know open violence, there is often a prior increase in militarization and the quantity of weapons flowing into the area. Militarization supposes a close relation between political and military elites, and sometimes the regime may actually be a military dictatorship. Men, and sometimes women, are subject to periods of compulsory military service. The police force grows in size, reach, and armed capability. A rhetoric of national security and secrecy, often embodied in censorship laws, limits freedom of expression and movement. A militarized society is necessarily undemocratic.

Cynthia Enloe notes the gendered decisions that sustain and flow from militarization: "When a community's politicized sense of its own identity becomes threaded through with pressures for its men to take up arms, for its women to loyally support brothers, husbands, sons and lovers to become soldiers, it needs explaining. How were the pressures mounted? What does militarization mean for women's and men's relationships to each other? What happens when some women resist those pressures?" (1993: 250). And, one might add, some men. For militarization often forces into imprisonment or exile those men who do not wish to fight.

Militarization is accompanied by high expenditure on arms. This is often at the expense of spending on public services, including health and education. In the main, poor countries spend a greater proportion of their national product on arms than rich countries. Daniel Volman (1998) has described the arming of the African continent. From his figures it is possible to total at least US$60 billion of sales from the superpowers to African countries between the 1950s and 1980s. That flow dried up but was followed by an unquantifiable and unchartable deluge of cheap and recycled weapons. As a result, he says, "Africa today is literally awash in arms, particularly guns and other light weaponry of the sort that have much more impact on the security and daily lives of civilians, especially women, than tanks and combat aircraft" (1998: 150).

Domestic violence often increases as societal tensions grow and is more common and more lethal when men carry weapons. In the buildup to the war in the former Yugoslavia, groups providing support to women victims of domestic violence in Belgrade reported that demand for their services increased significantly and that violence occurred particularly after militaristic TV programs that hyped up "national honor" (Maguire 1998). Croatian women noted a shift related to increased weaponry: "No more wooden sticks, shoes and other 'classic' instruments of violence, but guns, bombs etc. ... Everybody has weapons" (Boric and Desnica 1996: 136). The shadowy and overwhelmingly masculine world of arms dealing is often linked to trafficking in drugs and in women. Military and nonmilitary trade becomes entwined in what Georg Elwert (1999) has termed "markets of violence," the system by which the lead perpetrators of violence survive and reproduce themselves.

Divisive Shifts in Ideology

One warning sign of impending political violence or armed conflict is a shift in discourse, particularly in media representations. Words chosen, tunes sung, and images painted increasingly divide people from each other. They stoke the fires of national patriotism against a rival nation, point a finger at "the enemy within," or deepen the sense of ethnic belonging in opposition to some "other" from whom "we" are different and by whom our culture or our religion, our very existence, is threatened.

Divisive discourse is often accompanied by a renewal of a patriarchal familial ideology, deepening the differentiation of men and women, masculinity and femininity, preparing men to fight and women to support them. Nira Yuval-Davis (1997) has carefully analyzed the ways in which the discourses on gender and on nation tend to intersect and to be constructed by each other. The more primordial the rendering of people and nation, the more are the relations between men and women essentialized. Women are reminded that by biology and by tradition they are the keepers of hearth and home and are meant to nurture and teach children "our ways." Men by physique and tradition are there to protect women and children and the nation, often represented as "the motherland." Through this retelling of old gender tales, women are readied to sacrifice their husbands and sons, and men to sacrifice their lives.

The disintegration of the federal state of Yugoslavia in the early 1990s was preceded and accompanied by the reemergence of just such a gender ideology. Except by feminists, it was not heeded as a warning of war. Many women of the region have since described how the veneer of socialist modernization was stripped away and gender traditionalism refurbished by Croatian, Serbian, and other nationalist movements. Birthrates came to be seen as strategically important. Women were urged to leave paid employment and attend to their "natural duties." Maja Korac notes that "the first instances of control and violation of women's rights during the transition from state socialism to ethnic nationalism were restrictions on their reproductive freedoms" (1998: 22).

In such preconflict moments, an ethic of "purity" may grip people's minds and legitimate politically "cleansing" the state of its internal enemies and ethnically cleansing the land of people who are seen as alien. Purity is a dangerous ethic for women. In extreme forms of patriarchy men's honor is seen as depending on women's "purity" to the degree that women who seek to escape this strict code, or who inadvertently fall or are dragged from it, may be killed by their menfolk with impunity. The prevalence of such "honor killings" in the context of communal strife in India has been vividly described by Urvashi Butalia (1997). For women in such circumstances, the threshold of war is lower than for men.

WAR AND POLITICAL TERROR

Over the past century, more than 100 million people have died in wars (Turpin 1998: 3). This does not include the many murdered by politically repressive regimes or the victims of the terror sometimes evoked in response to them. It is a drastic increase over earlier centuries: the figure represents about three-quarters of estimated war deaths since 1500 AD. Turpin adds:

> These deaths are not randomly distributed throughout the world—most of the wars since the 1960s have taken place in the less-developed countries, particularly in Asia and sub-Saharan Africa. Military intervention, on the other hand, is perpetrated primarily by the former colonial powers, mostly by the United States, followed by Britain and then the USSR/Russia, Belgium, South Africa, and India. (1998: 4)

Let us look at three manifestly gendered elements of war: mobilization into the armed forces; the catastrophic disruption of everyday life; and brutalization of the body.

Mobilization

It is men who, overwhelmingly, have constituted the fighting personnel of national militaries, popular militias, political police forces, and armed gangs of warlords. Men take part in violence for many reasons—for money, for honor, patriotism, or brotherhood, in self-defense, for liberation, to liberate others. But male positioning in patriarchal gender systems and the masculine identities they generate underwrite all these reasons. Indeed, many versions of masculinity in the world's varied cultures are constituted in the practice of fighting; to be a "real" man is to be ready to fight and ultimately to kill and to die. It is often for the safety and honor of women and daughters that men are asked by their leaders to sacrifice themselves. Sometimes patriarchy requires them to kill these very women and children to keep them "safe." Urvashi Butalia (1997) reports interviews with Sikh men in India who recalled, sadly but proudly, how during Partition they "martyred" their own womenfolk to save them from being captured by Muslims and forced into Islam.

But representation is one thing, practice another. As Sara Ruddick puts it: "In all war, on any side, there are men frightened and running, fighting reluctantly and eager to get home, or even courageously resisting their orders to kill" (1998: 218). And armed forces have had and probably always will have women nurses, provisioners, and camp followers. Increasingly, too, women are choosing to enter or are being enlisted into national armies. In some militaries (the Israeli Defense Forces, for example), they are kept out of combat roles (Yuval-Davis 1985). In others, women do bear arms, by their own demand or, as in Libya, through an official concept of "modernization" (Graeff-Wassinck 1994). The US military has greatly increased the proportion of female recruits in recent years in order "to offset the end of the male draft and to forestall a reliance on black male volunteers" (Enloe 1994: 87). During the Gulf War, 40,000 US women were deployed to the Middle East (Enloe 1994).

Some women have bloodstained hands, therefore. They have participated in uprisings for national liberation, such as the widely celebrated Palestinian *intifada* against the Israeli occupation (Sharoni 1995). They have also committed atrocities, as, for example, in the ethnic war in Rwanda (Lentin 1997). The forces of the Liberation Tigers of Tamil Eelam, fighting for Tamil independence in Sri Lanka, include an entirely female elite battalion of suicide bombers. But research suggests that women do not gain equality through their active engagement in war, even at this extreme level of sacrifice (Peries 1998). Nor do the character, culture, and hierarchy of armed forces become more feminine because of women's presence. If they did, they would no longer fulfill their current function.

Disruption of Everyday Life

Today's armed conflicts have ended any distinction there may once have been between combatants and civilians as targets of war. Civilians made up half the casualties in World War II; the proportion has been as high as 90 percent in recent wars. Since men as a sex are more generally mobilized, "civilians" means predominantly women and children. Besides, war and terror have the effect—sometimes deliberately achieved, sometimes incidental—of rending the fine fabric of everyday life, its interlaced economies, its material systems of care and support, its social networks, the roofs that shelter it. This affects women, who in most societies have a traditional responsibility for the daily reproduction of life and community in ways that are both class and gender specific. The poorest are least able to escape the war zone or buy protection.

The 20-year civil conflict that followed Mozambique's independence struggle is an example. The combatants in this war, which resulted in one million dead and five million displaced, were the presiding government, led by the socialist movement Frelimo, and the counterrevolutionary Renamo, supported by the South African government. Ruth Jacobson analyzed this war from a gender perspective. Thousands of boys, some as young as seven, were forcibly recruited by both sides. "Mozambican women themselves," she says, "recount numerous instances of the highest self-sacrifice on the part of men seeking to protect their families" (1999: 180). Women's stories constantly point to the gendered nature of the outcomes of the conflict. For example, the collapse of primary health services led to appalling rises in maternal and child mortality and morbidity. Gendered mobility was most evident in the differentiation between the male and female population in rural areas (where 90 percent of the total population lived in the early 1980s). Men were more able, with sufficient warning, to flee to provincial towns and the capital city. Women, encumbered by dependents, were more likely to have to stay in situ, producing "taxes" in the form of food and providing domestic services to occupying forces (including those of government). As their workloads escalated, they became exposed to ever higher levels of debilitation.

Brutalization of the Body

It is perhaps in brutality to the body that the most marked sex differences occur in wars. Men and women die different deaths and are tortured and abused in different ways in wars, both because of physical differences between the sexes and because of the different meanings culturally ascribed to the male and female body. Jacobson (1999) notes substantial evidence of large-scale rape and sexual servitude in the war in Mozambique at the hands of Renamo troops and supporters.

Ruth Seifert has suggested three explanations for the widespread rape of women in war. First is the booty principle. It is an unwritten rule of war "that violence against women in the conquered territory is conceded to the victor during the immediate postwar period.

... Normally the orgies of violence toward women last from one to two months after a war and then abate (as in Berlin in 1945 and Nanking in 1937)" (1994: 58). Second, while rape serves to humiliate enemy women, it also "carries an additional message: it communicates from man to man, so to speak, that the men around the woman in question are not able to protect 'their' women. They are thus wounded in their masculinity and marked as incompetent" (59). This is a particularly powerful motivation in genocidal wars. Women analyzing the epidemic of rape in the wars associated with the breakup of Yugoslavia have noted how women's bodies have been used as "ethnic markers" in nationalist ideology (Meznaric 1994). When men also are raped or sexually humiliated, or their genitalia mutilated, the act is no less gendered: it is their masculinity that enemy men are deriding. The third explanation proposed by Seifert (59) is that rape (particularly gang rape and systematic rape) is sanctioned by officers, and engaged in by the rapists themselves, because it promotes soldierly solidarity through male bonding.

In warfare, but also in situations of political terror, the instruments with which the body is abused in order to break the spirit tend to be gender differentiated and, in the case of women, to be sexualized. Lois Ann Lorentzen studied the writings in which women political prisoners in El Salvador bore witness to their incarceration. They reflect, she says, "the specific circumstances of *women* in prison. ... In these 'secret' women's prisons, captors, guards and torturers were all male. Prisoners were female" (1998: 197). Sexual degradation, assault, and mutilation were the main forms of torture.

In some parts of the world, slavery is persisting or returning, and war is a primary source of slaves. Tens of thousands of women, mainly Dinkas, seized in the war in southern Sudan have been sold by their captors into sexual servitude (Halim 1998). The Japanese government has recently acknowledged what was effectively institutionalized enslavement during World War II, in the extensive network of military brothels established throughout the Asian theater of war for soldiers of the Imperial Army. The estimated 200,000 "comfort women," as they were known, included Chinese, Korean, Filipino, Malaysian, Indonesian, and Dutch women (Sancho 1997). [...]

POSTCONFLICT: THE WOUNDS THAT REMAIN

There is no abrupt cutoff line between war and postwar. For one thing, attempts to achieve ceasefire and reestablish peace are frequently a feature of every stage of the conflict. And it should be noted in passing that antimilitarist, antiwar and peace movements are as gendered as militarization and war themselves. Often women find a particular interest in defending everyday life from the depredation of armed forces, and a feminist analysis of war sometimes leads women to organize separately to challenge military leaderships.

The blurring of war and postwar is also evident when instead of true peace a ceasefire brings only icy noncooperation. Sometimes the postwar period is better called interbellum, a pause before fighting begins again. Survivors are traumatized and the trauma is gendered. Male wounded are doomed to a life of unemployment. Women and children in rural areas are especially vulnerable to losing limbs from uncleared land mines. Women bear infants with birth defects due to contamination from depleted uranium in battlefields where residues of radioactive weapons remain. I will focus here on three aspects of postconflict situations: displacement; economic and social reconstruction; and aid, justice, and reconciliation.

Displacement

Figures published by the United Nations High Commission for Refugees (UNHCR 1998) show a world population of refugees, including asylum seekers and as-yet-unsettled returnees who remain of concern to the UNHCR, of over 22 million. Some of these have fled famine, but the great majority were displaced in war. Of the world's long-term refugees, about half are female, half male. But sometimes the statistics of flight are strongly sex-skewed. In the ramshackle exodus from Kosova in 1999, women predominated because young men had either gone to join the Kosovan Liberation Army or been imprisoned or assassinated.

Life in refugee camps can be squalid, dangerous, and stultifying. The displaced live with the memory of an earlier life lost and in despair of ever recovering it. They pursue the agonizing search for missing friends and family. Many are deeply traumatized. Only the luckiest receive skilled psychosocial help of the kind pioneered, for example, by Medica Women's Therapy Centre in Bosnia (Cockburn 1998). In some refugee camps (such as the Palestinian camps bordering Israel) two new generations have been born to the original refugees. Postwar also means deformation of home life for families who are obliged to take in refugees. Some of those displaced in armed conflict or political terror are obliged to resettle in distant countries and learn new languages and new livelihoods. They have to painfully evolve new identities and new attachments—

a negotiated belonging to the host country, to the diaspora, and to a now distant home (Brah 1996).

The experience of displacement through war may differ for women and men. For women, mainly responsible not only for themselves but for rearing, controlling, and educating children, refugee camps and overcrowded lodgings are especially nightmarish. Female bodily processes—menstruation, gestation, parturition, lactation—become more burdensome, uncomfortable, and dangerous. Women and girls are vulnerable to molestation and rape from male police, local men, and even other refugees. Young men and boys risk being recruited into criminal gangs and paramilitary forces. Among the displaced who move to big cities, it is boys who are most often seen living rough in the streets. What happens to the girls? Many disappear into domestic sequestration or prostitution.

Economic and Social Reconstruction

After war, infrastructure must be rebuilt, mines cleared, vegetation reseeded, and livelihoods reinvented. Usually capital is lacking and a country incurs more debt to undertake reconstruction. It may even, like Iraq after the Gulf War, be subjected by other states to economic sanctions as a punishment for the sins of its leaders.

Like destruction, reconstruction presents itself differently to women and to men. All ex-combatants need retraining for employment, but women may also face ostracism in their community and betrayal by male comrades who expect them to revert to prewar gender roles. Many women will have become widows and single parents, dependent on their own earning power to support themselves and their children. In the absence of jobs of the kind they can do, training they can get access to, and capital, credit and land, many women fall deeper into the poverty they knew before war began. Prostitution is often their only hope of a living. Men may consolidate their gender power in such periods. A World Bank (1996) report shows that in El Salvador, for instance, men have benefited more than women from government land distribution programs. Considered a better risk by lenders, they get bigger bank loans.

The same World Bank report points out that men and women use resources in different ways—wood and water, for example. The environment is likely to have been damaged and neglected during the years of crisis. El Salvador may not, perhaps, compete in this respect with post-Gulf War Iraq, where there has been massive contamination by radioactive materials, oil, and chemicals. But in this small country too, the environmental havoc resulting from economic policies imposed by international financial institutions has been exacerbated by war and militarization. The military conflicts were battles over land and models of development, clashes between peasants and the capitalist-export sector. The militaries of both El Salvador and Guatemala followed Vietnam-style "scorched earth" policies where entire regions were deforested and burned, thus hastening environmental decline (Turpin 1998: 7). Despite the horrors of tyranny and war, women are sometimes empowered during such times. Take Chad, for instance. Until the outbreak of civil war in 1979, Chadian society was patriarchal, recognizing only men as breadwinners, property owners, heads of household, and decision-makers. The war changed that. Women invented new ways of making money for their families to survive. They started traveling and trading over long distances, developing commercial networks and savings schemes (Women's Commission of the Human Rights League of Chad 1998: 127).

But from all around the world come stories of women losing their hard-won autonomy when the crisis is over. Alya Baffoun has said of the Arab world: "[W]omen who have massively contributed in the nationalist movements of liberation have been relegated to political back scenes and inferior economic sectors, once the Nation-State has been established" (1994: 167). The story is repeated in almost every anti-imperialist struggle (Jayawardena 1986) and many resistance movements.

Consequently, the civil society rebuilt after war or tyranny seldom reflects women's visions or rewards their energies. The space that momentarily opens up for change is not often used to secure genuine and lasting gender transformation.

Aid, Justice, and Reconciliation

As war recedes, war zones often see an influx of international peacekeeping forces and humanitarian agencies. They halt the gunfire and feed the starving but are themselves sometimes a problem. UN peacekeeping roles may offer the chance of a less masculine military. But, as Cynthia Enloe points out, we know "amazingly little about what happens to a male soldier's sense of masculine license when he dons the blue helmet or armband of the United Nations peacekeeper" (1993: 33). Complaints have been leveled against UN personnel for using underage prostitutes and for rape.

International humanitarian agencies and nongovernmental organizations (NGOs) are indispensable in picking up the pieces of war, and women are more visible there than in many other spheres of employment. International agencies often operate downwards and outwards through regional and national organizations to local grassroots organizations (GROs) active in development. Women's contribution is strong at this level too. It is estimated that more than 200,000 grassroots organizations exist in Asia, Africa, and Latin America, more than half of them organized by women (Durning 1989, cited in Fisher 1996). But not all agencies have a policy to build local capacity, and some inadvertently create dependencies. Humanitarian activity can create social imbalances, for instance when uneven distribution of aid has fueled renewed conflict. Women often do the work in agencies and nongovernmental organizations without being involved at the decision-making level (Fisher 1996).

Hatred is the strongest survivor of war and of political repression. So processes of retributive justice, truth-speaking, and reconciliation are important for social healing. Crimes committed in war and tyranny, as we have seen, have a gender dimension. And until recently, rape has rarely been prosecuted through war tribunals as a violation of women's human rights. The Japanese government's guilt for the enforced prostitution of thousands of women in World War II was not acknowledged in the peace treaties that ended that war, nor did the United States and Allied forces take account of it when assessing reparations (Sancho 1997). It takes special diligence, in any case, to bring rape cases to court in a way that protects women witnesses from further harm.

There is no guarantee either that reconciliation processes will not be gender-blind. The South African Truth and Reconciliation Commission encouraged public debate on its terms of reference. Beth Goldblatt and Sheila Meintjes decided to use that opening to put forward a gender analysis. Their submission showed how women's position under apartheid meant that their suffering often took a form different from that of men. But they stressed that women, like men, are divided by race, class, and ideology—and that "women who were spies, informers, warders and even torturers were all strands in the complex web of our past" (1998: 44).

In postconflict moments there is much talk of strengthening civil society and democratic structures. Civil society benefits from widespread grassroots self-organization, where women are particularly active. But their energies are often used without recognition. Participatory democracy means including all voices, but women are seldom in positions of political power.

A GENDERED CONTINUUM OF VIOLENCE

Let us return, then, to the notion that militarization and war may usefully be seen as a continuum of violence, through which gender relations run as a kind of fuse. Several aspects of this became visible in the foregoing account. First, gender links violence at different points on a scale reaching from the personal to the international, from the home and the back street to the maneuvers of the tank column and the sortie of the stealth bomber: battering and marital rape, confinement, "dowry" burnings, honor killings, and genital mutilation in peacetime; military rape, sequestration, prostitution, and sexualized torture in war.

Second, in emphasizing cultures, and therefore continuity between relations and events, a gender analysis suggests that it is meaningless to make a sharp distinction between peace and war, prewar, and postwar. I have separated, for convenience, phases I call preconflict, conflict and postwar reconstruction. But we saw gendered phenomena persisting from one to the next. Gender is manifest in the violence that flows through all of them and in the peace processes that may be present at all moments too. To consider one moment in this flux in the absence of the next is arbitrary.

Third, the continuum of violence runs through the social, the economic, and the political, with gender relations penetrating all these forms of relations, including economic power. Gender relations are sometimes enacted in the most intimately social of human relations. But a gender perspective should not thereby be allowed to deflect attention from forces and institutions that operate economically and politically. Gender power dynamics are as characteristic of multinational corporations and of international financial institutions as they are of the family.

We know that the incidence and abuse of unequal power is a factor in violence by men against women. We also know that one way the major economic actors on the world scene exacerbate violence is by sustaining or deepening inequalities. Global processes, what some have called the New World Disorder, are creating a new and dangerous dynamic in the relationship between strong nations and powerful multinational enterprises and more vulnerable regions and markets. Wars in poor countries may be logical responses to economic marginalization and political disempowerment (Duffield 1990). Any increase in inequality, any widening of the gap between nations and classes, between men and women, weakens the inhibitions against aggression. It legitimates violence toward people considered worthless. And those who are made to feel of scant value sometimes resort to violence to gain self-respect or power. This, I believe, is what Galtung (1996: 80) means when he points to the violence that can be latent in unjust social and economic power structures.

The power imbalance of gender relations in most (if not all) societies generates cultures of masculinity prone to violence. These gender relations are like a linking thread, a kind of fuse, along which violence runs. They run through every field (home, city, nation-state, international relations) and every moment (protest, law enforcement, militarization), adding to the explosive charge of violence in them. If most, if not all, violence has a gender component, violence reduction calls for a feminist gendered strategy. It has to involve, first, an alertness to gender difference and specificity, to the way women and men may be positioned differently, have different experiences, different needs, and different strengths and skills, and how in different cultures these differences have different expressions. Second, our feminist strategic thinking for violence reduction calls for widespread consciousness of the power imbalance in gender relations, of the way patriarchal power infuses with violence institutions like the family, the military, the state; of the way gender power relations augment the violence in class and ethnically based associations. Finally, if violence is a continuum, our movements have to be alliances capable of acting in many places, at many levels, and on many problems simultaneously.

REFERENCES

Ahooja-Patel, Krishna (1991) "Introduction." In Jeanne Vickers (ed.), *Women and the World Economic Crisis*. London: Zed Books.

Baffoun, Alya (1994) "Feminism and Muslim Fundamentalism." In Valentine M. Moghadam (ed.), *Identity Politics and Women*. Boulder: Westview Press: 167–182.

Boric, Rada and Mica Mladineo Desnica (1996) "Croatia: Three Years After." In Chris Corrin (ed.), *Women in a Violent World*. Edinburgh: Edinburgh University Press: 133–152.

Brah, Avtar (1996) *Cartographies of Diaspora*. London: Routledge.

Butalia, Urvashi (1997) "A Question of Silence." In Ronit Lentin (ed.), *Gender and Catastrophe*. London: Zed Books: 92–109.

Chenoy, Anuradha M. (1998) "Militarisation, Conflict, and Women in South Asia." In Lois Ann Lorentzen and Jennifer Turpin (eds.), *The Women and War Reader*. New York: New York University Press: 101–110.

Cockburn, Cynthia (1998) *The Space Between Us*. London: Zed Books.

Duffield, Mark (1990) *War and Famine in Africa*. Oxford: Oxfam Publications.

Durning, Alan B. (1989) "Action at the Grassroots." Worldwatch Paper 88. Washington DC: The Worldwatch Institute.

Elwert, Georg (1999) "Markets of Violence." In Stephan Feuchtwang and Dieter Neubert (eds.), *The Dynamics of Violence*. Berlin: Duncker and Humblot: 85–102.

Enloe, Cynthia (1993) *The Morning After*. Berkeley: University of California Press.

Enloe, Cynthia (1994) "The Politics of Constructing the American Woman Soldier." In Elisabetta Addis, Valeria E. Russo , and Lorenza Sebesta (eds.), *Women Soldiers*. New York: St Martin's Press: 81–110.

Fisher, Julie (1996) "Sustainable Development and Women." In Jennifer Turpin and Lois Ann Lorentzen (eds.), *The Gendered New World Order*. New York: Routledge: 95–111.

Galtung, Johan (1996) *Peace by Peaceful Means*. London: Sage.

Goldblatt, Beth, and Sheila Meintjes (1998) "South African Women Demand the Truth." In Meredeth Turshen and Clotilde Twagiramariya (eds.), *What Women Do in War Time*. London: Zed Books: 27–61.

Graeff-Wassink, Maria (1994) "The Militarisation of Women and 'Feminism' in Libya." In Elisabetta Addis, Valeria E. Russo , and Lorenza Sebesta (eds.), *Women Soldiers*. New York: St Martin's Press: 137–149

Halim, Asma Abdel (1998) "Attack with a Friendly Weapon." In Meredeth Turshen and Clotilde Twagiramariya (eds.), *What Women Do in War Time*. London: Zed Books: 85–100.

Jacobson, Ruth (1999) "Complicating 'Complexity'." *Third World Quarterly* 20(1): 175–187.

Jayawardena, Kumari (1986) *Feminism and Nationalism in the Third World*. London: Zed Books.

Korac, Maja (1998) *Linking Arms*. Uppsala: Life and Peace Institute.

Lentin, Ronit (ed.) (1997) *Gender and Catastrophe*. London: Zed Books.

Lorentzen, Lois Ann (1998) "Women's Prison Resistance." In Lois Ann Lorentzen and Jennifer Turpin (eds.), *The Women and War Reader*. New York: New York University Press: 192–202.

Maguire, Sarah (1998) "Researching 'A Family Affair'." In Caroline Sweetman (ed.), *Violence against Women*. Oxford: Oxfam Publications: 60–66.

Meznaric, Silva (1994) "Gender as an Ethno-Marker." In Valentine M. Moghadam (ed.), *Identity Politics and Women*. Boulder: Westview Press: 76–97.

Peries, Sharmini (1998) "Metamorphosis of the Tamil Woman in the Nationalist War for Eelam." Unpublished Paper, Women in Conflict Zones Network Conference (December), Hendaya, Sri Lanka.

Ruddick, Sara (1998) "Woman of Peace." In Lois Ann Lorentzen and Jennifer Turpin (eds.), *The Women and War Reader*. New York: New York University Press: 213–226.

Sancho, Nelia (1997) "The 'Comfort Women' System During World War II." In Ronit Lentin (ed.), *Gender and Catastrophe*. London: Zed Books: 144–153.

Seifert, Ruth (1994) "War and Rape." In Alexandra Stiglmayer (ed.), *Mass Rape*. Lincoln: University of Nebraska Press: 54–72.

Sharoni, Simona (1995) *Gender and the Israeli-Palestinian Conflict*. New York: Syracuse University Press.

Turpin, Jennifer, and Lois Ann Lorentzen (eds.) (1996) *The Gendered New World Order*. New York: Routledge.

Turpin, Jennifer (1998) "Many Faces." In Lois Ann Lorentzen and Jennifer Turpin (eds.), *The Women and War Reader*. New York: New York University Press: 3–18.

Turshen, Meredeth, and Clotilde Twagiramariya (eds.) (1998) *What Women Do in War Time*. London: Zed Books.

UNHCR (United Nations High Commissioner for Refugees) (1998) *Refugees and Others of Concern to UNHCR*. Geneva: UNHCR.

Vickers, Jeanne (1991) *Women and the World Economic Crisis*. London: Zed Books.

Volman, Daniel (1998) "The Militarisation of Africa." In Meredeth Turshen and Clotilde Twagiramariya (eds.), *What Women Do in War Time*. London: Zed Books: 150–162.

Women's Commission of the Human Rights League of Chad (1998) "Women Denounce their Treatment in Chad." In Meredeth Turshen and Clotilde Twagiramariya (eds.), *What Women Do in War Time*. London: Zed Books: 118–128.

Woodward, Susan L. (1995) *Balkan Tragedy*. Washington DC: Brookings Institution.

World Bank (1996) *El Salvador: Moving to a Gender Approach*. Report No. 14407–ES (June 12). Washington DC: World Bank.

Yuval-Davis, Nira (1985) "Front and Rear." *Feminist Studies* 11(3): 649–675.

Yuval-Davis, Nira (1997) *Gender and Nation*. London: Sage.

12
Child Soldiers: Growing Up in a Guerilla Camp

Julia Dickson-Gómez

An estimated 300,000 children are actively participating in 36 ongoing or recently ended conflicts in Asia, Europe, Africa, the Americas, and the former Soviet Union. In Sierra Leone some 80 percent of all rebel soldiers were aged seven to fourteen (Boothby and Knudson 2000). The ready availability of weapons has contributed to the recruitment of child soldiers. The new generation of inexpensive assault rifles, with their lightweight designs, can be carried, stripped, and reassembled by children aged ten years or younger (Barnett 1999; Boutwell and Klare 2000). Nearly all these wars take place in developing countries where resources for health care and education are extremely limited. In such unstable environments, children are extremely vulnerable to forced or "voluntary" recruitment to armed groups. They may become separated from family members when fleeing from their homes, or parents or caretakers may be killed, leaving children alone and unprotected. Extreme poverty may lead other children to join for economic benefits to their families. Still others are kidnapped from their homes and forced to fight (Boothby and Knudson 2000). In all cases of voluntary or involuntary recruitment, children do not have many options, and they lack the maturity to make decisions of such magnitude.

This article explores the long-term effects of children's active participation in the war in El Salvador by looking at young adults who fought with the guerilla army as children and adolescents. [...]

CHILDREN AND WAR IN EL SALVADOR

El Salvador's civil war in the 1980s constitutes one of the largest population upheavals in recent history, with up to 40 percent of its 5.2 million population having relocated (Aguayo and Weiss 1988). Estimates of deaths in the twelve years of civil war have reached

80,000, a large percentage of whom were civilians not connected to either the revolutionary Farabundo Martí National Liberation Front (FMLN) or the Armed Forces of El Salvador. The early 1980s were characterized by large numbers of mutilation killings and "disappearances" designed to create terror in the population and suppress growing political organization and popular unrest among the Salvadoran people. In 1981, the government initiated aggressive attempts to depopulate rural areas in order to destroy what it perceived as the social and material base of the opposition movement. The Legal Aid office of the Archdiocese of El Salvador reported 12,501 killings of civilians not engaged in combat during 1981. In 1984 and 1985, the government escalated its attack against people in the war zones by beginning intensive bombardment of civilians using US technology. Many people were forced to abandon their communities and take refuge in the surrounding mountains for days or weeks at a time and to flee in long lines called *guindas*.

Children were often witnesses to mutilations and murders of their family members and neighbors during the early period of oppression. They were also occasionally victims. As one example among many, the execution by guillotine of seven children under 13 years of age was documented between June and August 1981 (America's Watch 1982). Children were also victims of government strategies to depopulate rural zones where they were caught in the crossfire. They were recruited by both the National Liberation Front and the government's Armed Forces or killed as suspected subversives or army deserters. In its 1987 report on Salvadoran human rights, America's Watch discussed the use of children by both sides of the conflict. Children were used by the Armed Forces as soldiers and informers; the same report criticized the guerilla's involvement of boys in the conflict (America's Watch 1987). The majority of women and girls who joined the National Liberation Front participated in supporting roles, cooking and sewing uniforms. Others took a more active role as medics or in logistics, carrying supplies and coordinating the movements of soldiers. A minority of women and girls fought as combatants.

Children's experiences of the war in the community studied here parallel the participation of children in the country at large. Many adolescents and young men died in the war. Others left with their families to live in the capital and never returned to the community after the war. A group of about 20 of these young men retained ties to the community and visited on weekends to drink *guaro* (hard liquor), play soccer, and swim. Many of these young men were also interviewed. While they were witness to the National Liberation Front's early organizing in the community and witnessed the mutilation killings of their neighbors and family members, most escaped life in the guerilla camps and subsequent participation as soldiers.

Many young men, both those living in the community as well as those who lived in San Salvador, recalled "meetings" called by the National Liberation Front, which was especially interested in youth, and held training exercises below the soccer field. They reported that they participated at first, that it made them "feel like a man." They were unaware of the seriousness of these activities, however, and repression soon followed. [...]

The sound of dogs at night alerted neighbors to the presence of armed men knocking on the doors of houses, looking for subversives or informants. Dead and mutilated bodies appeared on the streets.

Many families with the resources to do so left the community after months of this kind of terror. Others without resources remained in the community until the government's Armed Forces came one day, locked all the people they found remaining in the community in a church, and held them there for several hours. They murdered all those they found in the surrounding hills who were trying to flee. The community members were told that the army would return in a few days and that any found still living in the community would be killed. Those remaining left for the mountains to live under the protection of the guerillas. [...]

THE CASES

The young adults who are the focus of this article left with their families to live in the guerilla camps. They were constantly on the move, suffering hunger and sickness as they followed the guerillas with their parents and grandparents. They were often targets of military violence. Three of the young adults eventually decided to participate actively in the guerilla forces after having lived for a number of years as support population.

José

José, 20 years old, was living with his paternal grandparents and 16-year-old sister during the period of study. He had been raised by his grandmother since the time that he was a toddler when she, accusing his mother of neglect, removed him from his mother's care.

His mother and father were separated, and so his grandmother took on the responsibility of raising him, as men in rural El Salvador do not customarily take responsibility for raising their children. When José was four years old, his father was assassinated by members of a death squad, his mutilated body parts left on the side of the road as a warning to others. José lost four other paternal uncles in the same period and fled with his grandparents to the Cerro Guazapa where they lived under the protection of the guerilla camps. He spoke of fleeing with his grandmother in *guindas* and witnessed two massacres of civilians that he somehow managed to survive. In one of these, government troops positioned themselves on opposite embankments of a road and fired on the civilian population trapped in the middle. They lined up the bodies of the dead and survivors alike, doused them with gasoline, and set them on fire. He and his grandmother hid under a bush while listening to the screams. [...]

Samuel

Samuel's father was also assassinated by paramilitary troops when Samuel was only six years old. His family also moved to Guazapa to live in guerilla camps. He decided to join the guerillas at the age of 11 to help provide for his fatherless and impoverished family and to avenge the death of his father. He first worked as a messenger and then as a combatant. He left for a refugee camp with the rest of his family and then moved back to the community at the age of 15. He talked of often being stopped by government troops as he carried supplies (cooking oil, rice, and beans, often received as donations from the Catholic church) from the municipal township back to the community. Once he was imprisoned and then tortured with another adolescent as suspected "subversives" supplying the guerillas. The other boy was covered in honey and tied to a post on a fire ant hill. A day later he was shot and killed.

Elva

Elva is the only one of the young adults presented in this article not born in la Pepa. Her family lived in an area in the east of the country where much of the heaviest conflict occurred. Two of her brothers, who had begun to organize with the National Liberation Front, had "disappeared," and so she and the rest of her family moved to San Salvador when she was ten. The death squads were still looking for them in San Salvador because of another brother's involvement with the guerillas, and so she left for Cerro Guazapa when she was 13 years old. First she worked as "support personnel" making tortillas and cooking for the troops. Later, she was trained as a medic and still later carried a gun. She became pregnant at the age of 15 and left her baby son in the care of her mother while she went back to Guazapa. Within a year she met the man she lived with at the time of fieldwork and became pregnant. They left for San Salvador to live with her family and later returned to la Pepa.

Lucas

Lucas witnessed his father's decapitation at the age of seven. He was killed with seven other people by the Armed Forces as they were working on a farm. Lucas fled with his mother and two younger sisters to Guazapa to live in the guerilla camps. His youngest sister, one year old, died from malnutrition as they were fleeing in *guindas*. His mother suffered a nervous breakdown after this event. They were removed by the Armed Forces in the 1985 offensive on refugee camps. At this time, his mother, offered a visa to live in Canada, decided instead to return to the community. Lucas followed his mother and sister, assisting them planting fields and rebuilding their home. He married early, at the age of 16, because he felt that his mentally ill mother could not help him improve their lives.

EARLY WAR EXPERIENCES

All four of these young people had close family members who were assassinated when they were very young. All had fled with what remained of their families to live under the protection of the guerilla camps. As young children, they took no part in the decision to join the guerillas and were therefore not presented with any choice of whether to collaborate with the guerillas or to participate in the war.

> *Lucas*: We left here in 1981; in January of '81 my dad was assassinated. [pause] They killed him at work, on a farm. They killed him, shot him twice in the chest, and later when they saw that he hadn't died, they decapitated him. He wasn't the only one who died there on the farm. Other friends died, other friends of his who were working. There were three other people they killed there and later when we left the farm, we found that they had also killed old people. There were seven people in all who died.
>
> Then we saw. I saw him. I was maybe around seven then, and my sister saw him, who was two years old, and another who was one, and my mother, we saw when they knocked off his head and

we, as we were small maybe it didn't cause us many problems mentally, but my mother yes, because my mother was already suffering from her nerves, and it shattered her nerves more and she's mentally ill.

Then from there, the government's Armed Forces came and said all the people should leave because if they returned [pause], the next time they came on an invasion, if they found people they were going to make them dirt. They were going to cut them in pieces. Children, women, old people, whoever. They had us like twelve hours maybe in the church, detained. Well we lived through that threat and stayed here seven days more maybe, and later when we saw that the people were fleeing, who the guerillas told should go with them because if the *escuadron* [government death squad] came, they would kill them. So as I was small, my mom grabbed us by the hands and took us where we could leave most easily, because of the fear that they would kill us. We left for the hills because it was where we could escape.

While Lucas recognizes that his mother did not have many options, he also recognizes that she, because of the trauma she had suffered, was not able to make effective decisions or care for her children as well as she needed to under the circumstances. All the young adults expressed this feeling of greater responsibility for their older and traumatized caretakers, as well as some resentment over the adult responsibilities that they were obliged to assume too early in their lives.

Many youths in their descriptions of why they chose to join the guerillas seemed to reverse roles with the adults in their families as they took on the adult responsibilities of protecting their families and providing economically for them. For example, Samuel described why he joined the guerillas as follows:

First because in the house, well we have always suffered from the economic situation as one raised without a father hardly has even daily nourishment. And well, they told me that if I joined with them I would improve my family's economic situation. They gave me things: clothes, beans, corn, everything for my family. That's why I went with them.

For Elva and other girls, life in rural El Salvador has always meant assuming adult responsibilities: before, during, and after the war. Girls are expected to help raise younger siblings and are often responsible for making food for the family. Elva, like many other women, spoke of not being allowed to study and being burdened with childcare, housework, and even work in the fields at a very young age. However, girls are not expected to support their families economically in the absence of a father to provide for them. That burden falls on boys who must become the "man of the house" when the father is absent. For Elva, involving herself in a more active way in the National Liberation Front gave her an opportunity to study health care and to have freedom she was not afforded before the war. "I became very interested in health because it was a way for me to work to help the rest of the people and to improve our lives."

José spoke of joining to protect his grandparents who had cared for him since he was a toddler. He expressed the expectation of his own death due to his participation but wished to protect his grandparents from a similar fate. His involvement as a combatant allowed him to negotiate their removal to a refugee camp. His life was less important than the lives of his family members.

> *José*: After a time, after I "involved" myself, when I already was armed, they took my family to San Salvador. I requested that they take them there because I didn't want them to be there [in the camps]. They suffered too much. They had to flee running from one side to another. It's very difficult not to be able to defend yourself with a gun, and the army being on top of you, wanting to kill you. So I requested that they take them. They took my grandfather and grandmother to San Salvador to a refugee camp. [...]

These young men, like Lucas quoted above, may have felt a greater responsibility due to the psychological trauma their caretakers suffered, which greatly impaired caretakers' functioning. The picture presented by these young men, of children actively protecting traumatized adults, is in sharp contrast to other adults' characterizations of their children's experiences of the war, in which children's agency is minimized or denied. When asked to describe their children's experiences of the war, many parents said that they really had not had any. They were too young to understand what was happening as they were only toddlers or young children when in the guerilla camps. This insistence that the children had not suffered from the war came in spite of the fact that many of the mothers who gave birth in the guerilla camps told stories of giving birth in trenches or crude shelters made of plastic in storms without any medical attention. They also told of carrying toddlers and babies in *guindas*, of their young children being present when they were captured by the army or other security forces. They also told about being separated from their children when they were imprisoned or when they left them in the care of relatives living in safer areas. Parents also described how, when living in the city, their children would occasionally hear gunshots or airplanes overhead, as, for example, during the final offensive. Intermittent fighting and aircraft were also heard by children whose families repopulated the community before the end of the war. However, even after recounting such experiences, parents insisted that because their children were young and did not "understand," they were easily calmed and quickly forgot about the incidents. As one father expressed, "as they were really little, they didn't pay so much attention to that. No more than when they sometimes would get a little frightened and I with only telling them a little story would calm them down because, well right, they were really little."

The youths echoed these sentiments, saying that they were not as affected as their caretakers because of their young years. However, this assumed resiliency added to their sense of responsibility for their traumatized caretakers. The death, disappearance, or assassination of children was felt to be particularly traumatizing to mothers. Later active participation as a guerilla soldier was also felt to be "easier" by these youths than living with the relative helplessness of their mainly female or elderly caretakers.

José: My grandmother, she's about 80-something, I think, and she can't talk about the experiences that she has had during the war because she remembers her children who were killed. She had like eleven children, it seems, and at the start of the war our family was very big. I had a lot of uncles but as the *escuadron* [government death squads] came and killed them, took them in the night. She saw how the *escuadron* left a son all shot up and shattered. They left him unrecognizable. She saw that, all her other sons who were killed, she saw and that has stayed recorded in her head so that now, since then, she mentally falls apart. She was traumatized and it's understandable because it wasn't an easy thing. Today, if you talk of that, you make her want to cry still because it has stayed inside her. [...]

The selflessness of children in war has been described by Assal and Farrell (1992). [...] Children often fear losing their families in conditions of war more than they fear for their own lives. Likewise parents often put their children's lives before their own (see Quesada 1998; Reynolds 2000). Wartime experiences, Antonius Robben (2000) writes, lead to a disruption of "basic trust", as parents find themselves unable to protect their children and vice versa. [...]

The intimacy of home and family were invaded for these *campesinos* [refugees in camps], and lives were permanently altered as people lived in a prolonged state of emergency—living not in villages but temporary camps, fleeing from one side of the mountain to another, and families were separated. The destruction of basic trust occurred for all community members, adults and children, but was perhaps more devastating for children. [...]

RESENTMENT

While all the youths described mental trauma in their adult caretakers, which caused them to feel a great deal of sympathy toward them, they also expressed some amount of resentment at having to assume adult responsibilities at a very young age. Children did not have the resources to assume these responsibilities and were still dependent on the adults who could no longer protect them from the outside world. Lucas expressed resentment, although not blame, toward his mother because of her inability to make decisions or care for her children in the face of overwhelming trauma.

We stayed like a year in the refugee camp San Roque. From there we left for another refugee camp because there wasn't room for all the people. They had a meeting where they said that they wanted to see the people decide to go to Canada or Australia. And as I was still only about nine or ten years old, I still wasn't given the choice. So my mother said that no, that she wasn't going anywhere. That what she wanted was to return to her *canton* [local community]. All that ... affected us because maybe in another country they would have helped us more. Maybe she would have recovered from her mental illness, because maybe she would have found good doctors and they would have helped us. [pause] But she didn't want to, she stayed here and they took us to another refugee camp in Santa Ana.

Lucas attributed his mother's desire to return to her community of origin to her traumatization: this desire first manifested itself after her infant daughter died of malnutrition in a *guinda*, the occasion when he felt that she first became seriously mentally ill. Resentment was also expressed about the decision to join the guerillas, a decision that was made at least in part because of the decision-making vacuum caused by parental trauma.

> *Samuel*: After that I remember how they had assassinated my family and well, yes, I had to see what to do about that because it couldn't stay like that. We had to go to the guerillas. [...]

Children resent their early involvement not only or even mainly because their parents failed to protect them but also because they were unable to "save" their parents and themselves due to their own immaturity. This is clearly seen in the quotes above in which mothers and grandparents are seen as more vulnerable than the child in spite of their greater maturity. The children clearly wished to protect their caretakers even sometimes at the cost of their own lives. Even the man who wished his mother had made the decision to emigrate to Canada expressed this wish at least partly so that she could recover from her "traumatization." [...]

Obligations between parents and children are mutual and necessary for the survival of the family. The state, of course, understood the importance of these social bonds when they forced parents to witness the torture and assassination of their children, and children the rape of their mothers. [...]

ADOLESCENT SOLDIERS

The basic mistrust caused by the brutal murder of family members as well as continued genocidal crimes against everyone they knew and loved was also the cause of profound identity crises as children became adolescent soldiers. There was no future for these children, as they had no hope of living to adulthood and therefore could give no meaning to their lives apart from the conflict. They could imagine no role apart from the role of soldier and no meaning apart from revenge.

> *José*: Who had hopes of living? We all knew that we were going to die but just because of this we didn't stop trying to save our skins either because if we fled from one side to another, it was not

to die. But we knew that one of these days, we weren't going to save ourselves. I, from when I was little, I think that it harmed me a lot because when they killed my father I was like four years old and still I remember how they left him broken. Since the time that they killed my father I said, "Why? Why had they killed him?" I never found an explanation since he hadn't done anything bad to anybody... And the problem was after killing him, this wasn't enough. They went chasing all the people, the rest of the families, in general everyone here. ...Why is it that they were going to kill us? I never found an explanation for that.

When I was about 13, then you see things differently and well, from all that, imagine that they kill your family and all that. You say, "Well I have to do something. I'm going to have revenge" and with that you gather even more rage, of revenge, of incorporating and killing as well.

Grief was repressed out of necessity during the conflict. Many *campesinos* interviewed talked of being unable to cry or show any emotion when soldiers or members of paramilitary forces killed or tortured neighbors or even friends for fear that expression of such emotions might also label them subversives. [...] José talked about this after describing, rather emotionlessly, a particularly gruesome massacre that he witnessed at the age of six.

They put a bunch of people in line, sprinkled them with gasoline, and then burned them. Some people hadn't passed away yet. They burned everyone. It was something very disgraceful what they did. Very difficult and as you know [pause] if you have lived through that, you have to be a little, a little hard so that it doesn't bother you all the time. ...

The defense against experiencing grief that was necessary to "keep going" during the war is also necessary now. The war in many ways is not over for this young man as remembrance of trauma is too painful to face even today. [...]

BECOMING "ONE WHO KILLS"

Unresolved grief and fantasies of revenge were experienced by all the young people who lived as children in the guerilla camps, although these reactions were perhaps more severe in the young people who became soldiers because they spent more years in the camps. Becoming a soldier, however, created additional conflicts not faced by Lucas, who did not join the guerillas. In acting out revenge, the youths encountered a crisis in identity. As the young man quoted above put it, after joining the guerilla he was "no longer the same person, but already someone else." [...]

Becoming "one who kills," however, set up a further dilemma for children as they were now soldiers like those who assassinated and relentlessly pursued them and their families. Revenge was seen as a particularly troublesome motive for participation in combat because it was seen as similar to the "inhuman," "animal" motives of government forces. Elva even went so far as to deny similarities in the violence committed by the National Liberation Front and the government's Armed Forces:

> At no time I tell you sincerely that the idea was to kill soldiers. The idea was to look for the leaders who had put them there. Who ordered them. That's who we looked for. Unfortunately, the leaders couldn't come without soldiers. Some soldiers had to fall. ... [We guerillas] had moral principles. ... They [government forces] were in general, finish the guerillas, finish the population, finish the elderly, the children, finish almost half the population because they didn't have that idea that we had. And we protected a great part of the population. We protected and they never protected anyone. Where have you heard in all the history of the war that the army protected or had asylums for orphans or elderly? [...]

Ideological reasons were often invoked by these youths in descriptions of how they became involved in fighting for the guerillas as children. Framing participation in ideological terms was a way of contrasting one's participation in killing from those of the governmental forces. [...]

> José: When I was nine they started to tell me. Well more than anything it's not what they say, I suppose, because if you are living with the guerillas, you are going to do what they do, no? Because it's the army that defends you and you have to follow it because it has defended you all the time.
>
> Besides, the whole time you're by its side. And when you're 13 or 14 years old, an adolescent, even twelve years old, you're already prepared mentally, and physically to fight! Because mentally, look, I had an experience like this. When I was little,

all the children, from five years on, when they began to play, to run and all that, everyone played war. They made guns out of branches and planks. ... They knew that they had to fight. ... It's something like, something that you already carry in your blood as one grows. Because from when you were little, you see what they do, and you want to do it too, seeing that it was a just and noble cause. [...]

Many youths expressed great disillusionment with revolutionary ideology after the war and felt that not much of what had been promised by the guerilla leadership had been gained. This disillusionment was common for almost all *campesinos* in the community interviewed but was perhaps greater for youths because they had even less control and choice over their participation. [...] Growing up in guerilla camps in reality gave them few options other than becoming a soldier. When social justice was not achieved after the war, young adults felt betrayed. [...]

José: Some people blame them [a branch of the National Liberation Front] for not having done anything to help people who put in their grain of sand for the fight. I know plenty of *companeros* who are sorry they fought and say that if they ask them to fight in another war, they're not crazy enough to do it ... imagine, the war was fought supposedly for the land because the land before belonged to the rich. ... The people see it like this, if they fought for the land, it wasn't so that now they would come to negotiate with us. It needed to be given to the poor.

Women and girls generally felt this disillusion to an even greater extent than boys because they often faced additional betrayals by the National Liberation Front leadership. First, many women and girls suffered sexual victimization in the guerilla camps (Garaizabal and Vazquez 1994). Second, the greater gender equality promoted by the guerillas during the war has not materialized in peace. [...]

REINTEGRATION IN "PEACE"

The United Nations report on the impact of armed conflict on children recommends reintegrating children into everyday community and family activities as the best way to promote peace and the mental health of children who have suffered from armed violence (Machel 1996). Although a return to a situation close to peacetime normality is surely the best way to promote recovery and healing from war trauma, the situation in many countries even after the signing of formal peace agreements can hardly be considered stable. This is the case in El Salvador, where violent crime has continued to increase since the end of the war and the economic situation of the poor has also deteriorated. [...]

Very little is known about the fate of child soldiers after they leave armed groups. The media has focused on the more sensational aspects of their experiences: atrocities committed by child soldiers, use of drugs and alcohol to encourage fearlessness and ferocity, the sexual abuse many are subjected to. There has been concern about the long-term psychological results of such early experiences on children. [...]

It is difficult to differentiate between children who are victims of war and child soldiers because many soldiers and other children suffer the same sorts of experiences, for example, witnessing the assassination of family members or bombings. Many child soldiers are also victims before, during, or after their participation as soldiers. However, the experiences of child soldiers are unique not only in terms of the frequency of exposure to extreme violence and danger but also, as argued in this article, because they require unique adaptations and behaviors. Becoming an adolescent guerilla fighter (*guerrillero*) creates conflicts in addition to those typically suffered in war by children who do not become soldiers, as adolescent soldiers must behave in ways that they feel are morally incorrect, becoming an inhuman killer like the enemy. Situations of continuing economic deprivation and insecurity add to the difficulty these child soldiers have in creating meaningful lives as adults.

REFERENCES

Aguayo, S., and P. Weiss (1988) *Central Americans in Mexico and the United States.* Washington DC: Center for Immigration Policy and Refugee Assistance.

America's Watch (1982) *Report on Human Rights in El Salvador.* Washington DC: The Union.

America's Watch (1987) *The Civilian Toll, 1986–1987.* Edited by Anne Manuel. New York: America's Watch.

Assal, Adel, and Edwin Farrell (1992) "Attempts to Make Meaning of Terror." *Anthropology and Education Quarterly* 23(4): 275–290.

Barnett, L. (1999) "Children and War." *Medicine, Conflict and Survival* 15: 315–327.

Boothby, N., and C. Knudson (2000) "Children of the Gun." *Scientific American,* June: 60–65.

Boutwell, J., and M. Klare (2000) "A Scourge of Small Arms." *Scientific American*, June: 48–53.

Garaizabal, C., and N. Vazquez (1994) *El Dolor Invisible*. Madrid: Talasa Ediciones.

Machel, Graca (1996) *Impact of Armed Conflict on Children*. New York: United Nations Department of Public Information, Development and Human Rights Section.

Quesada, J. (1998) "Suffering Child." *Medical Anthropology Quarterly* 12(1): 51–73.

Reynolds, P. (2000) "The Ground of All Making." In V. Das, A. Kleinman, M. Ramphele, and P. Reynolds (eds.), *Violence and Subjectivities*. Berkeley: University of California Press: 141–170.

Robben, Antonius C. G. M. (2000) "The Assault on Basic Trust." In Antonius C. G. M. Robben and M. Suarez-Orozco (eds.), *Cultures under Siege*. Cambridge: Cambridge University Press: 70–101.

13
Girls Behind the (Front) Lines

Carolyn Nordstrom

Q: What did you do?
A: I held my M-16 on them.
Q: Why?
A: Because they might attack.
Q: They were children and babies?
A: Yes.
Q: And they might attack? Children and babies?
A: They might've had a fully loaded grenade on them. The mothers might have thrown them at us.
Q: Babies?
A: Yes.
Q: Were the babies in their mother's arms?
A: I guess so.
Q: And the babies moved to attack?
A: I expected at any moment they were about to make a counterbalance.

> Paul Meadlo, court-martial testimony
> in Hammer (1971: 161–162)

Behind the rhetoric of soldiers fighting soldiers that fuels military propaganda and popular accounts of war around the world, children are maimed, tortured, starved, forced to fight, and killed in numbers that rival adult civilian casualties, and they outnumber those of soldiers who die. These youthful casualties—some one and a half million in recognized armed conflicts in the past decade alone—are largely invisible; most of the military texts, the political science analyses, and the media accounts of war ignore the tactical targeting of children.

In over a decade of studying war, I have seen children as victims of war, lying maimed in hospitals or dead in bombed-out villages, and living or dying of starvation in refugee camps and on the streets after their families and homes have been attacked. I have seen children sold into forced labor and sexual servitude by international networks of profiteers who exploit the tragedies of war and the powerlessness of children. This constitutes a multibillion dollar transnational "industry."

Despite seeing all of this, I have witnessed only a very small percentage of *all* the children who are directly affected by war. In trying to find out what happens to other children in war, I discovered that the (very) little data that exist concern mainly boys. This prompts me to ask: Where are the girls?

The more I ask this question, the less I find an answer. Cynthia Enloe demanded a new sensibility in political studies when she insisted we ask: "Where are the women in politics, in conflict, and in political solutions?" (Enloe 1989, 1993). To answer Enloe's question, I found women, I could follow their stories. Not all women and their stories, by any means. But I could see women during the time I was in war zones: they told stories and traded and set up healing programs. But *girls* were largely, dangerously, invisible. Outside of families, they disappeared from sight; they had no agency to direct their lives, to talk and trade and set up healing programs, they never spoke on the radio, their words were not recorded in newsprint, political scientists did not quote them, non-governmental organizations (NGOs) did not interview them.

When one tries to track the plight of girls in war zones, one finds that the images of children in war are obviously circumscribed. While bombing victims are plentiful in military and media presentations, discussions of the torture of children by state security forces are rare. While starvation among refugee children is frequently analyzed and photographed, the rape of these children is far less evident. While forcefully conscripting children into militaries has been studied in both academia and popular documentaries, the contemporary slaving of war orphans has been far more hidden, especially when the buyers are westerners. Likewise, military texts seldom publicly document the strategic targeting of children, even though frontline realities show how frequent these strategies are pursued.

In the war zones I have visited, girls are actors in the drama and tragedy of war along with adults. They are targeted for attack, they devise escapes, they endure torture, they carry food to the needy, they forge a politics of belief and action. In general accounts of war—not the few excellent ethnographies focusing specifically on children—I look for children as actors, and usually find none. Girls, children, are acted upon; they are listed as casualties—they do not act. They are not presented as having identities, politics, morals, and agendas for war or peace.

Given the (few) excellent studies incorporating the stories and voices of children that do exist, the silence of nonadults in generalized presentations becomes all the more politically loaded. To give but a few examples: Veena Das's inclusion of children's realities during the 1985 rioting in India (1990); Ed Cairns's work on children and political violence in Northern Ireland (1995, 1987); Marcelo Suarez-Orozco's study of the strategies of torture directed specifically at children (1987); Neil Boothby's work with unaccompanied children in conflict conditions (Ressler, Boothby, and Steinbock 1988); R. W. Connell's (1971) book of children's voices describing their political identities. Dorothy Allison's novel, *Bastard Out of Carolina* (1993), based on her own childhood of severe physical and sexual abuse, throws open the question of how much experiential separation really exists between what is called war and peace in terms of human rights violations and the suffering of children (see also Allison 1994).

What we hear and do not hear about the world we occupy is no accident. If reality is socially constructed, if we are the architects of our world and the cultures that give it meaning and vibrancy, knowledge is a profound resource. Shaping knowledge, and a lack of knowledge, constitutes a basic element of power. Silences—spheres where knowledge has been kept from public awareness—are undeniably political. So, what lies behind the silence about children in war, and why does it happen?

FOLLOWING GIRLS' STORIES DURING THE WAR IN MOZAMBIQUE

My two years of trying to locate girls in the war zones of Mozambique have raised many questions about the very premises of war. In this section, I explore three locations where war impinges directly on the health and wellbeing of girls—the frontlines of war, the borders of war zones proper, and the peace process.

In 1991 I visited a town in north-central Mozambique during the war, which claimed some one million lives in a decade. I flew on one of the few emergency relief cargo planes that were trying to supply an entire country's needs. As I listened to local citizens' experiences of war and military occupation, one concern predominated: people stressed to me that every woman and girl in the town had been sexually assaulted during Renamo control. The townspeople told me that virtually all the women and young females had sexually transmitted diseases. For those infected with HIV, the war would claim casualties long after the peace accord had been signed. Such conditions—common both throughout Mozambique and in other wars around the world—have neither been labeled "rape camps" nor generated international awareness and outrage.

Few non-locals or foreigners visited this town. Shortly after my visit, the emergency supply planes were diverted elsewhere. With no telephones or communications equipment, the town fell to a silence in the landscape of war. The people's lives became invisible once again to the outside world.

Where war is the worst, where suffering is at its greatest, the least is known. It is simply too difficult to travel to the hotspots erupting in the world, too difficult to get people's stories on the frontlines. The sad truth is that no one knows what occurred in the hundreds of towns and villages in Mozambique (and in thousands of villages worldwide like them) when the violence closed down the links with the NGOs, the administrators, the reporters, and the researchers. When we ask the questions: Where are the girls? What is their experience of the war? No answer is possible. Even the most concerned researchers cannot track the lives of girls in such towns under fire.

Following the plight of girls across time as well as across war zones complicates an already difficult task. The one million people killed in the 15 years of war left some 200,000 to 300,000 orphans. During my fieldwork, I continually asked about the orphans: What became of them? Many simply shrugged their shoulders; local Mozambicans generally responded that someone took them into their own families. There is a strong tradition of such care in Mozambique. More than once I visited friends whose families had grown by a child or two from the last time I saw them: war orphans, they had taken them in.

But this is not the full story. Thousands of children were visible on the streets of the major cities. Virtually all of them were boys. I told people that not all children could have found homes, otherwise there would not be any street children. But when I asked where the girls were, the answers were vague. People claimed girls were easier to care for than boys, and thus they fit more readily into established families. Yet no one has followed the path of the hundreds of thousands of orphaned girls to find out what has really happened to them.

Although I met children who had been taken into caring homes, I also encountered girls who did not fare as well, and their stories are as much a part of war as the others. There is a great international network of illegal racketeering that is spawned in time of war and that we must recognize. One example of this occurred in 1991 while I was in Mozambique.

In the midst of a war where public violence is often associated with the armed forces, collective civilian actions stand out. In 1991, groups of civilians gathered in one of the suburbs of the capital city, Maputo, then stopped and overturned certain vehicles and beat their occupants. The media explanations focused on *feiticeiria*, African medicine used for ill gain. For example, body parts, often of children, are said to be used in the more powerful and dangerous medicines of *feiticeiria*. The general word on these disturbances in Maputo was that children from the area were being kidnapped and killed to make these medicines. Many of the cars targeted in the attacks had South African registrations. This happened when the South African apartheid government was aiding Renamo's war in Mozambique.

Having worked with African healers for over a year, I found this explanation to be false. When I examined the allegations of *feiticeiria* and the body parts racket, I found a different and more insidious truth behind these disturbances. A thriving international industry had emerged to sell Mozambican children into white South African homes as domestics or as sexual slaves. The attacks described by the media were actually launched against the people running children across the border. War orphans, refugees who had been separated from their families, the poor and the desperate were the targets of this trade in humans.

Curiously, while the stories of selling "body parts" in pursuit of "sorcery" were widely circulated in the media, the actual selling of living children was not covered. A handful of industrious journalists documented the sale of children into white South African homes and businesses, but the international media did not feature the stories. The reluctance to file the reports may have resulted from the rumors that news stories of such racketeering could ruin more than a journalist's career.

Networks that sell children internationally are not the result of the work of only a few amoral individuals. Business, government, and military officials worldwide have greased the wheels, and their own pockets, in such illegal enterprises, and blaming *feiticeiria* may be a safe way to discuss child disappearances. Lost are the links among war, network profiteers, illegal border transfers, and abusive labor practices. Exactly who did the selling and buying, and how, was not documented, either because the specifics were too difficult to obtain or too dangerous to print. As a result, the children's plight has not changed, and their experiences have remained largely unheard.

AFTER WAR

As a profound irony of war and peace-building, young girls found themselves to be vulnerable to the sexual predation of the thousands of peacekeepers who passed through Mozambique in the two years between the 1992 Peace Accord and the 1994 elections. Each transient carried with him his own values about his rights as a soldier, as a peacekeeper, and (since most peacekeepers were male) as a man. Many peacekeepers were dedicated to their jobs and to the rights of the Mozambicans, but some also abused the rights of girls (and boys).

International justice systems tolerate the sexual exploitation of children; no UN soldier has yet been prosecuted for child rape or prostitution (Fetherston and Nordstrom 1995). Attitudes that appear to rationalize soldiers acting in this way only make matters worse. For example, the head of the UN mission in Cambodia, Yasushi Akashi, was asked about the physical and sexual violation of women and girls by UN troops. He responded by saying that he was "not a 'puritan': 18-year-old, hot-blooded soldiers had a right to drink a few beers and chase after 'young beautiful things of the opposite sex'" (Fetherston 1995: 23). Akashi left Cambodia to direct the UN peacekeeping mission in the former Yugoslavia where his attitudes, in that powder keg of sexual violations, can have only fanned the flames of human rights violations.

These are international abuses, transcending different regions and peoples. While many nationalities were implicated in the sexual abuse of children in Mozambique, the Italians were considered the worst offenders (Fetherston 1995: 23). M. M. Poston, who studied these abuses, claims that while local Mozambican officials knew about the Italian soldiers, they were afraid to make complaints about UN personnel—a clear indication of the power relations at work (1994: 35).

A report was made, and some soldiers were sent home, though the numbers of soldiers discharged and their nationalities were kept quiet. The report stated that while the sexual trade in children did exist, it was not restricted to the UN soldiers. To many, this constituted a whitewash. But it points to a deeper injustice: the sexual abuse of children is a human rights abuse racket that extends across societies and nationalities. Young prostitutes in Mozambique told the BBC's Barnaby Phillips that there is no shortage of foreign clients. "They come from lots of different countries. But they are usually white. It is white men who like young girls best" (Phillips 1994).

A CAUTIONARY NOTE

We must be cautious against "othering" violence against children. The United States Advisory Board on Child Abuse and Neglect, in a two-and-a-half-year nationwide study published in 1995, found levels of fatal abuse and neglect far greater than even experts had previously estimated. The report, entitled *A Nation's Shame: Fatal Child Abuse and Neglect in the United States*, found abuse and neglect in the home a leading cause of child deaths. Possibly more shocking, most abused and neglected children are under the age of four. This abuse, claiming the lives of at least 2,000 children and seriously injuring more than 140,000 each year, has been declared a public health crisis.

In some cases, the level of abuse that children suffer in "peaceful societies" may rival, or surpass, that in countries at war, as the above report shows. We should not look at the abuse of children in war, in another country, in another culture, in a different context, as if that were somehow different, more barbaric, than the patterns of abuse that characterize our own everyday cultures, in peace or in war. What people tolerate in peace and in the domestic sphere configures what takes place in war. Rather than seeing "war abuses" or "child (s)exploitation" as "outside" the rules and boundaries of "average" or "normal" society, we should instead be asking what makes such behaviors possible wherever they are found, what patterns of in/tolerance link them, and how they can be changed.

FOLLOWING GIRLS' STORIES GLOBALLY

The silence about Mozambique is not unique. Consider the following:

> Approximately 2 million children have died in wars in the last decade; 4 to 5 million have been physically disabled; over 5 million have been forced into refugee camps; and more than 12 million were left homeless (UNICEF 1995: 2).

> More children are killed in wars today than soldiers (UNICEF 1995: 2). 28 million minors lived in war zones in 1995.

70 to 80 percent of the world's refugees are women and children (Lang 1995). Children account for half of all refugees. Upward of 80 percent of girl and women refugees are sexually assaulted (United Nations 1995: 47).

100 million anti-personnel mines have been sown in about 60 countries. Girls suffer land-mine casualties in the greatest numbers as their traditional labors—fetching water and firewood—expose them to greater injury (UN Economic Commission for Africa 1995).

The number of children under age 18 involved in prostitution probably exceeds 2 million. About 1 million children globally will be infected with HIV by the year 2000 (UNICEF 1995).

There are 100 million street children in the world. Many of these children "disappear, are beaten, illegally detained and confined, sexually exploited, tortured and systematically killed by agents of the state" (Millet 1994: 294).

As of 1995, 168 countries—home to 90 percent of the world's children—have endorsed the Convention on the Rights of the Child, making it the most widely ratified human rights convention in history. Children are thus forced to live at the epicenter of the following irony: The major civil and human rights abuses children face are perpetuated by adults, yet children must rely on adults to protect their rights.

Children have no direct access to United Nations forums and decision-making consuls, nor to direct representation in courts of law, nor to state policy-forming committees, nor to non-governmental organization grants. In fact, children may find it difficult to elicit police protection, to find a hospital on their own, or to learn what rights they have in the many local, national, and international laws and conventions. They are bound by laws made without their input, and governed by institutions they cannot control, which may or may not protect their rights. A child who faces abuse at the hands of an adult learns that not all adults uphold the laws of the land; yet they also learn that only adults can rectify the situation.

WARTIME/PEACETIME?

What are normally considered "war accounts" and "problems of peacetime" have been juxtaposed here to show that the distinctions between war zones and peace zones are not only blurred, they are interfused. The profiteering institutions that abuse children are not isolated to countries or to regions, to "war" or to "peace." The networks that make such trafficking possible are multinational industries with global linkages. Any hard and fast divisions between "war (zones)" and "peace (zones)" are not only misleading but also dangerously wrong. Such divisions obscure the processes by which abuses of power and privilege—and by extension the solutions to these abuses—can be carried out. Only by understanding how abuses are constructed across social and political settings can we work to dismantle them.

International systems that exploit children are carefully constructed and consciously used by people, maintained within societies, and often tolerated in legal practice despite actual laws. They exist, even flourish, across divisions and zones of contention. These systems of abuse put billions of dollars into specific people's pockets. These people benefit, or think they benefit, from exploiting or ignoring the exploitation of children.

Challenging the belief in the naturalness of separating "war (zones)" and "peace (zones)" helps clarify the mechanisms that support these systems of abuse. Social habits move fluidly across conflict zones; they are put into place by people whose actions resonate across war and peace. To put this point bluntly: Would we as readily accept the physical and sexual abuse of children in war if child prostitution did not flourish in many countries, if domestic violence and incest were not tacitly allowed simply because these crimes are very difficult to formally uncover and prosecute?

Many of those who take sex tours to take advantage of underage girls and boys are unlikely to find the abuse or exploitation of children in war, or in peace, a significant cause for concern. Those who are encouraged to use physical and sexual violence against noncombatants and youths in war also have families and personal lives themselves—and a number carry these kinds of abusive actions back home into their communities with them. Studies show that domestic violence (physical and sexual) increases dramatically during war, and that people in uniform show significantly higher rates of domestic and sexual violations in war and out (Nordstrom 1996). That legal systems have so rarely prosecuted violators of children's rights, and in fact have often persecuted the victims themselves in peace or in war, shows that this is not idiosyncratic but rather a system of social practices that permeate civil, judicial, governmental, and military structures (Asia Watch et al. 1993: 1).

This should not be overgeneralized: many people work diligently for human rights, and they have created institutional systems that help rectify the injustices perpetuated in the contemporary world. When we can answer the question of "where are the girls" with hard facts and not a few anecdotes, we will know these workers are succeeding.

SOLUTIONS

Ending the silences and gaps in the empirical data on the plight of girls in war and in "peace" is a major avenue for beginning to solve these problems. At no time has it been more true that what is not known cannot be solved.

Sadly, we do not have adequate information on what happens to girls in war and out. In war we need to ask: What percentage of casualties are girls? How many are tactically targeted for torture or terror-warfare? How many girls, as well as women, are in rape camps? What do they face, if they survive, when they return home? And because statistics on social and political violence are more political discourses than accurate accountings (how many armies readily admit that more children are killed in war than soldiers, or that children are tortured in political prisons?), we must do direct fieldwork and not rely solely on secondhand data.

We must follow these questions out from war to map the international systems of child exploitation: What children are "bought" by whom and sold to whom for what purposes? What governmental, business, and legal and illegal networks make this possible, and what are their interrelationships? Who benefits, and how? If public opinion continues to see the exploitation of children as the random product of antisocial fragments of society and not as a well-developed transnational industry, the mechanisms by which this industry can be dismantled will not become evident.

Finally, we must ask girls to tell their own stories of war, its impact on them, and ask for potential solutions rather than assume the right to speak for them. If people misrepresent girls' experiences and opinions, the latter have little recourse to correct any misinformation; they have virtually no access to publishing, media, public presentations, and formal organizations. It is woefully easy to silence children's own words and realities.

Children often have a well-developed moral, political, and philosophical understanding of the events in their lives and worlds. Years of research on the front lines of war have taught me that even very young children have profound opinions on conditions of justice and injustice, violence and peace in their lives. Children fight and are fought against. UNICEF broke ground in the survey it sponsored in southeast Rwanda after the genocidal conflict there. It found that almost 56 percent of the children interviewed had seen children kill people, and 42 percent saw children kill other children (UNICEF 1995: 28). And on the other side of the equation, children worldwide have been involved in sophisticated peace-building efforts. From Youth for Peace in Northern Ireland to the peace-building work of the YWCA of Sri Lanka and the youth groups of South Africa, children have been working to forge viable platforms for peaceful coexistence (Abitbol and Louise 1993). As adults, we have a real obligation to support these initiatives.

Examples worldwide show children to be far more politically aware, more morally developed, and more actively involved in conflict and its resolution than most portrayals suggest. Adults do not necessarily impart responsibility to youths in a one-way process. Responsibility can flow from youths to adults as well. But who holds the reigns of power?

REFERENCES

Abitbol, Eric, and Christopher Louise (1993) *Up in Arms*. London: International Alert.

Allison, Dorothy (1993) *Bastard Out of Carolina*. New York: Plume.

Allison, Dorothy (1994) *Skin*. Ithaca: Firebrand Books.

Asia Watch and The Women's Rights Project (1993) *A Modern Form of Slavery*. York: Human Rights Watch.

Cairns, Ed (1987) *Caught in the Crossfire*. Belfast: Appletree Press.

Cairns, Ed (1995) *Children and Political Violence*. London: Basil Blackwell.

Connell, R. W. (1971) *The Child's Construction of Politics*. Melbourne: Melbourne University Press.

Das, Veena (1990) "Our Work to Cry: Your Work to Listen." In Veena Das (ed.), *Mirrors of Violence*. Oxford: Oxford University Press: 345–398.

Enloe, Cynthia (1989) *Bananas, Beaches and Bases*. London: Pandora.

Enloe, Cynthia (1993) *The Morning After*. Berkeley: University of California Press.

Fetherston, A. B. (1995) "UN Peacekeepers and Cultures of Violence." *Cultural Survival Quarterly* 19(1): 19–23.

Fetherston, A. B., and C. Nordstrom (1995) "Overcoming Habitus in Conflict Management." *Peace and Change* 1: 94–119.

Hammer, Richard (1971) *The Court-Martial of Lt. Calley*. New York: Coward, McCaan and Geoghegan.

Lang, Hazel (1995) "Women as Refugees." *Cultural Survival Quarterly* 19(1): 54–58.

Millett, Kate (1994) *The Politics of Cruelty*. New York: W. W. Norton.

Nordstrom, Carolyn (1996) *Rape: Politics and Theory in War and Peace*. Working Paper No. 146, Peace Research Centre. Canberra: Australian National University.

Phillips, Barnaby (1994) "Mozambique: Teenage Sex for Sale." *BBC Focus on Africa*, 15(2) (April–June).

Poston, M. M. (1994) *Guns and Girls: UN Peacekeeping and Sexual Abuse*. MA Dissertation, School of Development Studies. University of East Anglia.

Ressler, Everett, Neil Boothby, and Daniel Steinbock (1988) *Unaccompanied Children in Emergencies*. New York: Oxford University Press.

Scheper-Hughes, Nancy (ed.) (1987) *Child Survival*. Boston: D. Reidel.

Suarez-Orosco, Marcelo (1987) "The Treatment of Children in the 'Dirty War'." In Nancy Scheper-Hughes (ed.), *Child Survival*. Boston: D. Reidel: 227–246.

UNICEF (1995) *Annual Report*. Paris: UNICEF.

United Nations (1995) *The World's Women 1995*. New York: United Nations.

United Nations Economic Commission for Africa (1995) "Statement of the First Regional Consultation on the Impact of Armed Conflict on Children." Addis Ababa, Ethiopia, 17–19 April.

US Advisory Board on Child Abuse and Neglect (1995) *A Nation's Shame: Fatal Child Abuse and Neglect in the United States*. Washington DC: US Department of Health and Human Services; available online at <http://ican-ncfr.org/documents/Nations-Shame.pdf>.

14

On the Run: Narrative of an Asylum Seeker

Solrun Williksen

For Ada and persons like her—asylum seekers, international runaways—terms like globalization, migration, identity, and experience are unknown. What such persons relate to is living from day to day after a problem has made them run away. They are not travelers in the sense of discovering places. "Home," in terms of "belonging" and "native soil," is what they have run away from. Their notion of life is mobile and may be merely related to the kitchen in the asylum seekers' home where they have their meals and chat together at the end of the day (Rapport 1997: 73–79). Their primary concern is less about a sense of identity than about an identity or ID card, though the card may only be given temporarily. Their dream is to possess a passport. If they tell their life stories at all, they tell about what happened before the "problem" occurred or after they had sought asylum in a given country.

This article is about Ada, a young asylum seeker in Norway. Ada does not talk about her country as "home"; she usually says "in X" (name of the country). When she meets with her fellow asylum seekers they talk a lot about "before" (when they were still in, for example, Eritrea, Nigeria, or Somalia) and "after" (waiting for an answer from the immigration department in Norway), but they seldom talk about the "problem" (that which made them run away). A friend of Ada's, a young man, said to me as we were drinking tea together: "The immigration people here asked me for my identity papers—they thought I'd thrown them away. Who'd think of looking for one's ID papers when a problem arises? You just run away." When I asked Ada if she knew the particular reason behind her fellow asylum seekers' request for a permit to stay, she just shook her head. "It's not common for people to talk about what's happened to them. People never talk about themselves like that. We keep our stories to ourselves." What they do talk about is the rumors about who was sent out of the country and in what way, and how the police came in the middle of the night to take people to the airport—children screaming, people hiding from the police. Questioned more closely, nobody had actually *seen* those things happen, but the stories lingered on as a theme of conversation, emphasizing their own precarious state. [...]

David Parkin discusses the importance of mementos as transitional objects in people's experience of displacement and says there is "very little data on what people take and what they have, within the often limited time for making such decisions and consultations and sometimes in the context of unspeakable violence" (Parkin 1999: 305). The young man I mentioned above had taken nothing with him at all; he was surprised about how anybody could even ask about identity papers in such a situation of crisis, and the same is the case with other young refugees with whom I spoke. When they come to the asylum seekers' home in Norway, the state equips them fully. They receive a parcel containing everything they need: clothes, toilet things, towels, sheets—even pots and pans, cups and plates. They keep these until their papers have been processed, and they are either sent to a place where they can live, study, or work, or alternatively are sent back to their own country or the country to which they first came in Europe, which, according to the [European Union] Schengen agreement, is the country that should carry the responsibility for them. Ada relates how overwhelmed she was by getting so many things and how good it was to be able to take the same things with her when she was transferred to another camp. At the very beginning of her flight, she took a little picture of her mother with her. This was left behind long ago when she had to continue her flight from the place she had thought was relatively safe. When she arrived in Norway she had nothing, and even her "private mementos of mind" (Parkin 1999: 308), her memories, were mixed up and confused.

With the help and generosity of Ada, I shall present part of a story of an asylum seeker, her story, both "before" and "after" the problem arose, and the story of the problem too. But of the flight itself, a horrendous run across continents, she can only retrieve bits and pieces from memory, and even what she can remember she cannot easily put into words. The story I tell in this article will alternately develop, reveal, and conceal Ada's experience as it unfolded during the first months after her arrival in Norway when we met and during the months we waited for her papers to be processed. [...] The form of the narrative I am presenting here will to a certain degree reflect the fluctuating quality and painstaking retrieval of memory—the repetitions, the ever-returning doubt and anxiety.

Ada says she would like to tell everything that has happened to her and that she wants to be honest with me. But when she tries, she gets stuck in some detail while the sequence is lost. She has, as I have mentioned, no mementos to support and evoke the stories of the past. [...] There are shops in the city selling African food. Ada goes there frequently to look around, buy cream for her hair, skin ointments, and—not to be forgotten—okra, the rather sticky vegetable that seems to invite a lot of good memories of walks to the gardens outside the village, of preparing meals, eating, laughing, in those days when things seemed uncomplicated, when she was still not "thinking," as she later said to me. "I just did what I had to do and in the evening I went to bed. I never thought about the past like I do now, or what's going to come later. Now, I think all the time." [...]

THE ARRIVAL

Early one morning in November, Ada awoke to the noises of the boat slamming into the quay, heavy shutters opening, and human voices, apparently calling out to each other. There were no familiar sounds. She had got used to not hearing any words she could understand. She struggled out from her hiding place behind a container in the hull of the ship and pulled her clothes straight. Then she made for the exit, quickly walking across the bridge in between two trucks driving ashore. In her jeans and sweater and short cropped hair, she could have been taken for a helping hand on board. She had a dark complexion, but then so many have that now, even in Norway. It was cold. She felt bewildered. Where was this? [...] She looked around. She felt the cold through her thin clothes and the pain of hunger in her stomach.

There came by an elderly woman walking with a shopping bag. Quickly, Ada went up to the woman and said, "Please can you take me home with you? I'm so hungry." The woman looked surprised, but not unkind. She said, "I can't give you the help you need. I'll take you to the police station." Hearing "police" the young girl started to cry and said, "Please, I'm scared of the police. Help me!" The woman said, "The police in this country aren't evil. They'll help you. They know what to do. Don't be scared." So they went to the police station. There for the first time she heard herself defined as "underage." What was that? She could not understand. She was

17. What age was she "under"? The police asked her all sorts of questions, and then took her in a car and they drove off. Less than an hour later she was in a big house with many rooms, with many young people. [...]

This place was an asylum seekers' center for young refugees about whom the authorities still had to make a decision. She learned yet another definition of herself: "asylum seeker." She had never realized that she was one. She had just fled blindly from situations that were intolerable, hoping to find a place where she could be safe. She was now an "underage asylum seeker." She was in a country where they considered people under 18 to be "minors." When the civil servant from the Department of Foreign Affairs explained this to the young asylum seekers in an information session, many of them laughed and all of them were puzzled. [...]

So far in her life, Ada had learned one important lesson: One is never "under" any age when it comes to suffering.

THE ENCOUNTER

[...] Mid-December 2002: I decided to go and pay a visit to an asylum seekers' home just outside one of the cities of Norway. I knew it was a so-called receiving center for minor refugees. The inhabitants talk about it as "camp" or "*mottak*."

They would have to stay there until their situation had been considered, and they had been taken for an elaborate interview at the Department of Foreign Affairs (in Norwegian: "Utlendings-direktoratet," always mentioned in the abbreviated form, UDI), where they would be registered and their legitimate status as asylum seekers would be looked into on the basis of how trustworthy their life story seemed. It is an interview that is feared by the asylum seekers. [...] Will they be believed when they explain what made them run, how hard it all was? Ada said, after a few weeks in Norway: "People here all talk about Iraq and the Middle East. It's war there. They say there's no war in X, so why are so many of us here? They'll never believe me!" When the asylum seekers tell each other about what happens at the interviews, the UDI looms large, the institution becomes a threatening and relentless personality that nobody has yet met and that they dread. [...]

During our [first meeting], a small Christmas party, Ada was lively and entertaining. She told about her flight in a casual, easy manner. It sounded like a fantasy tale, and we did not really grasp what it was all about. She said she had lost her sister during circumcision, but even this she said in a tone of voice as if it was not quite real. She laughed when she talked about her country: "crazy" X. Later I found out that Ada would often laugh when she told or thought about something that was incomprehensible. The line between laughter and tears was very thin.

[On another occasion] there was a note of despair in Ada's voice. She and others had been informed about the "big interview" that would take place with the UDI, immediately after New Year. It was serious, they understood. People could be deported. They must tell the truth. They were entitled to a guardian during the interview. Could I be that guardian? I said, "Yes." A relationship of commitment between us had now been established and she would have to tell me, if not the whole story, at least part of it. Ada needed to tell somebody about the suffering of being an orphan and a refugee. [...]

The interview that Ada was waiting for at the time and which all refugees go through after their arrival in Norway is considered a crucial event on the road to a legitimate identity. As I have indicated already, the interview is conducted by officials at the Department of Foreign Affairs (UDI). This is decisive in establishing the asylum seekers' "true" age and identity and reasons for fleeing his or her country. For minors, like Ada was at the time of the interview, the procedure should ideally not take any more than six months, though it is not easy to guarantee this because minors are arriving in great numbers every day. The minor has a right to a guardian during the interview, to see that the child is not getting exhausted. The guardian is appointed by the UDI, and if the minor already knows a person he or she trusts it can be arranged for this person to be made the guardian at the minor's request, as happened in Ada's case. The minor seeking asylum also has the right to a lawyer to appeal the case should the request for a stay permit be rejected.

I will point out that although part of the life story here is also represented in the report of the interview, my presentation here, particularly when Ada herself is talking, is based primarily on the numerous talks we have had at meals, at bedtime, and in many other casual situations where her past experience flows over and needs to be told. [...]

THE FLIGHT

As we were cooking dinner the night before the interview, she told me how "everything" started about a year ago. This was not the entertaining version we heard on Christmas Eve. "Everything started in January 2002. I came here in November 2002. So much has happened in those months, terrible things, but I am still alive." It began with her sister being married off to an elderly man, who was himself already married. A group of village women demanded that her sister be circumcised and they performed the circumcision. "These are elderly women. It's a kind of organization. One can just call upon them to come and do it, and they come. Some live in the village. Those who did it to my sister came from outside."

Three days later her sister started to bleed and then she died. "I don't remember how it all happened. Suddenly she was dead. But she said before she died, 'Don't let them do this to you! Don't let them kill you!' I told my uncle: 'You killed my sister.' I told him this in front of other people. He was furious. If he ever finds me he'll kill me."

She thought she might have had a kind of breakdown after the death of her sister. She knows she was in a hospital for about a week. Then she came home to her uncle and aunt. Nobody spoke with her, nobody showed her any sympathy or affection. She was alone with her grief. She thought she was about to go mad. It must have been two weeks or less after her sister died that the following happened. She was in bed in the evening when the man to whom her sister had been married came along to see her uncle.

He came with another man, a lawyer or something. They said that my uncle should give the money back that the man had paid for my sister. My uncle said he had already spent it. The man said he could take the other girl as compensation. So my uncle signed the paper.

Ada was scared. She remembered what her sister had said. The same night she crept out of bed and went to the cupboard where she knew her uncle kept his money. She took all the money that was there and quietly left the house. For a long time her uncle and aunt had been bad to her and her sister. They wanted to get rid of the two girls in whatever way possible. The uncle had said many times that they were a burden to him and that they ought to be grateful he had them in his house at all. She traveled by pickup taxi the rest of the night and finally arrived at the place where she heard her mother had lived as a young girl. With a little picture of her mother, the only one she had, she went around in the streets of the small town, asking people if they had known her mother. She met a woman who said, "Yes, I knew your mother a long time ago. I hear she's dead now. You can come and stay with me till you find other relatives." So she went and stayed with the woman, who had a husband and some little children.

The woman had a business of some kind. She traveled around, buying and selling things. Ada stayed in the household and looked after the children. One day the family received a message that the woman had died in an accident. The husband was beside himself with grief. Ada was left to look after the children.

One day they went to a place where the widower had a farm. They were going to pick up something. The children were playing, and Ada grew thirsty. She went to the nearby river (lake) and drank from it. The villagers became angry. They said she had committed an offence by drinking from the river (lake). It was a shrine, they said, and she would have to be sacrificed to the gods. They tied her to a tree and said they would come back for her the next morning. The man who had lost his wife was scared. He could do nothing. He left and she never saw him or the children again. It became dark and she was terrified. She screamed and screamed. The place they had left her was called the Dark Forest.

Suddenly a man came, carrying a gun. He said he was a hunter of big game. She told him what had happened and he untied the ropes. He said she could come with him, so she traveled with him to the city of B. It took many hours. First they walked through a little desert; later they took a bus to a big city. She remembers the color of the bus. It was white. For the rest she does not remember much of the long journey. In the city of B she stayed with the hunter and his wife and their two small boys. They were Muslims, and though she was not a Muslim, they were nice to her, but all the months she was with them she never went to church. She stayed inside the house and wept a lot. She helped with the household activities.

I don't remember much. I stayed inside. I wept. I thought of my sister. Sometimes I saw her face in front of me. I thought about her all the time.

THE TRUTH

The day after we had the long talk in the kitchen, early in the morning, we went for the official interview. It lasted for most of the day, with small breaks in order for Ada to recover from the dark memories that now came washing over her and made her shiver and cry. But her voice remained firm throughout, concerning the exact data she could remember.

She said to me before we went inside:
I don't want to say anything that isn't true. Yesterday I thought I shouldn't mention I'd been to Denmark and Spain, but I think I'd better do it. They took my fingerprints in Denmark. They'll find out.

Ada did not wear a wig that day. Her fairly straight, short hair made her look older. Her face was haggard with lack of sleep and from her worries. From time to time during the interview she would pull at her hair and bury her head in her hands. When the interview came too close to the most painful things she cried, and when we had our short breaks she would walk to and fro silently and stand by the window in the little waiting room, looking out. In the streets young people were walking, laughing, carrying a Coke or a schoolbag.

The questions were all asked in Norwegian and translated by an English-speaking interpreter. This seemed strange since we all understood English. However, it is the rule, since the interview follows a standard procedure that is meant to be the same for everybody, whatever their mother tongue is, or whatever other languages they speak.

"What was the name of the man your sister was married off to?"
"Leon."
"What was the color of the first bus you traveled in?"
"It was white."
"What was the name of the man who saved you from being sacrificed?"
"Mika."
"What was the name of his wife?"
"Ana."
"What was the name of the lake you drank from?"
"They called it the Big Lake."

And so the interview went on in order to establish the truth content of the narrative. Not once did Ada hesitate to give the exact information. When the long flight across Europe started, however, it all became blurred. Day and night fused, and so did countries and continents. She lost her points of orientation from the moment she left the city of B. She struggled to understand how she had managed to get from there to Copenhagen, then again from Spain to Norway.

They were not even places on her mental map. She had never heard of them before. Later when I showed her an atlas she was surprised how far she had traveled. What was the route between the places? She still could not find the answer. Talking again and again of the events leading up to the flight and what happened on Ada's arrival in Norway, she and I gradually accepted a blank space, a no-man's land, a vast non-place (Augé 1995) that is not only anonymous, but simply without characteristics. Cities were all the same, railway stations were all the same, boats were of different kinds, but in none of them did she travel as a regular passenger. They were different only in their possibilities for hiding places. [...]

Ada lost the few belongings and money she had at the railway station in Madrid when she dropped off to sleep for a few hours. People meet by accident, disappear again like in a fog, never to be seen again, even their names unknown or forgotten.

> If only I could remember the family name of the hunter's wife. She was kind to me. Maybe she's in a refugee camp somewhere. Maybe somebody could help me find her. Who was the man who took me away? Who was the man who gave me this identity card? I don't know. ... He just came and said I had to travel on alone. He took her somewhere else, with her little boy.

As it appeared later, the card was a false one, belonging to a black girl with Spanish citizenship. Ada had never seen either an ID card or a passport before and had no idea that one needed these documents to get into a country. She did not know about the importance of borders.

Traveling as refugees do, on the floor of cars, under containers in ships, hidden somewhere in a train, the sense of time and space is soon lost, and with this loss, memory becomes confused. There is nothing left to attach remembrance to anymore. We know from literature how important a sense of place is for memory. What Augé (1995) describes is the fragmentation of attention that the modern person experiences in the places that are outside of social interaction, like hotels, airports, supermarkets—in short, places where we are only in transit. But the persons Augé talks about are coming from somewhere and going somewhere. The supermarket or the airport is a brief stop in an otherwise ordered life with homes and schools and companies and universities. For refugees the places they pass through constitute a trajectory not only through nonplaces, but through a no man's land and spaces where no routines can be established. Ada traveled through continents and countries without knowing the names of any of them. Day and night were the same and the conception of time faded away. Her experience was one of anxiety and confusion:

> We were at the bottom of this car. There were many people in the car, but only the other woman, her son, and I were hidden. The driver of the car threw a blanket over us to cover us up. We could only get out for a few minutes after dark.

"Where was it?" I asked.

> I don't know. The trip took a long time, maybe two weeks. We only once got out of the car in daylight. The driver said for us to cover our faces as if we were Muslim women. So we understood that this must be a Muslim country. Some time later we got on this boat.

"Were the woman and the little boy still with you?"

> Yes, we hid under some containers. We didn't see any people. There weren't any passengers. It wasn't that kind of boat. I don't know what kind of boat it was.

THE FEAR OF SCHENGEN

For many weeks after the interview, from time to time Ada would come back to the details that had been written down by the interviewers. On the whole she was satisfied with what she had said, but certain themes had not been made clear enough. When they asked about her health she had forgotten to say that she had bad stomach aches and that she sometimes did not know what she was doing or where she was. Later the psychologist explained to us that these were among many other post-traumatic symptoms.

> Sometimes I don't know what I'm doing. I don't know where I am. It makes me scared. Am I mad? [...]

The interview made many things explicit, and it gave her a certain pride that she had been able to answer most of the questions. One of the interviewers had told her, "I'm not the one to decide on your case, but I do believe your story." Ada would repeat this to herself and to me from time to time. "You see, I told the truth. She believed me. It makes me feel good."

Having found acceptance for her narrative, not only from me, but from the interviewer at the UDI, she gained mental energy. As she managed to put more of the bits and pieces together and look at them in a detached light—most often when together with me—she obtained a temporary sense of wholeness. The abyss became less frightening. Part of her story had never been lived in the sense of consisting of conscious acts; it had simply been suffered through. [...]

We went to a crisis psychologist the other day. During the long session of trying to cast light on the dark areas in her memory, he advised her not to be scared, but to trust that by confronting the difficult periods, she would regain her memory, her sleep, and her stability. He assured her that she was not "mad"—a word she herself had been using many times to describe her anxiety. "Am I mad?" she would ask when suddenly she did not even remember what to do with the book she had in her hand or the food she was about to prepare. [...]

Ada has told what she can remember of the many things from her life before the flight, but from different angles and from different perspectives. The narrative is set in X and there are a lot of gruesome as well as funny details. She tells how her uncle took her to a place where criminals were hanged and people could come and see it. It was horrible, yet it seemed a normal thing at the time. Now she often thinks about it as something that must be bad for children. She showed me the marks she had all over her body, partly from "treatment" by a medicine man when she had stomach aches, partly from beatings by her uncle and aunt. She also remembers funny situations from school and from going to the market to help her aunt sell vegetables. She and her sister were always together. She felt strong then. [...]

The story of the flight itself, which had lasted ten months, is one of terror and big blank spaces of oblivion, or events she cannot find the words to portray. There are times and places she cannot account for at all; she just shakes her head and says she cannot remember. It is "gone." Time and again we try together to retrieve the memory of the long journey, but there are so few places and names to tie the experience to that we always end up with just a few turning points in the trajectory. We go through them systematically: it was the lake/river where she drank some water and was accused of sacrilege. The villagers tied her to a tree and threatened to sacrifice her to the angry God the next day. Later it was the city of B. She saw nothing of the city, just sat inside and wept. The couple was kind to her. They had two young boys. Then something dreadful happened there (later she found out that a civil war had started while she was there). The man and one of the boys were killed by a group of men breaking into the house. The woman called out, "Come, we run." Then they were on the floor of a car for a long time.

It was Denmark at some stage. Was it Copenhagen? She does not know. Then it was the railway station in Madrid, and then finally the small place on the coast of Norway where she asked the woman for shelter and food, and then the place where she is now. When I gave her an atlas to look at, she spent hours every night peering closely at the maps and asking me questions about countries and distances. Was Denmark so close to Norway? She now understood why it had taken her so long to get to Norway: she had started from Madrid! What happened then? There was this man who traveled with her on a train; later they parted. She did not know where he went, but he had been kind. [...]

She traveled on boats and trains and in cars; sometimes she paid, sometimes people let her come with them. By this time the widow had gone, and she was traveling alone. After a long time she arrived in a city with many white people, but also many black faces. A woman came up to her and asked her if she was from X. The woman said she could come and stay with her. She cannot remember what they talked about or how many days she stayed with this woman. She rested there. One day, the first day maybe—she is not sure—the woman said, "Shall we go and have a cup of coffee in a café? We can't stay indoors all the time." They sat down in the café. She cannot remember what they ate or drank.

Suddenly somebody came up behind her and asked if she had identity papers.

"How did you come to Denmark?" said the person. He was a policeman.

"Denmark," she thought, "Is that a town or a country?" She pulled out the paper she had been given by the man who took the woman and little boy away with him at that railway station a long time ago.

"So you're Spanish?" the policeman asked, looking at the paper.

She said "Yes." Where was Spain? She had no idea, but she kept affirming it: "Yes, I am Spanish."

"Then we have to send you back there," the policeman said.

They brought her somewhere where they took her fingerprints. After that they took her to a house, gave her a room, and she stayed there for several days. Was it a hotel? She does not know as she had never been to a hotel before, but it was nice and clean, though the room was small. Was it a prison? She does not know. The door was locked. Every time they left after asking her questions, they locked the door. There was a person there who looked after the place, a guardian or something. She asked him for paper and a pen so she could try and write down what had happened to her. He gave it to her, but said it was useless to do so as nobody would read it anyway. She would be sent back to Spain.

She wrote a lot on that paper, about why she left, about her sister who died, about all her suffering on the trip. She felt a certain relief from writing it all down. She wrote and wrote for many hours, but when she had finished the guardian said he could not give it to anybody to read. So she tore the paper and just cried and cried. She felt as if she had lost everything. When the police came to take her away again she said she did not want to go anywhere. She threw herself on the floor and said she did not want to leave. They put handcuffs on her and carried her to the car. There were three police officers, one of them a woman. They took the handcuffs off when they walked with her into the plane. All three of them went with her to Spain and they tried to talk nicely with her in the plane so nobody would understand what it was about. In Madrid (a place she had never heard of) they left her at the airport, and the Spanish officials turned a blind eye to her presence.

Later, other refugees she met at the railway station told her that the Spanish did not care. They let anybody into the country, but did not give them any help either. If they died, they died. [...] She soon experienced that herself. Soon after she left the airport, where nobody tried to stop her or ask for any papers, she found her way to the railway station in the city. [...] She found a bench to lie on, but did not dare to sleep. Finally, after several days (she believes, but days and nights are one continuous blur) she fell asleep and when she woke up all her belongings were gone. After this the story becomes very confused. She can remember that she went about in the street and asked for money. She does not know how she traveled onward, but a man came and said he knew of a country they could go to. They traveled together for some time. He was nice. He was from Turkey. [...] Suddenly he was gone and she was alone again.

When Ada talks about this part of her flight she seems to be more concerned with Denmark than with anything else that happened: "Oh, my God, Denmark. I will never go there. If they send me there I will die!" [...] For a long time after we met, every conversation would end up with her anxiety about being sent back to Denmark.

This became worse when she turned 18 and was sent to an asylum for adults. There the theme every day seemed to be the "Schengen agreement," which apparently says that the first country a refugee arrives in is the country that must take the responsibility. Ada says, "We all talk about 'Schengen agreement.' What is Schengen? Who is Schengen? We don't know. The only thing we know is that it's about sending us somewhere else—that nobody wants to keep us. We know Schengen is bad for us refugees." [...]

Sometimes she will cry, sometimes she just laughs in disbelief.

Those people in X, they're crazy. Circumcision is forbidden by law, but they all, government and everywhere, force their daughters to have it done. They're mad. My uncle's mad too. He didn't have it done on his own daughters, but to my sister. I told him, "You killed my sister. I shall tell the truth about you." [...]

She pulls her dress up and reveals scars upon scars. "This is from the time my uncle nearly killed me." She quietly covers herself again. "He said my sister and I would never find anybody else to look after us. We ought to be grateful to him. I wish I could show him that people can love me. He should see me now!"

The scars on her body will never disappear. "Look at these scars. I can never wear a skirt, look what they did to me, but I don't care as long as I can stay here and get an education. I can wear trousers." According to her the sadness in her heart will also remain. We talk a lot about how one can live on with great sadness, how things can still continue, how one can work and have children and yet know that the sadness is there, close by. [...]

* * *

Just as I was finishing this account, with Ada spending many days on the couch feeling "sick" and not able to stop thinking, we received a message from the UDI that she had been granted a stay permit. As of this moment, she has been admitted to a class for immigrant youths in which she will learn the language and the history of her new country.

REFERENCES

Augé, Marc (1995) *Non-Places*. London: Verso.
Parkin, David (1999) "Mementoes as Transitional Objects in Human Displacement." *Journal of Material Culture* 4(3): 303–320.
Rapport, Nigel (1997) *Transcendent Individual*. London: Routledge.

Part IV
Intimacies of Suffering

Intimacies of Suffering: Introduction

Uli Linke and Danielle Taana Smith

The memory archives of modern warfare repeatedly remind us of the intimate relation between militarism and sexuality. As recorded by the trauma scripts of war in the twentieth century, sexual terror is an integral part of military violence: rape enforces masculine visions of state power. In this world order, the state is embodied in the soldier and the body of the soldier becomes a physical extension of the state. Regimes of militarized masculinity thrive on the suffering of women and feminized others. In Part IV, we connect the gendered dimensions of war to the tactical deployment of sexual bodies as a form of terror. In militarized states, women are primary targets of massacres, mass-orchestrated rapes, and organized sale into sexual servitude. Militarism sustains codes of morality and sexuality that marginalize female survivors, yet another form of domination. These strategies of dehumanization, while criminalized by international law, are legitimated by governments and armies to create conditions of fear. With the emergence of new visual technologies, the brutalization of the enemy is simultaneously deployed to disseminate fabricated images of the abject other. The specter of the phantasmatic enemy, whose elusive presence haunts the national imagination, propagates a culture of fear that normalizes human rights violations.

The introductory essay by Elisabeth Jean Wood (Yale University) provides a comparative analysis of the occurrence of sexual violence during armed conflict. With acute awareness of the complexities of political institutions and social realities, Wood reexamines the patterns of rape in war in an attempt to account for variation across different settings. From a global comparison of cases, Wood suggests that sexual terror is not an inevitable accompaniment of military action. Sex in war varies in extent, brutality, and form, ranging from the rape of civilians to torture in detention. The evidence leaves no doubt that the use of sex by soldiers cannot be explained by recourse to notions of the natural or normal disposition of male behavior. Rather, as Wood concludes by careful attention to data, detail, and pattern, the militaristic use of sexual violence is strategic. When sexual terror occurs on a massive scale or in an identifiable pattern, it is not merely tolerated but authorized and perpetrated as part of a carefully orchestrated tactic of warfare. Sex belongs to the repertoire of violence deployed by some militias, often government forces, to terrorize, traumatize, and dehumanize civilian populations to achieve total domination.

By examining military institutions from a critical feminist perspective, Cynthia Enloe (Clark University) lays the groundwork for exposing the patriarchal foundations that endorse violence against women. Enloe documents the deliberate and systemic use of torture, sexual slavery, and rape during war, orchestrated to achieve strategic objectives, such as ethnic cleansing. How do governments utilize women's labor in the process of preparing for and fighting wars? How are women's lives militarized in the absence of armed conflict? Enloe points to the global proliferation of military bases that contributes to thriving prostitution industries. The example of US military bases in Okinawa, Japan, shows how military policies endorse the recreational use of prostitutes by American soldiers. In turn, however, militarism also normalizes the sexual objectification of ordinary women. Misogynist notions are put into practice off-base, in this case leading to the abduction and rape of Japanese schoolgirls by US soldiers. In militarized societies, Enloe argues, women's lives are permanently altered by abuse and terror. She concludes that opposition to militarism is fundamental to changing the conditions of fear under which women live.

Women's experience of war takes many forms: as soldiers, as victims of armed conflict, as mothers and single heads of households, as forced laborers, and as sex slaves. Sexual violence against women is often used as a weapon of war, both to dishonor the woman and the enemy. For example in Sierra Leone, rebel commanders forcibly recruited or took young women as "wives" and in Algeria women were seen as a legitimate military target and part of the war booty. In a somber account of militarized violence against women in Uganda, Meredeth Turshen (Rutgers University) documents that rape and sexual assault gain approval from government authorities as well as rebel forces not as mere concessions to the desire of soldiers but as systematic devaluation of the enemies' property. While physical brutalization, including rape, is meant to terrorize women and families in order to stifle the possibility of resistance, Turshen provides detailed descriptions of the strategic role of sexual violence by soldiers in the extortion of economic assets from local communities. In addition to authorized looting, theft of property, food, and livestock, women themselves are bartered, exchanged, and sold by soldiers for money, labor, and sex. In examining the long-term consequences of sexual terror, Turshen provides guidelines for women's protection, health care, and economic restitution that might ameliorate suffering in Uganda.

How do we as global citizens acknowledge the suffering of others? How is the social reality of terror archived in the "western memory museum"? Cultural critic and public intellectual Susan Sontag seeks answers by turning her attention to the visual record of torture. Photographs can undoubtedly document and memorialize atrocities, but images can also selectively distort political realities. With a focus on the public circulation of the torture photos taken at the Abu Ghraib detention camp in Iraq, Sontag examines the problematic of looking, seeing, and interpreting visual media in a society indifferent to the pain of others. The graphic images of Iraqi prisoners, perpetrator snapshots of naked male bodies engaged in coerced sex acts, initially created a public outrage. But the response by government officials evaded the debate about military torture by reframing discussions in terms of the illegal dissemination of pornography and the anticipated life-endangering consequences for American troops. According to Sontag, the actual perpetration of systematic sexual torture by the American military remained peripheral to public discourse. The spectacle of homoerotic images displaced attention from state-sanctioned torture to the fabricated figure of the "criminal-Muslim-terrorist," who is deserving of any punishment inflicted. By nurturing a culture of fear, and thereby shaping a complacent public, the state validated sexual violence for its strategic value in the "war on terror." In further connecting these practices to comparable cases, including racial lynching in US American history, Belgian brutalities in the Congo, and German atrocities during the Nazi era, Sontag shows that sexual torture cannot be regarded as anomalous or as exceptional.

15
War and Sexual Violence

Elisabeth Jean Wood

While sexual violence occurs in all wars, its extent varies dramatically. During the conflict in Bosnia-Herzegovina, the sexual abuse of Bosnian Muslim women by Bosnian Serb forces was so systematic and widespread that it was a crime against humanity under international law. In Rwanda, the widespread rape of Tutsi women comprised a form of genocide, according to the International Criminal Tribunal for Rwanda. Yet sexual violence in some conflicts is remarkably limited despite other violence against civilians. Even in some cases of ethnic conflict, sexual violence is limited; the conflicts in Israel/Palestine and Sri Lanka are examples. Some armed groups, such as those in the Salvadoran and Sri Lankan insurgencies, appear to effectively prohibit their combatants engaging in sexual violence against civilians.

The form of sexual violence varies as well. In some conflicts, it takes the form of sexual slavery; in others, state agents engage in sexualized torture of persons suspected of collaborating with insurgents; in others, combatants target women of particular groups during ethnic or political cleansing; in still others, individuals engage in it opportunistically; and in some conflicts, all or nearly all forms occur. In some wars, women belonging to particular groups are targeted; in others, attacks are much less discriminating. In some wars, only females are targeted; in others, males are as well. Some acts of wartime sexual violence are committed by individuals; many are committed by groups. Some acts occur in private settings; many are public, in front of family or community members.

In some settings, wartime sexual violence appears to magnify existing cultural practices; in others, patterns of sexual violence appear to be innovations. In some conflicts, the pattern of sexual violence is symmetric, with all parties to the war engaging in sexual violence to roughly the same extent. In other conflicts, it is very asymmetric as one armed group does not respond in kind to sexual violence by the other party. Sexual violence often increases over the course of the conflict; in some conflicts, it decreases.

Sexual violence varies in extent and form in civil wars as well as inter-state wars, among ethnic wars as well as nonethnic, and among secessionist conflicts (Wood 2006). Despite the challenges to gathering data on this sensitive topic, the variation does not appear to be a product of inadequately reported violence: there are well-documented cases at the low end of the spectrum of sexual violence as well as the high end. Recognizing the variation in the frequency and form of wartime sexual violence has important policy implications. In particular, if there are armed groups that do not engage in sexual violence despite other forms of violence against civilians, then rape is not inevitable in war as is sometimes claimed, and we have stronger grounds for holding responsible those armed groups that do engage in sexual violence. Consistent with recent international law, by "rape" I mean the penetration of the anus or vagina with any object or body part or of any body part of the victim or perpetrator's body with a sexual organ, by force or by threat of force or coercion, or by taking advantage of a coercive environment, or against a person incapable of giving genuine consent (ICC 2000, Article 8(2) (e) (vi)–1). Thus rape can occur against men as well as women. "Sexual violence" is a broader category that includes rape, nonpenetrating sexual assault, mutilation, sexual slavery, enforced prostitution, enforced sterilization, and forced pregnancy.

Focusing on sexual violence against civilians by combatants, I first summarize patterns of variation in form and extent across several war settings. In particular, I document the absence of sexual violence in some conflicts and on the part of some groups. I then assess whether the causal mechanisms identified in the literature (often implicitly) explain the variation. In the conclusion, I sketch an analytical framework for the study of sexual violence as part of armed groups' repertoires of violence and suggest avenues of research that should contribute to scholarly understanding of sexual and other forms of violence.

CONTRASTING THE PREVALENCE OF SEXUAL VIOLENCE: SELECTED CASES

In this section, I describe the pattern of sexual violence in several wars, including interstate as well as civil wars, ethnic as well as nonethnic conflicts, and wars in which sexual violence was very prevalent and where it was not.

World War II

As the Soviet army moved westward onto German territory in early 1945, large numbers of women were raped (Naimark 1995). Although women of various ethnicities were raped in the course of looting of villages and cities, German women were particularly targeted. As the Soviet army occupied Berlin in late April and early May 1945, thousands of women and girls were raped, often by several men in sequence, often in front of family or neighborhood, sometimes on more than one occasion (Beevor 2002). Soldiers sometimes detained a girl or woman for some days in her home or elsewhere and subjected her to repeated rape. Sexual violence gradually subsided as occupation authorities realized the harm being done to the Soviet postwar political project and gradually instituted stronger rules against fraternization in general and rape in particular.

The sexual violence by Soviet troops appears to be an exercise in collective punishment and perhaps the taking of "victor's spoils." Did the Soviet troops engage in such widespread sexual violence in retaliation for sexual violence by German troops? Sexual violence by German troops occupying Eastern Europe appears to have been widespread in some areas according to recent research in newly available archives (Burds 2009). The German military treated the rape of civilians by German soldiers on the eastern front much more leniently than on the western front where military courts imposed significantly more severe punishment (Beck 2002). According to Wendy Jo Gertjejanssen (2004), German soldiers raped girls and women of various ethnicities, including Jews, despite regulations against sexual relations with non-German women. Much sexual violence appears to have taken the form of forced prostitution as many girls and women were forced to serve in military brothels in cities and field camps. While some volunteered to serve in the brothels as a way to survive in the dire circumstances of the occupation, others were forced to serve under threat of death or internment. German military authorities also organized brothels in labor and concentration camps, which were visited by favored prisoners. Some girls and women were forced to serve in these brothels, others when offered the choice of internment or service in the brothels chose the latter. The scale of sexual violence in the concentration and labor camps (aside from the sexual humiliation of forced undressing and the violence against homosexuals, which often took the form of medical experiments) appears to have been limited, as the number of women in the brothels appears to have been a small fraction of the number interned in the camps.

Massive sexual violence also occurred in the Pacific theater. The "rape of Nanjing," the widespread violence by Japanese soldiers in the environs of the Chinese city of Nanjing for eight weeks beginning December 13, 1937, included extensive sexual violence. According to Iris Chang (1997), 20,000 to 80,000 women and girls were raped and then executed; that is, 8 to 32 percent of the approximately 250,000 female civilians present in the city at the time of the takeover. Among them were prepubescent girls, pregnant and elderly women, and Buddhist nuns; most were summarily executed afterward. Sexual violence in Nanjing also included various forms of sexual abuse of men, including rape, the forcing of men to have intercourse with family members or the dead, and the forcing of celibate men to have intercourse.

One result of the negative international publicity in the wake of the violence in Nanjing was the widespread implementation of the so-called "comfort women" system of military-organized and controlled brothels that accompanied Japanese forces (Goldstein 2001: 367). According to a 1993 study by the Japanese government that included a review of wartime archives and interviews with both military personnel and former "comfort women," more than 200,000 women from across East and Southeast Asia were recruited by force and deception to serve as on-call prostitutes subject to immediate violence if they resisted. In establishing the brothels, Japanese officials sought "to prevent anti-Japanese sentiments from fermenting [sic] as a result of rapes and other unlawful acts by Japanese military personnel against local residents in the areas occupied by the then Japanese military, the need to prevent loss of troop strength by venereal and other diseases, and the need to prevent espionage" (Japanese Cabinet Councillors' Office on External Affairs 1993: 14). Most of the comfort women were between 14 and 18 years old, and most were Korean.

Bosnia-Herzegovina

Sexual slavery was also a prominent form of sexual violence in the conflict in the former Yugoslavia in the early 1990s. According to a European Union investigation, approximately 20,000 girls and women suffered rape in 1992 in Bosnia-Herzegovina alone, many of them while held in detention facilities of various types (Goldstein 2001: 363; Enloe 2000: 140). The most authoritative investigation of sexual violence in the former Yugoslavia was carried out by a UN commission, which found that the "vast majority of the victims are Bosnian Muslims and the great majority of the alleged perpetrators are Bosnian Serbs" (UNSC 1994, Annex IX.I.C). The commission identified several distinct patterns of sexual violence, including against men. Among the characteristics stressed by the commission were an emphasis on shame and humiliation (many assaults occurred in front of family or in public), the targeting of young girls and virgins along with educated and prominent female community members, and sexual assault with objects. The commission concluded that while some cases were the result of the actions of individuals or small groups acting without orders, "many more cases seem to be part of an overall pattern. These patterns strongly suggest that a systematic rape and sexual assault policy exists, but this remains to be proved" (UNSC 1994, Annex IX: Conclusions). While not explicitly stated in the report, the inference is clear that the commission believed it probable that rape comprised part of the systematic ethnic cleansing on the part of the Bosnian Serb forces. Direct evidence that Bosnian Serb and possibly Serbian forces planned a campaign of sexual violence as part of ethnic cleansing of Serbian areas of the former Yugoslavia is lacking, but may emerge as the various trials at the International Criminal Tribunal for the Former Yugoslavia continue.

Sierra Leone

Sexual violence during the war in Sierra Leone, in contrast to Bosnia-Herzegovina, did not involve explicit ethnic targeting. According to the Truth and Reconciliation Commission of Sierra Leone, sexual violence was carried out "indiscriminately on women of all ages, of every ethnic group and from all social classes" (TRC [Sierra Leone] 2005, chapter 3b, par. 282). The commission found that:

> ... all of the armed factions, in particular the RUF and the Armed Forces Revolutionary Council, embarked on a systematic and deliberate strategy to rape women and girls, especially those between the ages of 10 and 18 years of age, with the intention of sowing terror amongst the population, violating women and girls and breaking down every norm and custom of traditional society. (TRC [Sierra Leone] 2005, par. 298)

The commission noted that some armed groups targeted young women and girls presumed to be virgins (see also HRW 2003), as well as those girls and women associated with other armed groups.

The violence was also extremely brutal (HRW 2003). Gang rapes often took the form of very young victims enduring rape, with rebel combatants lining up to take turns. Many of those who suffered sexual assault did so on multiple occasions. A particular form of sexual violence in Sierra Leone was the detention of girls and women, often for long periods of time, as slaves serving and sexually servicing a rebel camp or a particular rebel. The commission did not analyze patterns of sexual violence in detail and therefore makes a less compelling case for sexual violence as a systematic strategy than that advanced by the commission for the former Yugoslavia, which laid out specific patterns not easily accounted for except by such a strategy.

Other cases in which sexual violence appears to be very prevalent include the present conflict in Darfur, Sudan, where rape occurs frequently in the context of the campaign by militias and government forces to punish villages thought to be associated with rebel groups (Amnesty International 2004; Médecins sans Frontières 2005; International Commission of Inquiry on Darfur 2005). During the genocide in Rwanda, some Tutsi girls and women (as well as, in much fewer numbers, Hutu women thought to support Tutsis) suffered rape and mutilation before their execution. Estimates of the prevalence of sexual violence in Rwanda vary widely, but appear to merit inclusion in the high prevalence category (African Rights 1994; Human Rights Watch 1996; Sharlach 1999).

Given the high prevalence of sexual violence in these very different conflicts, one might conclude that sexual violence inevitably accompanies war. However, the following cases in which the incidence of sexual violence is remarkably low or sharply asymmetric compared to the above demonstrate that such a conclusion is incorrect.

Israel/Palestine

In the Israeli–Palestinian conflict, also an ethnic conflict characterized by the increasing separation of ethnically defined populations, sexual violence appears to be extremely limited. While the forced movement of Palestinians out of some areas in 1948 was accompanied by a few documented cases of rape (Morris 2004), at present neither Israelis nor Palestinians carry out sexual assaults despite the killing of Israeli civilians by Palestinian groups and of Palestinian civilians by Israeli security forces (Wood 2006). It could be the case that the intensive international monitoring of the conflict deters the practice of sexual violence, but both sides do not appear much deterred in their other practices despite their frequent condemnation by international actors.

Sri Lanka

Like Bosnia-Herzegovina, Sri Lanka is also a case of a secessionist ethnic conflict, but in Sri Lanka the level of sexual violence appears to be significantly less and is also highly asymmetric. When it does occur, it has generally been wielded by government forces against women associated with the insurgency. Police, soldiers, or security forces occasionally subject displaced Tamil women and girls to various forms of sexual assault, including gang rape and rape with foreign objects, after their arrest or detention at checkpoints, sometimes on the grounds that they or family members are suspected members of the Tamil insurgency (Amnesty International 1999, 2002). Various human rights groups report that sexual torture by police and security forces against male and female political and criminal detainees occurs frequently. Of particular interest is the relative absence of sexual violence against civilians by the Tamil insurgent group, despite their inflicting frequent civilian casualties during attacks on non-Tamil villages, assassinations of political and military leaders, and their forcing non-Tamil populations to leave areas of their control, as in 1990 when 90,000 Muslims were forced to leave the Jaffna peninsula at extremely short notice (Wood 2009). Despite the frequent recruitment by force of girls as combatants, the group does not appear to engage in sexual abuse within its own ranks (HRW 2004).

El Salvador

Sexual violence during the civil war in El Salvador, a nonethnic conflict pitting a leftist insurgency against an authoritarian government, was one-sided, and very low in comparison to Bosnia-Herzegovina and Sierra Leone. Government soldiers and security forces occasionally engaged in sexual violence, including gang and multiple rapes, against some suspected insurgent supporters (including some men) detained in both official and secret detention sites. Government forces carried out sexual violence while on operations early in the war, for example, some of the nearly 1,000 people killed by the Salvadoran military at El Mozote in 1981 were raped (Danner 1994). The final report of the UN-sponsored Truth Commission mentions only one incident of rape, carried out by government forces in a village in eastern El Salvador in 1981. However, the unpublished annex to the commission's report discussed sexual violence in more detail; all incidents were reported to have been carried out by state forces or agents (TC [El Salvador] 1993, Anexos. Vol. II, 8–10, 15). No incidents of sexual violence were attributed to the insurgent force. Sexual violence in the Salvadoran conflict was thus asymmetric, distinctly low compared to other cases, and declined over the years of the war.

The type of war (at the broadest level) does not explain the variation even among these few cases. Sexual violence varies in prevalence and form among civil wars as well as inter-state wars, among ethnic wars as well as nonethnic, among genocides and ethnic-cleansing cases, and among secessionist conflicts. Nor does the prevalence of sexual violence simply reflect the intensity of conflict; the prevalence of sexual violence in Bosnia-Herzegovina was remarkably high compared to the frequency of lethal violence, while it is disproportionately low in Israel/Palestine and sharply asymmetric in El Salvador and Sri Lanka.

Before continuing, however, a preemptive concern must be addressed. Perhaps the variation described above is merely an artifact of inadequate knowledge about the empirical patterns present in each case. The reported variation may reflect different intensities of domestic and international monitoring of conflicts rather than different prevalence rates; violence in some regions appears to garner more international attention than in others. But variation in sexual violence is sufficiently well documented across enough wars and armed groups to suggest that it is real and not solely an artifact of bias in reporting and observation or a reflection of variation in peacetime levels (Wood 2006).

EXPLAINING VARIATION IN WARTIME SEXUAL VIOLENCE

Several causal mechanisms that might explain the observed variation appear (often only implicitly) in the literature on sexual violence during war. In this section I assess whether these mechanisms in fact do so. Candidate explanations for the variation also come from the recent literature on mechanisms of collective violence (Wood 2006, 2008).

Opportunity

One hypothesis, often implicit, is that the oft-observed increase in sexual violence during war reflects increased opportunity. Institutions of social control are often weaker in war, particularly when young combatants fight far from their home, communities are scattered to distinct areas, norms of respect for elders are undermined by new sources of authority such as guns, and armed groups loot kitchens for supplies. This approach implies that the pattern of sexual violence should mirror those of other forms of violence (because opportunity to loot and rape is also opportunity to kill), that combatants should not target civilians of a particular ethnicity (unless opportunity depends directly on ethnicity), and that sexual violence should be higher on the part of groups that loot provisions. Some studies weakly confirm these implications (Mitchell and Gluch 2004; Morris 1996). And sexual violence in some conflicts does appear to vary with other forms of violence, the frequency increasing and decreasing in the same patterns across time and space.

More generally, however, variation in opportunity does not account for the observed variation in sexual violence. Many armed actors target particular groups in patterns not explained by opportunity; in both Bosnia-Herzegovina and Rwanda, perpetrators had roughly equal access to civilians of various ethnicities yet targeted particular ones. The Salvadoran insurgency depended closely on residents of contested areas for supplies but does not engage in systematic rape of civilians. And sexual violence does not always vary with other forms of violence; the Sri Lankan and Colombian insurgencies appeared to strictly limit sexual violence but engaged in other forms of violence against civilians.

Incentives

A distinct approach argues that wartime experience increases individual incentives to engage in sexual violence. There are several versions of this argument. Some scholars interpret wartime increases in sexual violence to the breakdown of patriarchal institutions during war (Brownmiller 1975; Enloe 1983). Arguments based on patriarchal social relations imply that sexual violence should be more prevalent in wars in which traditional gender norms are more disrupted. But in many civil wars, gender roles become less polarized because village hierarchies break down as the population disperses and women take on tasks normally carried out by men. It does not appear to be the case that sexual violence is higher when traditional norms are more disrupted. Contrary to the patriarchal thesis, in some conflicts patriarchal relations are so disrupted that there are significant numbers of female combatants in insurgent factions. Rather than the predicted high rates of sexual violence, rates appear to have been very low in two such cases: the insurgencies in Sri

Lanka and El Salvador. And women sometimes participate in sexual violence as in Rwanda, where women sometimes incited men to rape, and in the sexual humiliation of men detained by US forces in Iraq, Guantánamo, and Afghanistan.

A second argument that does account for such targeting is that of revenge: combatants target enemy civilians with violence in revenge for the violence suffered by their community. However, why revenge takes the form of sexual rather than other kinds of violence is usually not explained. Sexual violence is sometimes said to occur in retaliation for sexual violence previously suffered (or rumored to suffer) by co-ethnics, but as our cases showed, some armed groups do not respond in kind to sexual violence.

The militarized masculinity approach (Morris 1996; Goldstein 2001) does account for the targeting of enemy women and men, and with specifically sexual violence. In order to persuade men to fight and endure the hardships of war, societies develop members willing to stand fast under fire, usually via the development of sharp distinctions between genders: to become men, boys must become warriors. Leaders persuade soldiers that to be a real man is to assert a militaristic masculinity, with the result that soldiers represent domination of the enemy in highly gendered terms and use specifically sexual violence against enemy populations. Moreover, bonding among members of the small unit—the loyalty that enables warriors to fight under the terrifying conditions of war— also takes gendered forms, reinforcing the militaristic masculinity of training.

Wartime memoirs from some conflicts (for example, memoirs by US soldiers who served in Vietnam) offer anecdotal support for this approach. Particular types of small-unit bonding such as joint visits to brothels may play a role in the frequent occurrence of gang rapes in wartime. However, if this approach is to explain variation in wartime sexual violence, armies should promote different notions of masculinity, with armies that emphasize more militaristic notions of manhood responsible for higher levels of sexual violence. I am not aware of systematic comparisons of military training, norms, and practices across state militaries; the variation in sexual violence among state militaries appears significantly greater than the surprisingly limited variation in their training. Moreover, the militaristic masculinity approach does not specify well what mechanism underlies its link to sexual violence, whether armies inculcate new norms, provide incentives to reward compliance without internalization, or recruit only those attracted to militaristic practices.

Sexual Violence as Instrumental for the Group

In the explanations based on increased opportunity and incentive, sexual violence occurred for reasons of individual gratification or as a byproduct of supposedly necessary training. In contrast, some armed groups promote (or tolerate) sexual violence as an effective means toward group goals. While strategic sexual violence may not be explicitly ordered, it is (at least) tolerated; if any punishment occurs it is symbolic and limited, clearly for external consumption rather than deterrence. Such violence appears to take two broad forms. The first is sexual torture and/or humiliation of persons detained by an armed group. The second is widespread sexual violence as a form of terror or punishment targeted at a particular group, which frequently takes the form of gang (and often public) rape, usually over an extended period of time, most notoriously as part of some campaigns of "ethnic cleansing," to force the movement of entire populations from particular regions claimed as the homeland, and as part of some genocides.

The conditions for such instrumental promotion of sexual violence are not well identified in the literature. Some authors suggest particular cultural beliefs provide the relevant condition; where armed groups understand sexual violence as a violation of the family's and community's honor, they are likely to engage in sexual violence as a weapon of war (Enloe 2000). However, this appears to predict significantly more sexual violence than is in fact observed as such beliefs are present in many societies where massive sexual violence has not occurred, as in Sri Lanka, El Salvador, and Colombia. Moreover, such broad notions of cultural proclivity do not account for cases where one party to the war promotes sexual violence while the other does not.

Sanctions against Sexual Violence

An armed group's leadership may prohibit sexual violence for strategic, normative, or practical reasons (Wood 2009). If an organization aspires to govern the civilian population, leaders will probably attempt to restrain combatants' engagement in sexual violence against those civilians (though perhaps endorsing it against other civilian groups) for fear of undermining support for the coming revolution. Similarly, if an armed group is dependent on civilians, leaders will probably attempt to restrain sexual violence against those civilians. Other possible constraints against sexual violence may include dependence on international allies or on female combatants (Wood 2008).

Reasons for prohibiting sexual violence may reflect normative concerns as well as practical constraints. Members of a revolutionary group seeking to carry out a social revolution may see themselves as the disciplined bearers of a new, more just social order for all citizens; sexual violence may conflict with their self-image. A norm against sexual violence may take a distinct form; sexual violence across ethnic boundaries may be understood by leaders or combatants as polluting the instigator rather than humiliating the targeted individual and community. New social norms against the use of particular forms of violence and in favor of others may also be actively cultivated by an armed group as a matter of strategy or principle. The Salvadoran insurgency attempted to shape individual longings for revenge toward a more general aspiration for justice because revenge-seeking by individuals would undermine insurgent discipline and obedience (Wood 2003). Despite systematic celebration of martyrdom in pursuit of victory, the insurgency did not endorse suicide missions and explicitly prohibited sexual violence. The Sri Lankan insurgency carries out suicide bombing and, arguably, shapes desires for revenge toward that end, yet does not engage in sexual violence toward civilians despite its practice of ethnic cleansing.

Whether an armed group effectively enforces the leadership's decision to promote, prohibit or tolerate sexual violence by members depends on its willingness and ability to discipline members. However, under some, probably rare, conditions, the prevalence of sexual violence may be low without relying on hierarchical discipline, namely when sufficiently many combatants have themselves internalized norms against sexual violence.

CONCLUSION: A RESEARCH AGENDA

The literature on sexual violence during war has yet to provide an adequate explanation for its variation across wars, armed groups, and units. While many authors have distinguished between opportunistic and strategic sexual violence, the empirical pattern of variation is wider, including wars where sexual violence is remarkably low on the part of one or more parties to the conflict. In the light of comparative analysis, we do not adequately understand the conditions under which armed groups provide effective sanctions against their combatants engaging in sexual violence or those under which groups effectively promote its strategic use. To conclude, I offer a theoretical framework with which to approach the analysis of variation, as well as suggestions for further research (Wood 2008: 346–348).

In research on sexual violence, scholars should focus on distinct types of sexual violence (or combinations thereof) as the underlying mechanisms generating high or low prevalence may be different for each type. Major sub-types should include sexual torture (including of men), sexual slavery, sexual violence (particularly rape) in the context of ethnic or political cleansing (rape and displacement; rape and genocide), sexual violence (particularly rape) as collective punishment, and opportunistic rape.

Whether or not an armed group engages in sexual violence in general and particular forms in particular should be understood as a question about the groups' repertoire of violence, by which I mean the analogue for violence of Charles Tilly's notion of the repertoire of collective action. This broader concept suggests several avenues of research. While focusing on the variation in sexual violence, this essay has also shown that the repertoire of violence varies across conflicts and armed groups, and may vary across units within a group. More specifically, the repertoire of a particular group may be constant over time and space, with the relative incidence of different forms of violence remaining approximately the same. In other cases, the repertoire may not be constant, as disappearances and executions rise and fall together but sexual violence remains constant. An obvious implication is that scholars should collect and code for all kinds of violence, not just lethal violence.

To understand the repertoire of violence, I suggest that armed groups (both state and non-state) should be approached as complex organizations that (in a particular setting, with more or less success) define opportunities, enforce specific norms, shape particular incentive structures, embrace some strategies and condemn others (see Wood 2009). In focusing on why violence sometimes but not always takes sexual form, we should not assume that male combatants will rape given the opportunity; rather, the sexual aspect of violence should be explained, not presumed. This approach suggests a focus on four units of analysis and their interrelationships: the armed group leadership; its hierarchy; the small unit in which combatants have face-to-face relations; and the individual combatant.

Key to explaining the observed variation are the conditions under which armed groups, small units, and individuals develop sanctions and norms that effectively endorse or constrain combatants' engagement in sexual violence. The distinction between leaderships that endorse sexual violence as an effective form of terror against or punishment of a targeted group and those that do not is of course essential, as is their ability to enforce those choices. The norms and practices by individuals and small units are essential determinants of patterns of sexual violence, but should not be assumed to be static; rather, they evolve over the course of conflict. Individual combatants enter an armed group with (possibly heterogeneous) norms, preferences, and cultural practices concerning sexual violence. The initial socialization in their small unit, the brutalizing processes of witnessing, enduring, and wielding violence, and the pressure to conform to the evolving practices of their unit may reshape those norms, preferences and practices in fundamental ways.

This approach suggests a number of hypotheses that might guide scholarly research (see Wood 2006: 330–335). *First*, where armed groups depend on the provision of support (supplies, intelligence) from civilians and aspire to govern those civilians, they do not engage in sexual violence against those civilians if they have a reasonably effective command structure. *Second*, where norms held by individual combatants and small units, either condemning or approving sexual violence, are the same and are also endorsed by the armed group's leadership, sexual violence by that group will be either very low or very high, respectively. Specifically, where armed groups reinforce cultural taboos against sexual contact with the potential target populations, sexual violence against that population will be low; in the absence of such taboos, where armed groups promote sexual violence, violence will be high. *Third*, if an armed group prohibits sexual violence against a particular population, the less effective the military discipline of the group, the more likely combatants are to engage in sexual violence (unless they hold particularly strong norms against it). Thus ill-disciplined militias, ill-trained armies of conscripts, poorly trained military police, and little-supervised service troops are more likely to engage in sexual violence than well-trained troops (in the absence of a policy promoting sexual violence).

This approach raises questions as well. To what extent is sexual violence accounted for by a breakdown in command-and-control structure and morale versus a change in norms on the part of combatants? What accounts for the emergence of an organizational structure strong enough to enforce strategic decision by the leadership? How and why do small-unit norms evolve that enable sexual violence by its members? In what conditions does military victory, on the one hand, and military stalemate, on the other, contribute to sexual violence? To what extent do international norms and law constrain the practice of sexual violence? Why are men targeted in some settings but not in others? Democracies rarely engage in widespread rape but sometimes endorse limited sexual violence: What constrains democracies, and why do those constraints not prohibit all forms of sexual violence?

The ongoing brutality in Darfur and Democratic Republic of the Congo reminds us that sexual violence remains a horrifying aspect of war, one that occasions great suffering on the part of civilians—particularly women and girls—trapped in conditions of insecurity and terror. Yet, rape is not inevitable in war, as this essay's emphasis on negative and asymmetric cases has illustrated. Understanding the determinants of the variation in sexual violence may help those UN officials, members of non-governmental organizations, government, military, and insurgent leaders who seek to limit sexual violence and other violations of the laws of war.

REFERENCES

African Rights (1994) *Rwanda*. London: African Rights.

Amnesty International (1999) *Sri Lanka*. Online at: <www.amnestyusa.org/countries/sri_lanka/reports.do>.

Amnesty International (2002) *Sri Lanka: Rape in Custody*. Online at: <www.amnestyusa.org/countries/sri_lanka/reports.do>.

Amnesty International (2004) *Sudan, Darfur: Rape as a Weapon of War*. London: Amnesty International.

Beck, Birgit (2002) "Rape." In Karen Hagemann and Stefanie Schuler-Springorum (eds.), *Home/Front*. New York: Berg.

Beevor, Antony (2002) *The Fall of Berlin 1945*. New York: Penguin.

Brownmiller, Susan (1975) *Against Our Will*. New York: Ballantine.

Burds, Jeffrey (2009) "Sexual Violence in Europe in World War II, 1939–1945." *Politics and Society* 37(1): 35–73.

Chang, Iris (1997) *The Rape of Nanking*. New York: Penguin.

Danner, Mark (1994) *The Massacre at El Mozote*. New York: Vintage Books.

Enloe, Cynthia (1983) *Does Khaki Become You?* Cambridge MA: South End Press.

Enloe, Cynthia (2000) *Maneuvers: The International Politics of Militarizing Women's Lives*. Berkeley: University of California Press.

Gertjejanssen, Wendy Jo (2004) *Victims, Heroes, Survivors*. PhD dissertation, University of Minnesota.

Goldstein, Joshua A. (2001) *War and Gender*. Cambridge: Cambridge University Press.

HRW (Human Rights Watch) (1996) *Shattered Lives*. New York: HRW.

HRW (Human Rights Watch) (2003) "'We'll Kill You if You Cry': Sexual Violence in the Sierra Leone Conflict." *Human Rights Watch* 15(1A). New York: HRW.

HRW (Human Rights Watch) (2004) "Living in Fear: Child Soldiers and the Tamil Tigers in Sri Lanka." *Human Rights Watch* 16 (13C). New York: HRW.

ICC (International Criminal Court) (2000) *Elements of Crimes*. UN Doc. PNICC/2000/1/Add.2.

International Commission of Inquiry on Darfur (2005) *Report of the International Commission of Inquiry on Darfur to the United Nations Secretary-General.* Geneva: United Nations. Online at: <www.un.org/news/dh/sudan/com_inq_darfur.pdf>.

Japanese Cabinet Councillors' Office on External Affairs (1993) (E/CN.4/1996/137). In UNESCO, *Contemporary Forms of Slavery*, Appendix 9(a) (E/CN.4/Sub.2/1998/13, 1998).

Médecins sans Frontières (2005) *The Crushing Burden of Rape: Sexual Violence in Darfur.* Amsterdam: MSF.

Mitchell, Neil, and Tali Gluch (2004) "The Principals and Agents of Political Violence and the Strategic and Private Benefits of Rape." Unpublished paper.

Morris, Benny (2004) *The Birth of the Palestinian Problem Revisited.* 2nd ed. Cambridge: Cambridge University Press.

Morris, Madeline (1996) "By Force of Arms." *Duke Law Journal* 45(4): 651–781.

Naimark, Norman M. (1995) "Soviet Soldiers, German Women, and the Problem of Rape." In Norman M. Naimark, *The Russians in Germany.* Cambridge MA: The Belknap Press of Harvard University Press: 69–140.

Sharlach, Lisa (1999) "Gender and Genocide in Rwanda." *Journal of Genocide Research* 1(3): 387–399.

TC (Truth Commission) for El Salvador (1993) *From Madness to Hope. Report of the Truth Commission for El Salvador.* Reprinted in: *The United Nations and El Salvador, 1990–1995.* The United Nations Blue Books Series, vol. IV. New York: United Nations.

TCR (Truth and Reconciliation Commission) of Sierra Leone (2005) *Final Report.* Online at: <http://trcsierraleone.org/drwebsite/publish/index.shtml>.

UNESCO (1998) *Contemporary Forms of Slavery: Systematic Rape, Sexual Slavery and Slavery-Like Practices During Armed Conflict.* E/CN.4/Sub.2/1998/13.

United Nations Development Fund for Women (2005) *Gender Profile of the Conflict in Sri Lanka.* Online at: <http://www.womenwarpeace.org/sri_lanka/sri_lanka.htm>.

UNSC (1994) *Rape and Sexual Assault.* Annex IX of the Final Report of the United Nations Commission of Experts Established Pursuant to Security Council Resolution 780 (1992). S/1994/674/Add.2 (vol. V).

Wood, Elisabeth Jean (2003) *Insurgent Collective Action and Civil War in El Salvador.* Cambridge: Cambridge University Press.

Wood, Elisabeth Jean (2006) "Variation in Sexual Violence during War." *Politics and Society* 34(3): 307–341.

Wood, Elisabeth Jean (2008) "Sexual Violence during War." In Stathis Kalyvas, Ian Shapiro, and Tarek Masoud (eds.), *Order, Conflict, and Violence.* Cambridge: Cambridge University Press: 321–51.

Wood, Elisabeth Jean (2009) "Armed Groups and Sexual Violence: When is Wartime Rape Rare?" *Politics and Society* 37(1): 131–161.

WHO (World Health Organization) (2002) "Sexual Violence." Chapter 6 of the World *Report on Violence and Health.* Geneva: WHO.

16
Militarizing Women's Lives: When Soldiers Rape

Cynthia Enloe

Prostitution seems routine.
Rape can be shocking.

Prostitution can seem comforting to some. They imagine it to be "the oldest profession." Around a military camp prostitutes connote tradition, not rupture; leisure, not horror; ordinariness, not mayhem. To many, militarized prostitution thus becomes *un*newsworthy.

Rape, by contrast, shocks. It shocks, but then it loses its distinctiveness. Typically, when rape happens in the midst of war, no individual soldier-rapists are identified by the victims, by their senior command, or by the media (if it is there). The women who suffer rape in wartime usually remain faceless as well. They merge with the pockmarked landscape; they are put on the list of war damage along with gutted houses and mangled rail lines. Rape evokes the nightmarishness of war, but it becomes just an indistinguishable part of a poisonous wartime stew called "lootpillageandrape."

Thus when we try to increase the visibility of particular rapes committed by particular men as soldiers, we are engaging in a political act. It is an act that must be undertaken with self-consciousness, for there are two traps. The first: women must be listened to, but with an awareness that their stories are likely to be complex. Atina Grossman, a researcher who has begun the tricky task of uncovering the murky but explosive history of the widespread rapes of German women chiefly (though not solely) by Soviet troops in 1945 and 1946, offers a caveat. To anyone who mistakenly imagines that it is a simple undertaking to reveal "the truth" about militarized rape, even brutal wartime rapes or mass-scale rapes, Grossman warns: "Women's rape stories were framed in incredibly complicated ways, shaped by their audience and the motives behind their telling. Their experiences were ordered and given meaning within a complex grid of multiple images and discourses" (1995: 55).

The second trap: exposing militarized rapes does not automatically serve the cause of demilitarizing women's lives. Making visible those women raped by men as soldiers is usually a difficult task; but sometimes it is a task made dangerously easy. A woman outside the military who has been raped by someone else's soldiers can be remilitarized if her ordeal is made visible chiefly for the purpose of mobilizing her male compatriots to take up arms to avenge her—and their—allegedly lost honor. Today, long after the perpetration of their wartime rapes, Indian and Bangladeshi women are still trying to make adequate nonpatriarchal sense of those rapes in the ongoing evolution of domestic and international politics of nations and states (see Menon and Bhasin 1998). The challenge, therefore, is to make visible women raped by men as soldiers *without* further militarizing those women in the process.

Militarized rape has gained visibility on the stage of international politics in recent years because of the incidence of mass rape that occurred in Bosnia during its 1992–95 war and in Rwanda during its 1994 attempted genocide. Yet militarized rapes are far more diverse. Often, as in Haiti and Indonesia, action has been required through the organizing by women for women to uncover soldiers' systematic political uses of rape (Lerner 1998; Mydans 1998). Rape perpetrated by men as soldiers has been experienced by women in a variety of forms. [...]

There are as many different forms of militarized rape as there are subtle nuances in the relationships between militarized women and militarized men. Nonetheless, they share some important common features—features that will affect not only the rapist's sense of what he is doing and of what gives him license to do it but also the raped woman's responses to that assault. First, the male militarized rapist in some way imposes his understandings of "enemy," "soldiering," "victory," and "defeat" on both the woman to be raped and on the act of sexual assault. Second, consequently, the militarized rape is harder to privatize than nonmilitarized rape is, since it draws so much of its rationale from an imagining of societal conflict and/or the functions of a formal institution such as the state's national security or defense apparatus or an insurgency's military arm. Third, the woman who has endured militarized rape must devise her responses in the minutes, weeks, and years after that assault not only by weighing her relationships to the rapist and to her personal friends and relatives, to the prevailing norms of feminine respectability, and perhaps to the criminal justice system, but *in addition,* she must weigh her relationships to collective memory, collective notions of national destiny, and the very institutions of organized violence.

In this chapter I explore just three particular conditions under which rape has been militarized. These three forms seem especially important to understand because they have demanded so many feminists' attention in recent years:

1) "Recreational rape" as the alleged outcome of not supplying male soldiers with "adequately accessible" militarized prostitution;
2) "National security rape" as an instrument for bolstering a nervous state; and
3) "Systematic mass rape" as an instrument of open warfare.

SOLDIERS SEEKING RECREATION

Militarized rape and militarized prostitution are often treated by policymakers as if they were divided. [...] In actual practice, in the world of military policymaking, officials think of rape and prostitution *together*. Providing organized prostitution to male soldiers is imagined to be a means of preventing those same soldiers from engaging in rape. It was this sort of thinking, connecting rape to prostitution, that informed the Japanese imperial government's 1930s and 1940s "comfort women" policymaking. Strikingly similar thinking undergirds present-day British and American military sexual politics. Take the Okinawa rape case of 1995.

Okinawa had been militarily occupied by the Japanese before World War II, but the militarization reached new heights during that conflict. That militarization process was both patriarchally gendered and sexualized. According to recently discovered documents, the imperial army created a total of 130 military brothels on Okinawa. The women forced to work in these establishments were both Okinawan and Korean (Katsuko et al. 1997).

Okinawa suffered some of World War II's most devastating battles. More than one-fourth of the island's population—150,000 Okinawans—were killed in June 1945. The Battle of Okinawa became the Japanese and American forces' last major face-to-face engagement of the war (Kristof 1995). Every year, June 23 is marked by Okinawans as a day for both memorializing the dead and recommitting themselves to peace (Sturdevant and Stoltzfus 1992: 246). And yet Okinawa remains today one of the most thoroughly militarized places on earth. By agreements between officials in Washington and in Tokyo, much of Okinawans' most fertile and commercially valuable land has been given over to US military installations. Five years after the end of the Cold War Okinawans played host to 29,000 American troops.

The US government created bases for its own military purposes (at the peak of the Cold War there were 145 bases on the island). Okinawa became a linchpin in the American post-World War II Pacific defense strategy. In 1972, Okinawa was returned to Japanese control—Okinawans refer to it as the "reversion"—but the American bases remained. Reversion made Okinawans "Japanese," but the switch from US control to Japanese control did not reduce militarization. Although the island of Okinawa accounts for a mere 1 percent of Japan's total territory it has been host to 75 percent of the US bases. By the early 1990s, American bases took up 20 percent of Okinawans' land (Pollack 1996a). Islanders found that their land, livelihoods, and environment were shaped by US military priorities that meshed well with mainland Japanese political leaders' strategy for cementing their own alliance with the United States. Looking back on his island's history, one elderly Okinawan summed it up this way: "We were sacrificed. ... Japan thought that Okinawa was expendable, something it could leave behind, like the tail of a lizard" (in Kristof 1995).

Okinawans born after 1972 came to think of the US bases as an inevitable part of their local landscape. The thriving prostitution businesses around the bases scarcely seemed worth thinking about. They were just there. In the mid-1990s, high school students told a Japanese teacher who conducted annual opinion surveys that the presence of American soldiers made the students feel as though they were more "worldly" than their mainland Japanese peers. Teachers found it difficult to teach classes with the roar of American fighters flying low over the schools, but the children had learned to put their hands over their ears (Tomoko 1996: 32–37).

Some Okinawans saw the American troops as a source of commercial opportunity. Restaurants, souvenir shops, bars, tailor shops, tattoo parlors, and prostitution businesses grew up around the American bases. Their owners designed each enterprise to suit the tastes and desires of American military personnel. Local shopkeepers' livelihoods came to depend on the US–Japanese military alliance. A tattoo parlor can be militarized. So can a tailor shop.

Other Okinawans, however, felt powerless in their own homeland, once an outpost for Japanese imperialism, thereafter a launchpad for Cold War rivalries. The best organized resisters were anti-bases landlords who petitioned to have their land returned. Other

Okinawans' opposition was fueled by memories of past sexual assaults by US military men on Okinawan nonprostitute women. An example was the infamous "Yumiko-chan incident," when in 1955 an American serviceman raped and killed a six-year-old girl named Yumiko; others could not forget the May 1993 rape of a 19-year-old woman by an American soldier, a man who was never brought to trial (Pollack 1995a; Mercier 1996: 28). After this 1993 assault, six Okinawan women's groups launched a petition campaign. They called for a more thorough investigation of all forms of military violation of women's human rights "going back to the beginning." Moreover, they proposed "the initiation of counseling services for empowerment in order to restore the human dignity and bodies of women ravaged by both the Japanese and U.S. military" (Suzuyo 1996: 139). [...]

Thus when a twelve-year-old Okinawan schoolgirl from the village of Kin was abducted and raped in September 1995 by two American marines and an American sailor, some local residents were outraged but not surprised. Many more were shocked into a new consciousness altogether. Comments by Okinawan high school students capture the latter:

> I had taken the bases for granted till I came to know how frightening they are, but the fact that I have been ignorant frightens me more.

> Till this happened, I had no fear nor any special feeling living in Okinawa with its bases. But through learning Okinawan history I came to understand that the bases remain just like the scars of war.

> I have had no previous doubts about the bases because they were already here when I was born, but I have felt fear whenever I heard the planes overhead. (Tomoko 1996: 34)

Many Okinawans' initial response to the rape was to call for basic reforms in the Japan–US Status of Forces Agreement (SOFA). As is the case in South Korea, ordinary citizens' lives are affected by the fine print in the SOFA. Because militarization has been such a salient issue in Japanese political life, criticism in the wake of the Okinawa rape was aimed not only at American officials but at their Japanese counterparts. Both were charged with fostering the militarization of Okinawans' lives. Local critics accused Tokyo-based elected politicians and civil servants of having reduced Okinawa to merely a convenient card to be played in their foreign policy dealings.

The 1995 rape of the schoolgirl thereby was added to a list that included loss of hearing and loss of land. Okinawan nationalists—and their Japanese mainland male-led peace movement supporters—did what some Philippine and South Korean anti-bases nonfeminist nationalist activists had done: they perceived the sexual exploitation of local women by foreign soldiers as one more reason to reject the idea that military bases were the currency of development and diplomacy. These nationalists thought about colonialism and neocolonialism. They thought about militarism. Most of these nonfeminist anti-bases nationalists, however, did not think about misogyny. They did not think about masculinity. They did not think about prostitution. They did not think about violence against women in general.

It would take Okinawan feminists to challenge this anti-bases nationalist political myopia. But these women activists would find it hard to redirect their nationalist and peace activist allies' attention from the bases to the conditions of women.

None of the three young American men charged with the rape of the Okinawan sixth grader had had prior criminal records. The three were African American men who had grown up in poor families in Texas and Georgia; they had studied hard to pass the increasingly rigorous US military entrance exams and had looked to military service as a vehicle for expanding their career opportunities (see Smothers 1995a). The women in their lives could not believe that these young men, whom they knew so intimately, for whom they had held such high hopes, would violently assault another woman, much less a schoolgirl. The initial reaction of these mothers, sisters, and wives was to suspect the US military of scapegoating, of using three young black soldiers as fodder for diplomatic wrangling between American and Japanese officials (Smothers 1995a, 1995b). Given the long history of racism in the US military, this presumption was not unreasonable (Westheider 1996; Terborg-Penn 1995).

There were added reasons for skepticism about the motives driving the seeming willingness of the US base commanders to hand the three soldier-suspects over to Japanese courts. An exhaustive exercise in investigatory journalism by two American reporters of the *Dayton Daily News* had revealed that the US military's own criminal justice system for years had been systematically tolerating the behavior of military men accused of rape and other forms of sexual assault (from articles published October 1–8, 1996). One civilian police detective, who had pursued numerous sexual assaults involving American navy personnel in his home state of Florida, had reached this conclusion: "It's like the military tries to keep it hush-hush and keep it in their own family. ... I would hate for my wife or daughter to be in the military and be sexually assaulted and have them investigate. They don't have the expertise, the training, and sometimes, they don't have the heart" (Carollo 1995).

The mother of one of the three men accused in the Okinawa rape case did not want her son to enlist in the navy in the first place. On the other hand, Esther Gill did not want to be seen as the proverbial domineering mother. One role of the military in American gendered culture has been as a vehicle for young men's departure from the feminized home. Esther Gill felt the societal pressure to accept this cultural ritual:

> I as a mother didn't want to sacrifice my son to the military. ... But I had to cut the apron strings and the day he was leaving, the recruiting office van that came to the house to take him symbolized a hearse to me. (Smothers 1995b)

It was hard for these women to hear the Japanese prosecutors' charges, which soon overlapped considerably with a friend's description and with their sons' own postarrest confessions of what they had done that day on leave:

> The three men [plus a fourth who later left] had discussed hiring prostitutes but Seaman Gill had said he had no money and proposed the rape instead. At first, the others thought he was joking, but then the discussion grew more serious. He said Private Harp, "didn't do anything to stop it. He just let things go."
>
> [The] four servicemen rented a car. At some point, Seaman Gill, who was driving, began proposing a rape. The men went to a grocery store and Private Harp and Ledet went in to buy tape and condoms. At that point, the fourth serviceman realized that his colleagues were serious about the rape and left. ...
>
> The men then drove around looking for a victim. ... At about 8 p.m., they found the girl, stopped the car, and Private Ledet and Private Harp got out.
>
> Private Harp acted as if he was going to ask for directions. Private Ledet put his arm round the girl's neck from behind and Private Harp hit her in the face. Private Ledet shoved her into the car, the two Marines taped her eyes and mouth and tied her hands

and feet. Seaman Gill drove to a remote farm road surrounded by sugar cane fields. ...

The rape was over at about 8:20. The men drove away and left the girl, who went to a nearby home to call for help. (Pollack 1995b)

There was a dispute among the three men over which of them attempted rape, which of them achieved penetration, and which of them participated in the kidnapping but did not attempt rape.

These men's pretrial stories suggest that many soldiers think of prostitution as a routine recreational activity. Buying sexual services from a local woman has to be figured into a male soldier's weekly budget. Moreover, none of the personal accounts of war or the studies of US military prostitution suggest that any particular racial group within the military rejects prostitution as a recreational activity. The only American racial characteristic of the discos and massage parlors around the US bases in Okinawa that stands out is that Okinawa entertainment district's male clienteles are less racially segregated than those that patronize the bars that used to surround the US bases in the Philippines and that still encircle the US bases in South Korea (Sturdevant and Stoltzfus 1992: 256). In addition, while there have been heated debates among Japanese citizens in recent years about the prevalence of racism in Japanese culture, Japanese citizens reacting to the 1995 rape did not appear preoccupied with the particular race of the three American men charged. Rather, as longtime African American residents of Japan explained, what seemed to matter to most Japanese was that the three men accused of rape were foreigners and that they were representatives of the Washington–Tokyo security alliance (DeWitt 1995).

Right after the three enlisted men told their stories, a senior American officer, a middle-aged, male, white, four-star admiral, reiterated the military's well-worn distinction between—and connection between—military prostitution and military rape. He spoke as if he were saying the obvious. He did not speak as if he knew he was jeopardizing his entire career. He was.

Admiral Richard C. Macke, a 35-year navy careerist, commander in chief of the US Pacific Command, held a breakfast interview with reporters in Washington. It was November 1995. The Clinton administration was about to repeat its apology for the September rape to the Japanese government in the hope that this gesture would smooth the way toward delicate upcoming government-to-government renegotiations of the two countries' mutual security agreement. [...] At the breakfast on that November morning, it was thus not surprising that a journalist should ask Admiral Macke about the Okinawa rape. The admiral, who may have believed that he was speaking off the record, replied: "I think it was absolutely stupid, I've said several times. For the price they paid to rent the car, they could have had a girl" (Pine 1995).

Feminists in Okinawa and the United States used rather different historical contexts to make sense of the admiral's remarks. For Okinawan feminists, the Okinawa rape of 1995 was the latest chapter in the story of Okinawa's militarized history and of Okinawan women's own distinctive experiences of that colonized history. [...] For many American women in public office, the admiral's prostitution-is-a-given attitude revealed a cause of American women soldiers' repeated experiences of sexual harassment: a military that tolerates (maybe even fosters) prostitution is a military that will breed male soldiers who feel hostile toward women soldiers who refuse to act like sex objects. Foreign civilian women assaulted by these male soldiers were not themselves of immediate interest to these American advocates of women's rights.

Senator Dianne Feinstein, one of California's two women senators and a member of the Senate Foreign Relations Committee, was among those women politicians quickest to respond to Admiral Macke's breakfast comments: "I would say to Navy Secretary John Dalton, your guys still don't get it. ... Rape isn't about money and it isn't about sex. It's about power over women" (Pine 1995). [...] In their turn, some American senior officials in the executive branch also had learned to act quickly, before chain-of-command sexism was translated into the prime-time media headlines. Thus Admiral Macke was soon persuaded by his Defense Department superiors to take early retirement with a demotion shortly after his undiplomatic, though revealing, breakfast statement. This rapid bureaucratic response had the hoped-for result: a manageable political wake. According to one middle-level Defense Department official, while the admiral's forced retirement did prompt "some ink" to flow along the Pentagon corridors, it did not provoke any serious reconsideration of the policy presumption that the military's facilitation of prostitution served to protect respectable women and girls from rape by US male personnel (Enloe 1996). That presumption was left standing even as Admiral Macke packed his bags.

Back in Okinawa, Japanese and Okinawan feminists were crafting their own political analysis of the schoolgirl rape. They took into account the fact that, by the 1980s, a change had taken place in the ethnic makeup of the women working in the bars around the US bases in Okinawa. Before the 1972 return of Okinawa to Japanese control, most of the women were ethnic Okinawan; 15 years later, however, most were Filipinas who had immigrated in search of work. [...] Japanese feminists had been trying to create supportive alliances with feminists in the Philippines. The "comfort women" issue, the spread of sex tourism, the movement of American troops from one militarized entertainment district to another throughout Asia, US military men's sexual assaults on local women—each issue was providing a basis for a new kind of international politics among Asian women. But Japanese women engaged in this work had become aware that, just as relations between Okinawan women and other Japanese women were fraught with distrust and inequality, so too were those between Japanese women and women of the Philippines, South Korea, Taiwan, Australia, and Thailand. Thus the efforts by Okinawan feminists to reach out to Filipinas living in Olongapo were seen as part of their wider reimagining of Japan's place in Asia and their own place among Asian women. [...]

In March 1996, the Japanese court handed down its verdict. Navy Seaman Marcus Gill and Marine Private Rodrico Harp were found guilty of abduction and rape and given a seven-year sentence. Marine Private Kendric Ledet was found guilty of a somewhat lesser charge and sentenced to a six-and-one-half-year term in jail. Barbara Cannon, mother of Kendric Ledet, held a press conference to criticize the sentences, saying they were longer than the usual sentences handed down by Japanese judges in rape cases (*Far Eastern Economic Review* 1996: 13; Pollack 1996b). Okinawan and Japanese feminists, on the other hand, told the press that these sentences, like the majority of sentences meted out by the Japanese justice system in rape cases, were far too lenient. The feminists accused the Japanese political system of being continuingly unwilling to take seriously all kinds of violence against women (Radin 1996).

With the trials over and diplomatic apologies made and accepted, officials in Washington and Tokyo went about reconfirming their commitment to a military alliance. One major concession made by the United States government was to return to Okinawans land occupied by Futenma Air Base. This changeover would not, however, entail any reduction in the overall number of US military personnel on the island (Kristof 1996). While American base commanders issued orders that soldiers had to leave the entertainment district by midnight, high-level governmental declarations made no public mention of ongoing prostitution policy or of violence against women inside or outside any of the military institutions involved. Okinawans held local referenda in which a majority of voters expressed opposition to continued US military presence. But the Japanese government in Tokyo applied formidable public relations and behind-the-scenes pressure on residents and their elected officials, ultimately paying little heed to the referenda outcomes (see Inoue et al. 1997: 82–86). Japanese officials simultaneously met with their Washington counterparts to decide Okinawans' gendered militarized future. While numbers of US personnel were being reduced in the Pacific as a whole, those based in Okinawa were set to play a more vital role in strategic planning for the new century: American forces stationed in Okinawa were to become responsible for a region stretching from North Korea to Somalia; Japan's own Defense Force was due, under the new bilateral agreement, to play a more expansive role in supporting future US military operations. The American forces based on Okinawa would continue to be overwhelmingly male. They would still have to have rest and recreation. [...]

At the same time that the declining value of the dollar against the yen was keeping visits to local bars and discos too expensive for the lowest paid American military personnel, Japanese young women from the main islands were developing internationalized consumer tastes and new ideas about "adventure." Some came to Okinawa to have an "experience" with an American man. The American sailors and marines, in turn, seemed to undergo a reconceptualization of themselves; they made adjustments now to appear not just as commercial patrons but as potential boyfriends. In this new mode, single men living on base successfully persuaded US base commanders to change their policies about guests; as of 1997, single men as well as married men could invite nonmilitary guests to their rooms on the base (Enloe 1998). The particular dynamics of militarized sexuality, it seems, change with the evolution of internationalized gendered consumerism and with the fluctuations of the international currency markets. When the dollar regains its competitive edge against the yen, the sexual politics of militarized sexuality on Okinawa are likely to shift once more. [...]

RAPE AS AN INSTRUMENT OF NATIONAL SECURITY

If we concentrate too exclusively on either "recreational," prostitution-linked rape or on wartime rape, we risk missing how rape has been used to militarize women under regimes preoccupied with what they define sweepingly as threats to "national security."

- Chile and Argentina in the 1970s
- the Philippines in the 1980s
- Guatemala in the 1970s and 1980s
- Iraq, Israel, and India in the 1980s and 1990s
- Haiti, Indonesia, Bhutan, Zaire, China, and Turkey in the 1980s and 1990s

Government officials in each of these 13 countries have been accused of systematically using rape and the threat of rape to ensure what they thought to be national security (Makiya 1993: 295–300; Thornhill 1992: 28–34; Kumar 1995: 127–142).

It is not inevitable that rape will be wielded by all regimes that see internal political opposition through the prism of national security. [...] The conditions that do seem especially likely to produce militarized rapes in the name of national security are:

1) when a regime is preoccupied with "national security";
2) when a majority of civilians believe that security is best understood as a military problem;
3) when national security policymaking is left to a largely masculinized policy elite;
4) when the police and military security apparatuses are male-dominated;
5) when the definitions of *honor, loyalty,* and *treason* are derived from the institutional cultures of the police and the military;
6) when those prevailing institutional cultures are misogynous;
7) when men seen as security threats are imagined by security officials to be most vulnerable in their roles as fathers, lovers, and husbands; and importantly,
8) when some local women are well enough organized in opposition to regime policies to become publicly visible.

If the first seven of these eight conditions are permitted to develop, then militarized rape becomes more probable, even when the country is not engaged in open warfare. By the late 1970s, all eight conditions had become entrenched in countries otherwise as dissimilar as the Philippines and Chile. [...]

Militarized rape carried on by a government's male security personnel most often has served as a form of torture. One Canadian

survey of 28 former women prisoners who had fled Latin America—
from Chile, Argentina, Uruguay, Brazil, El Salvador, Honduras
and Guatemala—found that 64 percent had been sexually abused
during their detention and 44 percent had been "violently raped"
(Hollander 1996: 68). [...]

Chilean feminist anthropolgist Ximena Bunster-Burotto is one of
the few scholars to have investigated in detail how torturers have
used rape in the name of national security. [She] takes us into the
gendered world of a national security detention center. We see it
through the eyes of a recently arrested woman:

> She is then taken to another room, where a group of men undress
> her, literally tear her clothing and start slapping and beating her
> up continuously. ... During the course of this brutal battering,
> she is given orders to sit down—there is never a chair—so she
> falls to the floor. ... In the meantime she is the target of crude
> verbal abuse and vile ridicule of her naked body. She becomes the
> pathetic jester who amuses her torturers. ... Fun is made of the
> shape of the woman's breasts, her birthmarks, or the scars left on
> her abdomen after a cesarean birth. ... As interrogations continue,
> sexual torture is increased. (Bunster-Burotto 1986: 308–309)

Rape is deliberately integrated into an elaborately sexualized
scenario of verbal and physical abuse. The rapist's (and his
superior's) ultimate purpose is to rob the woman prisoner of all
sense of self-respect, even identity. The aftershocks can last for
years, perhaps decades. Military torturers investigated by Bunster-
Burotto appeared to believe that if they could take from the woman
all sense that she could control her sexuality and thus all sense that
she could protect her feminine respectability, she would be reduced
in her own eyes to a nonperson. As a nonperson, she would do as
she was told: she would tell them what they wanted to know; upon
release (if she survived), she would return to her home and confine
herself to playing a woman's "proper" role. As in the Philippines,
national security rape in Chile was an authorized public act designed
to push women back into their privatized societal roles. [...]

WAR, RAPE, FEMINISM, AND NATIONALISM

Feminist geographer Joni Seager created a map on global rape. This
double-page full-color map of the world documents the locations
of widespread rapes during militarized conflicts of the early and

mid-1990s: Rwanda, Georgia, Afghanistan, Angola, Mozambique, Cambodia, Peru, Djibouti, East Timor, Turkey, Sri Lanka, Burma, Kashmir (India), Kuwait, Liberia, Papua New Guinea, Somalia, Sudan, Bosnia, Haiti, Mexico (Seager 1997). To this list we can now add Kosovo. Different cultures, different religions, different political ideologies, different foreign allies, different modes of warfare, different military-civilian relationships—but in each situation the rapes of women were by men who thought of themselves as soldiers.

The sheer variety of wartime rape sites may lure us into reducing the cause of wartime rape to raw primal misogyny. And yet succumbing to this understandable analytical temptation carries with it several political risks: the risk that mere maleness will be accepted as the sufficient cause for wartime rape; and the risk that the operation of particular military hierarchies will be deemed not worth examining. [...] Assuming that such a diffuse and elemental misogyny is the sufficient cause of wartime rapes carries with it yet another risk: paying dangerously little attention to the war-waging objectives to which rape is put by strategists and to the specific gender division of labor undergirding the definition of those objectives. For instance, *if* military strategists (and their civilian allies or superiors) imagine that women provide the backbone of the enemy's culture, *if* they define women chiefly as breeders, *if* they define women as men's property and as the symbols of men's honor, *if* they imagine that residential communities rely on women's *work*—*if* any or all these beliefs about society's proper gendered division of labor are held by war-waging policymakers—they will be tempted to devise an overall military operation that includes their male soldiers' sexual assault of women.

Rape was elevated to the status of a serious political issue (versus merely war's inevitable, natural side effect) during the 1991–95 war in the former Yugoslavia. This elevation was caused by carefully garnered evidence suggesting that the rapes in this war were systematic.

For any string of occurrences to be "systematic" they must be found to be not random, not ad hoc. Occurrences that are systematic are those that fall into a pattern. That finding, in turn, suggests that those occurrences haven't been left to chance. They have been the subject of prior planning. Systematic rapes are *administered* rapes.

By contrast, the well-worn litany of "lootpillageandrape" implies that male soldiers rape women the way a tornado inhales barns and tractors: anything that comes in the path of warfare, it is imagined analogously, is susceptible to warfare's random violence. Men caught up in the fury of battle cannot be expected to be subject to rules of conduct, much less the fine print of memos. Grabbing a stray chicken or a stray woman—it is simply what male soldiers do as they sweep across the landscape.

This portrait of battle breeds complacency. It blots out all intentionality. ... [But] rape in war has been part of a deliberate *policy*, not just ethnicity-run-wild.

REFERENCES

Bunster-Burotto, Ximena (1986) "Surviving without Fear." In June Nash (ed.), *Women and Change in Latin America*. South Hadley: Bergin and Garvey Publishers: 297–326.

Carollo, Russell (1995) "Escaping Justice." *Dayton Daily News*, October 1.

DeWitt, Karen (1995) "In Japan, Blacks as Outsiders." *New York Times*, December 6.

Enloe, Cynthia (1996) Research notes, unpublished.

Enloe, Cynthia (1998) Research notes, unpublished.

Far Eastern Economic Review (1996) "Japan: Three Jailed for Rape." March 21: 13.

Grossman, Atina (1995) "A Question of Silence: The Rape of German Women by Occupation Soldiers." *October Magazine* 72, Spring: 43–63.

Hollander, Nancy Caro (1996) "The Gendering of Human Rights." *Feminist Review* 22(1): 41–80.

Inoue, Massamichi Sebastian, John Purves, and Mark Selden (1997) "Okinawa Citizens, US Bases, and the Dugong." *Bulletin of Concerned Asian Scholars* 29(4): 82–86.

Katsuko, Kakasu, and the Okinawa Women's History Group (1997) "Map of Japanese Military Brothels in Okinawa." *Okinawa: Peace, Human Rights, Women, Environment* 4, February: 4.

Kristof, Nicholas (1995) "Okinawa Ponders Lessons of a Larger Invasion than D-Day." *New York Times*, June 24.

Kristof, Nicholas (1996) "US Will Return Base in Okinawa." *New York Times*, April 13.

Kumar, Radha (1995) *The History of Doing*. London: Verso.

Lerner, Sharon (1998) "Haitian Women Demand Justice." *Ms. Magazine*, July/August: 10–11.

Makiya, Kanan (1993) *Cruelty and Silence*. London: Jonathan Cape.

Menon, Ritu, and Kamla Basin (1998) *Borders and Boundaries*. New Brunswick: Rutgers University Press.

Mercier, Rick (1996) "Lessons from Okinawa." *AMPO: Japan-Asia Quarterly Review* 27(1): 28–30.

Mydans, Seth (1998) "In Jakarta, Reports of Numerous Rapes of Chinese in Riots." *New York Times*, June 10.

Pine, Art (1995) "US Admiral Retires under Pressure: Retracts Okinawa Rape Remark." *Boston Globe*, November 18.

Pollack, Andrew (1995a) "Marines Seek Peace with Okinawa in Rape Case." *New York Times*, October 8.

Pollack, Andrew (1995b) "One Guilty Plea in Okinawa Rape; Two Others Admit Role." *New York Times*, November 8.

Pollack, Andrew (1996a) "Okinawans Send Message to Tokyo and US to Cut Bases." *New York Times*, September 9.

Pollack, Andrew (1996b) "3 US Servicemen Convicted of Rape of Okinawa Girl." *New York Times*, March 7.

Radin, Charles A. (1996) "Rape in Japan." *Boston Globe*, March 8.

Seager, Joni (1997) *The State of Women in the World Atlas*. New York: Penguin Books.

Smothers, Ronald (1995a) "Accused Marines' Kin Incredulous." *New York Times*, November 6.

Smothers, Ronald (1995b) "Protests by Relatives." *New York Times*, November 8.

Sturdevant, Saundra, and Brenda Stoltzfus (1992) *Let the Good Times Roll*. New York: The New Press.

Suzuyo, Takazato (1996) "The Past and Future of Unai, Sisters of Okinawa." In AMPO (ed.), *Voices from the Japanese Women's Movement*. Armonk: M. E. Sharpe: 133–43.

Terborg-Penn, Rosalyn (1995) *Discontented Black Feminist*. In Darlene Clark Hine, Wilma King, and Linda Reed (eds.), *We Specialize in the Wholly Impossible*. Brooklyn: Carlson Publishers: 487–503.

Thornhill, Teresa (1992) *Making Women Talk*. London: Lawyers for Palestinian Human Rights.

Tomoko, Nishi (1996) "The Bases Seen by Highschool Students." *AMPO: Japan-Asia Quarterly Review* 27(1): 32–37.

Westheider, James. E. (1996) *Fighting on Two Fronts*. New York: New York University Press.

17
The Political Economy of Violence: Women during Armed Conflict in Uganda

Meredeth Turshen

I couldn't run because I have two children. I stayed in the house with them. After a while someone pushed the door open and flashed a torch at me. I realized he was a soldier. He threatened me with death if I made an alarm or noise. He then dragged me aside from the sleeping children and raped me inside my own house. I was gang-raped by four soldiers who took their turn, one after another. In all I was raped eight times that same night so I almost became unconscious without ability or energy to walk.

> *A. B., 28 years old, Pawel Angany, Bungatira, Uganda,*
> *December 25, 1997 (Amnesty International 1999)*

The soldiers were looking for rebels. One saw me. He left the others. He caught hold of me and began to strangle me. Then he raped me. ... I told my mother-in-law. My husband wanted [me] to stay with [him] but his other wives refused [to allow] him to have sex with me. I went with my children to Gulu.

> *M. L., Omel Kuru, Uganda, October 1996*
> *(Amnesty International 1999)*

Rape is the most common act of violence against women in wartime. Frequently reported as social or interpersonal violence, rape is also an act of political violence because communities reject women who have been raped and strip them of their social standing. Their tarnished reputation has economic consequences in societies that base women's access to such resources as land on their relationships with fathers, husbands, brothers, and sons. Customary and statutory laws regulate those relationships and severely limit women's political power in much of Africa. Rape affects women's eligibility (to marry or remain married) and, ultimately, their ability to provide for themselves and their children. The families, both natal and by marriage, of women known to have been raped and sexually abused in civil conflicts may reject their daughters and any children born of rape. Women cast out in this way lose their access to an agricultural livelihood in rural societies. These consequences are common knowledge and, in the context of civil war, combatants make deliberate use of this social information.

Rape is also an act of economic violence (see Rupesinghe and Rubio 1994). Civil conflicts are in part about the transfer of economic assets from the weak to the strong, and can include large assets such as mines and plantations or personal assets such as labor power and possessions. Rapists commit economic violence against a woman when they steal her material possessions and seize control of her labor. In the context of civil war, combatants use rape strategically in order to acquire women's assets, some of which are needed for the prosecution of the war or are among the reasons for it. Thus women are central to civil war strategies and rape is more than an act of individual violence.

Urgent concerns for women who are victimized and impoverished by conflict have overshadowed analysis of women's value to men in civil wars. Women's value resides in their productive and reproductive labor power and in their possessions and access to valuable assets, such as land and livestock. While attempting to put rape during wartime on the international agenda, women's rights activists found it important to emphasize the massive scope of the problem by compiling all the evidence and presenting it together. Hopefully we have progressed to the point where it is possible to differentiate the many circumstances of rape and to present a more nuanced analysis of violence against women.

This article, the second in a series, focuses on economic and political violence against women during civil war (Turshen 2001). I argue that in Uganda, as in many other civil wars, both government and rebel forces used violence systematically to strip women of their economic and political assets. My purpose is to advance our thinking about gender violence during armed conflict. An expanded definition of violence as economic, political and social allows us to disaggregate information about rape and sexual abuse during conflict and to reach for a more refined analysis (Moser and Shrader 1999: 4). The article opens with a brief overview of the conflicts in Uganda, the case study that grounds the theoretical arguments and provides detailed descriptions of the role of violence in the extortion of women's assets. The next section explores two themes:

the construction of women as property, in which the assets available for transfer are women's productive and reproductive labor; and the connections between women and property, in which women's possessions are the primary assets coveted. (Of course, armies also want livestock and land but until recently, women could neither own nor inherit in most areas of Uganda.) The focus is on systematic violence and assumes that rape during armed conflict is a socially constructed experience, that it is produced by a series of deliberate policy decisions, and that it is therefore neither inevitable nor unchangeable. After locating systematic violence against women during armed conflict in specific, historical, social, political, and economic contexts, the final section tries to identify the kinds of policies likely to protect women or mitigate some experiences of violence.

BACKGROUND TO THE CONFLICTS IN UGANDA

Recent Ugandan history is exceedingly complex and strife-ridden, and bears the legacy of colonial policies of divide and rule that developed the country unevenly and encouraged regional rivalries. Since independence from Great Britain in 1962, Uganda has experienced a series of civil conflicts. The most important of these are: the 1966 Buganda crisis, in which Milton Obote deposed the Kabaka in a coup d'état; the brutal military regime of General Idi Amin Dada (1971–79), which massacred up to 500,000 civilians; the bloody conflicts during the second regime of Milton Obote (1980–85); and the brief reign of General Tito Okello Lutwa (1985–86), from which Yoweri Museveni's National Resistance Army (now the Uganda People's Defence Force) emerged victorious (Ngoga 1998). In the midst of this intense civil war, the International Monetary Fund imposed a structural adjustment program, which devalued the currency, drastically reduced government expenditures on social services, and pressed for the privatization of government services (Khiddu-Makubuya 1994: 152–153).

Since 1986, the year Museveni took power, the Uganda People's Defence Force has faced several challenges (Allen 1996). Uganda is also involved in the current Congo conflict, but the discussion here is limited to civil wars in Uganda. Alice Lakwena created the army of the Holy Spirit Movement in northern Uganda in 1986 with Acholi soldiers of the defeated Obote and Okello regimes (both Okello and Obote were northerners). After her defeat in late 1987, her father, Severino Lukoya, picked up the leadership, while her cousin, Joseph

Kony, created the Lord's Resistance Army, which is still harassing northerners from its base in southern Sudan (Behrend 1998). Other challenges emerged in western Uganda, Idi Amin's home region, from the West Nile Bank Front (Gersony 1997), and from the Allied Democratic Forces operating mainly in the district of Bundibugyo on the Congo border, displacing some 85,000 people there.

In these wars, soldiers hold civilian populations responsible for the abuses of previous regimes or hold them accountable for the movements and actions of the enemy; this explains in some measure their extreme brutality. For women, it means being vulnerable to both sides. Rose, a northerner separated from her husband, said:

> the National Resistance Army started questioning how those [Holy Spirit] rebels could move through the villages to come and attack them. In retaliation, most civilians in the villages were victimized. The [National Resistance Army] started burning houses, robbing properties and killing indiscriminately. Even the very old, blind and disabled, who could not run, were killed. The government was convinced that the rebels were our sons, so all of us were assumed to be rebels. (Bennett et al. 1995: 107–108)

The Ugandan government, dominated by southerners who fought Obote, Okello and the Acholi, is said by Amnesty International (1999) to abuse the civilian population. Sabina, a 36-year-old kidnapping victim of the Holy Spirit Movement, reported:

> The DA [District Administrator] said that the Gulu people were encouraging the rebellion; but I felt that such remarks were unfair because how can anyone expect a grown-up rebel son to listen to his parents' advice? [The DA] said that the villagers were the ones encouraging the killing, because they won't [raise] alarms when the rebels are raping women or when they have killed. Even if one [sounded the] alarm, the National Resistance Army soldiers never responded! (Bennett et al. 1995: 99)

Bironika, now in her late fifties, said the moment one was found, whether by the rebels or the government,

> they would either kill you or force you to take them to the Aloop (hiding places). If you led them to where they wanted, they would set you free but do a lot of damage to the people in hiding. [After] you would be haunted by the deeds of the armed forces you led.

Where lives were lost, you would be hated by most of the people in the community. So people took a lot of care not to be found [by either side]. (Bennett et al. 1995: 109)

The current war in northern Uganda pits government forces allied with the rebellious Sudanese People's Liberation Army against the Lord's Resistance Army, which receives military and material aid from the Sudanese government. The Acholi are caught in a war of proxies, a war between Uganda and Sudan. The paradox of this civil war is that Kony is fighting in Acholiland on home territory and his people bear the brunt of the destructive raids and abductions. Stella, a 15-year-old abducted by the Lord's Resistance Army, described it this way: "One day I asked our commander, 'Why are you killing mostly your own people, people from the North?' He said, 'We do not kill them because they are from the North, but because they are misbehaving'."

The northern war has displaced some 400,000 people in Gulu and Kitgum, the most affected districts. According to the United Nations (2000), many of the internally displaced seek protection in camps; according to Human Rights Watch (1997: 55), it is government policy to "encourage" civilians to leave rural areas and move to camps near military installations of the Uganda People's Defence Force. But for some women, the camps afford no escape from rape (Mooney and Mugumya 1998).

RAPE AS A WEAPON OF WAR

A number of authors (for example, Rhonda Copelon, Cynthia Enloe, and Radhika Coomaraswamy) usefully describe different kinds of rape and men's motivation to rape. Enloe (2000: 109) describes the rape of women held in military prisons by male soldiers serving as guards, rape by a group of invading soldiers to force women of a different ethnicity or race to flee their home regions, and rape of captured women by soldiers of one communal or national group aimed at humiliating the men of an opposing group. I agree with Enloe (2000: 110) that militarized rape is a distinctly different act because it is perpetrated in a context of institutional policies and decisions. Militarized rape is directly related to the functions of a formal institution such as the state's national security or defense apparatus or an insurgency's military arm. In this context, what propels individual soldiers to rape (both psychological motivation and material incentives) is less important than what leads military commanders to promote rape by their forces.

The cultural significance of raping "enemy" women—women of a different race, ethnicity, religion, or political affiliation—is prominent in analyses of rape in sectarian conflicts: "ethnic cleansing rape as practiced in Bosnia has some aspects particularly designed to drive women from their homes or destroy their possibility of reproducing within and 'for' their community" (Copelon 1995: 205). Copelon is saying that, implicitly or explicitly, military forces organize rape as a means of both intimidating and dispossessing their enemies. We can take this analysis of cultural significance, which rightly decries the instrumental use of women in the struggle for power, one step further and recognize that combatants mobilize ethnic, national or religious sectarianism as justification for such extra-legal activity as asset transfers. When combatants abduct women in the same way they commandeer non-human objects (regarding both as loot or war booty), their actions go beyond the use of rape to intimidate the enemy. They treat women as assets in part because they can put women to work to create additional resources. Duffield (1994: 52) suggests that the more direct or coercive the transfer of assets, the more likely is sectarianism to be mobilized as justification.

Ugandan women understand rape as a weapon of war. Sabina, the woman mentioned above who was abducted by members of the Holy Spirit movement, said the worst thing about the soldiers of the National Resistance Army was that they forced women to have sex with them one after the other.

The DA [District Administrator] claimed that it was the women who were encouraging the killings, spreading the AIDS virus and encouraging the rebels to reach Gulu town because they knew them all. He felt that all who had taken refuge in the town should be forced to go back home [saying], "the rebels are your sons and why should you run away from your bad products?" He also said that women should avoid getting contaminated with the AIDS virus. This annoyed me and I asked him, "How do we avoid getting infected with the AIDS virus?" According to me it is the government which is intentionally spreading the AIDS virus by raping women when they go for firewood. Is raping one of the government weapons to fight the women? All these sufferings are being inflicted upon us because of our children's misbehaviour. ... The DA asked me to prove if [the gang rape] was done by government soldiers. And I told him it was true because I saw a helicopter bring them food; the rebels never owned a helicopter! (Bennett et al. 1995: 99)

The unpredictability of rape serves to terrorize the community and warn all people of the futility of resistance—those targeted as victims as well as those who might wish to protect the intended targets. The Lord's Resistance Army considered rape, along with killing and torture, "a tactic of warfare, a means of intimidation and control over the population" (Amnesty International 1997: 20). Behind the cultural significance of raping "enemy" women lies the institutionalization of attitudes and practices that regard and treat women as property. Consider these customs as examples: some societies require grooms to pay for brides, compensating the wife's family for the loss of their daughter's productive and reproductive labor value; some societies recognize only male heads of household and give men exclusive control of the family's assets, including control of wives' labor and the products of that labor; and some societies encode (in customary or statutory law) women's lifelong status as minors under the guardianship of fathers, husbands, brothers or sons.

WOMEN AS PROPERTY, WOMEN AND PROPERTY

That Ugandan soldiers regard women as property is illustrated by the following report from the Luwero Triangle (an area in the center of the country comprising the districts of Luwero, Mpigi, and Mubende from which Museveni launched his drive for power, and where the war between Obote's troops and Museveni's guerillas was most intense). An Obote government soldier abducted a 14-year-old girl and took her to his base where he repeatedly raped her. When he was transferred, he sold her for one thousand Ugandan shillings (about one US dollar) to another soldier; this soldier sold her again for the same amount when he was transferred (ISIS-WICCE 1998: 31; Florence Butegwa, personal correspondence). This next incident also occurred during the war in the Luwero Triangle:

G and her twelve-year-old classmate had been taken from their school by two [government] soldiers who, laughing and joking between themselves, had slit open the girls' vaginas with their pangas [machetes] and had raped them on the open ground outside the school. ... G survived, and was taken after several weeks, by the soldier who had raped her, to be his 'wife', when he was stationed in the north of Uganda. She had stayed there for the remainder of the war and had been forced to act as a wife: preparing food, cleaning, working on the land and having sex when it was demanded. (Giller 1998: 140)

Soldiers of the Lord's Resistance Army also treat women as chattel, and men have the power to transfer "their" women to other "husbands"; these "imposed relationships are precarious ... women may pass through several men" (Amnesty International 1997: 18). Human Rights Watch (1997: 24) reports frequent, though unconfirmed, allegations that during the rebellions of the Holy Spirit Movement and Lord's Resistance Army, some Ugandan girls and boys were sold as slaves to the Sudanese in exchange for guns and food.

The abduction of women and girls to serve as porters, nurses, cooks, farmers, cleaners, launderers, tailors, and sex workers is perhaps the crudest form of asset transfer in civil war; in this case, the asset is women's productive labor. Sex work is productive labor (that is, prostitutes can earn money in the commercial sex industry).

Girls and women [abducted by the Lord's Resistance Army] are forced to carry out the range of domestic duties that in rural Acholi society might be expected of a wife. These include cooking, cleaning, and fetching water and food. If the Lord's Resistance Army rules are not followed, the head of the [military] family has the power to punish, often carried out by caning, the number of strokes reflecting the severity of the offence. ... Forced marriage means that girls are also forced to provide sexual services to their "husbands." They are effectively held as sexual slaves. (Amnesty International 1997: 17)

Susan was 16 years old:

I spent three months in Uganda and three months in Sudan with the rebels. In Uganda, we were made to do a lot of hard work—getting rice, pounding rice, hulling rice, stealing food, and gathering wild leaves and preparing food. (Human Rights Watch 1997: 23)

The Lord's Resistance Army abducted 15-year-old P. in 1996 and kept him for seven months:

In the morning, after waking up, we will move until midday. Then we will cook. Then we will move again until sunset. Sometimes we will move all day without having food. They made you carry heavy luggage. If you could not carry the luggage, they'll kill you. (Amnesty International 1997: 24)

In general, the Lord's Resistance Army observed traditional gender roles: they trained most boys to use weapons and fight, most girls to serve as domestics. But some boys also worked as farmers and porters and some girls became soldiers.

In guerilla warfare soldiers live off the land, and women's agricultural labor is a critical asset. All farm work is manual in the absence of mechanization, and people must transport everything on their heads. Ugandan women do 80 percent of the farmwork; it is their labor that raises the taxes (in money or kind) regularly collected by armed forces in areas they control.

M was forty-two when the soldiers entered her village [in the Luwero Triangle]. ... Despite her and her husband's plea for mercy, several soldiers raped M and her fifteen-year-old daughter on the mud floor of the room while her husband and the rest of the family were forced to watch and clap. ... M and her daughter had to work for the soldiers, gathering all the food from the shambas [farm plots]. The soldiers stole everything. (Giller 1998: 139–140)

When the Lord's Resistance Army needed food, it obtained rations by enforcing contributions from villagers terrorized into acquiescence, or by looting.

Soldiers can also alienate women's productive labor by denying the enemy the benefit of women's work. They can accomplish this by amputating limbs. Fifteen-year-old Patricia said: "They would make us cut people's legs off" (Human Rights Watch 1997: 23). [Rebels of the Lord's Resistance Army attacked St Mary's College, Aboke, in October 1996 and abducted 139 girls. One of their teachers, Sister Rachele, followed the rebels and pleaded for the release of the girls: 109 were set free, 30 were detained, of whom seven escaped (see Rubin 1998).] A 15-year-old student from St Mary's College wrote that in her Kitgum village she had seen people whose mouths and ears were cut and people whose hands and legs were cut off by the rebels (Human Rights Watch 1997: 94).

Combatants may use violence to alienate women's reproductive as well as productive labor in civil war. There are two aspects of reproductive labor to consider: rape to impregnate, making women bear children for the "enemy" community, and rape to prevent women from becoming mothers in their own community, by making them unacceptable to their community or by injuring them physically so that they are unable to bear children. Under customary law in many societies, the inability to bear sons jeopardizes a woman's land rights. Because rape deprives women (and their kin groups) of control over their bodies, it is by nature a property crime.

The relationship between the theft of property and violence against women is complex because most African women do not own property outright. During the second regime of Milton Obote (1980–85), government forces punished the population in the Luwero Triangle that supported Museveni's National Resistance Army. In a study of women's experiences in armed conflict in this period, ISIS-WICCE (1998: 26), an international non-governmental organization based in Uganda, found that 97 percent of respondents reported having their household property looted and/or destroyed:

> iron sheets were removed from the roofs of houses ... household property was looted as well as animals such as cows, goats, chicken and pigs. Harvested coffee, maize and other crops were taken or burned.

Women were forced to carry the loot to the government military bases. A woman in a discussion group in Mukulubita that met ten years later to discuss the war said,

> The moment [the government forces] entered one's house, they could do thorough checking. Those who had interest in women could do the raping while their husbands and fathers would be looking on. The government soldiers were mostly fond of women, chicken, cows and other material things like clothes and mattresses. The girls would be taken as wives. (ISIS-WICCE 1998: 24)

Rape is sometimes the violent accompaniment to the forcible extortion of resources. D. described her experience in a 1996 Lord's Resistance Army attack:

I was sitting in my home with my six-month-old baby. The rebels arrived. They picked the baby from me and threw him on the ground. He survived. My husband is a civil servant. He was there along with a man who had come to buy groundnuts. The rebels started beating them. They killed my husband. They did not kill the buyer, but he is now mentally deranged. Then they started raping me. My daughter was seven years old. They burnt her with fire, tortured her and asked her where my husband had put government property. I was also beaten on the head and lost my teeth. (Amnesty International 1997: 26)

PROTECTING WOMEN IN CONFLICT AND THE AFTERMATH

The examples of women treated as property illustrate the underlying gender biases that make women vulnerable during conflict and in the aftermath. Rape exacerbates women's vulnerability because of the many social and cultural issues related to women's "cleanliness" and "good behavior." Ugandans regard non-marital sex as abhorrent; families and future husbands reject women and girls who have been sexual slaves to soldiers. On returning to their communities the women experienced shame and humiliation; some were taunted by men who said they were "used products that have lost their taste" (Human Rights Watch 1997: 46). A study conducted in early 1997 of 36 married women raped by Lord's Resistance Army or government soldiers found that 30 had been rejected by their husbands or husbands' relatives; three had not been chased away but their husbands no longer supported them and expressed fear that they carried the HIV virus (Amnesty International 1997: 32). The AIDS epidemic has made women in polygamous households equally rejecting of co-wives who have been raped, as in the report by M. L. from Omel Kuru, cited at the beginning of this article.

When marriage and motherhood define women's lives, divorce leads to economic deprivation. Many Ugandan customary laws discriminate against women in the areas of divorce and devolution of property on death. In most areas in the country, women may not own or inherit property, nor may they have custody of their children under local customary law. Ugandan society stigmatizes single women with children as prostitutes. In extreme situations, this accusation becomes reality because many destitute, socially ostracized women do turn to commercial sex work to feed themselves and their children. In this context, the economic and political consequences of violence are dramatic: surviving rape and bearing the rapist's child means loss of family, community and livelihood. Women have strong incentives to mask or hide their experiences of sexual assault, if they can. A student from St. Mary's College wrote,

> When our school closed for a while after the abduction, the majority of the students, including me, tried [to attend] various schools country-wide, but the life and the atmosphere in these schools was not conducive. We were nick-named by our fellow students as "Kony Rebels" and many teachers and school administrators suspected us [of being] HIV+, and wherever we were, we were afraid of identifying ourselves as students of St. Mary's College, Aboke, or else they would try to isolate us. Teachers in these schools asked us to be tested for venereal disease. We did not know why such was suspected of us. ... It was recently that we found out why were being suspected as AIDS victims. It was following the abduction, when rumors spread that all the students of the school were raped by the rebels. I am kindly appealing to you, the members of Human Rights Watch, that the information [that all of the] students [were] raped was false. None of us [was] raped except two girls, and those who did it were killed by their commanders. (Human Rights Watch 1997: 95)

Concepts of virtue and family honor objectify women, as does the need to protect a woman's chastity or virginity for the reputation of her family in a community and for the successful arrangement of a girl's marriage. The premise that women have property in themselves, an interpretation of human rights promoted by women's rights activists, is an idea alien to most customary and colonial legal codes in Africa. Those codes do not acknowledge women's individual rights as their inalienable property or recognize that such rights provide structure to women's interpersonal interactions in communal life. This discrimination is changing; in recent years, South African courts, for example, have interpreted individual rights to include, among other things, women's control of their own body, which includes the right not to be bartered, traded, or sold like chattel, as well as the right to have one's bodily integrity respected, free from unwanted battery and rape.

The underlying gender biases that existed in society prior to the conflict and are exacerbated by violent conflict have important policy implications. Recognizing the practice of treating women as property makes it possible to explain a widely observed paradoxical phenomenon: on the one hand, communities will fight to protect their women, and families see rape as so awful that in some cases the family's honor can be restored only by killing the woman who was raped; and on the other hand, rape was, until very recently, invisible in national and international courts and the law afforded little legal redress for this crime. In Uganda, apart from a general law on assault, there are no laws to protect battered women, and violence against women, including rape, remains common (US Department of State 1997: 10). Public opinion and law enforcement officials continue to view wife-beating as a man's prerogative and rarely intervene in cases of domestic violence. Child abuse remains a serious problem, particularly the rape of young girls (US Department of State 1997: 11).

The political rehabilitation of women in the aftermath of conflict involves reestablishing women's standing in their communities, as community status is the first instance of women's citizenship. This entails the end of discrimination, the promotion of women's rights, and the reform of outdated and discriminatory laws. Ugandan women are working on all of these issues, and Parliament was considering a Domestic Relations Bill and a Domestic Violence Bill in 1999. The UN Secretary-General has called for ratification of the Convention on the Elimination of All Forms of Discrimination against Women without reservations, and the equalization of laws for men and women, particularly those relating to property, inheritance and divorce (United Nations 1998: 21).

HEALTH CARE

Some final points may be made about how to alleviate the suffering caused by rape and forcible abduction in wartime. With timely and sensitive medical treatment, including—crucially—the option to abort safely, most women can heal from the social, interpersonal violence of rape (see Giller 1998; Turshen 2000). But the collapse of public health services in conflict zones makes it virtually impossible to meet those needs, while the disproportionate allocation of public expenditure to the military practically guarantees that resources for rehabilitation will be inadequate (Macrae et al. 1996). In the war in the Luwero Triangle in the 1980s, most rural dispensaries were thoroughly looted and rural hospitals were left derelict (Johnston 1985: 101). In the same period, hospitals in the West Nile were looted first by Amin's retreating forces, then by guerillas, and again by the Uganda National Liberation Army (Dodge 1985: 108). Whereas doctors remarked on a rise in sexually transmitted diseases

(Bennett 1985: 49), no one paid particular attention to victims of rape. This is the story of a woman from Kikamulo.

> I was 30 years old and married when I was gang raped. I had temporarily separated from my husband amidst fleeing and insecurity when the village was attacked by government soldiers. I, together with a friend and my young sister, ran into the bush where I met my first ordeal. Six soldiers found me hiding and raped me one after another. ... My relatives discovered me later soaked in blood, urine, faeces and men's semen.
>
> I was torn everywhere and developed backache. Before I had recovered, I was again gang raped at a military checkpoint (roadblock). This time I was raped by 15 soldiers. This left me shattered. I was once again torn to an extent that I could not control my biological functions. The cervix was dislocated and the uterus started hanging out. Whenever I am bathing I have to push it back in.
>
> My vaginal part and anus is separated by just a thread of flesh such that when I get diarrhoea, I defecate from both the front and behind. I was oozing water and blood. (ISIS-WICCE 1998: 28)

This woman eventually obtained some medical treatment but her symptoms continue. Her story illustrates how damaging rape can be in wartime.

In the current war in northern Uganda, frequent rebel attacks have destabilized the countryside, wreaking havoc on health care; rebels desperate to get their hands on medicines have raided scores of health clinics.

> The health care system in the north, always rudimentary, has almost collapsed. Many of those who are wounded in the fighting receive little or no medical attention; as a result, figures giving the number of dead and wounded are almost certainly too low, since many deaths and injuries never come to the attention of the authorities. Rebel raids on clinics and dispensaries have diminished the store of medicines available, and the instability has caused many health workers to flee. This has disrupted most basic non-emergency services, including immunization campaigns. Officially, there are thirty rural health units in Gulu, but as of May 1997, only fourteen remained in operation. (Human Rights Watch 1997: 55)

In the western Ugandan districts of Bundibugyo and Kabarole where fighting continues between government troops and ADF rebels, women lack access to adequate health care. According to Lillian Nsubuga of the Uganda Media Women's Association, many pregnant women have stopped going to health centers for fear of encountering rebels on the way. Some pregnant women, who live in the 47 camps for the estimated 100,000 internally displaced people that are scattered all over the district, lost their babies as they struggled to reach the only hospital in the district, and a few died along with their babies. Women who go into labor during the night and need the attention of an obstetrician are particularly vulnerable to attack. Some non-governmental organizations have started to train traditional birth attendants in an effort to help pregnant mothers who may be unable to reach health centers. Serina Biira, the acting District Health Visitor for Bundibugyo, said the district needed at least 360 more midwives but funds and trainers were lacking. The World Harvest Mission, an international non-governmental organization, trained some 170 traditional birth attendants in Bundibugyo, but Nsubuga said that rebels had killed some people and others had fled for fear of being attacked; only a handful remain (Amin 1999).

ECONOMIC REHABILITATION

The economic dimensions of violence against women are harder to address than the health consequences or even the political consequences of loss of status or standing in one's community. The economic consequences of the loss of current assets and of the ability to generate future assets resonate for a lifetime. For African women whose economic self-sufficiency is tied to their community standing, the political and economic consequences of violence are inextricably intertwined.

Women do most of the agricultural work in Uganda, but own only 7 percent of the land. A majority of customary laws maintain that only men can own land and property; consequently, when a husband dies, his family asserts its claim and evicts the widow. In 1998 the Ugandan Parliament adopted a new Land Act, which stipulates that wives and husbands have equal say in family property and in its disposal. For the first time, a widow whose husband dies without leaving a will is entitled to 15 percent of the property. This critical provision is a major advance in the economic rehabilitation of war widows; the challenge is to enforce it. Too often custom drives legal interpretation, and few women are apprised of their new rights.

Restitution of stolen property is another aspect of economic rehabilitation. The UN Secretary-General wants warring parties in Africa to be held accountable for their actions. He recommends that combatants be held financially liable to their victims under international law when civilians are made the deliberate target of aggression, and that international legal machinery be developed to facilitate efforts to find, attach and seize the assets of transgressing parties and their leaders (United Nations 1998: 12). In this respect, it would be useful for the special rapporteurs of the Human Rights Commission to document specific losses when recounting stories of sexual violence.

In the case of the Lord's Resistance Army and some of the other rebel bands operating in Uganda that never acquired land, do not control mines or plantations, and consumed most of the property they stole, victims can gain little from the implementation of such laws. Weapons are possibly the most valuable asset that men bring back from war; foreign governments often supplied those guns or rebels stole them from their own government. Sometimes these weapons are the only prize of demobilization, and they contribute to the ongoing terrorization of women in the aftermath of conflict. Ugandan women complain that the government distributes war compensation to men, who have a penchant for liquid consumption of such payments; women would prefer to receive cattle or other tangible property. Edisa, mother of ten children, a survivor of the war in the Luwero Triangle, said,

> my husband ... went to town to find out about compensation from the government, but he never told me anything. You know most men never discuss money with women—probably because they think it will spoil their plans. If the compensation were to be given in the form of livestock then maybe we shall see [it], but if it is cash then the money [will] be diverted to other things. (Bennett et al. 1995: 96)

A just compensation that would avoid these gender disputes is free education, including adult literacy classes and vocational training. Education would help to rehabilitate women, especially war widows and their children, and relieve them of the onerous burden of paying school fees. The international community could subsidize education through a tax on arms sales. Debt relief would also enable governments to abolish school fees.

REFERENCES

Allen, Tim (1996) "A Flight from Refuge." In Tim Allen (ed.), *In Search of Cool Ground*. London: James Currey: 220–261.

Amin, M. (1999) "Uganda: Women Bear the Brunt of War." Interpress Service, Global Information Network, December 22.

Amnesty International (1997) *Uganda: Breaking God's Commands*. New York: Amnesty International.

Amnesty International (1999) "Uganda: Breaking the Circle." AFR 59/01/99, March 17.

Behrend, Heike (1998) "War in Northern Uganda." In Christopher Clapham (ed.), *African Guerrillas*. Oxford: James Currey: 107–118.

Bennett, F. J. (1985) "A Comparison of Community Health in Uganda with Its Two East African Neighbours in the Period 1970–1979." In C. P. Dodge and P. D. Wiebe (eds.), *Crisis in Uganda*. Oxford: Pergamon Press: 43–52.

Bennett, O., J. Bexley, and K. Warnock (eds.) (1995) *Arms to Fight, Arms to Protect*. London: Panos.

Coomaraswamy, R. (1998) "Report of the Special Rapporteur on Violence against Women, its Causes and Consequences." UN Commission on Human Rights E/CN.4/1998/54, January 26.

Copelon, Rhonda (1995) Gendered War Crimes. In Julie Peters and Andrea Wolper (eds.), *Women's Rights, Human Rights*. New York: Routledge: 197–214.

Dodge, C. P. (1985) "The West Nile Emergency." In C. P. Dodge and P. D. Wiebe (eds.), *Crisis in Uganda*. Oxford: Pergamon Press.

Duffield, Mark (1994) "The Political Economy of Internal War." In J. Macrae and A. Zwi (eds.), *War and Hunger*. London: Zed Books: 50–69.

Enloe, C. (2000) *Maneuvers: The International Politics of Militarizing Women's Lives*. Berkeley: University of California Press.

Gersony, R. (1997) "The Anguish of Northern Uganda, Section 2." Kampala: US Embassy, October 2.

Giller, J. (1998) "Caring for 'Victims of Torture' in Uganda." In P. J. Bracken and C. Petty (eds.), *Rethinking the Trauma of War*. London: Free Association Books: 129–145.

Human Rights Watch (1997) *The Scars of Death*. New York: Human Rights Watch.

ISIS-WICCE (1998) *Documenting Women's Experiences in Armed Conflict*. Kampala: ISIS-Women's International Cross Cultural Exchange.

Johnston, Alastair (1985) "The Luwero Triangle." In C. P. Dodge and P. D. Wiebe (eds.), *Crisis in Uganda*. Oxford: Pergamon: 97–106.

Khiddu-Makubuya, Edward (1994) "Violence and Conflict Resolution in Uganda." In K. Rupesinghe and M. C. Rubio (eds.), *The Culture of Violence*. New York: United Nations University Press: 144–177.

Macrae, J., A. Zwi, and L. Gilson (1996) "A Triple Burden for Health Sector Reform." *Social Science and Medicine* 42(7): 1095–1108.

Mooney, E., and H. Mugumya (1998) "Uganda." In J. Hampton (ed.), *Internally Displaced People*. London: Earthscan: 25–82.

Moser, C., and E. Shrader (1999) *A Conceptual Framework for Violence Reduction*. Washington DC: World Bank Latin America and Caribbean Region Sustainable Development Working Paper No. 2.

Ngoga, Pascal (1998) "Uganda: The National Resistance Army." In C. Clapham (ed.), *African Guerrillas*. Oxford: James Currey: 91–106.

Rubin, E. (1998) "Our Children are Killing Us." *The New Yorker*, March 23.

Rupesinghe, K., and M. C. Rubio (eds.) (1994) *The Culture of Violence*. New York: United Nations University Press.

Turshen, Meredeth (2000) "Women's Mental Health." In M. Turshen (ed.), *African Women's Health*. Trenton: Africa World Press: 83–106.

Turshen, Meredeth (2001) "The Political Economy of Rape." In C. Moser and F. Clark (eds.), *Victims, Perpetrators or Actors?* London: Zed Books: 55–68.

United Nations (1998) "The Causes of Conflict and the Promotion of Durable Peace and Sustainable Development in Africa." Report of the Secretary-General to the United Nations Security Council, April 16.

United Nations (2000) "Update Uganda." *Humanitarian Coordination Unit* 2(1), January 24.

US Department of State (1997) "Uganda Country Report on Human Rights Practices for 1996." Released by the Bureau of Democracy, Human Rights, and Labor, January 30.

18
Regarding the Torture of Others

Susan Sontag

I

For a long time—at least six decades—photographs have laid down the tracks of how important conflicts are judged and remembered. The Western memory museum is now mostly a visual one. Photographs have an insuperable power to determine what we recall of events, and it now seems probable that the defining association of people everywhere with the war that the United States launched preemptively in Iraq last year [in 2003] will be photographs of the torture of Iraqi prisoners by Americans in the most infamous of Saddam Hussein's prisons, Abu Ghraib.

The Bush administration and its defenders have chiefly sought to limit a public-relations disaster—the dissemination of the photographs—rather than deal with the complex crimes of leadership and of policy revealed by the pictures. There was, first of all, the displacement of the reality onto the photographs themselves. The administration's initial response was to say that the president was shocked and disgusted by the photographs—as if the fault or horror lay in the images, not in what they depict. There was also the avoidance of the word "torture." The prisoners had possibly been the objects of "abuse," eventually of "humiliation"—that was the most to be admitted. "My impression is that what has been charged thus far is abuse, which I believe technically is different from torture," Secretary of Defense Donald Rumsfeld said at a press conference, "and therefore I'm not going to address the 'torture' word."

Words alter, words add, words subtract. It was the strenuous avoidance of the word "genocide" while some 800,000 Tutsis in Rwanda were being slaughtered, over a few weeks' time, by their Hutu neighbors ten years ago that indicated the American government had no intention of doing anything. To refuse to call what took place in Abu Ghraib—and what has taken place elsewhere in Iraq and in Afghanistan and at Guantanamo Bay—by its true name, torture, is as outrageous as the refusal to call the Rwandan genocide a genocide. Here is one of the definitions of torture contained in a convention to which the United States is a signatory: *"any act by which severe pain or suffering, whether physical or mental, is intentionally inflicted on a person for such purposes as obtaining from him or a third person information or a confession."* (The definition comes from the 1984 Convention Against Torture and Other Cruel, Inhuman or Degrading Treatment or Punishment. Similar definitions have existed for some time in customary law and in treaties, starting with Article 3—common to the four Geneva conventions of 1949—and many recent human rights conventions.) The 1984 convention declares, *"No exceptional circumstances whatsoever, whether a state of war or a threat of war, internal political instability or any other public emergency, may be invoked as a justification of torture."* And all covenants on torture specify that it includes treatment intended to humiliate the victim, like leaving prisoners naked in cells and corridors.

Whatever actions this administration undertakes to limit the damage of the widening revelations of the torture of prisoners in Abu Ghraib and elsewhere—trials, courts-martial, dishonorable discharges, resignation of senior military figures and responsible administration officials and substantial compensation to the victims—it is probable that the "torture" word will continue to be banned. To acknowledge that Americans torture their prisoners would contradict everything this administration has invited the public to believe about the virtue of American intentions and America's right, flowing from that virtue, to undertake unilateral action on the world stage.

Even when the president was finally compelled, as the damage to America's reputation everywhere in the world widened and deepened, to use the "sorry" word, the focus of regret still seemed the damage to America's claim to moral superiority. Yes, President Bush said in Washington on May 6, standing alongside King Abdullah II of Jordan, he was "sorry for the humiliation suffered by the Iraqi prisoners and the humiliation suffered by their families." But, he went on, he was "equally sorry that people seeing these pictures didn't understand the true nature and heart of America."

To have the American effort in Iraq summed up by these images must seem, to those who saw some justification in a war that did overthrow one of the monster tyrants of modern times, "unfair." A war, an occupation, is inevitably a huge tapestry of actions. What makes some actions representative and others not? The issue is not whether the torture was done by individuals (i.e., "not by everybody") — but whether it was systematic. Authorized. Condoned. All acts are done by individuals. The issue is not whether a majority or a minority of Americans performs such acts but whether the nature of the policies prosecuted by this administration and the hierarchies deployed to carry them out makes such acts likely.

II

Considered in this light, the photographs are us. That is, they are representative of the fundamental corruptions of any foreign occupation together with the Bush administration's distinctive policies. The Belgians in the Congo, the French in Algeria, practiced torture and sexual humiliation on despised recalcitrant natives. Add to this generic corruption the mystifying, near-total unpreparedness of the American rulers of Iraq to deal with the complex realities of the country after its "liberation." And add to that the overarching, distinctive doctrines of the Bush administration, namely that the United States has embarked on an endless war and that those detained in this war are, if the president so decides, "unlawful combatants"—a policy enunciated by Donald Rumsfeld for Taliban and al-Qaeda prisoners as early as January 2002—and thus, as Rumsfeld said, "technically" they "do not have any rights under the Geneva Convention," and you have a perfect recipe for the cruelties and crimes committed against the thousands incarcerated without charges or access to lawyers in American-run prisons that have been set up since the attacks of September 11, 2001.

So, then, is the real issue not the photographs themselves but what the photographs reveal to have happened to "suspects" in American custody? No: the horror of what is shown in the photographs cannot be separated from the horror that the photographs were taken—with the perpetrators posing, gloating, over their helpless captives. German soldiers in World War II took photographs of the atrocities they were committing in Poland and Russia, but snapshots in which the executioners placed themselves among their victims are exceedingly rare, as may be seen in a book just published, *Photographing the Holocaust*, by Janina Struk. If there is something comparable to what these pictures show it would be some of the photographs of black victims of lynching taken between the 1880s and 1930s, which show Americans grinning beneath the naked mutilated body of a black man or woman hanging behind them from a tree. The lynching photographs were souvenirs of a collective action whose participants felt perfectly justified in what they had done. So are the pictures from Abu Ghraib.

The lynching pictures were in the nature of photographs as trophies—taken by a photographer in order to be collected, stored in albums, displayed. The pictures taken by American soldiers in Abu Ghraib, however, reflect a shift in the use made of pictures—less objects to be saved than messages to be disseminated, circulated. A digital camera is a common possession among soldiers. Where once photographing war was the province of photojournalists, now the soldiers themselves are all photographers—recording their war, their fun, their observations of what they find picturesque, their atrocities—and swapping images among themselves and e-mailing them around the globe.

There is more and more recording of what people do, by themselves. At least or especially in America, Andy Warhol's ideal of filming real events in real time—life isn't edited, why should its record be edited?—has become a norm for countless webcasts, in which people record their day, each in his or her own reality show. Here I am—waking and yawning and stretching, brushing my teeth, making breakfast, getting the kids off to school. People record all aspects of their lives, store them in computer files and send the files around. Family life goes with the recording of family life—even when, or especially when, the family is in the throes of crisis and disgrace. Surely the dedicated, incessant home-videoing of one another, in conversation and monologue, over many years was the most astonishing material in *Capturing the Friedmans*, the recent documentary by Andrew Jarecki about a Long Island family embroiled in pedophilia charges.

An erotic life is, for more and more people, that which can be captured in digital photographs and on video. And perhaps the torture is more attractive, as something to record, when it has a sexual component. It is surely revealing, as more Abu Ghraib photographs enter public view, that torture photographs are interleaved with pornographic images of American soldiers having sex with one another. In fact, most of the torture photographs have a sexual theme, as in those showing the coercing of prisoners to perform, or simulate, sexual acts among themselves. One exception, already canonical, is the photograph of the man made to stand on a box, hooded and sprouting wires, reportedly told he would be electrocuted if he fell off. Yet pictures of prisoners bound in painful positions, or made to stand with outstretched arms, are infrequent. That they count as torture cannot be doubted. You have only to look at the terror on the victim's face, although such "stress" fell within the Pentagon's limits of the acceptable. But most of the pictures seem part of a larger confluence of torture and pornography: a young woman leading a naked man around on a leash is classic dominatrix imagery. And you wonder how much of the sexual tortures inflicted on the inmates of Abu Ghraib was inspired by the vast repertory of pornographic imagery available on the Internet—and which ordinary people, by sending out webcasts of themselves, try to emulate.

III

To live is to be photographed, to have a record of one's life, and therefore to go on with one's life oblivious, or claiming to be oblivious, to the camera's nonstop attentions. But to live is also to pose. To act is to share in the community of actions recorded as images. The expression of satisfaction at the acts of torture being inflicted on helpless, trussed, naked victims is only part of the story. There is the deep satisfaction of being photographed, to which one is now more inclined to respond not with a stiff, direct gaze (as in former times) but with glee. The events are in part designed to be photographed. The grin is a grin for the camera. There would be something missing if, after stacking the naked men, you couldn't take a picture of them.

Looking at these photographs, you ask yourself, How can someone grin at the sufferings and humiliation of another human being? Set guard dogs at the genitals and legs of cowering naked prisoners? Force shackled, hooded prisoners to masturbate or simulate oral sex with one another? And you feel naive for asking, since the answer is, self-evidently, People do these things to other people. Rape and pain inflicted on the genitals are among the most common forms of torture. Not just in Nazi concentration camps and in Abu Ghraib when it was run by Saddam Hussein. Americans, too, have done and do them when they are told, or made to feel, that those over whom they have absolute power deserve to be humiliated, tormented. They do them when they are led to believe that the people they are torturing belong to an inferior race or religion. For the meaning of these pictures is not just that these acts were performed, but that their perpetrators apparently had no sense that there was anything wrong in what the pictures show.

Even more appalling, since the pictures were meant to be circulated and seen by many people: it was all fun. And this idea of fun is, alas, more and more—contrary to what President Bush is telling the world—part of "the true nature and heart of America." It is hard to measure the increasing acceptance of brutality in American life, but its evidence is everywhere, starting with the video games of killing that are a principal entertainment of boys—can the video game *Interrogating the Terrorists* really be far behind?—and on to the violence that has become endemic in the group rites of youth on an exuberant kick. Violent crime is down, yet the easy delight taken in violence seems to have grown. From the harsh torments inflicted on incoming students in many American suburban high schools—depicted in Richard Linklater's 1993 film, *Dazed and Confused*—to the hazing rituals of physical brutality and sexual humiliation in college fraternities and on sports teams, America has become a country in which the fantasies and the practice of violence are seen as good entertainment, fun.

What formerly was segregated as pornography, as the exercise of extreme sadomasochistic longings—as in Pier Paolo Pasolini's last, near-unwatchable film, *Salo* (1975), depicting orgies of torture in the Fascist redoubt in northern Italy at the end of the Mussolini era—is now being normalized, by some, as high-spirited play or venting. To "stack naked men" is like a college fraternity prank, said a caller to Rush Limbaugh and the many millions of Americans who listen to his radio show. Had the caller, one wonders, seen the photographs? No matter. The observation—or is it the fantasy?—was on the mark. What may still be capable of shocking some Americans was Limbaugh's response: "Exactly!" he exclaimed. "Exactly my point. This is no different than what happens at the Skull and Bones initiation, and we're going to ruin people's lives over it, and we're going to hamper our military effort, and then we are going to really hammer them because they had a good time."

"They" are the American soldiers, the torturers. And Limbaugh went on: "You know, these people are being fired at every day. I'm talking about people having a good time, these people. You ever heard of emotional release?"

Shock and awe were what our military promised the Iraqis. And shock and the awful are what these photographs announce to the world that the Americans have delivered: a pattern of criminal behavior in open contempt of international humanitarian conventions. Soldiers now pose, thumbs up, before the atrocities they commit, and send off the pictures to their buddies. Secrets of private life that, formerly, you would have given nearly anything to conceal, you now clamor to be invited on a television show to reveal.

What is illustrated by these photographs is as much the culture of shamelessness as the reigning admiration for unapologetic brutality.

IV

The notion that apologies or professions of "disgust" by the President and the Secretary of Defense are a sufficient response is an insult to one's historical and moral sense. The torture of prisoners is not an aberration. It is a direct consequence of the with-us-or-against-us doctrines of world struggle with which the Bush administration has sought to change, change radically, the international stance of the United States and to recast many domestic institutions and prerogatives. The Bush administration has committed the country to a pseudo-religious doctrine of war, endless war—for "the war on terror" is nothing less than that. Endless war is taken to justify endless incarcerations. Those held in the extralegal American penal empire are "detainees"; "prisoners," a newly obsolete word, might suggest that they have the rights accorded by international law and the laws of all civilized countries. This endless "global war on terrorism"—into which both the quite justified invasion of Afghanistan and the unwinnable folly in Iraq have been folded by Pentagon decree—inevitably leads to the demonizing and dehumanizing of anyone declared by the Bush administration to be a possible terrorist: a definition that is not up for debate and is, in fact, usually made in secret.

The charges against most of the people detained in the prisons in Iraq and Afghanistan being nonexistent—the Red Cross reports that 70 to 90 percent of those being held seem to have committed no crime other than simply being in the wrong place at the wrong time, caught up in some sweep of "suspects"—the principal justification for holding them is "interrogation." Interrogation about what? About anything. Whatever the detainee might know. If interrogation is the point of detaining prisoners indefinitely, then physical coercion, humiliation and torture become inevitable.

Remember: we are not talking about that rarest of cases, the "ticking time bomb" situation, which is sometimes used as a limiting case that justifies torture of prisoners who have knowledge of an imminent attack. This is general or nonspecific information-gathering, authorized by American military and civilian administrators to learn more of a shadowy empire of evildoers about whom Americans know virtually nothing, in countries about which they are singularly ignorant: in principle, any information at all might be useful. An interrogation that produced no information (whatever information might consist of) would count as a failure. All the more justification for preparing prisoners to talk. Softening them up, stressing them out—these are the euphemisms for the bestial practices in American prisons where suspected terrorists are being held. Unfortunately, as Staff Sgt. Ivan (Chip) Frederick noted in his diary, a prisoner can get too stressed out and die. The picture of a man in a body bag with ice on his chest may well be of the man Frederick was describing.

The pictures will not go away. That is the nature of the digital world in which we live. Indeed, it seems they were necessary to get our leaders to acknowledge that they had a problem on their hands. After all, the conclusions of reports compiled by the International Committee of the Red Cross, and other reports by journalists and protests by humanitarian organizations about the atrocious punishments inflicted on "detainees" and "suspected terrorists" in prisons run by the American military, first in Afghanistan and later in Iraq, have been circulating for more than a year. It seems doubtful that such reports were read by President Bush or Vice President Dick Cheney or Condoleezza Rice or Rumsfeld. Apparently it took the photographs to get their attention, when it became clear they could not be suppressed; it was the photographs that made all this "real" to Bush and his associates. Up to then, there had been only words, which are easier to cover up in our age of infinite digital self-reproduction and self-dissemination, and so much easier to forget.

So now the pictures will continue to "assault" us—as many Americans are bound to feel. Will people get used to them? Some Americans are already saying they have seen enough. Not, however, the rest of the world. Endless war: endless stream of photographs. Will editors now debate whether showing more of them, or showing them uncropped (which, with some of the best-known images, like that of a hooded man on a box, gives a different and in some instances more appalling view), would be in "bad taste" or too implicitly political? By "political," read: critical of the Bush administration's imperial project. For there can be no doubt that the photographs damage, as Rumsfeld testified, "the reputation of the honorable men and women of the armed forces who are courageously and responsibly and professionally defending our freedom across the globe." This damage—to our reputation, our image, our success as the lone superpower—is what the Bush administration principally deplores. How the protection of "our freedom"—the freedom of

5 percent of humanity—came to require having American soldiers "across the globe" is hardly debated by our elected officials.

Already the backlash has begun. Americans are being warned against indulging in an orgy of self-condemnation. The continuing publication of the pictures is being taken by many Americans as suggesting that we do not have the right to defend ourselves: after all, they (the terrorists) started it. They—Osama bin Laden? Saddam Hussein? What's the difference?—attacked us first. Senator James Inhofe of Oklahoma, a Republican member of the Senate Armed Services Committee, before which Secretary Rumsfeld testified, avowed that he was sure he was not the only member of the committee "more outraged by the outrage" over the photographs than by what the photographs show. "These prisoners," Senator Inhofe explained, "you know they're not there for traffic violations. If they're in Cellblock 1-A or 1-B, these prisoners, they're murderers, they're terrorists, they're insurgents. Many of them probably have American blood on their hands, and here we're so concerned about the treatment of those individuals." It's the fault of "the media" which are provoking, and will continue to provoke, further violence against Americans around the world. More Americans will die. Because of these photos.

There is an answer to this charge, of course. Americans are dying not because of the photographs but because of what the photographs reveal to be happening, happening with the complicity of a chain of command—so Major General Antonio Taguba implied, and Pfc. Lynndie England said, and (among others) Senator Lindsey Graham of South Carolina, a Republican, suggested, after he saw the Pentagon's full range of images on May 12. "Some of it has an elaborate nature to it that makes me very suspicious of whether or not others were directing or encouraging," Senator Graham said. Senator Bill Nelson, a Florida Democrat, said that viewing an uncropped version of one photo showing a stack of naked men in a hallway—a version that revealed how many other soldiers were at the scene, some not even paying attention—contradicted the Pentagon's assertion that only rogue soldiers were involved. "Somewhere along the line," Senator Nelson said of the torturers, "they were either told or winked at." An attorney for Specialist Charles Graner Jr., who is in the picture, has had his client identify the men in the uncropped version; according to the *Wall Street Journal*, Graner said that four of the men were military intelligence and one a civilian contractor working with military intelligence.

V

But the distinction between photograph and reality—as between spin and policy—can easily evaporate. And that is what the administration wishes to happen. "There are a lot more photographs and videos that exist," Rumsfeld acknowledged in his testimony. "If these are released to the public, obviously, it's going to make matters worse." Worse for the administration and its programs, presumably, not for those who are the actual—and potential?—victims of torture.

The media may self-censor but, as Rumsfeld acknowledged, it's hard to censor soldiers overseas, who don't write letters home, as in the old days, that can be opened by military censors who ink out unacceptable lines. Today's soldiers instead function like tourists, as Rumsfeld put it, "running around with digital cameras and taking these unbelievable photographs and then passing them off, against the law, to the media, to our surprise." The administration's effort to withhold pictures is proceeding along several fronts. Currently, the argument is taking a legalistic turn: now the photographs are classified as evidence in future criminal cases, whose outcome may be prejudiced if they are made public. The Republican chairman of the Senate Armed Services Committee, John Warner of Virginia, after the May 12 slide show of image after image of sexual humiliation and violence against Iraqi prisoners, said he felt "very strongly" that the newer photos "should not be made public. I feel that it could possibly endanger the men and women of the armed forces as they are serving and at great risk."

But the real push to limit the accessibility of the photographs will come from the continuing effort to protect the administration and cover up our misrule in Iraq—to identify "outrage" over the photographs with a campaign to undermine American military might and the purposes it currently serves. Just as it was regarded by many as an implicit criticism of the war to show on television photographs of American soldiers who have been killed in the course of the invasion and occupation of Iraq, it will increasingly be thought unpatriotic to disseminate the new photographs and further tarnish the image of America.

After all, we're at war. Endless war. And war is hell, more so than any of the people who got us into this rotten war seem to have expected. In our digital hall of mirrors, the pictures aren't going to go away. Yes, it seems that one picture is worth a thousand words. And even if our leaders choose not to look at them, there will be thousands more snapshots and videos. Unstoppable.

Part V

Normalizing Terror

Normalizing Terror: Introduction

Uli Linke and Danielle Taana Smith

Images of war and terror are continuously transmitted on television, on the internet, in print media, in cinema, and recreational games to become part of everyday culture. Whether disseminated as news, documentary truth, or entertainment, the ubiquitous encounters with war require a new form of visual literacy that not only highlights the intersection of the local and the global, but also recognizes the ways in which media technologies, national histories, and political ideologies intervene in the formation of a visual culture. In Part Five, we examine how Euro-American representations of trauma and terror are commodified and disseminated by the global media market. We emphasize how optical or perceptual encounters with militarized violence are consumed by ordinary citizens to reinforce a culture of war and a politics of fear. In this panoptic global order, ordinary people, transient subjects, and those imagined as threatening enemy-others move in mediatized spaces and carceral zones, in which terror, surveillance, and detention govern everyday life.

According to Arthur Kleinman and Joan Kleinman (Harvard University), suffering is an existential condition of human experience, a defining quality of human existence. Images of victimhood are trafficked by the global media market as a master trope of trauma situations with immense emotional and moral appeal. The visual trace of human misery has been commodified, as Kleinman and Kleinman argue in this essay. Those who do not themselves experience the pain of suffering are encouraged to witness the terror of poverty and displacement, but at a safe distance, from the comfort of their homes. But since images of the misfortune of others are always within reach, visual overexposure results in empathy fatigue. In turn, media industries spectacularize human trauma to shock a complacent public to awareness, often privileging images of suffering that not only dehistoricize and depoliticize local situations but also negate a sense of shared humanity. Other modes of representation used by global health organizations pathologize trauma to measure and standardize the cost of disability for allocating assistance. These objectifications as well as the silencing censorship imposed by political systems erase the social experience of suffering. In all such instances, as Kleinman and Kleinman suggest, atrocities are reified as normal or natural occurrences in the life of distant others, thereby further limiting our capacity to empathize.

Building on these analytic insights, Henry A. Giroux (McMaster University) suggests that the tragedy and suffering in New Orleans, in the aftermath of hurricane Katrina in 2005, is symptomatic of a crisis that extends far beyond matters of governance and the incompetence of the Bush administration. Beyond exposing a crisis of leadership, the catastrophe is, according to Giroux, part of a "biopolitics of disposability." It is a politics in which entire populations marginalized by race and class are regarded as useless, unproductive, unnecessary burdens on state coffers, and therefore expendable. The pictorial record lays bare what many people in the United States do not want to see: large numbers of poor black and brown people struggling to make ends meet within a social system that makes it difficult to obtain health insurance, childcare, social assistance, savings, and even minimum-wage jobs. Following Giroux, this new biopolitics is encoded by existential and material questions regarding who is going to die and who is going to live. It represents an insidious set of forces that has stripped away the sanctity of human life for those populations rendered "at risk" by global neoliberal economies and works to mark some groups as disposable, and privileges others. Giroux calls for a language of critique and possibility in order to create the conditions for multiple collective and global struggles that refuse to use politics as an act of war and the use of markets as the measure of democracy.

The concluding essay by Nicholas Mirzoeff (New York University) situates the Iraq war within a broader vision of how globalizing capital and resurgent nation states are creating what he calls an "empire of camps." This regime, according to Mirzoeff, is "not the exception to democratic society. Rather [camps] are the exemplary institution of a system of global capitalism that supports the West in its high consumption, low price consumer lifestyle" (2005: 145). The camps in question are the detention centers for migrants and refugees that are the true symbols of this new world order. As Mirzoeff asserts: "the empire of camps has no scruples, no moral agenda, and no desire to be seen or to make its prisoners visible, although surveillance is everywhere." "The camp is the panopticon for our time, at once the site of deployment of new visual technologies; a model institution for global culture—and a powerful symbol of the renewed desire of nation-states to restrict global freedom of movement" (see Chapter 21, p.315). In this panoptic order, the spectacle of September 11 provided a legitimating context for the consolidation of the empire of camps, generating xenophobia and attacks on multiculturalism around the globe. Mirzoeff explores ways in which this order of empire is enacted at the level of everyday life, where the deployment of visual media serves as a weapon: to terrorize and militarize social worlds and to normalize carceral regimes for the new millennium capitalism. But what happens after the so-called war on terrorism has faded away? What possible futures can we envision? Mirzoeff (2002: 25) moves us to ponder whether global capital will succeed in consolidating itself in a more reactionary form or whether there is a chance that we will be able "to look transversely across" the militarized gaze, "across the color-line, and across surveillance to see otherwise and learn"?

REFERENCES

Mirzoeff, Nicholas (2002) "The Empire of Camps." *Situation Analysis* 1, October: 20–25.

Mirzoeff, Nicholas (2005) *Watching Babylon: The War in Iraq and Global Visual Culture*. New York: Routledge.

19
Cultural Appropriations of Suffering

Arthur Kleinman and Joan Kleinman

Images of suffering are appropriated to appeal emotionally and morally both to global audiences and to local populations. Indeed, those images have become an important part of the media. As "infotainment" on the nightly news, images of victims are commercialized; they are taken up into processes of global marketing and business competition. The existential appeal of human experiences, their potential to mobilize popular sentiment and collective action, and even their capability to witness or offer testimony are now available for gaining market share. Suffering, "though at a distance," as the French sociologist Luc Boltanski (1993) tellingly expresses it, is routinely appropriated in American popular culture, which is a leading edge of global popular culture. This globalization of suffering is one of the more troubling signs of the cultural transformations of the current era: troubling because experience is being used as a commodity, and through this cultural representation of suffering, experience is being remade, thinned out, and distorted.

It is important to avoid essentializing, naturalizing, or sentimentalizing suffering. There is no single way to suffer; there is no timeless or spaceless universal shape to suffering. There are communities in which suffering is devalued and others in which it is endowed with the utmost significance. The meanings and modes of the experience of suffering have been shown by historians and anthropologists alike to be greatly diverse. Individuals do not suffer in the same way, any more than they live, talk about what is at stake, or respond to serious problems in the same ways. Pain is perceived and expressed differently, even in the same community (Good et al. 1991; Morris 1991; Scarry 1985). Extreme forms of suffering—survival from the Nazi death camps or the Cambodian catastrophe—are not the same as the "ordinary" experiences of poverty and illness (see Langer 1993; Scheper-Hughes 1993; Bourdieu 1993).

We can speak of suffering as a social experience in at least two ways that are relevant to this essay:

1) Collective modes of experience shape individual perceptions and expressions. Those collective modes are visible patterns of how to undergo troubles, and they are taught and learned, sometimes openly, often indirectly;

2) Social interactions enter into an illness experience (for example, a family dealing with the dementia of a member with Alzheimer's disease or a close network grieving for a member with terminal cancer).

As these examples suggest, relationships and interactions take part, sometimes a central part, in the experience of suffering (Kleinman and Kleinman 1991). Both aspects of social experience— its collective mode and intersubjective processes—can be shown to be reshaped by the distinctive cultural meanings of time and place. Cultural representations, authorized by a moral community and its institutions, elaborate different modes of suffering. Yet, local differences—in gender, age group, class, ethnicity, and, of course, subjectivity—as well as the penetration of global processes into local worlds make this social influence partial and complex.

It is this aspect of suffering that this essay addresses by way of an analysis of the cultural and political processes that contribute to professional appropriations of suffering, processes that have important moral implications. To what uses are experiences of suffering put? What are the consequences of those cultural practices for understanding and responding to human problems? And what are the more general implications of the cultural appropriations of suffering for human experience, including human experiences of suffering? [...]

PHOTOJOURNALISM AND PUBLIC HEALTH:
PROFESSIONAL APPROPRIATIONS OF THE IMAGES OF SUFFERING

In the April 13, 1994 issue of the *New York Times*, there was a full-page advertisement taken out by the *Times*'s owners in recognition of the three Pulitzer Prizes that it won that year. The *Times* described the award-winning picture in the following way:

To *The New York Times*, for Kevin Carter's photograph of a vulture perching near a little girl in the Sudan who has collapsed from hunger, a picture that became an icon of starvation.

When the photograph first appeared, it accompanied a story of the famine that has once again resulted from political violence and the chaos of civil war in the southern Sudan (*New York Times* 1993). The *Times'* self-congratulatory account fails to adequately evoke the image's shocking effect. The child is hardly larger than an infant; she is naked; she appears bowed over in weakness and sickness, incapable, it would seem, of moving; she is unprotected. No mother, no family, no one is present to prevent her from being attacked by the vulture, or succumbing to starvation and then being eaten. The image suggests that she has been abandoned. Why? The reader again is led to imagine various scenarios of suffering: she has been lost in the chaos of forced uprooting; her family has died; she has been deserted near death in order for her mother to hold on to more viable children. The image's great success is that it causes the reader to want to know more. Why is this innocent victim of civil war and famine unprotected? The vulture embodies danger and evil, but the greater dangers and real forces of evil are not in the "natural world"; they are in the political world, including those nearby in army uniforms or in government offices in Khartoum. Famine has become a political strategy in the Sudan (see Dreze and Sen 1991).

The photograph has been reprinted many times, and it has been duplicated in advertisements for a number of non-governmental aid agencies that are raising funds to provide food to refugees. This is a classic instance of the use of moral sentiment to mobilize support for social action. One cannot look at this picture without wanting to do something to protect the child and drive the vulture away. Or, as one aid agency puts it, to prevent other children from succumbing in the same heartlessly inhuman way by giving a donation.

The photograph calls for words to answer other questions. How did Carter allow the vulture to get so close without doing something to protect the child? What did he do after the picture was taken? Was it in some sense posed? Inasmuch as Kevin Carter chose to take the time, minutes that may have been critical at this point when she is near death, to compose an effective picture rather than to save the child, is he complicit?

Those moral questions particular to Carter's relationship (or nonrelationship) to the dying child were only intensified when, on July 29, 1994, a few months after the Pulitzer Prize announcement, the *New York Times* ran an obituary for Kevin Carter, who had committed suicide at the age of 33. That shocking notice of his death, written by Bill Keller (1994: 138), the *Times's* Johannesburg correspondent, as well as a longer article by Scott MacLeod in *Time* magazine on September 12, reported Carter's clarifications about how he took the photograph and what followed:

> ... he wandered into the open bush. He heard a soft, high-pitched whimpering and saw a tiny girl trying to make her way to the feeding center. As he crouched to photograph her, a vulture landed in view. Careful not to disturb the bird, he positioned himself for the best possible image. He would later say he waited about 20 minutes, hoping the vulture would spread its wings. It did not, and after he took his photographs, he chased the bird away and watched as the little girl resumed her struggle. Afterwards he sat under a tree, lit a cigarette, talked to God and cried. He was depressed afterward. ... He kept saying he wanted to hug his daughter. (MacLeod 1994: 72)

The *Times*'s obituary ends with a section entitled "The Horror of the Work," in which Jimmy Carter, Kevin's father, observes that his son "Always carried around the horror of the work he did." Keller implies that it was the burden of this "horror" that may have driven Carter to suicide. The article by Scott MacLeod in *Time* shows that Kevin Carter had lived a very troubled life, with drug abuse, a messy divorce, deep financial problems, brushes with the police, and was manic-depressive. We also learn that he had spent much of his career photographing political repression and violence in South Africa, and that he had been deeply affected by the shooting of his best friend and co-worker, Ken Oosterbrock, for whom, he told friends, he "should have taken the bullet" (MacLeod 1994: 73). His suicide note, besides mentioning these other problems, comes back to the theme of the burden of horror: "I am haunted by the vivid memories of killings and corpses and anger and pain ... of starving or wounded children, of trigger-happy madmen, often police, of killer executioners..." (MacLeod 1994: 73).

From MacLeod we also learn that Carter had been present at the execution of right-wing paramilitary men in Bophuthatswana; much to his annoyance he had missed the master image snapped by his colleagues of a white mercenary pleading for his life before being executed—a picture that also was reprinted by newspapers around the globe. The article in *Time* reports that Carter was painfully aware of the photojournalist's dilemma:

"I had to think visually," he said once, describing a shoot-out. "I am zooming in on a tight shot of the dead guy and a splash of red. Going into his khaki uniform in a pool of blood in the sand. The dead man's face is slightly grey. You are making a visual here. But inside something is screaming, 'My God.' But it is time to work. Deal with the rest later. ..." (MacLeod 1994: 73)

Time magazine's writer discovered that some journalists questioned Carter's ethics: "The man adjusting his lens to take just the right frame of her suffering ... might just as well be a predator, another vulture on the scene." MacLeod notes that even some of Carter's friends "wondered aloud why he had not helped the girl" (MacLeod 1994: 73).

It is easy to moralize about how Carter's professional success was a result of his failure to act humanely. To balance the account, we need to remember that many photographers and journalists have been killed this year covering some of the more violent political conflicts around the world. "Hardly career advancement," cautioned Bill Kovach, Curator of Harvard's Nieman Foundation, in response to an earlier version of this paper. Kevin Carter's career is as much a story of courage and professionalism as it is a tale of moral failure. Moreover, the photograph he created provided political testimony and drove people to act. Photojournalists like Kevin Carter contribute to a global humanitarian effort to prevent silence. That is a considerable contribution.

Having learned about Carter's suicide, the prize-winning image, an anonymously public icon of suffering at a distance, becomes part of close experience. Kevin Carter is transformed from a name on the side of the photograph to a narrative, a story that is emplotted with a classic example of Joseph Conrad's depiction of Africa as the heart of darkness, the site of social horror. Carter becomes a subject in the cultural story his photograph helped write by being transformed, infected more than affected, by what he had to bear.

But what of the horrors experienced by the little Sudanese girl, who is given neither a name nor a local moral world? The tension of uncertainty is unrelieved. Only now, with the story of Carter's suicide, the suffering of the representer and the represented interfuses. Professional representation as well as popular interpretations would have us separate the two: one a powerless local victim, the other a powerful foreign professional [or phrased differently] the "taking" of victimized social subjects by the more powerful photographer, "a privileged observer"—the "eye of power" (Mitchell 1994: 288, 324,

365, 420–421). Yet, the account of Carter's suicide creates a more complex reality. The disintegration of the subject/object dichotomy implicates us all. The theories of a variety of academic professions may help explain how Carter got us into this situation of bringing the global into the local, but they fail to explain how we will get ourselves out of the moral complexities he has intensified for us by projecting the local into the global (Hannerz 1993a, 1993b). We are left only with the unsentimentalized limits of the human condition— a silence seemingly without meaning, possibly without solace. And still the world calls for images: the mixture of moral failures and global commerce is here to stay (see Cavell 1994: 116).

Without disputing the photograph's immense achievement, it is useful to explore its moral and political assumptions (Kleinman and Desjarlais 1995; Desjarlais and Kleinman 1994; Kleinman and Desjarlais 1994). There is, for example, the unstated idea that this group of unnamed Africans (are they Nuer or Dinka?) cannot protect their own. They must be protected, as well as represented, by others. The image of the subaltern conjures up an almost neocolonial ideology of failure, inadequacy, passivity, fatalism, and inevitability. Something must be done, and it must be done soon, but from outside the local setting. The authorization of action through an appeal for foreign aid, even foreign intervention, begins with an evocation of indigenous absence, an erasure of local voices and acts.

Suffering is presented as if it existed free of local people and local worlds. The child is alone. This, of course, is not the way that disasters, illnesses, and deaths are usually dealt with in African or other non-western societies, or, for that matter, in the west. Yet, the image of famine is culturally represented in an ideologically western mode: it becomes the experience of a lone individual (see Mintz 1984). The next step, naturally, is to assume that there are no local institutions or programs. That assumption almost invariably leads to the development of regional or national policies that are imposed on local worlds. When those localities end up resisting or not complying with policies and programs that are meant to assist them, such acts are then labeled irrational or self-destructive. The local world is deemed incompetent, or worse.

This may seem too thoroughgoing a critique. Clearly, witnessing and mobilization can do good, but they work best when they take seriously the complexity of local situations and work through local institutions. Moral witnessing also must involve a sensitivity to other, unspoken moral and political assumptions. Watching and reading about suffering, especially suffering that exists somewhere else, has, as we have already noted, become a form of entertainment. Images of trauma are part of our political economy. Papers are sold, television programs gain audience share, careers are advanced, jobs are created, and prizes are awarded through the appropriation of images of suffering. Kevin Carter won the Pulitzer Prize, but his victory, substantial as it was, was won because of the misery (and probable death) of a nameless little girl. That more dubious side of the appropriation of human misery in the globalization of cultural processes is what must be addressed.

One message that comes across from viewing suffering from a distance is that for all the havoc in western society, we are somehow better than this African society. We gain in moral status and some of our organizations gain financially and politically, while those whom we represent, or appropriate, remain where they are, moribund, surrounded by vultures. This "consumption" of suffering in an era of so-called "disordered capitalism" is not so very different from the late nineteenth-century view that the savage barbarism in pagan lands justified the valuing of our own civilization at a higher level of development—a view that authorized colonial exploitation. Both are forms of cultural representation in which the moral, the commercial, and the political are deeply involved in each other. The point is that the image of the vulture and the child carries cultural entailments, including the brutal historical genealogy of colonialism as well as the dubious cultural baggage of the more recent programs of "modernization" and globalization (of markets and financing), that have too often worsened human problems in sub-Saharan Africa (Desjarlais et al. 1995: 15–33).

Another effect of the postmodern world's political and economic appropriation of images of such serious forms of suffering at a distance is that it has desensitized the viewer. Viewers are overwhelmed by the sheer number of atrocities. There is too much to see, and there appears to be too much to do anything about. Thus, our epoch's dominating sense that complex problems can be neither understood nor fixed works with the massive globalization of images of suffering to produce moral fatigue, exhaustion of empathy, and political despair.

The appeal of experience is when we see on television a wounded Haitian, surrounded by a threatening crowd, protesting against accusations that he is a member of a murderous paramilitary organization. The dismay of images is when we are shown that the man and the crowd are themselves surrounded by photographers, whose participation helps determine the direction the event will take

(Webb and Unger 1994: 50–53). The appeal of experience and the dismay of images fuse together in Kevin Carter's photograph, and in the story of his suicide. The photograph is a professional transformation of social life, a politically relevant rhetoric, a constructed form that ironically naturalizes experience. As Michael Shapiro (1988: xii) puts it,

> ... representation is the absence of presence, but because the real is never wholly present to us—how it is real for us is always mediated through some representational practice—we lose something when we think of representation as mimetic. What we lose, in general, is insight into the institutions and actions and episodes through which the real has been fashioned, a fashioning that has not been so much a matter of immediate acts of consciousness by persons in everyday life as it has been a historically developing kind of imposition, now largely institutionalized in the prevailing kinds of meanings deeply inscribed on things, persons, and structures.

This cultural process of professional and political transformation is crucial to the way we come to appreciate human problems and to prepare policy responses. That appreciation and preparation far too often are part of the problem; they become iatrogenic.

PATHOLOGIZING SOCIAL SUFFERING

When those whose suffering is appropriated by the media cross over to places of refuge and safety, they often must submit to yet another type of arrogation (Kleinman and Desjarlais 1995). Their memories (their intimately interior images) of violation are made over into *trauma stories*. These trauma stories then become the currency, the symbolic capital, with which they enter exchanges for physical resources and achieve the status of political refugee. Increasingly, those complicated stories, based in real events, yet reduced to a core cultural image of *victimization* (a postmodern hallmark), are used by health professionals to rewrite social experience in medical terms. The person who undergoes torture first becomes a victim, an image of innocence and passivity, someone who cannot represent himself, who must be represented. Then he becomes a patient, specifically a patient with a quintessential fin de siècle disorder (that is, posttraumatic stress disorder) (Young 1996, 1997). Indeed, to receive even modest public assistance it may be necessary to undergo a sequential transformation from one who experiences, who suffers political terror to one who is a victim of political violence to one who is sick, who has a disease. Because of the practical political and financial importance of such transformations, the violated themselves may want, and even seek out, the re-imaging of their condition so that they can obtain the moral as well as the financial benefits of being ill. We need to ask, however, what kind of cultural process underpins the transformation of a victim of violence to someone with a pathology? What does it mean to give those traumatized by political violence the social status of a patient? And in what way does the imagery of victimization as the pathology of an individual alter the experience—collective as well as individual—so that its lived meaning as moral and political memory, perhaps even resistance, is lost and is replaced by "guilt," "paranoia," and a "failure to cope"? [...]

In recent years, experts in international health and social development, for very appropriate reasons, have sought to develop new ways of configuring the human misery that results from chronic disease and disability. Faced with the problem of increasing numbers of cases of chronic illness—diabetes, heart disease, cancer, asthma, depression, schizophrenia—as populations live long enough to experience degenerative diseases and other health conditions of later life, health professionals have realized that mortality rates are unable to represent the distress, disablement, and especially the *cost* of these conditions. Therefore, they have sought to construct new metrics to measure the suffering from chronic illness, which in medical and public health argot is called "morbidity." These metrics can be applied, the experts claim, to measure the burden of suffering in "objective" terms that can enable the just allocation of resources to those most in need (Kleinman 1994).

One metric of suffering recently developed by the World Bank has gained wide attention and considerable support (World Bank 1993). [...] This metric of suffering was constructed by assigning degrees of suffering to years of life and types of disability. The assumption is that values will be universal. They will not vary across worlds as greatly different as China, India, sub-Saharan Africa, and North America. They will also be reducible to measures of economic cost. That expert panels rate blindness with a severity of 0.6, while female reproductive system disorders are evaluated at one third the severity, is surely a cause for questioning whether gender bias is present, but more generally it should make one uneasy with the means by which evaluations of severity and its cost can be validly standardized across different societies, social classes, age cohorts, genders, ethnicities, and occupational groups.

The effort to develop an objective indicator may be important for rational choice concerning allocation of scarce resources among different policies and programs. [...] But it is equally important to question what are the limits and the potential dangers of configuring social suffering as an economic indicator. The moral and political issues we have raised in this essay cannot be made to fit into this econometric index. Likewise, the index is unable to map cultural, ethnic, and gender differences. Indeed, it assumes homogeneity in the evaluation and response to illness experiences, which belies an enormous amount of anthropological, historical, and clinical evidence of substantial differences in each of these domains (see Rothman 1994; Morris 1991). Professional categories are privileged over lay categories, yet the experience of illness is expressed in lay terms.

Furthermore, the index focuses on the individual sufferer, denying that suffering is a social experience. This terribly thin representation of a thickly human condition may in time also thin out the social experience of suffering. It can do this by becoming part of the apparatus of cultural representation that creates societal norms, which in turn shapes the social role and social behavior of the ill, and what should be the practices of families and health-care providers. The American cultural rhetoric, for example, is changing from the language of caring to the language of efficiency and cost; it is not surprising to hear patients themselves use this rhetoric to describe their problems. Thereby, the illness experience, for some, may be transformed from a consequential moral experience into a merely technical inexpediency. [...]

Economic indexes of health conditions have their appropriate uses, of course. We need to formulate health and social policy with respect to priorities for limited resources. We need valid economic indexes of illnesses and their social consequences. [Metrics] can be useful in health-care reform and should not become, as they seemed in much of the recent debate on health-care reform in the United States, the only authorized construction of suffering for policy and programs. These economic measures need to be complemented by narratives, ethnographies, and social histories that speak to the complex, even contradictory, human side of suffering. Without this other side, the economistic measurement of suffering leaves out most of what is at stake for peoples globally.

ABSENT IMAGES: THE POLITICAL RHETORIC OF OPPRESSION

It is necessary to balance the account of the globalization of commercial and professional images with a vastly different and even more dangerous cultural process of appropriation: the totalitarian state's erasure of social experiences of suffering through the suppression of images. Here the possibility of moral appeal through images of human misery is prevented, and it is their absence that is the source of existential dismay.

Such is the case with the massive starvation in China from 1959 to 1961. This story was not reported at the time even though more than 30 million Chinese died in the aftermath of the ruinous policies of the Great Leap Forward, the perverse effect of Mao's impossible dream of forcing immediate industrialization on peasants. Accounts of this, the world's most devastating famine, were totally suppressed; no stories or pictures of the starving or the dead were published.

An internal report on the famine was made by an investigating team for the Central Committee of the Chinese Communist Party. It was based on a detailed survey of an extremely poor region of Anwei Province that was particularly brutally affected. The report includes this numbing statement by Wei Wu-ji, a local peasant leader from Anwei:

Originally there were 5,000 people in our commune, now only 3,200 remain. When the Japanese invaded we did not lose this many: we at least could save ourselves by running away! This year there's no escape. We die shut up in our own houses. Of my 6 family members, 5 are already dead, and I am left to starve, and I'll not be able to stave off death for long. (Central Committee 1961: 188–191)

Wei Wu-ji continued:

Wang Jia-feng from West Springs County reported that cases of eating human meat were discovered. Zhang Sheng-jiu said, "Only an evil man could do such a thing!" Wang Jia-feng said, "In 1960, there were 20 in our household, ten of them died last year. My son told his mother 'I'll die of hunger in a few days.'" And indeed he did. (Central Committee 1961: 188–91)

The report also includes a graphic image by Li Qin-ming, from Wudian County, Shanwang Brigade:

In 1959, we were prescheduled to deliver 58,000 jin of grain to the State, but only 35,000 jin were harvested, hence we only turned over 33,000 jin, which left 2,000 jin for the commune. We really have nothing to eat. The peasants eat hemp leaves, anything they can possibly eat. In my last report after I wrote, "We have nothing to eat," the Party told me they wanted to remove my name from the Party Roster. Out of a population of 280, 170 died. In our family of five, four of us have died leaving only myself. Should I say that I'm not broken hearted? (Central Committee 1961: 188–91)

Chen Zhang-yu, from Guanyu County, offered the investigators this terrible image:

Last spring the phenomenon of cannibalism appeared. Since Comrade Chao Wu-chu could not come up with any good ways of prohibiting it, he put out the order to secretly imprison those who seemed to be at death's door to combat the rumors. He secretly imprisoned 63 people from the entire country. Thirty-three died in prison. (Central Committee 1961: 188–91)

The official report is thorough and detailed. It is classified *neibu*, restricted use only. To distribute it is to reveal state secrets. Presented publicly it would have been, especially if it had been published in the 1960s, a fundamental critique of the Great Leap, and a moral and political delegitimation of the Chinese Communist Party's claim to have improved the life of poor peasants. Even today the authorities regard it as dangerous. The official silence is another form of appropriation. It prevents public witnessing. It forges a secret history, an act of political resistance through keeping alive the memory of things denied (see Scott 1992; Watson 1994). The totalitarian state rules by collective forgetting, by denying the collective experience of suffering, and thus creates a culture of terror.

The absent image is also a form of political appropriation; public silence is perhaps more terrifying than being overwhelmed by public images of atrocity. Taken together the two modes of appropriation delimit the extremes in this cultural process.

CODA

Our critique of appropriations of suffering that do harm does not mean that no appropriations are valid. To conclude that would be to undermine any attempt to respond to human misery. It would be much more destructive than the problem we have identified; it would paralyze social action. We must draw upon the images of human suffering in order to identify human needs and to craft humane responses.

Yet, to do so, to develop valid appropriations, we must first make sure that the biases of commercial emphasis on profit-making, the partisan agendas of political ideologies, and the narrow technical interests that serve primarily professional groups are understood and their influence controlled. The first action, then, is critical self-reflection on the purposes of policies and the effects of programs. We take that to be a core component of programs of ethics in the professions. Perhaps a more difficult action is to lift the veil on the taken-for-granted cultural processes within which those policies and programs, no matter how well-intended, are inevitably, and usually unintentionally, taken up and exploited. The idea that the first impulse of social and health-policy experts should be to historicize the issue before them and to critique the cultural mechanisms of action at hand goes against the grain of current practice. Nonetheless, that is a chief implication of our analysis. The starting point of policymakers and program-builders needs to be the understanding that they can (and often unwillingly do) do harm. Because that potential for harm lies latent in the institutional structures that have been authorized to respond to human problems that work behind even the best intentioned professionals, "experts" must be held responsible to define how those latent institutional effects can be controlled.

Humanizing the level at which interventions are organized means focusing planning and evaluation on the interpersonal space of suffering, the local, ethnographic context of action. This requires not only engagement with what is at stake for participants in those local worlds, but bringing those local participants (not merely national experts) into the process of developing and assessing programs. Such policymaking from the ground up can only succeed, however, if these local worlds are more effectively projected into national and international discourses on human problems. (This may represent the necessary complement to the globalization of local images. Perhaps it should be called the global representation of local contexts.) To do so requires a reformulation of the indexes and instruments of policy. Those analytic tools need to authorize deeper depictions of the local (including how the global—for example, displacement, markets, technology—enters into the local). And those methodologies of policy must engage the existential side of social life. How to reframe the language of policies and programs so that large-scale social forces are made to relate to biography and local history will require interdisciplinary engagements that bring alternative perspectives from the humanities, the social sciences, and the health sciences to bear on human problems. The goal is to reconstruct the object of inquiry and the purposes of practice.

Ultimately, we will have to engage the more ominous aspects of globalization, such as the commercialization of suffering, the commodification of experiences of atrocity and abuse, and the pornographic uses of degradation. Violence in the media, and its relation to violence in the streets and in homes, is already a subject that has attracted serious attention from communities and from scholars. Regarding the even more fundamental cultural question of how social experience is being transformed in untoward ways, the first issue would seem to be to develop historical, ethnographic, and narrative studies that provide a more powerful understanding of the cultural processes through which the global regime of disordered capitalism alters the connections between collective experience and subjectivity, so that moral sensibility, for example, diminishes or becomes something frighteningly different: promiscuous, gratuitous, unhinged from responsibility and action. There is a terrible legacy here that needs to be contemplated. The transformation of epochs is as much about changes in social experience as shifts in social structures and cultural representations; indeed, the three sites of social transformation are inseparable. Out of their triangulation, subjectivity too transmutes. The current transformation is no different; yet perhaps we see more clearly the hazards of the historical turn that we are now undertaking. Perhaps all along we have been wrong to consider existential conditions as an ultimate constraint limiting the moral dangers of civilizational change. [...]

REFERENCES

Boltanski, Luc (1993) *La Souffrance a Distance*. Paris: Metailie.

Bourdieu, Pierre (ed.) (1993) *La Misère du Monde*. Paris: Editions du Seuil.

Cavell, Stanley (1994) *A Pitch of Philosophy*. Cambridge MA: Harvard University Press.

Central Committee, Chinese Communist Party (1961) "Internal Report", Annals for Feng Yang County: 188–191.

Desjarlais, Robert, Leon Eisenberg, Byron Good, and Arthur Kleinman (eds.) (1995) *World Mental Health*. New York: Oxford University Press.

Desjarlais, Robert, and Arthur Kleinman (1994) "Violence and Demoralization in the New World Disorder." *Anthropology Today* 10(5): 9–12.

Dreze, Jean, and Amartya Sen (1991) *Hunger and Public Action*. New York: Oxford University Press.

Good, Mary-Jo DelVecchio, Paul E. Brodwin, Byron J. Good, and Arthur Kleinman (eds.) (1991) *Pain as Human Experience*. Berkeley: University of California Press.

Hannerz, Ulf (1993a) "Mediations in the Global Ecumene." In Gisli Palsson (ed.), *Beyond Boundaries*. Providence: Berg: 41–57.

Hannerz, Ulf (1993b) "When Culture is Everywhere." *Ethnos* 58: 95–111.

Keller, Bill (1994) "Kevin Carter, a Pulitzer Winner for the Sudan Photo, is Dead at 33." *New York Times*, July 29: 128. Online at: <http://www.nytimes.com/1994/07/29/world/kevin-carter-a-pulitzer-winner-for-sudan-photo-is-dead-at-33.html>.

Kleinman, Arthur (1994) "A Critique of Objectivity in International Health." In Lincoln C. Chen, Arthur Kleinman, and Norma C. Ware (eds.), *Health and Social Change in International Perspective*. Boston: Harvard University Press: 68–92.

Kleinman, Arthur (ed.) (1995) *Writing at the Margin*. Berkeley: University of California Press.

Kleinman, Arthur, and Robert Desjarlais (1994) "Ni patients ni victimes." *ACTES De La Recherche en sciences sociales* 104: 56–63.

Kleinman, Arthur, and Robert Desjarlais (1995) "Violence, Culture, and the Politics of Trauma." In Arthur Kleinman (ed.), *Writing at the Margin*. Berkeley: University of California Press: 173–190.

Kleinman, Arthur, and Joan Kleinman (1991) "Suffering and its Professional Transformations." *Culture, Medicine, and Psychiatry* 15(3): 275–301.

Langer, Lawrence (1993) *Holocaust Testimonies*. New Haven: Yale University Press.

MacLeod, Scott (1994) "The Life and Death of Kevin Carter." *Time*, September 12: 70–73.

Mintz, Alan (1984) *Hurban: Response to Catastrophe in Hebrew Literature*. New York: Columbia University Press.

Mitchell, W. J. T. (1994) *Picture Theory*. Chicago: University of Chicago Press.

Morris, David (1991) *The Culture of Pain*. Berkeley: University of California Press.

New York Times (1993), Pulitzer Prize-winning photograph of starving child in Sudan, by Kevin Carter, March 26: A3.

Rothman, Sheila (1994) *Living in the Shadow of Death*. New York: Basic Books.

Scarry, Elaine (1985) *The Body in Pain*. New York: Oxford University Press.

Scheper-Hughes, Nancy (1993) *Death Without Weeping*. Berkeley: University of California Press.

Scott, James C. (1992) *Domination and the Arts of Resistance*. New Haven: Yale University Press.

Shapiro, Michael J. (1988) *The Politics of Representation*. Madison: University of Wisconsin Press.

Watson, Rubie (1994) "Memory, History, and Opposition under State Socialism." In Rubie Watson (ed.) *Memory, History, and Opposition under State Socialism*. Santa Fe: School of American Research Press: 1–20.

Webb, Alex, and David C. Unger (1994) "Taking Haiti." *New York Times Magazine*, October 23: 50–53.

World Bank (1993) *World Development Report 1993*. New York: Oxford University Press.

Young, Allan (1996) "Suffering and the Origins of Traumatic Memory." *Daedalus* 125(1): 245–260.

Young, Allan (1997) *The Harmony of Illusions*. Princeton: Princeton University Press.

20
The Biopolitics of Disposability

Henry A. Giroux

Emmett Till's body arrived home in Chicago in September 1955. White racists in Mississippi had tortured, mutilated, and killed the young 14-year-old African American boy for whistling at a white woman. Determined to make visible the horribly mangled face and twisted body of the child as an expression of racial hatred and killing, Mamie Till, the boy's mother, insisted that the coffin, interred at the A. A. Ranier Funeral Parlor on the south side of Chicago, be left open for four long days. While mainstream news organizations ignored the horrifying image, *Jet* magazine published an unedited photo of Till's face taken while he lay in his coffin. Till had been castrated and shot in the head; his tongue had been cut out; and a blow from an ax had practically severed his nose from his face—all of this done to a teenage boy who came to bear the burden of the inheritance of slavery and the inhuman pathology that drives its racist imaginary. The photos not only made visible the violent effects of the racial state; they also fuelled massive public anger, especially among blacks, and helped to launch the Civil Rights Movement.

From the beginning of the Civil Rights Movement to the war in Vietnam, images of human suffering and violence provided the grounds for a charged political indignation and collective sense of moral outrage inflamed by the horrors of poverty, militarism, war, and racism—eventually mobilizing widespread opposition to these anti-democratic forces. Of course, the seeds of a vast conservative counter-revolution were already well underway as images of a previous era—"whites only" signs, segregated schools, segregated housing, and nonviolent resistance—gave way to a troubling iconography of cities aflame, mass rioting, and armed black youth who came to embody the very precepts of lawlessness, disorder, and criminality. Building on the reactionary rhetoric of Barry Goldwater and Richard Nixon, Ronald Reagan took office in 1980 with a trickledown theory that would transform corporate America and a corresponding visual economy. The twin images of the young black male "gangsta" and his counterpart, the "welfare queen," became the primary vehicles for selling the American public on the need to dismantle the welfare state, ushering in an era of unprecedented deregulation, downsizing, privatization, and regressive taxation. The propaganda campaign was so successful that George H. W. Bush could launch his 1988 presidential bid with the image of Willie Horton, an African American male convicted of rape and granted early release, and succeed in trouncing his opponent with little public outcry over the overtly racist nature of the campaign. By the beginning of the 1990s, global media consolidation, coupled with the outbreak of a new war that encouraged hyper-patriotism and a rigid nationalism, resulted in a tightly controlled visual landscape—managed both by the Pentagon and by corporate-owned networks—that delivered a paucity of images representative of the widespread systemic violence. Selectively informed and cynically inclined, American civic life became more sanitized, controlled, and regulated.

Hurricane Katrina may have reversed the self-imposed silence of the media and public numbness in the face of terrible suffering. Fifty years after the body of Emmett Till was plucked out of the mud-filled waters of the Tallahatchie River, another set of troubling visual representations has appeared that has both shocked and shamed the United States. In the aftermath of Hurricane Katrina, grotesque images of bloated corpses floating in the rotting waters that flooded the streets of New Orleans circulated throughout the mainstream media. What first appeared to be a natural catastrophe soon degenerated into a social debacle as further images revealed, days after Katrina had passed over the Gulf Coast, hundreds of thousands of poor people, mostly blacks, some Latinos, many elderly, and a few white people, packed into the New Orleans Superdome and the city's Convention Center, stranded on rooftops, or isolated on patches of dry highway without any food, water, or places to wash, urinate, or find relief from the scorching sun. Weeks passed as the flood waters gradually receded and the military and privatized rental-armies gained control of the city, and more images of dead bodies appeared on the national and global media. TV cameras rolled as bodies reappeared on dry patches of land as people stood by indifferently eating their lunch or occasionally snapping a photograph. The world watched in disbelief as images of bloated, decomposing bodies left on the street, or in some cases on the porches of once-flooded homes, were broadcast on CNN. A body that had been found on a dry stretch of Union Street in the downtown district of New Orleans remained on the street for four days. Alcede Jackson's 72-year-old black body was left on the porch of his house for two weeks. Various media soon reported that over 154 bodies had been found in hospitals and nursing homes. The *New York Times* wrote that "the collapse of one of society's most basic covenants—to care for the helpless—suggests that the elderly and critically ill plummeted to the bottom of priority lists as calamity engulfed New Orleans" (Rohde et al. 2005). Dead people, mostly poor African Americans, left uncollected in the streets, on porches, in hospitals, nursing homes, electric wheelchairs, and collapsed houses prompted some people to claim that America had become like a "Third World country" while others argued that New Orleans resembled a "Third World Refugee Camp" (Brooks 2005). There were now, irrefutably, two Gulf crises.

The images of dead bodies kept reappearing in New Orleans, refusing to go away. For many, the bodies of the poor, black, brown, elderly, and sick came to signify what the battered body of Emmett Till once unavoidably revealed, and America was forced to confront these disturbing images and the damning questions behind the images. The Hurricane Katrina disaster, like the Emmett Till affair, revealed a vulnerable and destitute segment of the nation's citizenry that conservatives not only refused to see but had spent the better part of two decades demonizing. But like the incessant beating of Poe's tell-tale heart, cadavers have a way of insinuating themselves into consciousness, demanding answers to questions that aren't often asked. The body of Emmett Till symbolized an overt white supremacy and racialized state organized against the threat that black men (apparently of all sizes and ages) posed to white women. But the black bodies of the dead and walking wounded in New Orleans in 2005 revealed a different image of the "racial state" (see Goldberg 2001), a different modality of state terrorism marked less by an overt form of white racism than by a highly mediated displacement of race as a central concept for understanding both Katrina and its place in the broader history of US racism. That is, while Emmett Till's body insisted upon a public recognition of the violence of white supremacy, the decaying black bodies floating in the waters of the Gulf Coast represented a return of race against the media and public insistence that this disaster was more about class than race, more about the shameful and growing presence of poverty and society's failure to help those in need. Till's body allowed the racism that destroyed it to be made visible, to speak to the systemic character of American racial injustice. The bodies of the Katrina victims could not speak with the same directness to the state of American racist violence, but they did reveal and shatter the conservative fiction of living in a color-blind society.

The bodies that repeatedly appeared all over New Orleans days and weeks after it was struck by Hurricane Katrina laid bare the racial and class fault lines that mark an increasingly damaged and withering democracy and revealed the emergence of a new kind of politics, one in which entire populations are now considered disposable, an unnecessary burden on state coffers, and consigned to fend for themselves. The deeply existential and material questions regarding who is going to die and who is going to live in this society are now centrally determined by race and class. Katrina lays bare what many people in the United States do not want to see: large numbers of poor black and brown people struggling to make ends meet, benefiting very little from a social system that makes it difficult to obtain health insurance, childcare, social assistance, cars, savings, and minimum-wage jobs if lucky, and instead offers to black and brown youth bad schools, poor public services, and no future, except a possible stint in the penitentiary. As Janet Pelz (2005) rightly insists, "These are the people the Republicans have been teaching us to disdain, if not hate, since President Reagan decried the moral laxness of the Welfare mom." While Pelz's comments provide a crucial context for much of the death and devastation of Katrina, I think to more fully understand this calamity it is important to grasp how the confluence of race and poverty has become part of a new and more insidious set of forces based on a revised set of biopolitical commitments, which have largely given up on the sanctity of human life for those populations rendered "at risk" by global neoliberal economies and have instead embraced an emergent security state founded on fear, class privilege, and updated notions of racial purity. This is a state that no longer provides Americans with dreams; instead, it has been reduced largely to protecting its citizens from a range of possible nightmares. In this instance, a biopolitics of disposability and bare life has combined with "the imploding history of biocapital" (Comaroff 2007: 37).

Within the last few decades, matters of state sovereignty in the new world order have been retheorized so as to provide a range of theoretical insights about the relationship between power and politics, the political nature of social and cultural life, and the merging of life and politics as a new form of biopolitics, that is, a politics that attempts to think through the convergence of life and politics. Central here is the task of reformulating the meaning of contemporary politics and how it functions now to regulate matters of life and death, and how such issues are intimately related to both the articulation of community and the social, and the regulation, care, and development of human life. Within this discourse, politics is no longer understood exclusively through a disciplinary technology centered on the individual body—a body to be measured, surveilled, managed, included in forecasts, surveys, and statistical projections. Under the new biopolitical regimes, the body is understood primarily as an object of power, but it is a body that is social and multiple, scientific and ideological. Biopolitics points to new relations of power that are more capacious, concerned with not only the body as an object of disciplinary techniques that render it "both useful and docile" but a body that needs to be "regularized," subject to those immaterial means of production that produce ways of life that enlarge the targets of control and regulation (Foucault 1997: 249).

While biopolitics, as taken up in the work of theorists such as Michel Foucault on the one hand, and Michael Hardt and Antonio Negri on the other, emphasizes the relations between politics and death, biopolitics, in their views, is less concerned with the primacy of death than with the production of life both as an individual and a social category. In Giorgio Agamben's formulation, the new biopolitics is the deadly administration of what he calls "bare life" and its ultimate incarnation is the Holocaust with its ominous specter of the concentration camp. In this formulation, the Nazi death camps become the primary exemplar of control, the new space of contemporary politics in which individuals are no longer viewed as citizens but are now seen as inmates, stripped of everything, including their right to live. The uniting of power and bare life, the reduction of the individual to *homo sacer*—the sacred man, who, under certain states of exception and without fear of punishment, "may be killed and yet not sacrificed"—no longer represent the far end of political life (Agamben 1998: 8). As modern states increasingly suspend their democratic structures, laws, and principles, the very nature of governance changes as "the rule of law is routinely displaced by the state of exception, or emergency, and people are increasingly subject to extra-judicial state violence" (Bull 2004: 3). The life unfit for life, unworthy of being lived, as the central category of *homo sacer*, is no longer marginal to sovereign power but is now central to its form of governance. Modern politics in this instance, as Jean Comaroff (2007: 22) puts it, "reveals how modern government stages itself by dealing directly in the power over life: the power to exclude, to declare exceptions, to strip human existence of civic rights and social value." State violence and totalitarian power, which in the past either were generally short-lived or existed on the fringe of politics and history, have now become the rule, as life is more ruthlessly regulated and placed in the hands of military and state power.

For Agamben, the coupling of the state of exception with the metaphor of bare life points to a biopolitics in which "all subjects are at least potentially if not actually abandoned by the law and exposed to violence as a constitutive condition of political existence" (Mills 2004: 47). Nicholas Mirzoeff has observed that all over the world there is a growing resentment of immigrants and refugees, matched by the emergence of detain-and-deport strategies coupled with the rise of the camp as the key institution and social model of the new millennium. The "empire of camps," according to Mirzoeff, has become the "exemplary institution of a system of global capitalism that supports the West in its high consumption, low-price consumer lifestyle" (Mirzoeff 2005: 145). Zygmunt Bauman calls such camps "garrisons of extraterritoriality" and argues that they have become "the dumping grounds for the indisposed of and as yet unrecycled waste of the global frontier-land" (Bauman 2003: 136). The regime of the camp has increasingly become a key index of modernity and the new world order. The politics of disposability not only generates widespread violence and ever-expanding "garrisons of extraterritoriality" but also has taken on a powerful new significance as a foundation for political sovereignty. Biopolitical commitments to "let die" by abandoning citizens appear increasingly credible in light of the growing authoritarianism in the United States under the Bush administration.

Under the logic of modernization, neoliberalism, and militariza-tion, the category "waste" includes no longer simply material goods but also human beings, particularly those rendered redundant in the new global economy, that is, those who are no longer capable of making a living, who are unable to consume goods, and who depend upon others for the most basic needs. Defined primarily through the combined discourses of character, personal responsibility, and cultural homogeneity, entire populations expelled from the benefits of the marketplace are reified as products without any value, to be disposed of as "leftovers in the most radical and effective way: we make them invisible by not looking and unthinkable by not thinking" (Bauman 2004: 27). Even when young black and brown youth try to escape the biopolitics of disposability by joining the military, the seduction of economic security is quickly negated by the horror of senseless violence compounded daily in the streets, roads, and battlefields in Iraq and Afghanistan and made concrete in the form of body bags, mangled bodies, and amputated limbs—rarely to be seen in the narrow ocular vision of the dominant media.

With the social state in retreat and the rapacious dynamics of a market fundamentalism, unchecked by government regulations, the public and private policies of investing in the public good are dismissed as bad business, just as the notion of protecting people from the dire misfortunes of poverty and sickness, or the random blows of fate, is viewed as an act of bad faith. Weakness is now a sin, punishable by social exclusion. This is especially true for those racial groups and immigrant populations who have always been at risk economically and politically. Increasingly, such groups have become part of an ever-growing army of the impoverished and disenfranchised—removed from the prospect of a decent job, productive education, adequate health care, acceptable childcare services, and satisfactory shelter. As the state is transformed into the primary agent of terror and corporate concerns displace democratic values, the exercise of power increasingly becomes about evading social responsibilities. With its pathological disdain for public life and its celebration of an unbridled individualism and acquisitiveness, the Bush administration does more than undermine the nature of social obligation and civic responsibility; it also sends a message to those populations who are poor and black—society neither wants, cares about, nor needs you. Katrina revealed with startling and disturbing clarity who these individuals are: African Americans who occupy the poorest sections of New Orleans, those ghettoized frontier-zones created by racism coupled with economic inequality. Excluded from any long-term goals and a decent vision of the future, these are the populations, as Zygmunt Bauman points out, who have been rendered redundant and disposable in the age of neoliberal global capitalism.

Katrina reveals that we are living in dark times. The shadow of authoritarianism remains after the storm clouds and hurricane winds have passed, offering a glimpse of its wreckage and terror. The politics of a disaster that affected Louisiana, Alabama, and Mississippi is about more than government incompetence, militarization, socioeconomic polarization, environmental disaster, and political scandal. Hurricane Katrina broke through the visual blackout of poverty and the pernicious ideology of color-blindness to reveal the government's role in fostering the dire living conditions of largely poor African Americans, who were bearing the hardships incurred by the full wrath of the indifference and violence at work in the racist, neoliberal state. Global neoliberalism and its victims now occupy a space shaped by authoritarian politics, the terrors inflicted by a police state, and a logic of disposability that removes them from government social provisions and the discourse and privileges of citizenship. One of the most obvious lessons of Katrina—that race and racism still matter in America—is fully operational through a biopolitics in which "sovereignty resides in the power and capacity to dictate who may live and who may die" (Mbembe 2003: 11–12). Those poor minorities of color and class, unable to contribute to the prevailing consumerist ethic, are vanishing into the sinkhole of poverty in desolate and abandoned enclaves of decaying cities, neighborhoods, and rural spaces, or in America's ever-expanding prison empire.

In the aftermath of Hurricane Katrina, the biopolitical calculus of massive power differentials and iniquitous market relations put the scourge of poverty and racism on full display. But any viable notion of biopolitics has to be about more than subjection, crisis, abjection and apocalypse. The politics of exclusion only yields a partial understanding of how power works. To confront the biopolitics of disposability, we need to recognize the dark times in which we live and offer up a vision of hope that creates the conditions for multiple collective and global struggles that refuse to use politics as an act of war and markets as the measure of democracy. Making human beings superfluous is the essence of totalitarianism, and democracy is the antidote in urgent need of being reclaimed. Katrina should keep the hope of such a struggle alive for quite some time because for many of us the images of those floating bodies serve as a desperate reminder of what it means when justice, as the lifeblood of democracy, becomes cold and indifferent in the face of death.

REFERENCES

Agamben, Georgio (1998) *Homo Sacer*. Stanford: Stanford University Press.
Bauman, Zygmunt (2003) *Liquid Love*. London: Polity.
Bauman, Zygmunt (2004) *Wasted Lives*. London: Polity.
Brooks, R. (2005) "Our Homegrown Third World." *Los Angeles Times*, September 7.
Bull, M. (2004) "States Don't Really Mind Their Citizens Dying (Provided They Don't All Do It at Once): They Just Don't Like Anyone Else to Kill Them." *London Review of Books*, 16 December.

Comaroff, Jean (2007) "Beyond the Politics of Bare Life." *Public Culture* 19(1): 197–219.

Foucault, Michel (1997) *Society Must Be Defended*. New York: Picador.

Goldberg, David. T. (2001) *The Racial State*. Malden: Blackwell.

Mbembe, A. (2003) "Necropolitics." *Public Culture* 15(1): 11–40.

Mills, C. (2004) "Agamben's Messianic Biopolitics." *Contretemps* 5, December: 42–62.

Mirzoeff, Nicholas (2005) *Watching Babylon: The War in Iraq and Global Visual Culture*. New York: Routledge.

Pelz, J. (2005) "The Poor Shamed Us into Seeing Them." *Seattle Post-Intelligencer*, September 19.

Rohde, D., D. G. McNeil Jr., R. Abelson, and S. Dewan (2005) "154 Patients Died, Many in Intense Heat, as Rescues Lagged." *New York Times*, September 19.

21
Empire of Camps

Nicholas Mirzoeff

On September 11, I was on the South Pacific island of Moorea en route to Australia. It was not until September 12 that I first learned of the attack on the World Trade Center, alerted by my confused daughter's unsuccessful efforts to find French cartoons on television. As I stared at the instantly unforgettable images, I kept turning to look out of the window at what was for my British eyes the almost equally unreal sight of palm trees and white sand beaches. Caught between the exoticism of the Orientalist holiday-of-a-lifetime and the anti-modern spectacle of September 11, I experienced the full vertiginous affect of the visual subject in the empire of camps. ... As it turned out, Australia and Britain, where I have happened to spend the last year, were excellent locations to develop my understanding of the empire of camps (Mirzoeff 2002: 20).

BUILDING THE EMPIRE OF CAMPS

One of the first nations to implement a detain-and-deport policy was Australia, long haunted by the fear of Asia. Since 1992, everyone seeking asylum or refugee status in Australia has been sent to remote refugee camps, which have been convincingly linked to the nineteenth-century camps for Aboriginals. The new internment camps are not reforming institutions but simply serve as detention centers. Australia's notorious "White Australia" policy had been implemented after Federation by means of the Immigration Restriction Act (1901), in order to keep Asian workers out of the country. The neoconservative administration led by John Howard saw an opportunity to revive its fortunes by reverting to a state-led hostility to immigrants. In August 2001, Howard refused the MV *Tampa* permission to dock on the Australian territory of Christmas Island because the vessel was carrying several hundred refugees rescued from a sinking boat. While Howard anticipated the ensuing controversy, he could not have known that the events of September

11, 2001 were about to hand him a blanket endorsement of detain-and-deport Orientalism. It did not matter that most of the refugees affected were Afghanis and Iraqis fleeing the very regimes that Australia has since gone to war to overthrow. All were subsumed as Orientals, and hence the object of rejection, by being named "sleepers for terrorism," a charge that proved as effective as it was impossible to refute. Emboldened by the popular support for their stance, the Australian government has now implemented what it calls a "Pacific solution" by refusing to bring refugees to mainland Australia at all. Instead refugees are kept in camps on small Australian islands or, preferably, in other Pacific nations while awaiting an almost interminable "processing." Howard literally bribed the financially strapped government of the small Pacific island of Nauru to accept such asylum seekers by flying out a suitcase full of cash for their use in late 2001.

Those refugees who do make it to Australia, or who were already there, are being interned in remote camps. The low structures of the camps do nothing to draw attention to themselves and have no central viewpoint or command post. They are located in remote areas, such as the Woomera camp in South Australia, situated some 300 miles from the nearest city, Adelaide, on a vast rocket-testing site, once used by the British and US militaries and still in service today. Their location is meant to emphasize that they are not part of the nation-state and that their inmates will not achieve asylum, let alone citizenship. In this way the relics of the Cold War closed system have become components for the new global closed-circuit culture, exemplified by the extraordinary US detention center at Guantanamo Bay, Cuba. Its first incarnation was appropriately named Camp X-Ray, a place beyond normal vision, in which mere flesh cannot be seen. Now most prisoners are incarcerated in the blandly named Camp Delta, living in cells eight feet by seven feet with only three 20-minute periods for exercise a week. Unsurprisingly, detainees made 24 suicide attempts in the first two years of the camp's operation, a problem common to all the detain-and-deport centers. Woomera is presently surrounded with fences and coils of razor wire that will soon be replaced with an electrified fence, delivering a "non-fatal electronic shock" to anyone trying to escape. As such construction goes ahead it becomes clear that the camps are intended not as a temporary response to an imagined crisis but as permanent features of the legal system. They mark a radical reversal of state policy to foreigners, or, as the United States likes to call them, aliens.

These camps are not the exception to democratic society. Rather they are the exemplary institution of a system of global capitalism that supports the west in its high-consumption, low-price consumer lifestyle. I call this regime the "empire of camps." Conservative thinkers in the United States have become surprisingly comfortable with the term "empire" as a response to 9/11 and new books on the subject are published almost every week. George Bush has compared the occupation of Iraq to that of the Philippines in 1898, an avowedly civilizing mission of the old school—and one also promoted by inaccurate "intelligence." My use of the term "empire" was at first appropriated from Michael Hardt and Antonio Negri's instant classic *Empire* (2000) that analyses the new geopolitics of globalization. But Hardt and Negri's vision of a decentered empire has come to be overtaken by the assertion of a more familiar model of empire controlled by a particular nation-state. Drawing on the work of Claude Nicolet, a historian of the Roman Empire, Irit Rogoff has defined empire as "the spatialization of a concept which is played out through the evolution of technologies of mobility and surveillance and through a consciousness of boundaries that expand far beyond the self" (Rogoff 2000: 22). While empire has a wide range of meanings, this definition is very pertinent to the empire of camps. The camps in question are the internment camps for migrants and refugees that are the symbol of the new world order. Critics from Giorgio Agamben to Angela Davis and Paul Gilroy have understood the camp as a key index of modernity. Agamben, for example, writes that "the birth of the camp in our time appears as an event that decisively signals the political space of modernity itself" (Agamben 1998: 174–175; also see Gilroy 1999; Davis 2003). The refugee camp marks a new twist, in that modernity, for while they are, of course, very similar to detention and concentration camps of earlier periods (if not to the extermination camps of the Nazis), it is important to register that they are also something new.

The camp is the panopticon for our time, at once the site of deployment of new visual technologies; a model institution for global culture—and a powerful symbol of the renewed desire of nation-states to restrict global freedom of movement to capital and deny it to people. To this end, the empire has used a degree of force that would have been unthinkable without the enabling context of September 11. For all its religious overtones, the empire of camps has no scruples, no moral agenda, and no desire to be seen or to make its prisoners visible, although surveillance is everywhere. The grand, architectural sweep of the panoptic prison, the department store and the military barracks, has been replaced by the low-rise internment camp, the strip mall and the anonymous delivery of "smart" weapons. In an important example, US high schools now operate behind metal detectors and with closed-circuit TV surveillance, unable to rely on traditional discipline. In one extraordinary case, high school pupils in private Jesuit colleges funded by the Bill and Melinda Gates Foundation are sent to work for businesses for five days a month without recompense. The school receives funds for their labor that are used to support operating costs (Schemo 2003). The *maquilladora* factories turning out cheap products for the US economy on the Mexican side of the border are another key example of this low-wage high-surveillance economy. While the department store and the arcade were the commercial outlets of panopticism, the camp retails via the strip mall, the outlet store and the suburban superstore. Here appearances are sacrificed to the cash nexus: you get the steak cheaply but you have to supply the sizzle yourself.

Now the empire of camps has further challenged what seemed to many, in the first stages of this era of globalization, to be the revenge of the nomads by reclassifying the nomad as a person fully incapable of being emancipated into citizenship. As such the detainees are kept in a realm of the undead, under total observation but out of sight. This politics of ghostly subjection requires a re-emancipation of time and space. Detainees, even children, are given nothing to do and have no information as to what may happen to them. Nothing could be further from the rational exchange of information that structured the panopticon. Arguably, the Orientalist theory behind the camps denies rationality to the inmates in any event, reinforced by the western theory that Islam and the terrorism it is supposed to engender are anti-rational belief systems. For whereas the panoptic institution at least aspired to reform their inmates, the camps are specifically intended to generate, in the words of the Australian government's own human rights advisory group, "a miasma of despair and desperation" (Barkham 2002: 24–31). Inmates are then offered deportation with a small cash incentive in the belief that they will feel that anything is better than their detention. In 2003, the British government proposed taking children of refugees who refuse to leave into care as hostages to ensure their parents' departure, prompting protests even from the Conservative opposition.

As Alison Bashford and Carolyn Strange (2002) have argued, these camps owe as much in inspiration to quarantine procedures as they do to prisons as such. Building on legislation passed in 1908 that gave the Australian government extensive powers of detention, a system of quarantine was established that maintained leper colonies on remote islands as recently as the 1960s. The rhetoric of hygiene that motivated quarantine procedures was also a key part of the rationale of eugenics that sought to breed "imperfections" out of society, by force if necessary. These insistent and circular implications—prison implies quarantine which implies eugenics which implies internment camps—form the logic of the detain-and-deport model of social order. Foucault saw quarantine as one model for the disciplinary society, based on measures to control outbreaks of social and medical disorder: "Behind the disciplinary mechanisms can be read the haunting memory of 'contagions,' of the plague, of rebellions, crimes, vagabondage, desertions, people who appear and disappear, love and die in disorder" (Foucault 1977: 198). Quarantine, then, is always as much a means of social control as it is a medical matter. These procedures are still very much part of the present. It is instructive to see how the SARS outbreak, concurrent with the war in Iraq, was quickly brought to heel by quarantine procedures in China, Hong Kong and Toronto, the leading sites of infection, while the anthrax attacks of 2001 remain a mystery. For the biological weapon anthrax was delivered in modern fashion by mail, whereas the SARS virus, although clearly spread by air travel, could be contained in very traditional manner by incarcerating the sick. At the same time, the Bush administration is claiming credit for promoting initiatives against AIDS in Africa, even though it has requested only two-thirds of the relevant budget item. In an exclusionary model of discipline, quarantine and disease control are paradigmatic, not the reforming prison.

In Australia, the camps have been met with principled and courageous protests, such as a series of wire-cutting protests at Woomera that allowed inmates temporary freedom. Echoing the Australian Freedom Buses of the 1960s that culminated with the granting of citizenship to Aboriginal peoples for the first time in 1967, the Imaginepeace Busketeers attacked the fences of the camps, flew kites over the wire, or passed flowers and messages over the dividing line between the alien and the citizen. Unlike in the 1960s, governments welcome such protests as an opportunity to demonstrate their determination and rigor. When a family facing deportation from Britain in 2002 sought refuge in a mosque, the police had no compunction in breaking down the door to drag them out. The imprisoned refugees in Woomera and in the British camp of Yarl's Wood have resorted to burning down their huts in protest. Built at cost of £100 million, Yarl's Wood was opened in January

2002 to house over 1,000 asylum seekers. Home Secretary David Blunkett hoped to deport over 2,500 people a month from Yarl's Wood and contracted the center out to the private Group 4 Security firm. Their conduct was so poor that even a government prosecutor later referred to them as a "national laughing stock." The first riot was provoked as early as February 2002, when Younis Igwegbe, a Nigerian woman, was prevented from going to chapel on a Sunday. Other inmates took her side and things escalated to the point where the entire center was burned to the ground—no sprinkler system had been installed (Morris and Allison 2003). In similar protests, other detainees at Woomera and the French camp at Sangatte have sewn their mouths closed. In March 2002 twelve inmates at Woomera symbolically dug their own graves and lay in them as a protest. The poet Abas Amini, a Kurdish refugee in Britain, sewed both his mouth and his eyes closed to protest his ordered deportation to Iran in May 2003. Such resistance nonetheless mimics and reinforces the intent of the camps. Commenting on the protests at Woomera, the Australian minister for immigration, Philip Ruddock, said: "Lip-sewing is a practice unknown in our culture. It's something that offends the sensitivities of Australians." That is to say, the very protest by the detained refugees was proof of their barbarism and unfitness for Australian citizenship. The guards at the camp expressed the connections being implied perfectly when they called the protesters "terrorist motherfuckers" (Pugliese 2002). The inmates from around Asia are now all terrorists and they are characterized as sexual deviants outside the boundaries of "civilized" behavior as both practitioners of political violence and "primitive" protests like lip-sewing.

The goal of the camps, then, is to render their inhabitants into the undead, people with no social existence. While the panopticon wanted its prisoners visible at all times, the camps want their inmates to be permanently invisible. The Bush administration has invented a new category of criminal, the "enemy combatant," who can be detained at will because their presumed actions render them without value. In her dissent to the July 9, 2003 ruling by the Fourth Circuit Court of Appeals that upheld the practice (under appeal to the Supreme Court at time of writing), Judge Diana Gribbon Motz argued that the decision allowed "the indefinite detention, without access to a lawyer or the courts, of any American citizen, even one captured on American soil, who the Executive designates an 'enemy combatant'" (Hentoff 2003: 35). The case concerned Yaser Esam Hamdi, an American citizen captured in Afghanistan in

2001. Subsequently, he was held in a military brig and not charged or allowed any access to lawyers, let alone others in the outside world, on the basis of a two-page statement by an official in the Defense Department, until a sudden reversal in December 2003. Such procedures recall the early modern practice of the *lettre de cachet* in which the absolute monarch of France was able to order the secret detention of any person he regarded as a threat. Two centuries after the storming of the Bastille, the practice was revived in France at the refugee camp at Sangatte, where people attempting to claim asylum in Europe were detained in primitive conditions. Reporter Djaffer Ait Aoudia quoted an anonymous displaced person in the camp as saying: "We are already dead. Sangatte is the cemetery of the living" (Aoudia 2002: 14). Bentham's fear that the ineffective panopticon would turn its inhabitants into ghosts is now government policy. Sangatte itself is now a ghost, as the British and French governments closed it in December 2002 in favor of detaining their refugees at a further remove. The new European strategy to limit refugees and asylum seekers has been borrowed from Australia's Pacific solution. Following British instigation, the European Union is now building a similar remote camp in Croatia, at the village of Trstenik, 30 miles from Zagreb near the town of Dugo Selo. It will hold up to 800 people. The £1 million center will take refugees arriving at British ports and airports from the Balkans and Eastern Europe. No doubt the hope is that this undesirable location will persuade the refugees to accept meager deals to be shipped home or to other, as yet undetermined, countries who might be willing to take them.

As one might expect given the context of re-masculinizing the nation-state, the empire of camps is intensely gendered. The camps figure the migrant as male, fecklessly abandoning a family somewhere in the global ghetto, adopting an apparently feminist rhetoric with impressive cynicism. The British Labour immigration minister (since re-shuffled), Lord Rooker, declared in May 2002 that: "Most asylum seekers are single men who have deserted their families for economic gain." These remarks were then quoted with approval by the anti-immigration tabloid the *Daily Express* as a validation of its xenophobic campaign. Taken at face value there is an obvious problem with the idea of single men being blamed for abandoning their families, unless the Labour Party has suddenly adopted a Chinese respect for its elders. By leaving their country of origin, non-western men become single, unlike, for example, western soldiers or colonial civil servants. As such, their identity becomes suspect and they are in a certain sense instantly convicted of being deviant by the western nation-state. Orientalism has long attributed extravagant and queer sexuality to the East. In Richard Burton's lengthy appendix to his 1885 translation of *The Arabian Nights,* the widest possible geographical definition of the Orient, ranging from Southern Europe via the Middle East and North Africa to the South Seas, was held to be the homeland of what he called "Sotadism," or sodomy. This deviant zone ran right through what Burton called Mesopotamia, the site of modern Iraq, as it includes the sites of ancient Sodom and Gomorrah. This psycho-geography—the association of geographical space with particular psychic affects—resonates in our own time because digital culture has operated according to what Wendy Hui Kyong Chun has called a "hi-tech Orientalism" of its own, from William Gibson's 1984 novel *Neuromancer,* via the Asianized Los Angeles of *Blade Runner* (the director's cut, 1991) to the Asian affect of the *Matrix* film series (Chun 2002: 250–252). Such apparently random acts as the murder of a British police officer pursuing a supposed terrorist suspect by a young Algerian man in January 2003 are given meaning by this psychogeographical determinism. In this view, much circulated by British tabloid media, young Islamic men pursue economic or terrorist ambitions with local cost to their abandoned families and global consequences such as September 11. Keeping these men in place sustains both the global economy by maintaining a low-wage female workforce within the "family" structure that western theorists deem indispensable and prevents the spread of terrorists, newly defined as any Islamic migrant.

PANOPTICON INC.

The camps are themselves the center of an expanding transnational industry. The first level of opportunity is the privatization of detention and other corrections worldwide. Even greater is the opportunity presented by the denationalization of the nation-state in Iraq to rebuild what the American army and air force destroyed, while enabling the modernization of the oil fields, a market that has been cornered by the multinational Halliburton. Had the so-called road map succeeded, there would have been another such market in Palestine. As this mode of capitalizing destruction is still in its infancy, let's here consider the private prison empire. The British camp at Yarl's Wood was initially run by the private security firm Group 4, while all five Australian camps for detainees were managed by Australasian Correctional Management, a subsidiary of the US penal giant Wackenhut Corrections. Wackenhut, now renamed the GEO Group, manages 61 correctional and detention centers in North America, Europe, Puerto Rico, Australia, South Africa and New Zealand, generating annual revenues in excess of $500 million and a 14.1 percent profit increase in 2001. According to its own website, Wackenhut deals in "prisoner transportation, electronic monitoring for home detainees, correctional health care and mental health services." Like any other multinational, Wackenhut sends its capital where profits are to be made and is subject to the monopolizing character of globalization, leading it in 2002 to close an "unprofitable" prison in Arkansas in favor of a 3,024-bed facility in South Africa. So successful were these strategies that Wackenhut was itself taken over by the $2.5 billion Danish corporation Group 4 Falck (PR Newswire 2002a), resulting in a dramatic 97 percent increase in net income in the first quarter of 2002 for Wackenhut as a separate division within Group 4. More generally, this concentration of private corrections has engendered the unnoticed creation of a global empire of incarceration in the hands of corporations, not governments (PR Newswire 2002b). Wackenhut claims 24 percent of the global market for private corrections (www.wcccorrections. com), while its rival, the Corrections Corporation of America (www. correctionscorp.com) claims to operate more corrections facilities in the US than all but four states and the federal government. This carceral regime has its own communications network, relying on websites like www.corrections.com to keep it posted with new technology, and allow it to swap ideas on bulletin boards and catch up with the news.

A crisis in American prisons seems possible, as the withdrawal of private prisons has coincided with the execution of punitive sentencing laws, generating a vast explosion in prison inmate numbers. With prisons already full, some nonviolent offenders are being freed, sent into drug treatment programs, or not imprisoned in the first place because there is nowhere to put them. Even in jail-happy California, nonviolent offenders in Los Angeles were released early in 2003 as the county, facing a $170 million budget deficit, was caught between its desire to incarcerate drug users and illegal immigrants, as well as three-time offenders, and the limits of state budgets in the current recession. Nonetheless Wackenhut posted an optimistic forecast of continued expansion to its website in 2003, due to the war on terrorism and the continued determination of the federal government to maintain detention as its primary strategy.

Indeed, in 2003 the US federal system became the largest single incarcerator, holding over 172,000 inmates compared to roughly 160,000 in both California and Texas. As the states seek to reduce their prison populations, Attorney General John Ashcroft instructed federal prosecutors in September 2003 to set aside plea bargains and aim for the sternest possible penalties. Wackenhut and other private prison corporations win either way. Its share price rose by more than 50 percent in the first six months of 2003, allowing it to repurchase all shares from Group 4 Falck by August 2003. At the same time, Wackenhut sold its British operations at a profit to its former partner Serco and renamed itself the GEO Group, with headquarters in Boca Raton, Florida. The *South Florida Business Journal*, which covers the area, represents GEO's profit as the result of "opening its Lawrenceville Correctional Facility in Virginia in March, a strengthened Australian dollar, [and] improved occupancy rates." The GEO Group/Wackenhut's share price (GEO continues to use the old Wackenhut designator on the New York Stock Exchange) has more than doubled since these maneuvers, which gives some indication of how powerful market flexibility is for the new global corporations. It is difficult to understand what is in fact happening in these flows of capital. How Wackenhut repurchased itself is hard to comprehend in commonsense terms. Meanwhile, due to a cut in budget, Texas and six state prison systems are offering their inmates a reduced-calorie diet with only two meals a day on holidays and weekends, making it clear who the losers are in this game.

CAMP IRAQ

From the point of view of its own citizens, Iraq is now functioning as a camp. Large portions of the country are under constant curfew, and thousands are being detained, often in Saddam's old prisons. Media reports in early 2004 suggested that some 13,000 people were being held without charge or the possibility of trial in Iraq. Within Camp Iraq is the camp of camps, the so-called "Sunni triangle," the middle third of the country that contains the capital, Baghdad. The camp effect can be observed at several levels. In everyday life, the sense of loss in the popular mood, the devastation of public services; and the restrictions on personal movement deprive Iraqis of citizenship in their own country. While these conditions may be seen as temporary, the occupation is an extraordinary effort to convert a nation-state previously functioning as a command economy into a denationalized zone for global capital. Whether as a state of transition or permanent condition, the country has become a supervised and hostile refugee camp on the model of Israel's permanent war with the Palestinians in the Gaza Strip and on the West Bank.

At the time of writing, Iraqi everyday life has become notably worse since the war and occupation began. Supplies of water and electricity remain extremely uncertain, while even gasoline is very hard to come by in this oil-rich nation due both to deliberate sabotage and the dilapidated equipment of the Iraqi oilfields. Although the war was declared over by George W. Bush in May 2003, there was no effort to restore regular telecommunications until US intelligence determined that the insurgents were not communicating by phone. At the same time, this policy had the effect of cutting off ordinary Iraqis from the outside world. The consequences were noticeable. When US forces were attacked in Samara in November 2003, they claimed to have killed 54 *fedayeen* or militiamen. Locals claimed, by contrast, that only seven or eight bystanders had been killed. Robert Fisk of the London *Independent* verified that only nine bodies were in the mortuary but the US military claimed that fighters' bodies would not be sent to such an official facility. Of course, one cannot distinguish the truth of these accounts at a distance but the simple existence of conflicting accounts adds a degree of complexity that US officials would prefer to suppress. Nonetheless bystanders are killed almost daily in shoot-outs between the US military and the Iraqi opposition forces, as well as by car bombs and suicide bombers. One Iraqi anonymously quoted in the *New York Times* placed his people firmly in the empire of camps: "Saddam Hussein killed all the Iraqis. Even the ones who are alive are now dead" (Fisher 2003: A17). This despair is extending to the occupying troops, with three suicides by US soldiers being reported as of November 2001 and some 500 requiring mental health treatment (Packer 2003: 72). In the Bush administration's 2003 request for $87 billion to refinance Iraq, it was noticeable that $500 million was budgeted for the construction of several new high-security prisons, as opposed to only $100 million for new housing in a country devastated by two decades of war. Both provisions were later removed by Congress as a symbolic gesture of oversight, reducing the cost by a nominal $1.7 billion, while the loss of new housing further depleted the benefits of this package for ordinary Iraqis.

Restrictions on personal movement are now similar to those in the West Bank. Traffic barriers and curfews have become a part of Iraqi everyday life since the beginning of the occupation in May 2003, just as they are in Palestine. Increased traffic control in Baghdad has led to school runs of a few kilometers taking hours, in a fashion all too familiar to Palestinians who have to use a separate road network to Israelis. In December 2003, the US army instigated a new high-profile assault on the insurgency that culminated with the arrest of Saddam Hussein. News reports described the way in which Iraqi towns and villages were turned into de facto camps. For example, the 7,000 inhabitants of Abu Hishma were subjected to a 15-hour curfew, a razor-wire fence, and identity cards with text in English only, after an attack on American forces was determined to have come from their town. The razor fence allows only one way in and out of the town and carries the extraordinary sign: "The fence is here for your protection. Do not approach or try to cross, or you will be shot." One local man said to a *New York Times* reporter: "I see no difference between us and the Palestinians" (Filkins 2003: A1). Veteran intelligence reporter Seymour Hersh suggested that the US is taking advice from the Israelis on counter-insurgency policy and that some Israelis may be secretly deployed as advisers (Hersh 2003: 48). In this view, it is no coincidence that concurrent with the occupation of Iraq has been the construction of a high barrier by Israel along an arbitrary line of security that exceeds its 1967 borders (Weizman 2003). Towns such as Qalqilya are surrounded on three sides, creating a Palestinian ghetto. As has happened consistently since the United States became "Israelized" in its adoption of exclusionary security state policies, Israel has refused American entreaties to desist from this practice. As there is a similar barrier along the US border with Mexico at San Diego that stretches for miles at a height of 16 feet, it could also be said that the Americans initiated the policy.

While these strategies are held to be short-term responses to the insurgency, the longer-term strategy for Iraq—insofar as there is one—is for it to become a denationalized zone for the operation of global capital. Saskia Sassen (2002) has argued that globalization entails a "denationalizing" of time and space. In Sassen's view, this denationalization has hitherto taken place for the most part in certain privileged global cities as a series of exemptions that "makes possible the hypermobility of financial capital on the global scale" (Sassen 2002: 18–24).

The detain-and-deport system of the empire of camps reinforces this mobility of capital in two decisive ways. First, it restricts the workforce to those locales desired by capital. To meet this demand, a migrant workforce of no fewer than 100 million people has been created in China (Eckholm 2003: A1). Working for between $50 and $120 a month, this fluid industrial reserve army of globalization produces the low-cost goods the new economy needs. Now with the invasion of Iraq we have seen the denationalization of the nation-state, in part to ensure the free flow of primary, extractive resources, in this case oil. Even if some of the political actors did not believe this to be their motive, the effect of the war has been to collapse the possibility of Iraq acting as a legal personality, while restoring the oil reserves of the country to the international market. Second, it restores the privilege of the one-third world over the two-thirds world, such that the perquisites of the Western nation-state have been reinforced to a remarkable extent by the denationalization of the two-thirds world's nation-states. Finally, the wholesale privatization of Iraqi government assets, widely considered to be in breach of the conventions of occupation, has transformed the Iraqi economy from state-controlled centralism to the current orthodoxy of deregulated market capitalism almost overnight. Even the occupation has been privatized with over 10,000 private military contractors operating in Iraq at the end of 2003. For example, the British firm Global Risk Strategies has more than 1,000 personnel in Iraq, including Gurkhas, Fijian militiamen and, allegedly, ex-SAS men (Traynor 2003: 1). The relics of the old British Empire are now being used to support the new regime of empire. However, this is not just an ideological project but one with substantial financial rewards. The US military estimates that at least $30 billion of the $87 billion appropriated by the Bush administration to sustain the occupation of Iraq will go to private corporations. In this sense, the Iraq war was fought as a key part of the consolidation of reactionary globalization, rather than for the now-discredited rationale of eliminating weapons of mass destruction.

REFERENCES

Agamben, Giorgio (2000) *Homo Sacer.* Trans. Daniel Heller-Roazen. Stanford: Stanford University Press.

Aoudia, Djaffer Ait (2002) "Inside Sangatte." *Observer*, May 26: 14.

Barkham, Patrick (2002) "No Waltzing in Woomera." *Guardian Weekend*, May 25: 24–31.

Bashford, Alison and Carolyn Strange (2002) "Asylum Seekers and National Histories of Detention." *Australian Journal of Politics and History* 48(4): 509–527.

Chun, Wendy Hui Kyong (2002) "Othering Space." In Nicholas Mirzoeff (ed.), *The Visual Culture Reader.* New York: Routledge: 243–254.

Davis, Angela Y. (2003) *Are Prisons Obsolete?* New York: Seven Stories Press.

Eckholm, Erik (2003) "Tide of China's Migrants: Flowing to Boom, or Bust?" *New York Times*, July 29: A1.

Filkins, Dexter (2003) "Tough New Tactics by US Tighten Grip on Iraqi Towns." *New York Times*, December 7: A1.

Fisher, Ian (2003) "Iraqi Says He Stalks and Kills Baath Party Men, With Toll at 12." *New York Times*, May 1: A17.

Foucault, Michel (1977) *Discipline and Punish*. Trans. Alan Sheridan. Paris: Gallimard.

Gilroy, Paul (1999) *Against Race*. Cambridge MA: Harvard University Press.

Hardt, Michael, and Antonio Negri (2000) *Empire*. Cambridge MA: Harvard University Press.

Hentoff, Nat (2003) "Who Made George Bush Our King?" *Village Voice*, July 30–August 5: 35.

Hersh, Seymour (2003) "Moving Targets." *New Yorker*, December 15: 48.

Mirzoeff, Nicholas (2002) "The Empire of Camps." *Situation Analysis* 1, October: 20–25.

Morris, Steven, and Rebecca Allison (2003) "Yarl's Wood: Tinderbox That Sent Asylum Plans up in Flames." *Guardian*, August 16. Online at: <http://www.guardian.co.uk/uk/2003/aug/16/immigration.immigrationandpublicservices>. Accessed June 2009.

Packer, George (2003) "After the War." *New Yorker*, November 24: 72.

PR Newswire (2002a) "Wackenhut Corrections Comments on the Merger of the Wackenhut Corporation with Group 4 Falck." Online at: <http://www.prnewswire.com/>. Accessed May 30, 2002.

PR Newswire (2002b) "Wackenhut Corrections Reports First Quarter Results." Online at: <http://www.prnewswire.com/>. Accessed May 30, 2002.

PR Newswire (2003) "Press release." Online at: <http://www.prnewswire.com/cgibin/stories1?ACCT=105&STORY=/www/story/08-07-2003/00 01997160>. Accessed September 29, 2003.

Pugliese, Joseph (2002) "Penal Asylum." *borderlands e-journal* 1(1). Online at: <http://www.borderlandsejournal.adelaide.edu.au.vol1no1_2002/pugliese.html>.

Rogoff, Irit (2000) *Terra Infirma*. New York: Routledge.

Sassen, Saskia (2002) "The Global City." In Gerfried Stocker and Christine Schopf (eds.), *Unplugged: Art as the Scene of Global Conflicts, Ars Electronica 2002*. Ostfildern-Ruit: Hatje Cantz Publishers: 18–24.

Schemo, Diana Jean (2003) "Charities Pledge $19 Million to Jesuit Model Schools." *New York Times*, 21 May. Online at: <http://www.nytimes.com/2003/05/21/us/charities-pledge-19-million-to-jesuit-model-schools.html>.

Traynor, Ian (2003) "The Privatisation of War." *Guardian International*, December 10: 1.

Weizman, Eyal (2003) "Ariel Sharon and the Geometry of Occupation." Online at: opendemocracy.net (September): accessed October 30, 2003.

Notes on Contributors

David L. Altheide is a regents' professor in the School of Justice and Social Inquiry at Arizona State University. He received the 2005 George Herbert Mead Award for lifetime contributions from the Society for the Study of Symbolic Interaction. His publications include *Creating Fear: News and the Construction of Crisis* (Aldine de Gruyter/Transaction 2002), which focuses on the news media's constructions of a discourse of fear. This book received the 2004 Cooley Award, as the best book for the year in the tradition of symbolic interaction, from the Society for the Study of Symbolic Interaction. Another recent book, *Terrorism and the Politics of Fear* (AltaMira 2006), examines the role of the mass media and propaganda in promoting fear and social control. Altheide examines how terrorism discourse has pervaded public life and informed political "talk" in his forthcoming book *Terror Post 9/11 and the Media* (Lang).

Susan J. Brison is an associate professor of philosophy at Dartmouth College where she also teaches in the Program in Women's and Gender Studies. She has held visiting positions at Tufts University, New York University, and Princeton University, and has been a Mellon Fellow at New York University and an NEH-funded member of the Institute for Advanced Study (Princeton). Brison is the author of articles in anthologies and in scholarly journals such as *Ethics*, *Hypatia*, and *Legal Theory*. She has also published in the *Sunday New York Times Magazine*, the *Guardian*, the *Chronicle of Higher Education*, and the *San Francisco Chronicle*. Brison is co-editor of *Contemporary Perspectives on Constitutional Interpretation* (Westview 1993), and author of *Aftermath: Violence and the Remaking of a Self* (Princeton University Press 2002).

Noam Chomsky is an institute professor and professor of linguistics (emeritus) at the Massachusetts Institute of Technology. He revolutionized the scientific study of language with the publication of *Syntactic Structures* in 1957. Subsequent principal linguistic works include *Current Issues in Linguistic Theory* (1964), *The Sound Pattern of English* (with Morris Halle, 1968), *Language and Mind* (1972), *Studies on Semantics in Generative Grammar* (1972), *Some Concepts and Consequences of the Theory of Government and Binding* (1982), and *Knowledge of Language* (1986). In addition to his work as an educator and linguist, Chomsky has written and lectured widely on philosophy, intellectual history, contemporary issues, international affairs, and US foreign policy. He was an early and outspoken critic of US involvement in the Vietnam War and has written extensively on many political issues from a libertarian socialist point of view. Among his political writings are *American Power and the New Mandarins* (1969), *Peace in the Middle East?* (1974), *Manufacturing Consent* (with E. S. Herman, 1988), *Profit over People* (1998), and *Rogue States* (2000). In his controversial bestseller *9-11* (2002), Chomsky analyzes the World Trade Center attack and, while denouncing the atrocity of the event, traces its origins to the actions and power of the United States.

Cynthia Cockburn is a visiting professor in the Department of Sociology at City University, London, and active in the international antimilitarist network Women in Black. Her research and writing are focused on the intersection of peace and gender studies. Since 1995, she has worked closely with women peace activists in conflictual countries based on qualitative action-research. Her publications on these themes include *The Space Between Us: Negotiating Gender and National Identities in Conflict* (Zed Books 1998) and *The Post-War Moment: Militaries, Masculinities and International Peacekeeping* (co-edited with Dubravka Zarkov; Lawrence and Wishart 2002), which has chapters on the Netherlands as a "peace-keeping" country and Bosnia as a "peace-kept" country. Another work is *The Line: Women, Partition, and the Gender Order in Cyprus* (Zed Books 2004), which features women resisting partitions—of ethnicity and gender. A recent project, *From Where We Stand* (Zed Books 2007), involved mapping and analyzing feminist opposition to war as a growing, global, social movement. Cockburn's current research is on the relation between socialisms, anarchisms, pacifisms, and feminisms in the antiwar movements in several countries.

Julia Dickson-Gómez is an associate professor of psychiatry and behavioral medicine at the Medical College of Wisconsin and fellow at the Center for AIDS Intervention Research. Initially trained as a medical anthropologist, Dickson-Gómez has conducted extensive research on the effects of war on families in a rural community in El Salvador. As a post-doctoral fellow at Arizona State University, she gained expertise in HIV and drug use research. Dickson-Gómez has carried out a wide range of studies on the relationship between violence, drugs, and sexuality in El Salvador. Her recent research interests include HIV prevention among active drug users in the United States and El Salvador. Dickson-Gómez is currently conducting a NIDA-funded research project focused on the effects of community structural factors on the organization of crack selling and social context of crack use in San Salvador, El Salvador, and how differences in the context of drug selling and drug use affect the HIV risk of crack users. She is principal investigator of a four-year NIDA-funded study to explore differences in access to housing among drug using and non-drug-using low-income urban residents, and the effects of their housing status and stability on their HIV risk.

Cynthia Enloe is a research professor of international development and women's studies at Clark University. Enloe's teaching and research emphasize the interplay of women's politics in the national and international arenas, with special attention to how women's labor is made cheap in globalized factories and how women's emotional and physical labor has been used to support governments' war-waging policies, and how many women have tried to resist both of those efforts. Racial, class, ethnic, and national identities and pressures shaping ideas about femininities and masculinities have been common threads throughout her studies. Enloe serves on the editorial boards of several scholarly journals, including *Signs* and the *International Feminist Journal of Politics*. Among her nine books are: *The Morning After: Sexual Politics at the End of the Cold War* (1993); *Bananas, Beaches and Bases: Making Feminist Sense of International Politics* (2000); *Maneuvers: The International Politics of Militarizing Women's Lives* (2000); and *The Curious Feminist: Searching for Women in a New Age of Empire* (2004), all published by the University of California Press. Her most recent book is *Globalization and Militarism: Feminists Make the Link* (Rowman and Littlefield 2007).

Henry A. Giroux currently holds the Global TV Network Chair Professorship at McMaster University, Ontario, in the English and Cultural Studies Department. His primary research areas are cultural studies, youth studies, critical pedagogy, popular culture, media studies, social theory, and the politics of higher and public education. In 2002, he was named as one of the top 50 educational thinkers of the modern period in *Fifty Modern Thinkers on Education: From Piaget to the Present* as part of Routledge's Key Guides Publication Series. In 2005, he received an honorary doctorate from Memorial University in Canada. He is on the editorial and advisory boards of numerous national and international scholarly journals, and he serves as the editor or co-editor of four scholarly book series. He has published numerous books and articles and his most recent books include: *Take Back Higher Education* (co-authored with Susan Searls Giroux; Palgrave Macmillan 2004), *The University in Chains: Confronting the Military-Industrial-Academic Complex* (Paradigm 2007), *Against the Terror of Neoliberalism* (Paradigm 2008), and *Youth in a Suspect Society: Democracy or Disposability?* (Palgrave Macmillan 2009).

Doug Henry, a medical anthropologist, is an associate professor of anthropology at the University of North Texas. His research and writing emphasize the interaction of culture, health, society, and illness. Henry has conducted extensive field research on violence, refugees, and international relief during conflict and disaster in Sierra Leone and elsewhere in Africa. From 2005 to 2006, Henry worked as a consultant for AIDS education and prevention in Texas. His most recent work in medical anthropology includes studies in areas such as sleep disorders and treatment-seeking behaviors, program evaluation through "cost-benefit analyses," and structural violence and the public health of young gay and bisexual men. His articles and essays have been published in edited collections and in journals such as *Medical Anthropology Quarterly*, *African Geographical Review*, *Anthropological Quarterly*, *Journal of Gay and Lesbian Psychotherapy*, *Ageing International*, *Practicing Anthropology*, *Human Organization*, and *Social Science and Medicine*.

Arthur Kleinman, a medical anthropologist, is the Esther and Sidney Rabb Professor of Anthropology at Harvard University and was chair of that department from 2004 to 2007. From 1991 to 2000 he chaired Harvard Medical School's Department of Social Medicine and from 1993 to 2002 he held the Maude and Lillian Presley Professorship at Harvard Medical School. He continues to be Professor of Social Medicine and Psychiatry at Harvard Medical School. Since 1968, Kleinman, who is both a psychiatrist and an anthropologist, has conducted research on Chinese society, first in Taiwan, and, since 1978, in China, on depression, somatization, epilepsy, schizophrenia and suicide, and other forms of violence. Kleinman is the author of six books, editor or co-editor of 28 volumes and special issues of journals, and is author of more than 200 research and review articles and chapters. His chief publications are *Patients and Healers in the Context of Culture*; *Social Origins of Distress and Disease: Neurasthenia, Depression and Pain in Modern China*; *The Illness Narratives*; *Rethinking Psychiatry*; *Culture and Depression* (co-editor); *Social Suffering* (co-editor); and his most recent book, *What Really Matters* (Oxford University Press 2006).

Joan Kleinman, a sinologist, has worked as a research associate in the medical anthropology program at Harvard University. Her research and writings have focused on issues of health, illness, and suffering in China and among Chinese communities in East Asia. Her studies on the culture of medicine have appeared in collaborations with Arthur Kleinman and are based on field research in China, Taiwan, and North America.

Uli Linke is a professor of anthropology at the Rochester Institute of Technology. Her principal areas of interest include the political anthropology of the body, visual culture, violence and genocide, and the politics of memory and suffering. She has conducted extensive fieldwork in Europe, with long-term projects in Germany. Linke has held academic positions at the University of Toronto, the Central European University in Budapest, Rutgers University, and the University of Tübingen, Germany. Her major publications include *Blood and Nation: The European Aesthetics of Race* (University of Pennsylvania Press 1999), *German Bodies: Race and Representation After Hitler* (Routledge 1999), and *Denying Biology* (co-editor; University Press of America 1996). She has written more than 50 essays and articles which have appeared in scholarly journals such as *Comparative Studies in Society and History*, *Journal of Anthropological Theory*, *Anthropology Today*, *American Anthropologist*, *History and Anthropology*, *Transforming Anthropology*, and *New German Critique*. Among her recent essays are "The Limits of Empathy" in *Genocide* (Hinton and Lewis, eds., Duke University Press 2009) and "Contact Zones: Rethinking the Sensual Life of the State" (*Anthropological Theory* 2006). Her current projects include border militarism and the black male body in contemporary Europe (in *Europe in Black and White*, forthcoming).

John MacArthur, MD, MPH is an Infectious Diseases Team Leader at the USAID Regional Development Mission—Asia (Bangkok, Thailand). John earned his medical degree from Georgetown University. He has trained in family and community medicine at the University of California at San Francisco and preventive medicine at Johns Hopkins School of Hygiene and Public Health. He holds a Master of Public Health in International Health from Johns Hopkins and served as an Epidemic Intelligence Officer at the Centers for Disease Control and Prevention (CDC) where he later served in the Malaria Branch. A Captain in the US Public Health Service, John has been detailed to USAID's regional mission in Thailand since September 2005.

Liisa H. Malkki is an associate professor of anthropology at Stanford University. Her research interests include: the politics of nationalism, internationalism, cosmopolitanism, and human rights discourses as transnational cultural forms; the social production of historical memory and the uses of history; political violence, exile, and displacement; the ethics and politics of humanitarian aid; child research; and visual culture. Her field research in Tanzania explored the ways in which political violence and exile may produce transformations of historical consciousness and national identity among displaced people. This project resulted in *Purity and Exile: Violence, Memory, and National Cosmology among Hutu Refugees in Tanzania* (University of Chicago Press 1995). In another project, Malkki explored how Hutu exiles from Burundi and Rwanda, who found asylum in Montreal, Canada, imagined scenarios of the future for themselves and their countries in the aftermath of genocide in the Great Lakes region of Africa. Malkki's most recent book, *Improvising Theory: Process and Temporality in Ethnographic Fieldwork* (with Allaine Cerwonka) was published by the University of Chicago Press in 2007. Her current book-length project (based on fieldwork from 1995 to the present) examines the changing inter-relationships among humanitarian interventions, internationalism, professionalism, affect, and neutrality in the work of the Finnish Red Cross in cooperation with the International Committee of the Red Cross.

Joseph Masco is an associate professor of anthropology at the University of Chicago. His research explores the intersection of science studies, US national security culture, mass media, and critical theory. He is the author of *The Nuclear Borderlands: The Manhattan Project in Post-Cold War New Mexico* (Princeton University Press 2006), which received the 2008 Rachel Carson Prize (Society for the Social Studies of Science) and the 2006 Robert K. Merton Prize (Section on Science, Knowledge and Technology, American Sociology Association). He is currently working on a book examining the evolution of the national security state in the United States, with a particular focus on the interplay between affect, technology, and the public sphere in the articulation of threat.

Lucia Ann McSpadden, a cultural anthropologist, has lived and worked in Mexico, Japan, Nepal, and Uppsala, Sweden, where she served as Research Director of an international peace research institute, the Life and Peace Institute (LPI). In the United States, she developed a multiethnic curriculum for Head Start, investigated community development on a Native American reservation and worked extensively with congregations resettling African refugees. McSpadden has conducted long-term field research in Eritrea (northeast Africa) and is a founding member of both the Committee on Refugee Issues of the American Anthropological Association and the International Association for the Study of Forced Migration. She was project leader of a multinational study on the role of NGOs in the repatriation of refugees and has published widely on human rights issues and humanitarian approaches to complex human emergencies in the aftermath of war and political violence. Her publications include *Negotiating Return* (LPI 2000), co-edited volumes *Women, Violence, and Nonviolent Change* (WCC 1996), *Negotiating Power and Place at the Margins* (American Anthropological Association 1999), and the more recent book *Meeting God at the Boundaries* (UMGBHE 2003, 2006). McSpadden has designed and facilitated cultural competency and anti-racism workshops for church and community organizations as well as for humanitarian aid organizations in Europe. Currently she is an adjunct faculty working with international students at the Pacific School of Religion.

Nicholas Mirzoeff is a visual culture theorist and professor in the Department of Media, Culture and Communication at New York University, the Steinhardt School of Culture, Education and Human Development. He is best known for his work developing the field of visual culture and for his many books and his widely used textbooks on the subject. These include two edited volumes, *Diaspora and Visual Culture: Representing Africans and Jews* (Routledge 2001) and *The Visual Culture Reader* (Routledge 1998, 2002). Mirzoeff's other books include *Bodyscape* (Routledge 1995), *An Introduction to Visual Culture* (2nd revised ed., Routledge 2009), *Seinfeld: A Critical Study of the Series* (British Film Institute 2007), and *Watching Babylon: The War in Iraq and Global Visual Culture* (Routledge 2005). To further examine the idea of watching the war, Mirzoeff has initiated a public series seminar which focuses on war and violence, in particular on the Iraq war. Mirzoeff was awarded the 2006 Steinhardt Challenge Grant and was the Visiting Canterbury Fellow, University of Canterbury, New Zealand in 2005. His newest book, *The Right to Look: A Counterhistory of Visuality* is forthcoming from Duke University Press in 2010.

Carolyn Nordstrom is a professor of anthropology at the University of Notre Dame. Her principal areas of interest are the anthropology of war and peace, transnational extra-legal economies, and gender, power, and globalization. She has conducted extensive fieldwork in war zones worldwide, with long-term interests in southern Africa and South Asia. Her books include: *Global Outlaws: Crime, Money, and Power in the Contemporary World* (UC Press 2007); *Shadows of War: Violence, Power and International Profiteering in the 21st Century* (UC Press 2004); *A Different Kind of War Story* (University of Pennsylvania Press 1997); *Girls in Warzones* (Life and Peace Institute 1997); and the edited volumes *Fieldwork Under Fire* (1995) and *The Paths to Domination, Resistance, and Terror* (1992), both published by the University of California Press. She has authored dozens of scholarly articles, and has recently been awarded the John D. and Catherine T. MacArthur and John Simon Guggenheim Fellowships as well as numerous other grants, including from the US Institute for Peace.

Danielle Taana Smith is an associate professor of sociology at the Rochester Institute of Technology. Her research focuses on the effects of global violence and the resulting displacements of people. Her fieldwork among Liberian refugees in Rochester examines survival strategies adopted by the refugees throughout camps in West African countries. Her study follows the refugees after resettlement, and explores the complex processes of healing and readjustment as refugees are resettled in the US and other western nations. She documents the continuing traumatization of refugees who have escaped the violence of war, but find themselves resettled in decaying and violent urban centers that lack the basic infrastructures to enable refugees and long-term city residents to become economically self-sufficient. Smith has published articles in anthologies, edited volumes, and a range of scholarly journals such as *Race, Gender, and Class*, *Journal of Global Awareness*, *Journal of Black Studies*, *Economic Development Quarterly*, *Development and Society*, and the *Journal of Health and Social Policy*. She is currently completing a book manuscript on the psychological, social and economic obstacles that refugees encounter as they attempt to construct new lives in the urban United States.

Susan Sontag (1933–2004), an essayist, short-story writer, novelist, and human rights activist, was a leading commentator on modern culture, whose innovative essays on such diverse subjects as camp, pornographic literature, fascist aesthetics, photography, AIDS, and revolution gained wide attention. Born in New York City in 1933, she grew up in Tucson, Arizona, and attended high school in Los Angeles. She received her BA from the College of the University of Chicago and did graduate work in philosophy, literature, and theology at Harvard University and St Anne's College, Oxford. Her books, all published by Farrar, Straus & Giroux, include four novels, *The Benefactor*, *Death Kit*, *The Volcano Lover*, and *In America*; a collection of short stories, *I, etcetera*; several plays, including *Alice in Bed* and *Lady from the Sea*; and nine works of nonfiction, starting with *Against Interpretation* and including *On Photography*, *Illness as Metaphor*, *Where the Stress Falls*, and *Regarding the Pain of Others*. Sontag's last essays include "Regarding the Torture of Others," which situates the abuse of prisoners in Iraq in the context of US history and slavery and the cultural spectatorship of suffering.

Miriam Ticktin holds a joint position as an assistant professor of anthropology and international studies at the New School for Social Research. Her research interests include the critical study of humanitarianism, migration, camps and borders, sexual violence, and anthropology of science, medicine, and ethics. Her work is centered in

France, Europe and North Africa. She is currently completing a book manuscript, *Between Justice and Compassion: The Politics of Immigration and Humanitarianism in France*, which is about the fight for social justice of undocumented immigrants in France. She is also co-editor (with Ilana Feldman) of *In the Name of Humanity: The Government of Threat and Care* which explores new conceptions of the category of humanity (forthcoming from Duke University Press).

Meredeth Turshen is a professor in the Edward J. Bloustein School of Planning and Public Policy at Rutgers University. Her research interests include international health and she specializes in public health policy. She has written four books, *The Political Ecology of Disease in Tanzania* (1984), *The Politics of Public Health* (1989), and *Privatizing Health Services in Africa* (1999), all published by Rutgers University Press, and *Women's Health Movements: A Global Force for Change* (Palgrave Macmillan 2007). Turshen has edited five other books, *Women and Health in Africa* (Africa World Press 1991), *Women's Lives and Public Policy: The International Experience* (Greenwood 1993), *What Women Do in Wartime: Gender and Conflict in Africa* (Zed Books 1998), which was translated into French as *Ce que font les femmes en temps de guerre: genre et conflit en Afrique* (L'Harmattan 2001), *African Women's Health* (Africa World Press 2000) and *The Aftermath: Women in Postconflict Transformation* (Zed Books 2002). She serves on the Board of the Association of Concerned Africa Scholars, as Treasurer of the Committee for Health in Southern Africa, as contributing editor of the *Review of African Political Economy*, and is on the editorial board of the *Journal of Public Health Policy*.

Solrun Williksen is a professor (emeritus) of social anthropology at the Norwegian University of Science and Technology, Norway. She was educated at the University of Oslo, where she received a masters' degree in psychology and anthropology, with Fijian language as a field of specialization. She also holds a doctoral degree in social anthropology from the University of Oslo. She lived in Fiji for several years during the 1970s and 1980s when she also conducted her fieldwork for her doctoral thesis. She has published her work in a wide range of scholarly journals, including the *Journal of the Polynesian Society*, *Ethnos*, *The Australian Journal of Anthropology*, *Ethnography*, and *Bijdragen*. Her main work has been on Fijian culture, but in later years her interest has turned towards issues of integration and ethnicity in Norwegian society.

Elisabeth Jean Wood is a professor of political science at Yale University and a professor of the Santa Fe Institute. She is currently writing a book on variation in sexual violence during war. She is the author of *Forging Democracy from Below: Insurgent Transitions in South Africa and El Salvador* (Cambridge University Press 2000) and *Insurgent Collective Action and Civil War in El Salvador* (Cambridge University Press 2003). Among her recent articles are "Sexual Violence during War: Toward an Understanding of Variation" in *Order, Conflict, and Violence* (Kalyvas et al., eds., Cambridge University Press 2008), "Armed Groups and Sexual Violence: When is Wartime Rape Rare?" (*Politics and Society* 2009), and "The Social Processes of Civil War" (*Annual Review of Political Science* 2008). She serves on the editorial boards of *Politics and Society*, the *American Political Science Review*, and the Contentious Politics series of Cambridge University Press. At Yale Elisabeth teaches courses on comparative politics, political violence, social movements, and qualitative research methods.

Slavoj Žižek, philosopher, psychoanalyst and political analyst, is researcher at the Institute of Sociology at the University of Ljubljana, Slovenia, and the international director of the Birkbeck Institute for the Humanities, University of London. Since his publication *The Sublime Object of Ideology* in 1989, Žižek has published more than a dozen books, edited several collections, published numerous philosophical and political articles, and maintained an extensive speaking schedule. Since the 1990s, his work has taken on an increasingly engaged political tenor, culminating in books on September 11, terror and violence. His most recent books include *Violence: Big Ideas/Small Books* (Verso 2008), *In Defense of Lost Causes* (Verso 2008), and *The Monstrosity of Christ: Paradox or Dialectic?* (with John Milbank; MIT Press 2009).

Index

Compiled by Sue Carlton